D1431433

The Sources of
Soviet Naval Conduct

The Sources of
Soviet Naval Conduct

Edited by

Philip S. Gillette
Willard C. Frank, Jr.
Old Dominion University

Foreword by

Rear Admiral Ronald J. Kurth, USN
President, Naval War College

Lexington Books
D.C. Heath and Company/Lexington, Massachusetts/Toronto

Library of Congress Cataloging-in-Publication Data

The Sources of Soviet naval conduct / edited by Philip S. Gillette,
  Willard C. Frank, Jr. ; with a foreword by Ronald J. Kurth
      p.   cm.
    ISBN 0-669-21073-0 (alk. paper)
      1. Sea-power—Soviet Union. 2. Sea control. 3. Soviet Union.
  Voenno-Morskoĭ Flot.   I. Gillette, Philip S.   II. Frank, Willard C.
  VA570.S68   1990
  359'.03'0947—dc20   89-13108
                                                                       CIP

Published simultaneously in Canada
Printed in the United States of America
Casebound International Standard Book Number: 0-669-21073-0
Library of Congress Catalog Card Number: 89-13108

The paper used in this publication meets the minimum requirements of American National
Standard for Information Sciences—Permanence of Paper for Printed Library Materials,
ANSI Z39.48-1984. ∞™

Year and number of this printing:

89 90 91 92 10 9 8 7 6 5 4 3 2 1

For Nancy and Mary

Contents

Foreword
Soviet Change and Assessing Naval Conduct

Rear Admiral Ronald J. Kurth, USN

There is simply no true understanding of the sources of any Soviet conduct *today*, naval or otherwise, without an understanding of what the General Secretary, Mikhail Gorbachev, has been doing at home. The major factor affecting the sources of Soviet naval conduct has shifted away from the former goals of Soviet foreign policy toward new goals generated largely by Soviet domestic policy. Furthermore, a major influence on U.S. naval conduct, as with U.S. foreign policy, is the course of events taking place on the Soviet domestic scene. As a consquence, this introduction properly turns its attention to the General Secretary's effort at change based on *novoe myshlenie* (new thinking).

The simple truth, a Russian friend in Moscow recently said, is that the great Soviet experiment in modeling a new society had failed—and that the Russians now had to cope with that overpowering reality. He was talking about Marxism, the revolution, Leninism, Joseph Stalin, Nikita Khrushchev, Leonid Brezhnev, the party, central economic planning—the whole works. That is the problem in its most stark and perhaps extreme relief.

What dramatized the increasing stagnation of the Soviet socialist state was the renewed success of capitalism. It was not just that West Germany and Japan had sprung from the ruins of war to become economic successes with high standards of living, although the new successes of capitalism included those histories. It was still more poignant in Moscow that Third World countries, striving with sometimes agonizing aspirations for development, were dumping the Soviet model for market economies. To comprehend the full impact of the apparent change of fortune for the Soviet model, one need only recall a speech that became the center of attention just under three decades ago.

On June 11, 1960, a former president of the United Nations General Assembly, Dr. Charles Malik of Lebanon, delivered a speech in Williamsburg, Virginia, that severely jolted most everyone in the United States. The speech was widely published and widely read. The *U.S. News and World Report* reprinted the speech in its edition of July 4, 1960—yes, July fourth—under the banner "Is It Too Late to Win Against Communism?" Dr. Malik, who was reputed to be a kindly man, was then the ambassador of Lebanon to the United States. He had been an academic, a mathematician, physicist, and philosopher. He said:

> Communism started from zero forty-three years ago, and today it rigidly controls one-third of mankind and has penetrated and softened up in varying degrees the remaining two-thirds. Was this phenomenal development inevitable? . . .
>
> Backing international communism materially is the second most industrially advanced state in the world, the Soviet Union, which might at the present rate of development surpass the United States in two decades.
>
> The simple fact that the free world has not succeeded in forty years in pushing back the tide of communism by one inch from where it really got political control leaves the strong impression that we are here dealing with an irresistible and irreversible thrust which will inevitably inherit and transform in its own image all the kingdoms and cultures of the earth. Is this creeping tide of communism completely irreversible?

Those who remember this speech will recall that Dr. Malik called for the abandonment of the policy of containment for something much more active. Malik's words are less than three decades old. Yet now, to some some of us, after only four to five years of Gorbachev, Dr. Malik's words may sound like very distant history. For, in response to serious problems, the communist, or Marxist-Socialist, states are undergoing immense change. Immediately upon assuming power in March 1985, General Secretary Gorbachev and his associates began to take action that showed clearly that they understood their country's failure. Mr. Gorbachev launched one of the greatest programs of reform in Russian and Soviet history.

Mikhail Gorbachev is the first of the new generation of Soviet leaders; he is not cut from the old cloth. He did not experience the transitions of the 1920s, he was not threatened by the purges of the 1930s, nor is he a veteran of the Great Patriotic War. He was in school at Moscow State University when Stalin died, and no doubt he was excited as a young man by the reforms that Khrushchev attempted. Khrushchev's efforts were precursors of his own in many important respects; but those of Gorbachev appear to be better thought-out and much better organized. He may be, as Gromyko is reported to have said, a man with a nice smile but iron teeth. Whether or not Gorbachev knows exactly where his reforms will lead (and I doubt that he does), he is a superb tactician.

For Soviet leaders before Gorbachev, the benchmark for Soviet progress was always the United States. The Soviet leadership was obsessed with catching and then surpassing the United States. Originally, in the 1930s, catching the United States had an economic context. Many of us can remember—and the youngest among us may have seen on late-night television—a movie with Greta Garbo starring as a beautiful Soviet commissar. On a trip to Europe (Paris, if I remember right), she spouts statistics about Soviet increases in steel production, as the male lead, Melvin Douglas, tries desperately to involve her in romance.

The competitive context changed some after World War II. With the onset of nuclear weapons, the Cold War, the fading colonialism, and the birth of tens of new nations in the Third World, the Soviet mood turned more toward military and diplomatic competition with the United States. Soviet spirit for competition grew with the success of Sputnik at a time when the United States was a poor second in rocket technology. Subsequently, the pursuit of parity in strategic weaponry, while preserving predominance in conventional arms, became *the* important Soviet goal. The Soviets so completely engulfed themselves in the competitive effort that they failed to grasp that the development of weaponry in the West was only ancillary to the development of ever-increasing economic, technological, and industrial strength. The Russian leadership could not seem to escape the narrowness of their competitive focus. The Soviets were surrendering a possible chance to develop a modern economy in order to achieve parity in weapons and to search for advantage in the Third World. Once they judged themselves at the great threshold of parity, they became mesmerized by the apparent successes for socialism as the United States lost the war in Vietnam, plunged itself into societal chaos, and muddled through difficult executive administrations. Led by Leonid Brezhnev—a collegial trustee as General Secretary but in ever-increasing poor health at the end of the 1970s—the Soviet leadership had trouble recognizing how much the world had changed.

The developed world had become an economic and technological marvel of communications and consumerism from which the Soviet leadership had excluded their nation. The Russian people increasingly recognized their exclusion. They had paid by sacrifices in their standard of living and quality of life for Russia's crowning as a superpower—a status based on military might. As the Russian population increasingly coveted Western fashions, American music, and Japanese elecctronics as symbols of higher standards of living, it became disenchanted and apathetic, unmotivated and unproductive. The Soviet ship of state began to take on water, and Brezhnev and company either could not see this or ignored it.

However, one man had the courage to recognize publicly what was happening, and he became General Secretary in March 1985. By April, he had convened a plenum of the party; and with like-minded men, who for some time had seen the ship listing, he initiated reform.

Mikhail Sergeevich Gorbachev has spent the succeeding years showing his countrymen—and us—what he wants to do about it. In plenums, in a party congress, in a party conference, in central committee meetings, in scores of Politburo meetings, and most recently before the Congress of People's Dep-

uties and the Supreme Soviet, he attacked, savagely at times, the falsely sac-
rosanct, more correctly inept, record of the party leadership and the government bureaucrats that had led to what he has repeatedly documented publicly
as the country's lame and severely handicapped economic circumstance. Nor
has the military escaped his biting criticism; and criticism was a new experience for the saviors of the homeland in the Great Patriotic War. Gorbachev
has repudiated the policies of Leonid Brezhnev and his cronies, whose complacency and privileged self-indulgence, he alleges, allowed it to happen. He
spelled out his concepts for radical change as he worked at the same time to
consolidate his hold on power. He rid the Soviet government of those senior
Soviet colleagues who appeared to be a threat to his power or were rigid in
their attachment to the failed policies of the past.

Gorbachev's efforts at reform have been first-class theatre for the Krem-
linologists of the world as he has publicly laundered the party's dirty linen
and moved among the people like a Western politician running for popularly
elected office. He believes that the Soviet Union's economy must look more
like those of the West and the Pacific: self-sustaining through efficient organization, effective management, and a productive work force. Furthermore,
the Soviet Union must move into the world of modern economies by better,
more efficient capital investment. The Soviet Union, he says, is a wasteland
of half-completed construction projects. And he finds many of those projects
completed to be redundant or too costly. He has sought an infusion of high
technology into enterprises that are to be managed in a more decentralized
way. He wants to make local managers responsible for profitable operations
by giving them and their labor-force higher wages—likewise decrementing
the pay of those whose efforts fail to be profitable. He wants to manage to
the bottom line like a capitalist, although he insists socialism was always
meant to work that way. For, he asserts, *that* is what Lenin had in mind.

Gorbachev quotes Lenin about a Soviet society that should be built on
personal interests, personal incentives, and business principles. The trouble,
argues the reformist Gorbachev, is that Lenin's model for Soviet development
was corrupted in the course of past leadership. Gorbachev wants a revolution
in management; and more importantly, he wants a revolution in the mind-
sets of socialist workers—a revolution, he admits, of magnitude and importance comparable to the Great October Revolution. For that to happen, he
needs to win the hearts and minds of the Soviet people, and for that purpose,
he has taken his case to them. Ultimately, he has termed the pillars of his
platform *glasnost'* (openness or publicity), *perestroika* (restructuring), and
democratization. He has made clear that the Soviet Union must use *glasnost'*
in order to achieve *perestroika*, and must use openness and popular participation in order to achieve the new thinking necessary for restructuring.

It is interesting to note that in the beginning of the Gorbachev period,
the Soviet press would not talk of reforms and only talked about restructuring. Americans tend to throw such words around rather carelessly because,

for us, they have neither ideological content nor implications. However, the Soviet press was initially skittish about the word *perestroika,* for the translation of such a word was sensitive, because in the Soviet Union the subject of economics is ideological. Consequently, the word *reform* might have implied that something based on Marxist ideology was basically wrong and had to be changed. Even worse, the word reform could have connoted a change meant to make something good out of something bad or something which *turned* bad. Marxism in the Soviet Union is an *infallible* philosophy. It accounts for the inevitable course of history, and it is the basis for a state structure grafted onto a people by force of arms. It is a philosophy that has trouble with being judged wrong, for the legitimacy of the state comes into possible question. For these reasons, the connotation of a word has special importance.

Quickly, however, the Soviet sensitivity about the implications of words had to change as Mr. Gorbachev's program became increasingly more radical than that of the program of *uskorenie* (speeding up) with which he started.

The increasing radicalization of the Gorbachev effort can be seen in that part of his program he has called *glasnost'*. In its early context, *glasnost'* meant "openness" or "publicity," but it was shaded with the sense in which the party uses the word propaganda. For the party, propaganda is the use of information to develop a desired point of view. When the point of view is preconceived, the information used is preselected. Therefore, in a political structure adhering to such a theory regarding use of information, *glasnost'* did not mean what the U.S. media would mean by openness or publicity. It did not mean that any subject was open to full review regardless of consequences simply because pursuit of truth is a value in itself. In the West, particularly in the United States, all shades of fact and opinion are thought to deserve sunlight because we pursue truth through the collision of contending views on what the truth is. Perhaps we believe that truth can only be approximated. We also believe that an informed citizen ought to be able to determine that approximation and that the state must allow the citizen to do that or the state risks becoming a tyranny. It is this philosophy that plunges us into controversy in the United States over issues of censorship, state secrets, and the withholding of information. Things are different in the Soviet Union.

Glasnost' meant to tell the truth, or some of the truth, for a specific set of reasons and within limits. Lenin talked about *glasnost'* as a tool for controlling management and the directors of enterprises. Gorbachev has been very much interested in that meaning for *glasnost',* but more importantly he has had to accommodate *glasnost'* of increasingly radical content in the context of Soviet experiences.

Mr. Gorbachev believes that Soviet society became apathetic, alienated, and demoralized in the 1970s, such that it became unproductive. So *glasnost'* became his technique for using criticism and information in the pursuit of a specific goal: to breathe sufficient fresh air into Soviet society so that the

Soviet people might once again become motivated, supportive, and productive—for without those qualities Gorbachev perceived that the Soviet Union to be on the road to becoming a second-rate power. He ties open and honest treatment of shortcomings to a healthy means of policing the economy and ensuring a sense of reponsibility among workers and managers. He wants intelligent workers who have access to information and who are critical because he believes that progress toward a modern, technologically advanced economy demands those qualities. The Brezhnev era became stagnant because, in part, it fell victim to its own control of information.

However, the practice of *glasnost'* has changed. Since *glasnost'* became intertwined with the plunge into democratization, the world has been treated to an ever more interesting show. Before the Congress of People's Deputies and more recently the Supreme Soviet, Gorbachev, his wife Raisa, and his ministers—D.T. Yazov of Defense and V.A. Kriuchkov of the KGB (Committee for State Security), among others—have been the subject of the new *glasnost'*. If Gorbachev had not planned on this extent of public cross-exmination, and I think he did not, then questions arise. It is not that the pursuit of truth is harmful, even for a Soviet communist state, for it is not. Rather, this example of *glasnost'* raises the question of how much change Soviet society can absorb, and at what pace, before Gorbachev and his program falter. Should he and his program falter, the results may seriously affect the sources of all Soviet conduct, including naval conduct. For navalists, that fact should require continued sharp focus on Soviet domestic circumstances.

The history of reform in Russia has seen more failure than success. There has repeatedly been more to correct than there has been endurance to a reform effort. Therefore, if one turns to the past to predict the future, the outlook for Secretary Gorbachev is grim. Nevertheless, Russian history not withstanding, Western democracies as well as the American public have been seized with optimism over the possibilities for the Soviet Union under Mr. Gorbachev. The phenomenon has been labeled *Gorbymania*. This optimism (for example, that the reasons underlying the Cold War have disappeared) is encouraged in Western democracies by the scarcity of funds and competing fiscal requirements—all of which press to diminish defense spending. These circumstancces set the stage for Western naval forces of diminished size before there is any clear evidence of Soviet success in domestic reforms. The optimism may be unfounded, and if it is, Soviet domestic developments could generate cataclysmic change and influence of still greater proportions on the sources of naval conduct, Western as well as Soviet. It is therefore reasonable and prudent to keep a careful eye on Soviet domestic developments as well as to maintain an optimum naval posture. These points, I would argue, are important to remember when assessing the sources of Soviet naval conduct.

Preface

In the Soviet Union an era of "new thinking" is unfolding under the leadership of Mikhail Gorbachev. For the moment at least, Soviet military doctrine is defined as defensive. A new world war seems remote, and security is pursued through arms control. A revolution in technology is also underway, particularly in advanced conventional weapons, and we are facing the possibility of a postnuclear world in strategy. Yet traditions and habits of mind are hard to break, and future Soviet military posture will likely be the result of tension between continuities and changes.

In the midst of these dynamics sits a large and capable Soviet Navy. Its roles for the future remain uncertain, as are their implications for Western security. In an era of rapid change, it is prudent for us to seek out the sources of Soviet naval conduct. How can we assess future Soviet naval strategy and behavior? How might we assess seemingly contradictory signals from the Soviet Union on how its naval forces might be employed?

One way to approach these questions is to examine the conditions, proclivities, and forces that shape how we and the Soviets think about the Soviet Navy and its roles and missions. Whereas other studies focus on hardware and capabilities, this book examines the broader and enduring contexts, mind-sets, and tendencies that, whether Gorbachev succeeds or fails, will likely combine with developments and innovations to inform future Soviet naval conduct. Many of the chapters in this book are updated revisions of papers presented at a conference held by Old Dominion University in May 1987.

We wish to thank Old Dominion University, Computer Dynamics, Inc., the Jonathan Corporation, and Metro Machine Corporation for the support that made this book possible. We are much indebted to Gary S. Newsome, whose insightful eyes helped with editing K.C. Jacobsen, who carefully read the manuscript; and Elaine Dawson, a whiz at word processing. Finally, we owe a debt of gratitude to Charles O. Burgess, Daniel E. Sonenshine, Richard A. Skinner, Admiral Harry D. Train II, and the Honorable G. William Whitehurst for their encouragement and support throughout this project.

Recurring Abbreviations and Acronyms

ABM	Antiballistic missile
ASW	Antisubmarine warfare
C³	Command, control, and communications
CinC	Commander in chief
CINCLANT	Commander in chief, Atlantic Command
CPSU	Communist party of the Soviet Union
ICBM	Intercontinental ballistic missile
INF	Intermediate-range nuclear forces
KGB	Soviet Committee for State Security
Komsomol	Young Communist Youth League
MAD	Mutual assured destruction
MIRV	Multiple independently targetable reentry vehicle
NATO	North Atlantic Treaty Organization
NARKOMVMF	People's Commissar of the Navy
NEP	New Economic Policy
NKVD	People's Commissariat of Internal Affairs; the Stalinist secret police and intelligence service
POL	Petroleum, oils, and lubricants
RKKA	Workers' and Peasants' Red Army
RVSR	Revolutionary Military Council of the Republic
SALT	Strategic Arms Limitation Talks
SDI	Strategic Defense Initiative
SLOC	Sea-lines of communication
Spetsnaz	Soviet special operations forces
SSBN	Ballistic missile nuclear-powered submarine
SSGN	Guided (cruise) missile nuclear-powered submarine
SSN	Attack nuclear-powered submarine
START	Strategic Arms Reduction Talks
Stavka	Headquarters of the czarist and Soviet military high command
TVD	Theater of military action
UN	United Nations

Part I
National and Military Strategy and Foreign Policy Settings

William H.J. Manthrope and Ken Booth present two contexts for an understanding of Soviet naval conduct. Manthrope discusses in chapter 1 how Soviet national and military strategy determine naval conduct. He stresses the cultural, historical, and ideological influences that produce more continuity than change in Soviet national and military strategy. Booth, on the other hand, shows in chapter 2 the disastrous course of Soviet policy under Leonid Brezhnev that led to Mikhail Gorbachev's foreign policy of limiting the damage to Soviet influence around the world while lessening tensions and cost through arms control. Although Soviet policy at the moment is reluctant to be overly assertive, the Soviet Navy has been a successful instrument of policy in the Third World and is available to be so again.

1

A Background for Understanding Soviet Strategy

William H.J. Manthorpe, Jr.

S oviet naval conduct has long puzzled many observers in the United States. The way in which the Soviet Navy is employed and when, where, and how it operates are quite different from the employment and operations of the U.S. Navy. Certainly Soviet naval employment and operations differ from what various U.S. naval strategists and operational commanders believe they should be—or, at least, would be if those U.S. authorities were commanding the Soviet Navy. This raises the question: Why is the Soviet Navy employed and operated so differently from the U.S. Navy? In other words, what are the sources of Soviet naval conduct?

At one time many U.S. naval thinkers believed that the Soviet Navy was employed in a limited role and operated when, where, and how it did not only due to geographic constraints but especially because it lacked extensive maritime experience and sophisticated naval technology. It was assumed in the United States that once those deficiencies were overcome and the Soviet Navy had developed into an oceangoing fleet, it would be employed and operated like the U.S. Navy—despite geographical limitations. But over the years, as the Soviet Navy has matured into a blue-water navy, this has not occurred.

Today the U.S. Navy maintains high readiness to support steady-state naval operations; the Soviet Navy maintains high readiness for surge operations. While the U.S. Navy operates its strategic missile submarines in broad ocean areas, the Soviet Navy increasingly confines its nuclear-powered ballistic missile submarines (SSBNs) to restricted bastions in peripheral waters. While the U.S. Navy maintains and exercises about a third of its general purpose naval forces in a forward-deployed deterrent posture, the Soviet Navy forward deploys less than 10 percent of its general purpose forces and exercises the remainder in sea-denial or sea-control barriers covering the approaches to the Soviet Union and SSBN bastions.

In the light of these persistent differences in employment and operations, it is necessary to look beyond the capabilities and limitations of the Soviet Navy in order to determine the sources of observed Soviet naval conduct. It is not necessary to look very far, for the employment and operations of the navy in peace and war are dictated by Soviet national strategy and military strategy. Clearly Soviet strategy is the immediate and direct source of Soviet naval conduct. In that case, an understanding of Soviet strategy should offer insights into Soviet naval conduct. Yet to understand this strategy, it is necessary to look more broadly and deeply at the national factors that shape it.

This chapter offers such a background for understanding Soviet strategy. It highlights the cultural, historical, and ideological factors that create the mind-sets, establish the national goals, and shape the political-military decision making that are the foundation of Soviet national strategy. It describes the various components of Soviet military science, the military command and control system, and military decision-making processes that guide the formulation and execution of Soviet military strategy.

Each of these topics can be covered in sufficient detail to indicate how it shapes the fundamental characteristics of Soviet strategy. Thus, by covering the unique, national factors that provide the basis for Soviet strategy and, then, by describing the fundamental characteristics of Soviet strategy itself, both the secondary (indirect) and primary (direct) sources of Soviet naval conduct can be revealed.

Slavic Civilization

The Russians have long been isolated from the West. Their civilization has different roots and developed separately. It originated in Byzantium rather than Rome. It was greatly influenced by prolonged interaction with Asiatic peoples rather than the freewheeling entrepreneurial and diplomatic intrigues of the Italian Republics. It was stimulated and preserved by orthodoxy rather than experiencing the artistic, moral, and individualistic influences of the Renaissance and Reformation. Russia eventually opened a window to the West, but it was not changed by the philosophical and constitutional thoughts of the English, American, and French revolutions. Rather, it remained in self-imposed isolation from the West, censoring ideas and restricting travel.

But Russia has never been isolated from the West in terms of access to technology. Peter the Great made his opening to the West to get naval and other technology to spur Russia on its way to becoming a modern, powerful nation. Lenin went to the West for military and civilian technology to build Soviet power. Stalin used Western arms to preserve the Russian homeland and expand the Soviet empire. Recent Soviet rulers have used Western technology to challenge the West in space.

This isolation from and yet, dependence on the West has given the Soviets feelings of superiority and pride—and also inferiority and embarrassment.

The Soviet people believe in the superiority of their communal way of life, social progress, and cultural achievements. They take great pride in the sacrifices they have made to create and defend a new political and economic system. But they experience feelings of inferiority when they recognize their exclusion from international political and economic power and their lower material and technological standard of living. They are embarrassed by their dependence on the West for food, good-quality products, and high technology.

Russian History

The history of Russia and the Soviet Union is the story of repeated invasions and prolonged occupations by almost every neighboring nation from all directions. The original *Rus'* was created by invader-occupiers from the north. Then came the Mongol hordes and the 500-year Tatar yoke. The Turks, Swedes, Poles, French, Germans, Japanese, and British subsequently invaded Russia. As a result, today, the Soviets see themselves as surrounded by enemies—all of them now allied with the United States. The Soviets well remember that U.S. forces, including sailors and marines, landed in and occupied portions of northern and Far Eastern Russia from 1918 to 1920 in support of opponents of Soviet rule.

Furthermore, throughout its history, whether Russian or Soviet, the nation has been unprepared for those invasions. Its armed forces have had to fall back and defend on their own territory, and the people suffered for years before the invaders were driven from the land.

As a consequence, between wars, the nation adopted a policy of continental expansion. It extended its political influence and military power beyond its borders to create buffer states around the Russian homeland. Then it gradually increased control over those buffers and eventually absorbed them. That policy created more wars, the need for another ring of buffers, and more expansion—eventually leading to the formation of a continent-spanning empire.

Marxist-Leninist Ideology

Their ideology teaches the Soviets that they are engaged in a long-term class struggle between two antagonistic and irreconcilable political, economic, and social systems, each dedicated to the destruction of the other. Ideology also teaches that communist victory is inevitable. History and time, they believe, are on their side. Just as popular republics eventually replaced absolute monarchies in the course of past history, so will "socialist democracies" replace "capitalist oligarchies" in the future. Furthermore, the Soviets believe that victory can be accomplished by what they call "peaceful" means, which include ideological propaganda, political subversion, diplomatic intrigue, economic pressure, state-sponsored terrorism, and wars of national liberation fought by surrogate forces. To the Soviets, "peaceful" means are anything short of what they call "armed conflict."

"While ideology assures them that victory is inevitable, Soviet leaders recognize that progress is required to demonstrate both the validity of the inevitability theory and the validity of their policies as Soviet rulers. As this progress is made, the Soviets believe that eventually, when the capitalist-imperialist structure is about to crumble, the West will attack the Soviet Union in order to save itself. That will be the decisive point in history when the Soviet Union must defend itself and destroy the enemy to achieve the inevitable victory.

Soviet Mind-sets

This kind of civilization, history, and ideology engenders in the Soviet people and, especially, in their traditional leaders certain underlying mind-sets that can be diagnosed as a psychosis about national power. The symptoms caused by their culture are a sense of isolation and schizophrenic swings between delusions of grandeur and an inferiority complex. They have feelings of resentment over dependency and of insecurity. Their history makes them paranoid about the threat, gives them a persecution complex and fear of attack, and thus creates a fortress mentality. Their ideology pushes them to adversarial relationships and creates a need to demonstrate power. All of this results in aggressive behavior.

Soviet National Goals

Culture, history, and ideology have created a set of five Soviet national goals:

1. To strengthen the Soviet system and preserve rule by the communist party and the elite.
2. To defend the Russian homeland and the Soviet state from outside interference.
3. To avoid war.
4. To maintain dominance over the land and sea areas beyond Soviet borders.
5. To extend Soviet influence worldwide.

The pursuit of these goals constitutes Soviet national strategy.

The Soviet Union's preferred method of implementing national strategy gives priority to the twin goals of extending Soviet influence worldwide and maintaining dominance over a defensive perimeter beyond Soviet borders by employing political, economic, and more aggressive "peaceful" means backed up by massive military power for coercion and intimidation. By that method, the Soviet Union plans to make incremental progress toward the inevitable victory while also meeting its goal of avoiding war and ensuring the defense of the homeland. This preferred method of implementing Soviet national strategy is what the Soviets call "peaceful competition," while the West sees it as Soviet adventurism and expansionism.

Yet the Soviets also recognize that implementing their national strategy always requires them to concentrate on the twin goals of strengthening the Soviet system to preserve the rule of the party and the elite and of defending the homeland. The means of meeting these goals has been the creation of a garrison state with a controlled society, command economy, and massive military establishment. This is seen by the Soviets as "defense of the homeland and the revolution," but to the West it constitutes the Soviet threat.

Soviet national strategy is to employ both the preferred and required methods simultaneously. Which method receives emphasis depends on which goals are more important at the moment, given the politics in the Soviet Union and the world situation.

There is good historical evidence that the Soviets have always had this dual, flexible strategy for pursuing their national goals. In the early days of Soviet power, it was reflected in the classic debate over whether the party should pursue "world revolution"—external goals—or concentrate on "building communism in one country"—internal goals—first. In more recent years it has been reflected in the competing calls to pursue "equal participation in world affairs"—external goals—or "equal security"—internal goals.

Soviet Political-Military Planning and Decision Making

The implication of the dual methods of pursuing Soviet national strategy is that Soviet political-military planning and decision making involves continual risk-gain assessments. Soviet leaders are always assessing how far they can go in implementing their national strategy by the preferred peaceful competition strategy before they will be forced by Western reaction to fall back on their required strategy for defending the revolution and their homeland.

Soviet political-military strategic thinking has its origins in Slavic thinking patterns reinforced by Marxist-Leninist training. Typical Slavic thought processes are deductive, starting from broad philosophical principles and proceeding to specifics in an attempt to solve problems. Marxism-Leninism, while it professes to be a science, is really a religion in which thinking must proceed from broad dogma (the works of Lenin) to specifics in order to solve a problem.

Thus, Soviet political-military strategic thinking is grounded in Marxist-Leninist philosophy on war and the army, or basically Lenin's interpretation of Carl von Clausewitz supplemented, depending on the era, by the views that other political leaders such as Mikhail Frunze, Joseph Stalin, or Leonid Brezhnev have drawn from their wartime experiences. It also embodies a belief in the laws of war. The Soviets believe that those laws are natural laws of the universe, just like the laws of physics. They believe that they are objective laws, existing regardless of whether others believe them. They believe further that the laws of war are historical and can be shown to have influenced past military events. The first law of war is that the nature and type of war depends on the political objectives of the war. There are four to six other laws of war. They state that the course and outcome of war depend on the correlation of forces and means between the opposing two sides in terms of the economic power, scientific power, national will, and, most important, military power at the outset of the war and the military potential to carry on the war.

In their strategic risk-gain decision making, Soviet political planners or decision makers, adhering to the first law of war, state the nature and type of war they would be willing or might have to fight to gain their political objectives. Then they turn to the intelligence services, other experts, and the military to ascertain the risk of fighting that kind of war. Those advisers, guided by the other laws of war, look at the scientific, the economic, and, particularly, the various military correlations of forces and attempt to calculate the correlation of societal forces and military means needed to ensure a successful course and outcome of the war under consideration and the level of correlation that could be made available at various times throughout the crisis or conflict. The calculations of relative economic, scientific, and other forces help the political decision makers decide whether to emphasize the preferred or required method of pursuing national strategy in the period leading up to the war and to plan the timing of the war. The military's calculations of the correlations of military means required to meet the threat and the forces actually available provide the basis for military advice to the political decision makers.

Soviet Military Science

Soviet military science, the basis for the development of Soviet military forces and the formulation and execution of Soviet military strategy, is traditionally defined as a system of knowledge of the nature, types, and laws of war and the methods of preparing for and waging war. It is an academic discipline and the realm of military academics—doctors and candidates of military science—researching and writing about military affairs. The study of Soviet military science has a sociopolitical branch and a military-technical branch.

In the sociopolitical work of military science, some military academicians interpret, update, and apply Marxist-Leninist philosophy on war and the army to the current situation and problems. Other academics are theorists trying to understand and define the nature and types of war. The linkage between political thinking about war and soviet military science is a common belief in the laws of war. Based on an acceptance of the historical nature of the laws of war, Soviet military historians study past campaigns and battles to discern factors that have repeatedly contributed to success and victory. This is an attempt to discover law-governed patterns or evidence of the laws of war at work. Finally, based on these updated interpretations of Lenin, increased understanding of war, and discovery of new law-governed patterns, Soviet military theorists develop new concepts and ideas about preparing for and waging war.

In the military-technical branch of Soviet military science, mathematicians, systems analysts, and operations researchers work to test and apply those concepts and ideas about war. They model appropriate historical battles, attempt to quantify various aspects of law-governed patterns, and relate theories to modern technology. From this work they develop models and algorithms useful for understanding and planning modern combat and forecasting future operations and requirements.

All this is not done as an academic exercise. Soviet military science is conducted under the auspices of the Military Scientific Directorate of the General Staff. The results of military scientific work are used by the General Staff to recommend military doctrine to the political leadership, to develop the principles of military art for guidance of the operational forces, and to form a basis within the General Staff for strategy development, force planning, and decision making.

Many in the West confuse the writings setting forth the results of this research of Soviet military science with statements of Soviet military doctrine. It is easy to spot Soviet military-scientific discussion because it always focuses on the past or future, not the present, and is written by a military academic and first summarized by a general officer.

Soviet Military Doctrine

Soviet military doctrine traditionally has been defined as a system of scientifically based views and guiding principles that are the authoritative and official statements of the party and the state on the nature of war and the methods of preparing for and waging war. In other words, Soviet military doctrine is the politically endorsed result of Soviet military science.

On its own initiative, based on the work of Soviet military academics, or in response to direction from above, the General Staff proposes new or modified military doctrine. It is reviewed and approved by the Defense Council and is promulgated by the Presidium of the Supreme Soviet as a law of the Soviet Union.

Most Soviet military doctrine is not publicly stated and must be inferred from open references and actions. Nevertheless, if the Soviets are willing to make it available publicly, military doctrine can be identified easily. It consists of broad general statements about the current nature and type of war that are made first by an individual at the top of the party. Then those same words appear repeatedly in the writings of Soviet military leaders. This is especially true when the Soviets want their doctrine to be clear to the West for propaganda purposes or as a deterrent.

Despite the occasional use of a doctrinal statement for its political or deterrent effect in the West, Soviet military doctrine plays an even more important role. The purpose of doctrine is to ensure a unity of views between the political leadership and the military concerning what kind of wars the Soviet Union will fight and how they will be fought.

Soviet military doctrine should not be confused with military policy, is defined as party political actions taken to strengthen Soviet defense capability and direct the armed forces. Essentially it is the party management activity that sets the objectives and tasks for the organization and development of the armed forces. Soviet military policy is developed by the Central Committee and embodied in the party platform or party statements emanating from party congresses or conferences. It embodies party guidance on fiscal, personnel, organizational, morale, discipline, and other matters.

Soviet Military Art

The principles of Soviet military art are the practical application of Soviet military science and the reflection of military doctrine at the operational level. They are general principles and recommendations for commanders and staffs to follow when organizing or controlling forces and conducting operations. They are formulated by the General Staff to ensure that Soviet military planning and operations exploit law-governed patterns and adhere to military doctrine. The principles are taught in military academies and listed in the field regulations of the Soviet Army and the combat regulations of the Soviet Navy.

Soviet Military Command and Control

Many assert that the Soviets have centralized command and control. Rather, it can be postulated that they have centralized control over strategy development and implementation but decentralized command for strategy execution.

Control is centralized in the few people who make up the Politburo. In peacetime, the Politburo itself makes foreign policy or crisis response decisions to guide governmental actions. A few members of the Politburo serve on the Defense Council, which, according to the Soviet constitution, is the highest executive organ of Soviet government. The Defense Council approves military strategy and military development—that is, all those other efforts required to create and maintain the armed forces of the Soviet Union. A few members of the Politburo, also serving in government on the Presidium of the Supreme Soviet, have the constitutional authority to mobilize the Soviet armed forces and declare war.

During wartime, some members of the Politburo, probably the same people who are on the Defense Council, form the Supreme High Command (VGK). The VGK is responsible for wartime grand strategy and direction of military strategy. The remaining members of the Politburo and other important members of the Central Committee form what has been known in wartime as the *Stavka,* or headquarters, of the VGK. The *Stavka* provides the political, economic, and military support to carry out the strategy of the VGK. The General Staff of the Soviet armed forces provides strategic decision-making support to the VGK and, once a strategy has been selected, directs and controls its implementation. *Stavka* support and General Staff direction is not only from afar but often involves the presence of their representatives at the headquarters of the commanders executing the strategy.

On the other hand, Soviet military command is decentralized. There are five combat arms of the Soviet armed forces: the ground forces, strategic rocket forces, air forces, air defense forces, and naval forces. The leaders of those forces are deputy ministers of defense with functional responsibilities. In peacetime, they are responsible for carrying out all aspects of military development, training, and mobilization of their forces. In wartime, as deputy ministers of defense, they have no operational role; they become members of the *Stavka* and provide military advice and support to the VGK.

Operational command of the Soviet armed forces rests with the supreme commanders (GKs) of the theaters of military action (TVDs). Since the late 1970s, theater commands have been active in peacetime. Today, there are theater commanders, staffs, and headquarters to develop the plans and exercise the forces for Soviet wartime strategy. In wartime, they command forces made up of elements of all Soviet combat arms within the theater to execute Soviet military strategy.

Soviet Military Planning and Decision Making

Calculations of the correlation of forces are the basis for Soviet military planning and decision making at every command level and across the entire spectrum of conflict. The Soviet General Staff uses calculations of the correlation of forces in strategic planning and decision making. A Soviet operational staff calculates the correlation to support the commander's decision making. Furthermore, at any time during crisis or war, the staffs are not only calculating the strength relative to the enemy in the current situation but are calculating the future potential relative strength based on variables such as expected losses, availability of reserves, or use of nuclear weapons. This is done in order to forecast and plan ahead in an attempt to ensure a favorable course and outcome to the conflict.

Soviet staffs at all levels calculate the correlation of forces to develop and test the courses of action they propose to their commanders. They compare their own forces with the enemy forces and, for various alternative courses of action, forecast the outcome of an engagement between those two forces. These calculations are made by a whole range of algorithms and models derived from the work of Soviet military science. They include coefficients for the quantity and quality of Soviet and enemy forces, the time available to those forces to position themselves and carry out their mission, and even coefficients for other factors, such as the quality of the commanding officer derived from indicators such as tour length and previous command experience. This staff process is becoming increasingly automated, although the Soviets continue to emphasize that the commander, not the staff or computer, must select the appropriate course of action.

In peacetime, Soviet staffs use this process for preplanning. They calculate the correlation of forces for various expected situations and threats in order to develop war plans, to allocate forces in support in those war plans, and even to establish requirements for the development of new systems that will improve their capability to carry out the war plans. The developed plans are then prepackaged, distributed to the operational forces, exercised repeatedly in peacetime, and kept ready for wartime execution in response to a code word.

In crisis or wartime, the Soviets must recalculate the correlation of forces against the actual threat in the actual situation in order to plan mission execution and determine force requirements. If the actual threat is the same as the expected threat, decision making becomes simpler for the Soviets. To plan mission execution and establish force requirements, they merely turn to the war plans that they have prepackaged and exercised repeatedly with the forces already allocated. But if the actual threat is quite different from the expected threat, decisionmaking becomes complicated. The Soviets must revise their plans and reallocate their forces, a process that requires time and communications, thereby providing the enemy with warning and the opportunity for countermeasures. It is also a process that might be slowed by the inertia of commanders who would prefer to fight in ways they have already planned and exercised.

Characteristics of Soviet Strategy

Soviet national strategy originates from long-standing cultural, historical, and ideological influences that create a mind-set, establish national strategic goals, shape the methods by which those goals are pursued, and guide political-military planning and decision-making. Thus, it is a long-term strategy concerned with the entire spectrum of conflict, from peace to war termination. It is an integrated political, economic, and military strategy that is implemented by two methods simultaneously. But there is flexibility to give emphasis to whichever method is appropriate in the light of national politics and the international situation.

The Soviets' preferred method of implementing national strategy is one of making incremental gains by so-called peaceful means backed up by military superiority for coercion and intimidation. This is intended to bring to the Soviet Union superpower status. Nevertheless, the Soviets recognize that they are always required to implement national strategy by a method that ensures the defense of the revolution and homeland against both internal and external threats. Thus, the Soviet political-military leadership is always making risk-gain assessments between how long and how far they can pursue their preferred externally oriented strategy before they will have to fall back and give emphasis to their required, mainly internal, strategy.

The formulation and execution of Soviet military strategy is based on Soviet military science, military doctrine, military art, and within the Soviet military centralized control and decentralized command system by correlation-of-forces-based planning and decision-making procedures. Thus, Soviet military strategy is centrally developed by the General Staff and controlled at the highest political levels. Military doctrine and party military policy provide political guidance and political constraints for the development of Soviet military strategy. The result is a unified national military strategy.

Since formulation of military strategy is based on the continuing theoretical and historical research and mathematical analysis of military science, it will always be evolving. Because of the underlying reliance on the correlation of forces concept, a strategy-force match is ensured, and the strategy is responsive to all expected threats.

Soviet military strategy will be executed by regional theater commanders using combined armed forces. Execution in response to expected situations or threats will be fast but inflexible. Response to the unexpected will take longer. The principles of Soviet military art provide consistent guidance for strategy execution to the operational level.

Thus, based on cultural, historical, and ideological influences and national mind-sets, goals, and decision making derived from them, Soviet national strategy has taken on certain fundamental characteristics. Because of unique national processes for the development and implementation of Soviet military strategy, it too has taken on certain fundamental characteristics. It is those unique national factors and the resulting characteristics of Soviet strategy that have been, respectively, the secondary and primary sources of past Soviet naval conduct.

Turning from the Past to the Future

Today dramatic changes are occurring in the Soviet Union. How will these changes affect Soviet national and military strategy and, thus, Soviet naval conduct? The answer depends on whether these are truly fundamental, mainly methodological, or simply superficial changes in the underlying national and unique factors that shape Soviet national and military strategy and in the basic characteristics of those strategies.

Changes in Factors Shaping Soviet National Strategy

To bring about fundamental change in the factors underlying Soviet national strategy would require reversing many of the ingrained attitudes of Slavic culture, the accepted lessons from the experience of Russian history, and the imperatives of Marxist-Leninist ideology—all of which create the national mind-set that shapes Soviet national goals. Even in this time of great turmoil, it is unlikely that more than a thousand years of culture and history will be overcome or seventy years of propagated ideology will be undone.

There would seem to be no personal motivation for the instigator of all this potential change, General Secretary and President Mikhail S. Gorbachev, to do so. He is, after all, an ethnic Slav who was evacuated from his home as a youth to avoid the Nazi invasion and occupation. He is married to a Marxist-Leninist philosopher, was selected as a protégé by the long-term head of the Committee on State Security (KGB), and was nominated as general secretary by the man who conducted foreign affairs for all of his predecessors. With such a cultural heritage, historical experience, and Marxist-Leninist pedigree, it is unreasonable to expect any fundamental change in Gorbachev's mind-set or his acceptance of the underlying Soviet national goals that dictate Soviet national strategy.

Gorbachev, however, has received a legacy of economic, industrial, and bureaucratic stagnation, plus a heavy burden of military power and commitments from the Brezhnev era and subsequent interim regimes. He understands that these inherited conditions place great limitations on his ability to sustain progress toward achieving Soviet national goals by the preferred method of implementing national strategy through "peaceful competition" with the West. Indeed, he recognizes that political and economic stagnation at home pose the greatest threat to the Soviet Union's ability to achieve its national goals.

Thus, Gorbachev has concluded that it is necessary to make methodological changes in the implementation of Soviet national strategy. He has deemphasized the external, preferred method of implementing Soviet national strategy. Rather, he has focused on the required, internal method of implementing national strategy by concentrating on the goal of strengthening the Soviet system and preserving control by the party and elite. To achieve that goal, however, he cannot employ the usual means of further developing the garrison state. His means must be internal political, economic, and industrial reforms that will, of necessity, reduce the priority and resources given to military power. Since the goals of avoiding war and defending the homeland remain no less important, the means of achieving them must be by pursuing arms control rather than by continuing the arms race.

To bring about this methodological change in implementing Soviet national strategy and to develop new means of implementation, Gorbachev must make methodological changes in the Soviet policymaking process. His program to do so involves *glasnost'* and *perestroika*. *Glasnost'* means giving "publicity" to problems, issues, and proposed solutions in order to generate support for *perestroika*, which means "restructuring" the party and government policymaking bureaucracy as well as "rebuilding" the economy and industry. Thus, Gorbachev's program is proceeding on two levels. On the superficial level of *glasnost'*, changes are being made in the ways things are discussed and described in order to create a climate for subsequent changes; and on the methodological level of *perestroika*, changes are being made in the way the bureaucracy does its work, the economy is planned, and industry performs.

Gorbachev's success in bringing about change is more apparent at the superficial level of *glasnost'* than at the methodological level of *perestroika*. There is much more open discussion of past problems, new concepts to be applied, proposals to be adopted, and directives to be implemented than there are ongoing or completed reforms. The conservative opposition that exists could slow or preclude the adoption and implementation of his efforts.

Thus, the turmoil that is occurring in the Soviet Union today does not yet represent fundamental change in the factors underlying Soviet national strategy. Rather, Gorbachev has been forced to make a methodological change in the implementation of that strategy.

Changes Affecting the Factors Shaping Soviet
Military Strategy

In order to help him bring about methodological change in Soviet national strategy, Gorbachev has surrounded himself with a coterie of civilian advisers on national security affairs. This civilian group has introduced new political thinking in the sphere of international relations to challenge the traditional military dominance over thinking about Soviet national security affairs.

These civilians have been studying, writing, and advising Gorbachev on the same topics—Marxist-Leninist philosophy on war, military history, military theory, and the correlation of forces—that have long been the preserve of military academicians and Soviet military science. Based on their "new thinking," the civilians have developed a national security rationale that supports Gorbachev's need to shift scarce resources from the military to the economy and industry while maintaining military parity by arms control.

Accordingly, the Soviet military have been told to adopt a new "defensive doctrine" and size their forces to "reasonable sufficiency." The Defense Council has made changes in the formal definition of Soviet military doctrine. Rather than the traditional description of military doctrine as being concerned with preparing for and conducting war, doctrine is now described as being concerned with the prevention of war, defense, and repelling aggression. Wide publicity has been given to these changes as indicative of Soviet adoption of a defensive doctrine. Meanwhile, Gorbachev has emphasized the concept of reasonable sufficiency as the basis for party military policy and has led the party to temper its commitment to provide resources for the military. This defensive doctrine and reasonable sufficiency of forces have been declared as the official doctrine and policy of the Warsaw Pact and the Soviet Union.

This effort of Gorbachev and his civilian advisers to get the military to adopt a defensive military doctrine and adhere to a policy of reasonable sufficiency of forces stimulated a major public debate between the civilian advisers and military leaders. The debate was not about whether Soviet military doctrine is now defensive or whether Soviet military policy is now one of reasonable sufficiency. That has been decided and promulgated, top-down. Rather, the debate was about how those concepts and words should be interpreted at the practical level.

Over the next several years, the Soviet Union will be developing and finalizing the Five-Year Plan beginning in 1991. During that time the Defense Council must make a myriad of individual decisions about the specific operational implementation of defensive doctrine and the specific force levels and composition that constitute reasonable sufficiency, as well as the resource allocations required to support them.

Until those decisions are made, Gorbachev's concepts of a defensive doctrine and reasonable sufficiency will remain only superficial changes in the way doctrine and policy are stated. It will be several years before it will be possible to determine the degree to which those superficial changes bring about methodological changes in the various components of Soviet military science and strategic military decision making that guide the way the Soviet Union develops and executes its military strategy.

Conclusion

Based on cultural, historical, and ideological influences and on national mind-sets, goals, and decision making derived from them, Soviet national strategy has taken on certain fundamental characteristics. Because of unique national processes for the development and implementation of Soviet military strategy, it too has taken on certain fundamental characteristics.

While there is change in the Soviet Union, none of the underlying influences on Soviet national strategy have changed, nor have any of the processes shaping the development and implementation of Soviet military strategy been abandoned. Rather, Gorbachev is trying to bring about methodological change in how the Soviet Union implements its national strategy and executes its military strategy. So far, he has clearly changed the method of implementing national strategy by shifting emphasis from the preferred method to the required method. His efforts to change the methods by which military strategy is executed at the operational level, from offense to defense, and at the resource level, from plenty to sufficiency, are still superficial. But over the next several years, those desired methodological changes may be accomplished. Despite this change, the fundamental characteristics of Soviet national and military strategy acquired over the years have not changed. They remain the direct sources of Soviet naval conduct.

2

The Foreign Policy Context:
Brezhnev's Legacy and
Gorbachev's Talents

Ken Booth

I n March 1985 Soviet foreign policy came to the end of a particularly difficult period. For over five years, there had been a depressing parallelism for the Soviet Union between its ailing leaders and its declining effectiveness in international affairs. In the first half of the 1980s, foreign policy had been characterized by the immobilism of Leonid Brezhnev's last years, the stricken hopes of Yuri Andropov, and the funereal caretakership of Konstantin Chernenko. Following the deaths of this trio, a new generation stepped forward under Mikhail Gorbachev. Since that time we have had the promise—though many in the West have seen it as a threat—of a sustained period of energy, sophistication, and stability in the Kremlin.

Gorbachev's Inheritance

The international position Gorbachev inherited in 1985 was not an enviable one, though this was not how it was portrayed by the leaders of the major Western states, notably President Ronald Reagan and Prime Minister Margaret Thatcher, who were at the forefront in propagating images of a threatening and successful Soviet Union. Yet the state of Soviet foreign relations in the first half of the 1980s bore little resemblance to the new cold war images. Nor did Soviet standing in the world match the inflated claims of Moscow's propaganda.

The theory and practice of foreign policy is preoccupied with the problem of images, that is, the perceptions and misperceptions that individuals and groups have about the objective situation. Images shape behavior. Policies are invariably made and nations interact on the basis of a less than perfect understanding of reality. Nowhere have clashing images been of more political

I wish to thank Randall Forsberg, Caroline Kennedy, and Nicholas J. Wheeler for help on the initial draft of this chapter.

importance than over the issues surrounding Soviet foreign policy. The Western debate has polarized during the last decade around two sets of images, the ideological and the empirical.

In the first half of the 1980s, ideological images dominated the agenda in the West of both policymaking and public debate. These images, however, bore only a superficial relationship to reality. They painted a picture of the Soviet Union as the focus of evil in the world; it was, in Reagan's famous phrase, the "empire of evil." From this perspective, a threatening image of Soviet external behavior was projected. The Soviet Union was seen as a country that through the 1970s had accumulated (and was still accumulating) unprecedented military potential while diplomatically purporting to support détente. The Helsinki Final Act had been signed, but within the Soviet Union's own boundaries and those of its Eastern European satellites, human rights continued to be trampled. In the Third World, the Soviet Union was seen as ignoring world opinion while engaging in political and military expansionism and adventurism. Confident of its growing military strength, the Soviet Union seemed increasingly ready to employ military pressure of one sort or another to extend its influence. It exploited opportunities to further its long-term ambitions. Across the globe—in Africa, the Middle East, Central America, and Southeast Asia—there seemed to be a relentless Soviet strategic momentum in the second half of the 1970s. Pickings were even thought to be available in the West, where West European disaffection with U.S. leadership seemed to offer an opportunity to drive a wedge into the nuclear core of the North Atlantic Treaty Organization (NATO). At the end of 1979, the Soviet intervention in Afghanistan helped to bring together all the pieces of this ideological image. For the first time since it had rolled up Eastern Europe in the aftermath of defeating Nazi Germany, the Kremlin had decided to inject large numbers of its own troops into a country that was not accepted as part of the Soviet bloc. After decades of being a relatively weak actor on the world stage, the arrival of Soviet troops in Afghanistan seemed to prove that the Soviet superpower now had both the military strength and the geopolitical confidence to further the regime's traditional global ambitions.

The ideologically derived image of the state of Soviet foreign relations was erroneous. It was not the image as seen at the time by most Soviet specialists in the West, nor did it depict the world as viewed from the Kremlin walls. In contrast with this image of growing Soviet power and success, the empirical view drew attention to the fact that Soviet foreign relations had become decidedly uncomfortable. In the first half of the 1980s, the Soviet Union was a harassed socialist superpower. Its leaders knew that while their armed forces were formidable, their utility was limited. They knew that they had made some gains in the Third World in the 1970s—in Angola, Ethiopia, Mozambique, Vietnam, and elsewhere—but they were aware that their relations with these countries were not secure springboards for wider ambitions.

They knew that there were serious cracks behind the superpower facade. The Soviet Union was threatened by dangerous trends in Eastern Europe (for example, the growth of Solidarity in Poland); there were chronic economic problems at home; constraints existed on its influence-building potential almost everywhere; and the strategic power of this "one-dimensional superpower" rested on technology that was second rate in comparison with that of the United States. As a result of these weaknesses and the growing hostility of much of the outside world, the Soviet Union in the early 1980s was, and felt, more insecure than at any other time since the Cuban missile crisis.

The bleak outlook was disappointing to the aging leaders of the Soviet Union, and even more so to the next generation of leaders waiting in the wings. In broad ideological terms, the Kremlin had always seen the period since 1917 as one in which a transformation was taking place from an outdated capitalist order to a new communist one. But history has been moving with depressing slowness for the descendants of the Bolsheviks. Over the years, no Soviet leader has denied the possibility of a world communist order, but the time scale for the achievement of this goal has been extending since the early years of postrevolutionary innocence. As recently as Nikita Khrushchev, it was still possible for a Soviet leader to talk about the Soviet Union's overtaking the United States economically within twenty years or so and achieving communism in the foreseeable future. No longer do Soviet leaders have that optimism. More recently, the Soviet position has been encapsulated in the quip that "communism is like the horizon: the closer one seems to approach it, the further it recedes."

The role of ideological goals in Soviet foreign policy remains a complex issue, but several general themes are evident. First, Soviet ideology is not a static set of ideas.[1] The ideology—or rather the set of interrelated beliefs which make it up—has and will continue to evolve. It has never simply been the body of ideas expressed on paper by the classical theorists. It has also been what the party leadership of the day says and does; and in some respects the ideology by this process has become less radical with the passage of time. Second, different aspects of the ideology serve different functions. These might be classified as philosophical, programmatic, and behavioral. The philosophical aspects of the ideology analyze and explain the forces that shape humans and society, history and economics, and the nature of world politics. The programmatic aspects are those that indicate the revolutionary goals and the tactics of communist takeovers. The behavioral aspects of the ideology are concerned with socializing its supporters, legitimizing Soviet behavior, helping to bind the adherents together, and establishing the boundaries of acceptable thought and behavior.

When these two propositions are put together—that Soviet ideology changes and that its different elements have different functions—it is evident how complex the possible interrelationships are between ideology and foreign policymaking and execution. The theme running through this chapter is that the philosophical and behavioral aspects of Soviet ideology are still significant but that the programmatic aspects are less so. This means that Soviet spokesmen continue to think and talk ideologically and that their words and actions are both somewhat limited and justified by ideological precepts; however, when it comes to foreign policy programs, the development of the Soviet state has gradually come to be shaped by more objective realities than doctrine. While Soviet leaders probably continue to believe in world revolution as an ultimate goal, it is now more a utopian dream than the active plan of the early postrevolutionary period. There has been little sign that such revolutionary objectives have dominated Soviet policymaking in recent times or even that the Soviet Union could cope with world revolution if it did come about. For the Soviet Union, as for all other states, policymaking tends to be incremental and reactive. In the adverse international conditions of the early 1980s, this meant a foreign policy characterized by damage limitation.

In the light of the terrible history suffered by the peoples of the Soviet Union, security—physical, territorial, political, and psychological—has always been at the premium. Soviet leaders since Stalin have not had to fear old-style invasion, but they have had and do have many other insecurities. They fear, to different extents, the loss of authority in Eastern Europe, the potential dangers of losing control in a multinational state, borderland instability, and the nuclear confrontation with their most powerful enemies getting out of hand. In the extreme, these problems could result in the collapse of the power of the Communist party of the Soviet Union, the breakup of the Soviet empire, or even the catastrophe of a nuclear war. These were all distant worst-case possibilities in the first half of the 1980s, but these possibilities were more thinkable than the problem of welcoming the growth of communism across the world.

Brezhnev's Foreign Policy Legacy: A Regional Survey

The difficult inheritance to which Gorbachev succeeded was in part the result of Soviet behavior. How much so is a matter of dispute. Soviet commentators, like those of other nations in a similar position, naturally tend to blame their problems on the hostility and mischief making of others rather than upon their own words and actions. But from the viewpoint of mainstream Western opinion, the Kremlin brought trouble on its own head in the 1975–1985 decade. Would there have been the breakdown in arms control had the Soviet Union shown more flexibility? Would relations with the United States have deteriorated had the Soviet Union not supported national liberation movements so aggressively in the 1970s? Would Japan have proved so defiant had the Soviet Union been less heavy-handed in general and in particular with respect to the Kurils? Would the mistrust of so many states have been less, especially in the Islamic world, had Soviet troops not gone into Afghanistan? And what of the state of relations with China had not the Soviet Union backed Vietnam so vigorously? The list of such questions could go on.

Soviet commentators would recognize some errors in their behavior, but for the most part, their explanation of the 1975–1985 period would be more in terms of external hostility than of their own mistakes: they saw themselves surrounded by ideological and national adversaries intent on securing advantages in the inexorable struggle between systems and states. With some exceptions, the Soviet (and before that Russian) approach to the outside world has been ethnocentric and paranoid. Such outlooks are no less real for being in the mind. But the Soviet characterization of a hostile world was not far from actual reality. This will be evident in the regional survey below. The picture that will be revealed contrasts radically from that projected by the Reagan and Thatcher governments in the first half of the 1980s.

The United States

In the first half of the 1980s, the Soviet Union's relationship with the world's most powerful nation was worse than at any other time since the Cuban missile crisis of 1962.[2] The process of superpower détente, which had developed in a promising direction in the early 1970s, finally collapsed at the end of 1979 with the Soviet intervention in Afghanistan and the U.S. Senate decision not to ratify the Strategic Arms Limitation Talks (SALT) II Treaty. The process had been ailing for at least five years, with the gathering mutual mistrust encouraging both sides to place unilateral gain before mutual restraint.

The détente relationship had been an important one for the Soviet Union. At the end of the 1960s, Leonid Brezhnev and his colleagues had hoped to use the relaxation of tensions with the United States to secure trade agreements, credits, and technical assistance from the West. Unwilling to institute radical economic reforms at home, the Kremlin hoped to get the capitalist world to prop up a socialist system that was failing to feed its people satisfactorily, failing in industrial performance, and failing to create an efficient distribution system for that which was produced. For a time détente worked well for the Soviet leadership, but by the mid-1970s, the returns were proving less than had been hoped. By the end of the decade, Soviet observers had come to explain the decline of détente with a set of arguments that were an exact mirror image of those being used in the United States.[3]

From the Soviet viewpoint, the United States had not lived up to the requirements of a détente relationship. In Moscow's eyes, the United States had not sunk into the "decade of neglect" as later claimed by the U.S. right. Instead it had been engaged in a vigorous arms race, one of development rather than deployment, of qualitative rather than quantitative change. In addition, the United States had failed to deliver on the economic and arms control agreements supported by the Kremlin. Diplomatically the United States had been very critical of Soviet behavior in areas where the latter believed that what they were doing was legitimate (for example, support for national liberation struggles) or where criticism was thought to be inconsistent with trying to strengthen détente (notably the pressure on the Soviet Union's human rights policy). In short, from the Soviet viewpoint, the United States lived up to neither the spirit nor letter of détente.

From the mid-1970s onward, U.S. behavior was increasingly tough and uncompromising in the eyes of the Kremlin, so much so that it was calculated that there was not too much to lose by moving troops into Afghanistan. Washington reacted strongly, as it did to the imposition of martial law in Poland two years later. U.S. reactions appeared to be both hypocritical and unduly hostile in Moscow's eyes; after all the United States had not been averse to using military force to prop up its friends, and it supported military governments. Nevertheless, U.S. opinion was increasingly outraged at what it saw as growing Soviet aggressiveness.[4] Already in 1979, the NATO allies had agreed to install what Moscow considered to be threatening new "strategic" missiles in Western Europe; in Moscow this was deemed to be an escalation of the arms race to match the Soviet Union's own intermediate nuclear forces (INF) modernization. In 1980 the U.S. Senate failed to ratify SALT II, and Ronald Reagan was elected president. With his anti-Soviet and anti–arms control beliefs, President Reagan promised (threatened in Soviet eyes) to revitalize the United States and restore it to what the country saw as its rightful position of "number one" in international politics, and notably in military affairs. Soviet leaders had plenty of cause for anxiety; they knew from long experience that the United States always wins arms races, and they feared how a Reagan White House might demonstrate that power.

After Reagan became president, Soviet relations with the United States deteriorated rapidly. U.S. defense spending rocketed. Talk of U.S. nuclear strategy shifted from deterrence to war fighting and prevailing, and U.S. naval strategy adopted an aggressive posture. The United States threatened to leap far ahead in the technological arms race. The development of deep-strike capabilities for NATO doctrine and of emerging technology were capped by the announcement in 1983 of the Strategic Defense Initiative (SDI) (and continued reassertions that it was nonnegotiable). Soviet appeals for détente were rejected. In place of talk about cooperation, the White House called for sanctions against the Soviet Union. Furthermore, there were overt and covert U.S. attempts to push back Soviet gains in the Third World made in the 1970s. In all major areas of the superpower relationship, the Soviet Union felt confronted and threatened, and there were few signs that the situation would improve.

China

Soviet leaders had been facing a second cold war in their relations with China since the 1960s. The scale of the Soviet Union's China problem is something observers in the West find difficult to understand.[5] The ingredients are a 6,000-kilometer border with a country of about 1 billion people of an alien race and culture. In addition, there have been historical conflicts between the two states, notably because of Chinese claims on the vast territories that were taken from them by czarist Russia. On top of all this there has been an overlay of ideological hostility between the two socialist giants; for a quarter of a century, the quarter of humanity bustling on the Soviet Union's southern border has represented alternative views about communism.

Sino-Soviet relations went into further decline in the late 1970s when Chinese relations with the United States and Western Europe began to open up. From the Kremlin's perspective, this represented a worrying coalescence of hostile forces, especially since it was accompanied by increased efforts to modernize Chinese industry and military capabilities. Although the latter have remained relatively primitive by Soviet standards, the Chinese now have a handful of long-range missiles and other delivery systems, and they have probably reached the point at which they could inflict unacceptable damage on the Soviet Union in the event of war.[6]

The long cold war with China, which in 1969 threatened to escalate following the border clashes on the Ussuri, not only became less comfortable from the Soviet point of view; it also came to be seen as wasteful materially and playing into the hands of the United States diplomatically. Soviet hopes of a rapprochement with China were dim in the first half of the 1980s, but even efforts at normalization proved unsuccessful. Talks failed as often as they started because the Chinese terms were unacceptable to the Soviet Union. Thus, for Brezhnev and his immediate successors, the Soviet Union's China problem remained a heavy drain on Soviet military and diplomatic resources.

Japan

Soviet problems with China were given an extra edge as a result of the normalization of China's own relationship with the other East Asian power, Japan. The latter's economic success in the 1970s stood in sharp contrast to the sorry state of the Soviet economy. To make matters worse for the Kremlin, Soviet relations with this burgeoning economic superpower had been deteriorating for several years.

Starting in the late 1970s, Japan became a growing problem for Soviet foreign policy. Tokyo ignored Moscow's warnings and signed a treaty of friendship with China; it reaffirmed its alliance with the United States; it would not sign a peace treaty with the Soviet Union on the latter's terms; it continued to raise the vexing question of the Soviet-occupied Kuril islands; there was periodic talk of the constitution's being revised in order to strengthen its armed forces; Japan reacted vigorously against the Soviet intervention in Afghanistan; the shooting down of a Korean airliner in 1983 led to a further exacerbation of relations; and the United States pressed its dynamic Far Eastern ally to translate more of its economic wealth into military potential. Japanese prime minister Yasuhiro Nakasone in 1983 made a remark about turning Japan into an unsinkable aircraft carrier in support of the West.[7] For Soviet defense planners thinking "worst cases," Japan was an increasingly powerful and hostile member of the encircling anti-Soviet Western-Chinese bloc.

By the first half of the 1980s, therefore, the Soviet Union had poor relations with the United States, China, and Japan—that is, with the world's most influential superpower, the other leading communist power, and the nation with the most dynamic economy in Asia, respectively. To make matters worse, these centers of power seemed to be developing a more coordinated anti-Soviet stance. But if Soviet foreign policy was proving unsuccessful in its relations with the world's major power centers, it was also failing to make headway elsewhere.

The Third World

The Third World—that varied mixture of ex-colonial less-developed countries that became such a feature of world politics after the World War II—has been a considerable disappointment to the Soviet Union. When the latter entered into the international politics of the Third World, it had many advantages, but it subsequently failed to capitalize on them.[8]

As he contemplated this emerging field of international struggle in the mid-1950s, Khrushchev had reason to think that the Soviet system would be the wave of the future. Great Britain with its colonial past, and the United States with its string of alliances with local strongmen, were seen as the enemies of change in the Third World. The Soviet Union, in contrast, had a head start in winning hearts and minds. Its propaganda had always been identified with anti-imperialism, while its own hands were clean of both an overseas empire or alliances with distant dictators (the Soviet empire in Eastern Europe is rarely seen as relevant in such discussions). Despite its advantages, the Soviet wave of the future never reached as far as was expected in the Third World.

The reasons for the lack of Soviet success are not difficult to discern. Soviet leaders have always had limited economic power; they often appeared manipulative in their military aid diplomacy, and they were sometimes unsophisticated in their dealings with local countries. Additionally, Third World nationalism, alternative sources of economic assistance, and the patchwork of regional conflicts seriously hampered Soviet efforts at spreading influence. In the course of time, Soviet ideology lost much of whatever attractiveness it had originally possessed. In some parts of the world, especially Latin America and the Middle East, religion was a major barrier. It was significant that when Iran threw off Western materialism, the people turned not to Soviet materialism, but to Islam. And even where "socialism," "Marxism-Leninism," or "communism" was espoused by governments or communist parties in the Third World, most groups preferred their own brand or were attracted to China's. The Soviet model lacked universal attraction.

A major indicator of the lack of Soviet success in influence building across the world has been the historic decline of the world communist movement, in both image and reality. Who, apart from right-wing ideologues, can now conjure up the threat of monolithic communism that was such a powerful force in the thinking of the cold war period? As time has passed this threat has declined in significance and for practical political purposes has long been irrelevant. In addition to the inherent problems of finding unity in any international grouping, the failure of international communism owed much to the Soviet Union's own behavior. The latter sank nail after nail into the movement's coffin: Stalinist attempts to maintain Soviet domination and orthodoxy in the movement, the invasion of Hungary, the Sino-Soviet split and all its associated recriminations, the military repression of "socialism with a human face" in Czechoslovakia, and the intervention in Afghanistan. In some parts of the world, particularly Eastern Europe and Southeast Asia, states committed to communism have represented bigger enemies to each other than they have to neighboring noncommunist states. Soviet problems with socialist neighbors Poland and China led to the now famous gibe that the Soviet Union, in Brezhnev's later years, was the only country in the world surrounded by communist enemies.

In contrast to the image projected by some in the West of Soviet success in the Third World in the 1970s, the Third World was not falling into the grasp of the Soviet Union.[9] Under Brezhnev, the Soviet Union certainly made some gains, but it also suffered losses, and its gains were of uncertain value and permanence. To some sectors of Western opinion, the growth of any Soviet relationship—diplomatic, cultural, or economic—with a Third World nation appeared and appears threatening and expansionist. But as the world's second largest power, it was only to be expected that the Soviet Union would attempt to develop relationships with countries in all regions; whether that relationship could be defined as a threat depended on its character and extent. The frequent exaggeration of the degree of success and threat represented by Soviet policy in the Third World can partly be explained by the fact that until the mid-1950s, the Soviet Union had played a minimal role; previously there had been a virtual Western monopoly of interest and power.

Consequently, if one gauges Soviet relations with Third World countries not against this background of noninvolvement but instead against its political advantages and its authority as one of the two superpowers, then one can only conclude that the Soviet record by the late 1970s, after over thirty years of effort in the Third World, was unsuccessful.

Africa in the 1970s throws into sharp relief the contrast between the image and reality of Soviet influence-building success. In the second half of the 1970s, the Soviet Union was widely portrayed as having become a significant power in the politics of Africa.[10] This was not the case. Only three of the fifty states in Africa voted in support of the Soviet Union at the United Nations (U.N.) following the latter's intervention in Afghanistan, and only a handful of the forty-seven members of the Organization of African Unity (Angola, Ethiopia, and Mozambique) could have been described as Soviet clients. Some Western countries, such as France, remained much more influential than the Soviet Union in the international politics of the continent, while the West in general, through its domination of the international economy, was overwhelmingly more powerful in determining the general pattern of African affairs.

The chief Soviet concern about the Third World in the late 1970s and early 1980s focused on their southern flanks. Geopolitically it is not sufficiently recognized in the West that the Middle East and Southwest Asia occupy the same relationship to the Soviet Union as Central America does to the United States. The distance between Washington and Managua or the Panama Canal is roughly comparable to that between Moscow and Jerusalem and the Persian Gulf. Since the late 1970s, the Soviet Union's southern borderlands have been characterized by instability and war to a far greater extent than the southern borderlands of the United States. The fall of the shah and the rise of the Ayatollah Khomeini, the Lebanon crisis, the growth of Islamic fundamentalism, the spread of terrorism, the Iran-Iraq War, the continuing Israeli-Arab dispute: these were only the major flash points in this chronically troubled region.[11] Despite its reputation for being able to fish in troubled waters, the Soviet Union was unable to exploit these troubles to its own advantage. On the positive side, it developed its relationship with Syria. But on the negative side, it was maneuvered out of the central diplomacy of the region through the 1970s; its policies were opposed by such important regimes as those of Egypt and Iran; and it incurred the hostility of most of the Islamic world by its military attempt to defend the gains of socialism in Afghanistan. The United States remained the major external influence on the region.

The intervention in Afghanistan in 1979 proved to be a historic blunder for the Soviet Union.[12] Tempted to defend a friendly government against internal attack, the Soviet Union in the first half of the 1980s became as bogged down as the United Stated had been in undertaking a similar task in Vietnam over a decade earlier. The main difference was that Soviet discomfort was far less public at home and abroad. But like the United States, the Soviet Union continued to invest its efforts in a war that, from the outside, it seemed it could not win. Casualty figures were high, as were other costs, including a diplomatic price in terms of international prestige. The war in Afghanistan was a great boon to the Soviet Union's critics. Meanwhile, the evidence suggested that if Soviet troops had been pulled out, the Marxist regime in Kabul would have collapsed. Just like the United States in Vietnam fifteen years earlier, the Soviet Union in Afghanistan in the first half of the 1980s did not seem to be able to win militarily but believed for the moment that it could not afford to lose. There were occasional signs from Soviet leaders and spokesmen in Geneva and elsewhere that they would have liked to have withdrawn, but there were no signs of an exit route acceptable to all parties.

Other examples of Soviet adventurism or expansionism in the Third World were not as costly as Afghanistan but were still unprofitable.[13] Angola, which had been so important in undermining U.S. support for détente, proved to be a disappointment to the Kremlin. In the early 1980s, the civil war rumbled on. The country cost the Soviet economy a great deal to support, and the Popular Movement for the Liberation of Angola (MPLA) government showed an unfortunate independence of mind in its search for foreign backers. Ethiopia was also a disappointment. Soviet support for the Marxist regime there had excited Western fears about Soviet ambitions on the Horn of Africa in the late 1970s, but by the mid-1980s the region was attracting world headlines, not because it became a hotbed of communism but because it became the scene of tragic famine. Ethiopia became another heavy drain on Soviet resources that promised little in the way of material or political benefits to the Soviet Union. The same was true, but to a lesser extent, about the Soviet relationship with Vietnam following the North's victory over the South in 1975. Vietnam offered the Soviet Union naval facilities and regional support, but economically it proved to be yet another burden on the Soviet budget. Furthermore, Vietnam's military intervention in Kampuchea provoked the mistrust or hostility of other countries in the region. Naturally this mistrust spilled over onto Vietnam's superpower backer. Thus the price of the Soviet relationship with Vietnam was not only financial, it was also diplomatic. The Soviets and the Vietnamese believed that they would be useful to each other, but no sign of mutual regard developed. In Ho Chi Minh City, Russians came to be called "Yankees without dollars."[14]

Of all the Soviet Union's associates in the Third World, Cuba has been of special significance, but the balance sheet again is mixed.[15] Like other countries organized according to socialist principles, Cuba has faced enormous economic difficulties, and like the other struggling countries, has also been supported by the Soviet Union. By the mid-1980s this had reached a figure of $11 million a day.[16] Unlike the others, however, Cuba has proved to be a vigorous ally. It sent troops to support Soviet-backed national liberation struggles in Africa in the 1970s. But Fidel Castro has not proved to be an easy ally. His revolutionary enthusiasm has generally outrun that of the Soviet leaders, and his behavior has at times led to a U.S. backlash that has disadvantaged his Soviet backers. The Kremlin has not been sorry to see instability in South and Central America, but with the exception of the steps leading to the Cuban missile crisis, Soviet leaders have trodden very carefully in what they, as well as Washington, choose to see as the backyard of the United States.

After committing thirty years of resources and effort, the Soviet Union has relatively little to show in the Third World. By the mid-1980s it could count among the pro-Soviet group of countries only Afghanistan, Angola, Cuba, Ethiopia, Mozambique, South Yemen, Vietnam, and a couple of less-committed countries, notably Syria. The future of the ruling regimes of these countries was uncertain, as was that of their long-term relationship with the Soviet Union; these clients, together or separately, did not promise to be stepping-stones to world influence. For the most part, Third World countries acted in support of Soviet interests only when it served their own purposes. Western observers frequently mistake Soviet influence for mutual shared interests. The Soviet Union, of course, can help Third World countries undertake policies that are hostile to particular Western interests (such as supplying arms to North Vietnam or supplying intelligence to Argentina), but the evidence suggests that none of this can buy secure long-term influence. Starting in the mid-1950s, the Soviet Union entered the international politics of the Third World with many advantages; thirty years later an empirical assessment leads to the conclusion that it missed the bus.

Western Europe

Ironically, one of the few hopeful areas for Soviet foreign policy in the first half of the 1980s was Western Europe, which historically had offered infertile ground for the growth of Soviet influence. Here again Soviet hopes proved to be disappointed.

There were potential pickings for Soviet policymakers in the growing anti-U.S. and antinuclear mood in many parts of Western Europe following NATO's 1979 decision to deploy U.S. cruise and Pershing II missiles and in reaction to the election and posturing of Ronald Reagan. Anti-Americanism and antinuclear attitudes were fueled more by the words and actions of the Reagan administration than by those of the stony-faced Kremlin. Despite the latter's efforts and strained transatlantic relations in the first half of the 1980s, Western European defense plans continued. The right-wing parties of Margaret Thatcher in Great Britain and Helmut Kohl in West Germany were successful in general elections; cruise and Pershing II missiles were deployed; France's first socialist president, François Mitterand, proved to be more

Gaullist than his predecessors; and although capitalist economies were under strain during these years, by Soviet bloc standards Western Europe as a whole was prosperous and technologically advanced. Viewed from the inside, the European Economic Community was full of bickering, and it advanced at only a snail's pace. Viewed from the Kremlin (and from the lifetime's perspective of one of Soviet Russia's aging leaders), the contrast between the crisis-ridden and economically struggling Western Europe of the 1930s and the peaceful, prosperous, and relatively united Western Europe of fifty years later must have been truly remarkable. In its continuing vitality, democracy, and economic success, Western Europe represented a standing challenge to the sorry state of the communist dream in the Soviet Union and Eastern Europe.

The Soviet Union not only failed to win over the center and right of opinion in Western Europe, it also lost ground with radicals on the left. Leftward-leaning opinion in Western Europe looked with decreasing enthusiasm toward Moscow. The growth of the Eurocommunist phenomenon in the mid-1970s had marked a further significant defection by a substantial part of the Socialist world from Soviet aspirations for ideological authority.[17] But even Eurocommunism itself had lost momentum by the 1980s.

Soviet hopes of building influence across the spectrum of Western European political opinion in the late 1970s and early 1980s remained unfulfilled. Indeed, politically and economically, the Kremlin was for the most part on the defensive. Even the Soviet penchant for propaganda could not counter the West's diplomatic and propaganda offensive against Soviet behavior at home and abroad. Soviet spokesmen in the early 1980s had to work hard to meet the Western challenge over its intervention in Afghanistan, the Soviet record on human rights, and allegations of Soviet cheating on arms control. To make matters worse, Soviet behavior sometimes played into the hands of their adversaries, as was notably the case with the downing of a Korean airliner in 1983, a major propaganda coup for the Reagan White House.

In absolute military terms, the Soviet Union was more powerful than ever before in the early 1980s, but its impressive order of battle did not readily translate into politically usable power. Soviet military might could do little to counter the failures. Furthermore, few in Western Europe seemed to believe that the Soviet Union would engage in a cosmic gamble and one day use its weaponry to attack westward. Indeed, various knowledgeable sources began to question NATO's prevailing image of Soviet conventional military supremacy.[18] Whatever the state of the balance, much Western opinion wondered why the Soviet Union should ever undertake the awful risk of invading and trying to occupy Western Europe when it was already experiencing such difficulties maintaining control over its empire in the eastern half of the continent.

Eastern Europe

There might have been Soviet disappointment at the lack of success in Western Europe in the early 1980s, but there were deep Soviet fears about the way the situation was developing in Eastern Europe. Although in strictly military terms the Warsaw Pact had never been stronger than it was at the end of the 1970s, the Soviet management of the region was threatened by a series of interacting problems. Nationalism, severe economic difficulties, and political stagnation created a situation that both the local regimes and the Kremlin found difficult to handle. After a generation of economic growth, stagnation in Eastern Europe led to cracks in the system.

In the early 1980s, Poland was the focus of Soviet problems. There, as the *Economist* put it at the time, "The withering away of the communist party, under the glare of the Soviet empire's first genuine workers' movement, has put a question mark over the empire's whole ideology."[19] It was not only in the area of ideology where developments in Poland threatened the authority and legitimacy of the Communist party of the Soviet Union. Political and ideological challenges also ultimately threatened the physical domination of the Soviet Union over this critical region.[20] This fear was raised by the prospect that the Polish crisis might bring victory for Solidarity and that similar defections from Soviet norms would spill over into other countries. It was imperative for the Soviet Union that the growth of Solidarity be checked; the desperate measure of martial law was, from the Soviet viewpoint, a notable, albeit surprise, success. The Kremlin knew that Soviet military intervention in Poland to maintain socialism would have been costly and dangerous. It would have been yet another symbol of the Soviet Union's historic failure to spread its system. The worst outcome was averted because the Polish military intervened first, but it was an ominous warning.

The rest of Eastern Europe presented a patchwork of different problems for Soviet policymakers.[21] Although Rumania criticized the Soviet Union over its policy in Afghanistan, it nevertheless behaved in a less maverick fashion in foreign affairs than hitherto, in part because of its own growing economic vulnerability. Hungary, in contrast, successfully experimented with a more liberal approach to economic affairs while following the Soviet Union faithfully in foreign policy. The German Democratic Republic (DDR) remained loyal to Moscow in both domestic and foreign policy, but the pull of West Germany on this linchpin of the Soviet bloc remained a long-term worry for the Kremlin. The German problem, although quiet, remained at the heart of the continent's security problems. Loyalty to the Soviet Union was not an issue in the case of Bulgaria and Czechoslovakia, but neither country showed the socialist system in a positive light. Although events elsewhere in Eastern Europe were nowhere as dramatic as in Poland, it was evident that the region would face a period of prolonged strain as political and economic factors interacted in uncertain ways both within and across borders. It was a potentially turbulent mix. The Eastern European regimes, together with the Kremlin, attempted to keep matters under control by a variable combination of marginal economic reform, tolerance, punishment, and rewards, but no leader in the region could have been ignorant of the underlying and unsettled tensions and frustrations in their countries.

If there had to be change in Eastern Europe, the Kremlin wanted to manage it. The theme of integration within the Council of Mutual Economic Assistance (Comecon) was one response. More important, the Warsaw Pact had evolved over the years into an important control mechanism.[22] But even here there were problems in the early 1980s. There was a small but significant amount of opposition in the DDR and Czechoslovakia to the siting of new Soviet missiles in Central Europe in response to NATO's INF deployment. There were also some reports that the Soviet Union might face problems when the Warsaw Pact came up for renewal in 1985. Despite all this, the Soviet Union continued to exercise control in the region effectively, if not effortlessly. The memory of the use of overwhelming military force in 1956 and 1968 continued to provide brutal warnings to the Eastern European countries of the dangers of moving too quickly beyond the bounds of Soviet-defined orthodoxy. Although the threat of force remained in the background, it was one that Soviet leaders seemed increasingly reluctant to exercise. It nevertheless continued to be an impressive instrument of policy, as the two decades of stagnation in Czechoslovakia testified.

Despite the various constraints, it was certain that there would be change in Eastern Europe. This change would take place at different rates in different countries and would take different forms. No doubt the ideal Eastern European future from the Kremlin's perspective was a region of pro-Soviet socialist regimes; however, the Polish crisis could not have encouraged Kremlin optimism in that regard. The Kremlin must have feared that any process of change would mean that the problems of control would grow rather than recede. Short of a war against one of its main adversaries, the prospect of losing political and military control over this vitally important region was the Kremlin's most serious foreign policy concern in the early 1980s.

Continuity and Change under Gorbachev

Clearly Gorbachev's foreign policy inheritance was not an enviable one. For most of the period since his arrival in Moscow in 1978, the Soviet Union had been a harassed socialist superpower. During the Brezhnev years the Soviet Union had become respected as a superpower in a military sense and had achieved strategic parity with the United States. Nevertheless, the balance sheet of Brezhnev's period of rule contained many negative features, including a range of counterproductive policies and apparent successes that proved to be burdens. Toward the end of the Brezhnev era, the strains were showing in both domestic and foreign affairs. The state was in crisis. Change was clearly necessary if this "incomplete superpower" was not to follow the path of its aging leadership.[23]

When set against this background, Gorbachev's behavior was not difficult to explain. While Gorbachev's innermost thoughts remain uncertain, it has been evident to all close observers that he is an extremely intelligent man and seems all the more impressive when set against the declining powers of his predecessors.[24]

In his first two years, Gorbachev tackled some of the more obvious symptoms of Soviet stagnation rather than the underlying problems. Since then, however, Soviet reform has accelerated. At the June 1987 Central Committee Plenum, major economic reforms were posted, and, twelve months later, political reform headed the agenda.

"Openness" and "democratization" are seen in the Kremlin as socialist instruments rather than liberal goals, but they have gone much further than could have been imagined when Gorbachev became leader. It takes time for new orthodoxies to become established; but as *perestroika* becomes more of an orthodoxy, it will work its way down the party line. Ideological evolution has gone alongside other changes as Gorbachev, now president as well as general secretary, and his supporters have elaborated a new theoretical framework.

The light being shined on the Soviet system's previous failings and excesses has been remarkable to witness. And although the changes in political and economic arrangements do not amount to a dismantling of socialism, they do promise the prospect of a significantly different political form—socialism with a consumer's face. Restructuring could be reversed (Gorbachev himself has admitted that new thinking is not yet irreversible), or changes in degree could yet become changes in kind. It is too soon to say what the outcome will be. Nevertheless, there can now be no doubt about Gorbachev's own commitment to radical reform.

In foreign affairs, the most impressive feature of Gorbachev's behavior in his first years in office has been his rationality and pragmatism. When he came to power, the objective needs of Soviet external relations were evident: the damage of the preceding years had to be reversed; a breathing space was required to reconstruct the economy at home; the costly arms race had to be controlled; it was necessary for several reasons to reduce international tensions; it would be helpful to pry apart the growing coalition of powerful hostile forces; policy in the Third World needed to be more discriminating; it was desirable to gain or regain a Soviet foothold in important regions; a more positive image needed to be created and projected in international affairs; it would be useful to begin or to improve diplomatic contact with a variety of states; attention had to be paid to the modernization of Eastern

Europe in both economic performance and political control; and relations needed to be normalized with the major power centers in the world and improved with a number of key regional powers. Furthermore, like all other Soviet leaders, especially new ones, Gorbachev hoped to use his foreign policy to strengthen his position at home. These, then, were the requirements of the situation when he became general secretary of the Communist party of the Soviet Union (CPSU) in March 1985. So far he has responded to them with the tactical authority of a chess master and the image-making skill of the most successful Western politicians.

Given the years of hibernation and stagnation in Soviet foreign policy in the early 1980s, any policy showing flair and initiative was likely to be regarded as newer than it actually was. This has been the case since 1985. Almost all of Gorbachev's initiatives have in fact been attempted before: the peace theme, collective security in Asia, the idea of a Middle Eastern settlement, radical nuclear disarmament proposals, naval disengagement schemes, new diplomatic openings—all of these ideas, and others, have long been part of the Soviet foreign policy menu. In addition, the scope for radical change in Soviet foreign policy was limited because of a mixture of objective and subjective factors that could not be wished away: Soviet economic weaknesses, U.S. hostility, Chinese mistrust, the economic strength of Japan and Western Europe, Third World nationalism, and the patchwork of regional disputes across the world. The scope for change was also limited by domestic preoccupations and whatever constraints were imposed by skeptical colleagues within the Kremlin. To date, the Soviet system has not long suffered risk takers in either foreign or domestic affairs.

Continuities were strong in the first period of Gorbachev's foreign policy. Several themes were either resurrections of ideas advanced in Brezhnev's period or were somewhat cosmetic. The growing involvement in the international economy, evident in the foreign trade reforms to ease links between foreign firms and Soviet enterprises, was a continuation of the turn from autarky signaled during the heyday of détente in the early 1970s. One waits to see what the stress on "interdependence" actually means in practice. Interdependence can be a mixed blessing, as members of Comecon have found with "integration." When superpowers talk about interdependence, they tend to look forward to everybody's dependence on them. One aspect of the interdependence theme has been the stress on various global problems involving scientific exchange. This could be merely cosmetic, but it could be a signal of a real desire for cooperation in other fields.

Gorbachev has had a remarkable impact on the atmosphere of international relations within a very short time, despite continuity. Clearly, "changing the atmospherics" was crucial for Gorbachev. The Soviet Union had been on the defensive in winning international opinion in the early 1980s, and whether for narrow self-interested reasons or to further more visionary projects, the new general secretary needed to project a more moderate, credible, and trustworthy image of his country. He succeeded quickly and well. He was greatly aided by the appointment of a cohort of affable, accessible, and urbane spokesmen who contrasted markedly with the stern representatives of the past. Gorbachev gave this media packaging of Soviet foreign policy special importance, but the idea was not new. Propaganda has always had a high priority in the Soviet Union, and even before Gorbachev became leader, attention was being given to a modernized press corps, improved communications, and greater exposure to Western media. In 1978, Brezhnev had created the International Information Department in the Central Committee to specialize in image management for foreign consumption.[25] Gorbachev developed this to good effect, and *Time* magazine was justified in talking about Gorbachev's "charm offensive."[26] Atmospherics can aid deception or help create the conditions for agreement. But as we know from the "spirit of Geneva" and the "spirit of Camp David" in earlier decades, atmosphere can rapidly change. For the moment, Soviet image management has never been more sophisticated or more successful.

The charm offensive has helped restore Soviet prestige and has done so in the most effective fashion; it would not have been so successful, however, if there had not been a convergence of projected image and actual behavior. The reasons for believing that Gorbachev is genuine and not simply engaging in an old-style peace offensive or massive *dezinformatsiia* are various: the consistency of the efforts; the Soviet reassessment of past behavior (which has resulted in a rewriting of the history of issues such as the blame for the cold war); the domestic risks he is running; the wide scope of the discussion; the commitments made by individuals; and the actions that have been taken in accordance with the new ideas. There can be no doubt that Gorbachev is a man with a vision and not merely a propagandist.

Gorbachev's approach has been new and startling in the most vital area of all, security.[27] He soon began to stress the theme of common security, which had been so loudly proclaimed by Western liberals through the early 1980s. This is the idea that nations should not try to strengthen their security at somebody else's expense and that a stable peace rests not on weapons but on a satisfactory political relationship. Gorbachev has supported his words on this idea by extensive arms control initiatives and an unprecedented willingness to be flexible. His approach has been startling because it contrasts so fundamentally with traditional Soviet strategic culture; prominent in the latter has been the equating of stability with preponderance, the tradition of military overinsurance, and the importance of negotiating from strength.[28]

Has there developed, then, a distinctively Gorbachevian foreign policy? There have been few new policies, but there have been new aspects of style and presentation; and the energy, sophistication, and intensity of approach are different from anything seen in years. But there are also signs of real new thinking in his belief in common security and defensive defense—and in the glimmerings of a better understanding of how the Soviet Union looked to others and a better understanding of the limitations of Soviet power. It could be that Gorbachev is the first empathetic and pessimistic Soviet leader. For these reasons alone, he may be the most successful.

Soviet Foreign Policy since 1985: A Regional Survey

If Gorbachev's innermost thoughts must remain hidden, his foreign policy actions were apparent and showed a distinctly rational response to all the problems facing the Soviet Union. Moreover, within a short space of time, he secured a remarkable turnaround from the state of Soviet external relations in the first half of the 1980s. A survey of the world's regions illustrates the magnitude and breadth of Gorbachev's advance on all fronts.

The United States

From the outset Gorbachev's intentions toward the United States seemed to be to reduce tension and wind down the enormously expensive and wasteful military competition between them. This would enable him to achieve his priority goals, which in the short and medium term were on the domestic front. Initially Gorbachev seemed to think that this could best be achieved by giving relations with the United States a lower priority than that accorded by his predecessors. This changed during 1986.

Arms control became the centerpiece of Soviet initiative toward the United States, based on Gorbachev's proposals of January 1986.[29] While the immediate background of Soviet–United States relations was far from encouraging given the confrontational character of the Reagan presidency, Gorbachev pursued his aims with energy and flexibility. He presumably hoped that something might yet be achieved with Reagan, who was facing a variety of pressures that might tilt him toward a more accommodating relationship with the Soviet Union. Even if he failed with the White House, a more flexible and accommodating Soviet Union might impress the Democratic-controlled Congress and also be a positive input into the next U.S. presidential election, whose initial skirmishing was already on the horizon. In addition, even if the United States proved obdurate on arms control, strains might be encouraged in the Western alliance since arms control had a higher priority in Western Europe than in Washington. Whether Reagan proved responsive to Gorbachev's flexibility, therefore, there were advantages to be gained by an active and sophisticated Soviet arms control policy. This, in fact, is what was tried with success in 1986–87.

Gorbachev sprayed the Western allies with initiatives (including the tossing back of some of their own). They found him difficult to handle. His approach was far more flexible than any of his predecessors on such issues as

INF and SDI. His efforts culminated in the signing of the INF treaty in December 1987 and his historic unilateral disarmament announcement at the U.N. in December 1988. In addition, the public presentation of the Soviet case became more effective; for example, unilateral gestures were made as tokens of seriousness. His tactics have been dazzling. He has shown remarkable flexibility and openness on issues such as intrusive verification, the possibility of asymmetrical cuts, and meaningful exchange of data. Doubts have been largely removed about his commitment to disarmament and arms control. When negotiations took place, there was a greater willingness to compromise. In the past the Soviet Union had always been serious about arms control on its own terms; under Gorbachev it was showing that its terms could be moderated in the interests of accommodation.[30] As a result of Gorbachev's arms control initiatives, the Reagan White House was thrown back on the defensive. President Reagan, buffeted by the Iran-contra scandal and other failures, became a late convert to arms control as a result of weakness, not strength. Despite being forced onto the defensive, the U.S. government did not allow Gorbachev to rest. He was pressed on human rights and regional issues (perhaps to deflect attention from his initiatives on the arms control front), and the maintenance of U.S. strategic programs (notably SDI) reminded Gorbachev of the dangers and costs of another round in the arms race.

On the whole, the Western doubters have expected results to come too quickly from the Soviet Union. There are several inherent obstacles to quick results in arms control because of the long lead times of military programs and the entrenched positions of military (and militarized) bureaucrats.

Gorbachev clearly is serious about disarmament and arms control, and for the strongest possible reasons; he believes they will serve a variety of major Soviet interests. On the economic front, cuts in conventional forces will save money and release manpower. Arms control might reduce particular military threats to the Soviet Union (cruise and Pershing II missiles, SDI, and emerging technology). Arms restraint also conforms with what might be emerging as a new defensive orientation in Soviet military doctrine. In contrast, a high-technology arms race would not only place the superpowers on a dangerous path toward collision, it would also be economically draining to the Soviet Union. There might be political benefits in proposing arms control since this might open up some cleavages within NATO. Above all, arms restraint is necessary to help produce that easing of international tension that is so important for the furtherance of pressing domestic problems. Similar arguments might have been used in earlier times, but the Soviet economic situation was not as serious. This is no longer the case, and as a result, the Soviet Union of Gorbachev seems to have abandoned its traditional commitment to what in the West has usually been called military overinsurance and which Gorbachev now calls superabundance.

Gorbachev continued to try to normalize the Soviet Union's relationship with the West by deideologizing it, appearing and acting in a constructive manner, meeting points of disagreement, and generally depriving Western ideologies of an enemy. Gorbachev was fortunate in his timing; his period of leadership coincided with "Reagan II" and a United States concerned about its domestic problems, rather than the first-term "Reagan I," who had been concerned to "restore" the United States to what his country thought its rightful position in international affairs.

China

From the outset the Gorbachev Kremlin adopted a significantly friendlier tone toward China. Hints were given that solutions were possible to the outstanding problems between them, and this followed a period when, according to the Chinese, the Soviet Union had refused to discuss these issues. Moscow suggested that improvement was possible not only in economic but also in political relations.

Fortunately for the new Soviet leadership, the problems preventing better relations with China did not seem to be looming as large as they had in previous years. In his much-publicized speech at Vladivostok in July 1986 and on other occasions, Gorbachev addressed the three major obstacles that had been regularly raised by the Chinese. He withdrew troops from Afghanistan and Mongolia. He also offered the Chinese concessions over the delineation of the Ussuri river boundary. By indicating the possibility of an agreement on such issues, Gorbachev was reducing the Chinese sense of a Soviet threat, and so leaving them the opportunity to concentrate more fully on their own program of domestic reform. With progress in these other areas, the matter of Soviet support for Vietnamese action in Kampuchea became the major obstacle. The Chinese had demanded for some time the withdrawal of Vietnamese troops from Kampuchea before it would reestablish the same party-to-party links with Moscow that it had developed with the parties in Eastern Europe. The Soviet government could only do so much, but progress took place over Kampuchea.

The Chinese had adopted a wary wait-and-see attitude toward the new Soviet leader, but Gorbachev had changed the situation. As a result of his efforts the normalization of the Sino-Soviet relations was on the table and led to a summit in May 1989. Gorbachev could scarcely have done more.

Japan

There were close parallels between Soviet policy toward China and toward Japan. In both cases relations had deteriorated, and in both cases Gorbachev gave early hints that it might be possible to settle outstanding disputes.[31]

Gorbachev seems to have attached considerable importance to better relations with Japan from the outset, with good reason. With Soviet-Japanese relations being so strained over the previous decade, there were benefits from relaxation : diplomatic (some loosening of the growing Western-Chinese-Japanese coalition), strategic (the discouraging of the trend toward the militarization of Japan), and economic (the involvement of Japan in the Soviet Union's domestic reconstruction). As a token of his desire for improved relations, Gorbachev demonstrated a new sensitivity to Japanese security needs, and he strengthened his words with some modest practical gestures. These included an early visit to Japan by Foreign Minister Eduard A. Shevardnadze and the easing of Japanese access to ancestral graves in the Kurils.

The Japanese, like the Chinese, were attentive to Moscow's new diplomacy, though under the premiership of Yasuhiro Nakasone, the Japanese government remained deeply hostile toward the Soviet Union. In both major East Asian powers, therefore, the Soviet Union had a great deal of mistrust to overcome. The Soviet leadership faced the prospect of having to continue on its chosen path with patience.

The Third World

Soviet policy in the Third World in the first half of the 1980s had been beset by difficulties following the ostensible "successes" of high Brezhnevism in the 1970s. Under Gorbachev, Soviet policy in the Third World pursued a policy of restraint, discrimination, and responsibility. The high-profile unilateralist policy of the Brezhnev years was abandoned. In its place the U.N. was given a new prominence, and progress occurred toward the settlement of some of the major international disputes (notably the withdrawal of Soviet troops from Afghanistan). The primacy being accorded to Soviet domestic affairs did not mean that the Third World was ignored: instead, it suggested that the Soviet leadership would more carefully calculate costs and benefits.

The result of these developments was to move toward a position in which the Third World was becoming a much less salient issue on the superpower agenda. The Soviet Union was not retreating into isolation, however; indeed, Soviet diplomacy was active during 1987–1988 in developing ties with a range of countries regardless of their ideology. Gorbachev played down power politics and committed himself to the idea of freedom of choice on the matter of social system. Like Khrushchev before him, Gorbachev did not want to compete with the United States by military means; instead he wanted to attract countries to the Soviet model by force of example. Given the Reagan administration's position on many important North-South issues—and also its hostile attitude to the U.N.—Gorbachev's new Third World policy gained him considerable international credit. It remains to be seen whether Gorbachev can maintain his chosen course with more consistency than Khrushchev.

Within the Third World, the traditional geopolitical priority of the Middle East remained the major area of Soviet concern. But Gorbachev also showed that he intended to give particular attention to the economically booming Asian-Pacific region. Africa and Latin America were accorded a lower priority on the agenda, as had been the case historically.

A more discriminating Third World policy implied that the Soviet Union would have to support potential winners rather than losers. Nowhere were the implications of this more apparent than in Africa and Latin America. In Africa, the regimes that the Soviet Union backed in the 1970s continued to suffer natural and man-made crises, and Gorbachev distanced himself from them. This was also the case in Central America, where even the Reagan administration's complaints against Soviet involvement became muted. The Soviet Union soon came to be described as behaving with relative restraint. In Nicaragua, for example, Soviet commitments were reduced. Gorbachev's visit to Cuba produced no new commitments and did not inflame U.S. sensitivities.

The unstable Middle East, in contrast, proved to be an area of higher profile Soviet activity under Gorbachev. Following Moscow's marginalization on the diplomatic front in the 1970s, the Soviet Union began a slow climb back after 1985.[32] Of particular significance was the Soviet attempt to become involved in the organization of a regional peace conference. The Reagan administration, which had suffered severe failures in the region, said that it would not veto such a prospect. In order to play such a role, the Soviet Union would have to try to rebuild diplomatic ties with Israel. This was attempted and represented the most novel Soviet move in the region during Gorbachev's first years in office.[33] Having access to Israel would assist any Soviet attempt to play honest broker between the states of the region, while Israel made the resumption of diplomatic ties a condition for accepting a Soviet role in any international peace conference. An additional dimension to the Soviet-Israeli relationship was the development of the Jericho missile by Israel, capable of reaching Soviet territory. In addition to the Soviet activity in the Arab-Israeli dispute, attention was also paid to the five-year-long Iran-Iraq War. Here the Soviet Union played a limited role in supporting efforts to bring about peace, though competing interests made it difficult to follow a consistent line.

Soviet attempts to become involved in multilateral efforts to stabilize the Middle East have been supported by a general attempt to restore Soviet regional influence. This has included the cultivation of relations with the conservative Persian Gulf Arab states—notably Oman and the United Arab Emirates. Better relations have also been pursued with Saudi Arabia, and with some success. The Saudis have shown a new willingness to reassess their relations with the United States as a result of U.S. policies toward Lebanon and Libya and the White House's Iran-contra scandal.[34] The image of Soviet moderation, commitment to peace, and anti-imperialism was projected by its revival of the idea of superpower naval limitations in the Mediterranean, the Indian Ocean, and the Persian Gulf. U.S. military power in the Middle East had become a focus of concern in the Arab world because of the attacks on Libya in April 1986.[35] The Kremlin reacted to the bombing in a minimalist fashion. It postponed planning talks for the summit with the United States in order to appease those Arab states with which it was building up relations, but this was the least response it could have made. Otherwise the Kremlin distanced itself from Colonel Muammar Qaddafi and thus from the association with terrorism; it identified with the people of Libya rather than the leader; and it did not take any risks to protect him.

If the Soviet Union pursued a policy of quiet diplomacy aimed at restoring influence in the Middle East, its efforts at influence building in Asia attracted rather more attention. The Asian security theme that Gorbachev and his spokesmen developed at Vladivostok and elsewhere included ideas about nuclear-free zones, naval reductions, a regional security conference, and troop reductions on the Sino-Soviet border and in Afghanistan. Gorbachev also talked about the possible reduction of the Soviet military presence in the region as a whole, and he promised that if the United States gave up its bases in the Philippines, its action would not go unanswered. The implication of this seemed to be that a U.S. withdrawal would be matched by a Soviet withdrawal from Cam Ranh Bay. Washington responded negatively.

The idea of a collective security system for Asia, first proposed by Brezhnev in June 1969, had been vague at the outset and has remained so.[36] Gorbachev's relaunching of the proposal can be seen as but a further stage in a long-term strategy to legitimize the Soviet wish to be accepted as a rightful Asian power. Skepticism remains among the countries of Asia, though perhaps Gorbachev's quiet diplomacy and presentational flair may yet prove more successful than the efforts of his predecessors.

Soviet influence-building efforts in Southeast Asia in the late 1960s and early 1970s largely failed, after earlier looking so promising. This was partly because of local suspicion toward the concept of collective security and very active concern about the support the Soviet Union was giving to Vietnam. By the early 1980s, the problem of Vietnam remained a serious impediment to Soviet policy in the region. The relationship clearly illustrates the way in which having to choose sides in regional conflicts can hamper wider influence-building aspirations. The foreign minister of Singapore dismissed the visit of Soviet foreign minister Shevardnadze to Southeast Asia early in 1987 as "all part of the offensive of the Soviet Union in this part of the world."[37] Officials of the Association of South East Asian Nations (ASEAN) emphasized that it was Soviet aid that had sustained Vietnam's position in Kampuchea and that they were waiting to see how far the Kremlin was willing or able to exert influence on Hanoi in order to negotiate a settlement. For the moment, Gorbachev tried to ride two horses; the Soviet Union continued to prop up its militarily significant but economically struggling ally while at the same time attempting to cultivate (for trading as well as diplomatic purposes) the economically successful pro-Western members of ASEAN.

The wariness of the ASEAN countries toward the Soviet Union has been echoed by countries elsewhere in the Asian-Pacific region. Australia is a good example. Despite Shevardnadze's being the first Soviet foreign minister ever to visit Australia, this was not enough to counteract various negative images of Soviet policy in that unthreatened but security-conscious country; these included the buildup of Soviet naval forces in the West Pacific over previous years and the increased Soviet diplomatic and commercial interest in the South Pacific (marked by fishing agreements with various island states). The Australian response to this growing Soviet activity was to announce increased defense cooperation with the South Pacific island states.[38]

Whereas Soviet policy in the Pacific played somewhat into the hands of Australian defense planners searching for a threat on which to focus their efforts, no similar problems attended Soviet-Indian relations. New Delhi was the target for Gorbachev's first visit to an Asian capital, and it confirmed the shared interests of the two countries.[39] It appeared to observers that the Soviet organizers had put much thought into the public relations aspect of the visit. The meetings between the leaders underlined the mutually beneficial character of Soviet-Indian relations, and all the signs suggested that this was how matters would remain.

Unlike other Asian countries and the West, India had not been openly concerned by the Soviet war in Afghanistan. To Indian policymakers there could have been worse governments in Kabul than the one supported by the Soviet Union, and the diversion the war created for Pakistan's forces eased India's defense problem. Other countries did not adopt India's attitude. As a result, the war in Afghanistan created a serious problem for Soviet diplomacy in its dealings with most other states. It proved a diplomatic embarrassment, as well as what Gorbachev called a "bleeding wound." He set out with more vigor than his predecessors to resolve the situation by political means. Again, Gorbachev proved himself to be more radical than the skeptics imagined. Although a difficult and unsettled postwar situation was inevitable in Afghanistan—one that would cause the Soviet Union embarrassment, if not trouble—Moscow was not deflected from its intention to withdraw.

During his first years in office, therefore, Gorbachev tried to project a different image of Soviet policy in the Third World, to become more discriminating in his choice of foreign associates, to wind down costly commitments, to erase mistakes, and to avoid taking new commitments. However, there was no sign that the Soviet Union was withdrawing from the competition for influence, and when necessary, toughness was displayed. The Soviet Union continued to express solidarity (at least verbally) with those embattled regimes struggling against the anticommunist forces backed by the Reagan doctrine. But no extra commitments were made: military assistance to Nicaragua did not increase, and that to Ethiopia and Mozambique declined. Quiet diplomacy characterized what the Soviet Union did but also did not do: it did not stir up trouble in Pakistan or exploit the instability in the Philippines. In the Middle East, it became identified with processes aimed at ameliorating the major conflicts in the region. Meanwhile, the Soviet Union started to play a more responsible role in the United Nations.

In the Third World, as elsewhere, Soviet policy under Gorbachev has been rational, incremental, and pragmatic. Effective politics is the art of doing what is acceptable as well as what is merely possible, and in this respect the new Soviet regime and its spokesmen have been very successful. No allies or associates have been abandoned, but instead relations have been maintained at steady levels. Meanwhile, rather than being burdened by association with a string of ideologically sympathetic but economically crippled countries, the Soviet Union has sought trade and influence with more effective regional actors. While many of the tactics that have been employed have been tried before, they have been carried out with more attention, greater flexibility, and more sensitivity to local attitudes. As a result, there is more responsiveness to Soviet initiatives. Soviet policy in the Third World has been carried out more effectively under Gorbachev than under his immediate predecessors, but the traditional problems and constraints remain.

Western Europe

In the countries of Western Europe, as elsewhere, what was most striking about Soviet foreign policy after March 1985 was not the details of the proposals but rather the changed image that was projected. In Europe Gorbachev stressed that he wanted détente and gave the impression that a great deal could be achieved. These were welcome words in Western Europe, where détente never developed the negative connotations it did in the United States. Western Europe was a major target of the Soviet charm offensive. Western European opinion was significantly affected by the new words coming from Moscow; there was a widespread willingness to believe that they were more than merely propaganda. Public opinion polls in Europe showed Gorbachev to be a more popular and trusted leader than Ronald Reagan.[40]

Positive images of the Soviet Union were also developing at the official level, as well as with public opinion. The most notable development here was the apparent revolution in the opinions of Great Britain's prime minister, part of whose reputation had been made on her cold war ("iron lady") attitudes. Even before Gorbachev became leader, Margaret Thatcher had described him as somebody with whom the West could do business. Some minor agreements were made between Great Britain and the Soviet Union as gestures of cooperation and doing real business, but on major issues (notably nuclear disarmament) there was disagreement. Public relations apart, presumably Gorbachev does not believe complete nuclear disarmament is possible; but unlike Thatcher the Soviet leader seems to believe that radical denuclearization will improve international security.

While trying to exploit the chemistry between Reagan and Thatcher, Gorbachev has also been engaged in a somewhat contradictory effort to loosen the ties that bind Western Europe and the United States. It is doubtful whether the Kremlin wants a complete withdrawal of the United States from Western Europe because of what this might provoke in terms of a German-dominated (possibly nuclear) Europe. But it would prefer a less threatening confrontation, and some loosening of the transatlantic ties might help achieve this. Where possible, Soviet spokesmen have made a distinction between the United States and Western Europe when discussing Soviet-Western relations, and they also paid special attention to the major European countries and their sensitivities. They expressed understanding of the British and French security needs in Europe, laid stress on political and economic rather than military relations, offered to reduce troops in Eastern Europe, welcomed visits by Western European leaders, and talked of denuclearizing Europe and shifting military postures in a defense-only direction. By such actions Gorbachev hoped to strengthen his notion of a "common European home."

Gorbachev's most difficult Western European relationship continued to be with the Federal Republic of Germany. However, a visit by Chancellor Helmut Kohl in November 1988 went well. Mutual interests were identified, and numerous agreements were signed. Kohl raised the issue of German reunification, but Gorbachev ruled out boundary changes; Gorbachev thereby underlined that he did not become leader of the Politburo to preside over the dismantling of Soviet security. And in June 1989 Gorbachev returned the visit with great success.

Whatever Gorbachev means by the "common European home," the further development of the European Community represents a potential barrier to his hopes for any family approach to European issues. If this development proves to be a success, and if at the same time Eastern Europe fails to improve its economic performance, then a capitalist curtain will divide the continent at just the time that the old iron curtain is becoming decreasingly relevant. As the European Community has grown, the Soviet Union has come to terms with its rising power in the world political economy. This was consistent with Gorbachev's stress on interdependence. However, in the light of the threatened new curtain after 1992, Gorbachev does not want the European Community to move too far too fast—and certainly if that implies that it will take on a political (and perhaps therefore in time a military) dimension. This no doubt is one of the reasons that Gorbachev has been seen to give special attention to Thatcher. The British prime minister is the most powerful of the opponents of the trend toward Western European unity. At the opposite extreme of the European landmass, Gorbachev has found another leader who favors decentralization; it is good tactics that he should inflate her international importance.

One of the effects of Gorbachev's policies toward Western Europe has been to weaken the Western European image of a Soviet military threat. In this respect arms control proposals have been of primary importance. Gorbachev's apparent desire to stabilize the conventional force balance, his recognition that asymmetries exist in the military strength of the two alliances and should be eradicated, his calls to change military doctrine in a defensive direction, his interest in reducing the numbers of nuclear weapons, his stress on common security, his assertion that no war can be a continuation of politics, his speeches implying that the Brezhnev Doctrine is obsolete,[41] his repetition of the idea that security is mutual, his desire to base the Soviet military machine on reasonable sufficiency—all of these developments, and others, made a significant dent in the old stereotypes about the cold war. By seeming to change the military relationships between the two halves of the continent, Gorbachev has been changing the basis for the international politics of Europe. Major milestones in this respect were the May 1987 proposals of the Warsaw Pact for conventional forces restructuring, the December 1987 INF ("double zero") treaty, and the December 1988 speech at the U.N. promising unilateral Soviet troop and weapons withdrawals and reductions. Some Western Europeans remained skeptical about the import of Gorbachev's words and his ability and willingness to put them into practice. In contrast, a growing number came to be impressed by his vision and convinced of his seriousness. They recognized that he could and might be knocked off course, but they believed that he had done as much as was reasonable in the time available, that some of the changes he signaled could not be achieved overnight, and that it would be difficult for the Soviet Union to move much further without the West's showing a greater willingness to reciprocate.

As well as seeking to improve relations with the Western European power centers (attention was also given to France and Italy), the new mood in the Kremlin has also been directed at Europe's left. Moscow became more accessible, and the reforms posted by Gorbachev were welcomed by the major socialist parties in the West. The British Labour party was told that if it secured office and put its nonnuclear defense policy into operation, there would be positive reciprocation by the Soviet Union in the form of commensurate reductions and changes in targeting. At the grass-roots level, the peace movements in Western Europe had much to cheer in Soviet arms control initiatives since Gorbachev has embraced many of the ideas they advanced so vigorously in the early 1980s, notably those of common security, denuclearization, and nonprovocative defense. Further to the left, the new mood in Moscow opened up the doors to the Eurocommunists, whose voices were given some space in the Moscow press. The convergence of their ideas and Gorbachev's could not but improve the Soviet image among Europe's left, but these very ideas weakened the prospect of the spread of Soviet control. So although the dominant political mood in Western Europe has continued to be conservative, Gorbachev has made significant inroads in improving the responsiveness of both the political right and left.

As a result of this activity, Moscow since March 1985 has steadily become the scene of state and other visits and the focus of new ideas. It has become the center of European diplomacy in a way it has not been before.

Eastern Europe

Unfortunately for Gorbachev, some of the same domestic reforms that have made his leadership attractive and relatively successful in Western Europe have caused anxiety among the ruling groups in Eastern Europe. It is ironic that if Gorbachev only a few years ago had been an Eastern European leader pursuing the same policies, he would have provoked considerable disquiet in both the Kremlin and among his more conservative Warsaw Pact allies. The Moscow spring that he has created might well have led to direct military pressure on him in the name of the Brezhnev doctrine. Whether Gorbachev's policies will help release the pressures in Eastern Europe in a stabilizing fashion or will provoke dramatic revolution is, in world political terms, of more significance than the success of *perestroika* within the Soviet Union itself. In addition to all the other uncertainties there is the problem of the future role of Soviet forces in the region—and the actual operational status of the Brezhnev doctrine. The role of the Soviet military presence in Eastern Europe is crucial for the future of both the Eastern and Western parts of the continent. Proposals about Soviet troop withdrawals were expected through 1987–1988, but they were not expected to be announced unconditionally or in the numbers laid out by Gorbachev in his December 1988 U.N. speech. Although a substantial force will remain, the withdrawal of large numbers of Soviet men and equipment from Czechoslovakia, the DDR, and Hungary promises (or threatens) to result in significant changes in the political and economic relations among the Warsaw Pact allies.

As ever in Eastern Europe, there is a danger of matters getting out of control as a result of spillover and imbalance between domestic and foreign policies, between reform and revolution, between freedom and responsibility, between cohesion and development, and between nationalism and anti-Sovietism. We are confronted by an era of question marks in Eastern Europe. If reform becomes revolution, how will Gorbachev respond? Is the Brezhnev doctrine still operational? Can a new "organic" relationship develop between the socialist countries? Gorbachev presumably hopes that he can control what he has helped unleash, but he cannot guarantee it. If he fails, the results could be disastrous for himself and others.

Not without cause, Eastern Europe is widely regarded as the most dangerous region of instability in international politics for the foreseeable future. On the one hand, the way the situation develops in Eastern Europe could provide the shortest route to Gorbachev's political downfall and acute insecurity throughout Europe. Alternatively, if Gorbachev can help transform the region peacefully and quickly into an economically more successful group of countries—with more freedom to run their own affairs, greater involvement with the West, and a more normalized relationship with the Soviet Union—then without doubt the new Soviet president will be firmly in the running for the title of the twentieth century's greatest statesman.

The Military and Naval Dimension

One aspect of Soviet policy that attracted relatively little attention during Gorbachev's first period in office—in part because of Gorbachev's intention to divert attention away from it—was the Soviet military instrument. This, however, more than human rights or economic reform at home, is what ultimately concerns most outsiders: the Western powers and the Soviet Union's neighbors look forward to predictably moderate external behavior from Moscow. The immediate signs were favorable, though these were still early days and special circumstances.

The priority tasks of modernizing the economy and energizing the Soviet system were clear in all of Gorbachev's early efforts. As a result, the military establishment had to face the prospect of tougher resource allocation battles than in the past. This could be expected to cause strain, though modernizers within the military may value economic reform and some military belt tightening on the ground that in the long run such measures are necessary in order to create a more effective military machine for the high-technology future. Both reformers and conservatives exist in the Soviet military establishment.

Relaxing international tension and easing the defense burden were clearly a high priority for Gorbachev. There were several straws in the wind concerning the latter. Gorbachev made it clear that the defense budget was adequate for the job (he advertised the notion of reasonable sufficiency); he stressed the primacy of domestic reform over military needs, arguing that the struggle was in the economic and scientific arena, not the military one; he asserted that security was more effectively achieved through political rather than military means; the defense minister, Marshal Sergei Sokolov, was not promoted to the Politburo; military figures were not prominent at Chernenko's funeral; war was ruled out as a rational instrument of policy; and *glasnost'* extended to an attack on a senior general in *Pravda*.[42]

Common security and its associated notions of disarmament and defensive deterrence have naturally led to some opposition from within the Soviet military; some of Gorbachev's ideas appear to be alien to traditional Soviet strategic culture. As a result, resistance has been encountered from "old thinkers" within the military as well as within the party. Nevertheless, Gorbachev has maintained his objective of pinning down the defense budget to one of reasonable sufficiency. The armed forces, like other sectors of society, must feel the impact of *perestroika.*

During 1987–1988 Gorbachev's new thinking in the strategic realm became clearer, though it will inevitably take time before some of the changes come into effect. Whether they do come into effect will also depend in part on whether the West reciprocates. Although military resistance to some of his ideas became more evident in 1987–1988 in comparison with 1985–1986, Gorbachev did succeed in replacing some of the old guard within the military establishment, there was some evidence of the military falling in line, and slowdowns have been reported in some weapons programs. Furthermore, there is reason to suppose—as Michael MccGwire suggests in his *Military Objectives in Soviet Foreign Policy*—that some of the developments under Gorbachev are extrapolations of existing ideas.[43] Consequently, even in the event of Gorbachev's period in office proving to be short-lived, it is possible that part of his revolution in the military field would survive.

Change is proving difficult for President Gorbachev in such a conservative country as the Soviet Union and especially in relation to the conservative elements in the armed forces. It is evident to his supporters and to outsiders that his commitment to maintaining Soviet security is no less than that of any of his predecessors. The difference between the new and the old thinkers is that the former believe that severe restraint on arms can bring security as well as political and economic benefits.

If Gorbachev did start out seeking to reduce the military influence and the military burden, then it was only logical to suppose that at least in the short term he would play down the importance of the military instrument in Soviet foreign policy. His stress on the political bases of security is significant in this respect. Yet his attitude to the use of force has not yet been tested. His policy toward Afghanistan merely showed that he believed that some wars could not be won at an acceptable price. Apart from Afghanistan, however, there was no reason to suppose that the man with "iron teeth" (in Andrei Gromyko's famous remark) would not defend what had been gained by his country or would ever show weakness. These are not the characteristics of Politburo leaders. In the direct East-West military competition, Gorbachev's words and some actions (the unilateral nuclear test moratorium, for example) suggested that he understood the limited utility of nuclear weapons in an era of parity and sufficiency. He stressed, like those before him, that the Soviet system would ultimately prove its advantages not by force of arms but by force of example. Many in both East and West regard this as the only rational response to a post-Clausewitzian era in the international politics of advanced industrialized states.

If there is a role for direct militant action in the future, it will be in the Third World. It is here where the Soviet Navy could have its biggest role. Since the late 1960s, the navy has been a moderately successful instrument in a largely unsuccessful foreign policy.[44]

Although Soviet priorities will remain elsewhere than in the Third World, it will continue to pursue its interests there with persistence. It will not cease to compete because of disappointments in the past. Moreover, lessons will have been learned. The domestic emphasis, however, does imply an interest in reduced tension and so too in policies that do not provoke a Western backlash as occurred in the 1970s. Consequently, current needs allied to traditional caution suggest that we should be sanguine about the prospects for Soviet adventurism in the Third World. This conclusion is another reason for thinking that the "rise" of the Soviet Navy may have peaked.

The choice of Admiral Vladimir Chernavin to replace the venerable Admiral Sergei Gorshkov in December 1985 was significant. Chernavin had argued for a combined arms approach (an integrated rather than an independent role for the navy) and for greater fighting efficiency; he was the man for the moment. Efficiency is crucial when a service cannot expect more resources. Instead of the expansion of the Soviet Navy, we can expect to see the old pattern of integrated defense and a new commitment to intensified fighting effectiveness. In the debates about cost-effectiveness and resource allocation, the expensive naval instrument will inevitably come under sharp scrutiny. As it is, we have not been seeing a continued growth of amphibious forces and logistic support, an outcome forecast and feared by many Western naval observers in the 1960s and 1970s.

The circumstances under which Admiral Gorshkov won the debate for his balanced fleet in the 1970s have passed. At that time there were opportunities opening up in the Third World, the "Vietnam syndrome" dominated the United States, and the Soviet Union had achieved a satisfactory correlation of forces (codified in SALT I) with its main adversary.[45] The situation was very different a decade later: the Soviet leadership that had overseen the rise of the Soviet Navy had left the scene, and there may well develop an "Afghanistan syndrome" in the Soviet leadership. Moreover, Soviet activism in the Third World was one of the factors that had provoked anti-Sovietism in the West and elsewhere, which in turn had led in the case of the United States to Reaganism and an unprecedented military buildup. Finally, the new Soviet leadership quickly showed itself more committed to the national economic struggle at home rather than national liberation struggles overseas.

These arguments suggest that Admiral Gorshkov's successor will not oversee any further expansion of Soviet power projection forces beyond those already in the planning process. Nevertheless, the Third World will remain an area of instability that will sometimes offer opportunities for external intervention and superpower competition. It is possible that the depth of U.S.

hostility toward the Soviet Union displayed during the Reagan years may lead a new and more vigorous Soviet leadership—once it has its own house in order—to make the Third World an area of contest with the United States. Meanwhile, they will defend any gains against U.S. pressure (as manifest in the Reagan doctrine), and, when possible, they will grasp targets of opportunity. The development of more impressive warships may shape the will to try to influence events in distant seas.

For the time being, however, Gorbachev's words, Soviet interests, and traditional Soviet caution combine to suggest that militant behavior will be avoided. Furthermore, impressive weaponry does not necessarily indicate an intention to use it, nor does risk taking necessarily increase because one invests more in insurance. So far, Gorbachev has been lucky; he has not had to handle any major crisis. If events were going badly for him at home or in Eastern Europe, he might become edgy and uncertain; he might miscalculate; he might be prone to take greater risks. Indeed, the situation and his hold on the reins of power might depend on a willingness to act toughly. There is no reason to suppose he would not do what he thought necessary, however tough that action was.

Conclusion

In his first years in office, Mikhail Gorbachev has proved himself an intelligent tactician who stands head and shoulders above his immediate predecessors. He has done exactly what the difficult circumstances require. It has become more apparent that Gorbachev is "a man in a hurry," and understandably so. His sense that time is short has led to what sometimes appears to be a loss of a sense of priority (everything is crucial), and this has sometimes led to an impression of unpredictability. In addition some of the problems he faces have been caused by his successes rather than his failures. Some of his "new thinking" has deserved the adjective "new," at least in the Soviet context. In the area of foreign policy, this is especially the case with notions of common security and interdependence. It is also now decreed that one must not identify peaceful coexistence with the class struggle; the latter is no longer said to be the determining tendency of the present age.

In the short term, Gorbachev turned around the difficult foreign policy inheritance Brezhnev left. The further development of his foreign policy will depend on three interrelated considerations. First, it will rest on the results. To date Gorbachev has not set a foot wrong, and he has cultivated a positive image. But if there were to be a series of mistakes, crises, and unexpected obstacles—the stuff of politics—he may come to be seen in a different light. Trust will go, both at home and abroad. Furthermore, if achievements are not forthcoming, his domestic critics will be emboldened. The second and related consideration is his need for support at home. Soviet foreign policy begins in the struggle for power in the Kremlin. Gorbachev's policies must command support, and some Western observers believe that his future may be limited. The security of Gorbachev's leadership remains in doubt, with individuals in a variety of important groups being suspicious of the far-reaching changes he had outlined. Within the Soviet military, the party apparatus, the bureaucracy, the work force, and middle management, President Gorbachev has provoked opposition to his policies. Common sense and history suggest that it is a potentially formidable grouping. In addition, the problem of the nationalities has grown, and economic restructuring has yet to produce the goods. These are formidable problems that could undermine his authority. On the other hand, how far can his domestic reforms go without stimulating those political and economic forces (pluralism, nationalism, and economic liberalism) that will not merely change the system but will abolish it? Third, and finally, the further development of his foreign policy will lie in the hands and minds of Western policymakers. Western responses and initiatives will play a major part in determining Gorbachev's political future, and so perhaps the character of Soviet foreign policy.

A division of opinion still exists on the question of whether a successful Gorbachev would be a threat or a promise to Western interests. There are those in the West who are clear that Gorbachev should be helped. They advocate, for example, a new "Marshall Plan" to help the recovery of the Eastern European economies. Several countries in Western Europe have been keen to do as much business with the Soviet Union as possible, and the German foreign minister, Hans Dietrich Genscher, has been the most prominent statesman pursuing this line. Such advocates argue that if help is given to the Soviet Union and is successful, not only will it improve the standard of living in the Soviet Union, but it should also draw the Soviet economy into that of the West. This would make it much less likely that we would see a regression to earlier, more militant manifestations of Soviet behavior.

It would be unwise for the West to make hasty judgments about Gorbachev's foreign policies. There is a danger of both overselling him (through wishful thinking) and of underselling him (through implicit enemy imaging). If Gorbachev is seen as just a modern Bolshevik with a charm offensive, then a chance will be missed to put East-West relations on a more stable political and military footing. On the other hand, if we exaggerate the new thinking in Moscow and oversell the moment of hope embodied in Gorbachev, then we risk making the same error that was made in the early 1970s when détente was oversold. As in the early 1970s, if future relations fail to match unrealistic expectations, then a backlash will occur against the notion that it is possible to live in a relationship of greater stability (and less cost) with the Soviet Union. What is needed is more consistency on the part of the West in its dealings with the Soviet Union, in terms of both perceptions and performance. We need what Marshall Shulman in the early 1970s called a "Western philosophy of coexistence."[46]

This is a crucial period for those who believe that industrial societies have an interest in demilitarizing the common conflict and moving toward a wider acceptance of the notion of common security. There has never been a better chance in recent years to move forward, and there may not be a better one for many years if this opportunity is lost. Although many questions about Gorbachev remain to be settled, nobody in the West could have hoped (let alone predicted) that the Soviet system would yield from the corridors of Brezhnevism an individual able to promise so much in terms of the international security interest. If the traditional vicious circle of the East-West conflict is ever to be turned into a spiral of better relations, Western statesmen must not miss the opportunity to test Gorbachev's intentions to the full.[47] They must at the same time accept that there are limits on how far and how quickly he can act; they should look for moderation in Soviet foreign policy, but they must not make radical changes in domestic policy a condition for positive responses. Above all, they must have the confidence to take the risk that if Gorbachev is successful in building a modern and effective socialist state, the West will not lose in the competitive coexistence that will ensue. There is nothing to lose by exploring positively (and quickly) the bases for a less confrontational and less militarized East-West relationship. By failing to respond to Gorbachev, we will lose a rare opportunity to develop processes pointing toward a more stable peace.

Notes

1. An excellent brief starting point for developing an understanding of the role of Soviet ideology is still Karen Hurst Dawisha, "The Roles of Ideology in the Decision-Making of the Soviet Union," *International Relations* 4 (November 1972): 156–175. Standard references include R.N. Carew Hunt, *The Theory and Practice of Communism: An Introduction* (New York: Macmillan, 1957); Alfred G. Meyer, *Marxism, The Unity of Theory and Practice* (Cambridge: Harvard University Press, 1954) and *Leninism* (Cambridge: Harvard University Press, 1957); and Bertram D. Wolfe, *One Hundred Years in the Life of a Doctrine* (New York: Dial, 1965).

2. The most substantial survey of U.S.-Soviet relations in the 1970s and first part of the 1980s is Raymond L. Garthoff, *Detente and Confrontation: American-Soviet Relations from Nixon to Reagan* (Washington, D.C.: Brookings, 1985).

3. See Marshall D. Shulman, "U.S.-Soviet Relations and the Control of Nuclear Weapons," in Barry M. Blechman, *Rethinking the U.S. Strategic Posture* (Cambridge, Mass.: Ballinger, 1982), 77–100.

4. For an argument that U.S. policy in the 1980s was in part based on an inaccurate perception and presentation of Soviet behavior in the 1970s, see Ken Booth

and Phil Williams, "Fact and Fiction in U.S. Foreign Policy: Reagan's Myths about Detente," *World Policy Journal* 2 (Summer 1985): 501–32.

5. See, for example, O.B. Borisov and B.T. Kolokov, *Soviet-Chinese Relations 1945–1970* (Bloomington: Indiana University Press, 1975); Herbert Ellison, ed., *The Sino-Soviet Conflict: A Global Perspective* (London: University of Washington Press, 1982); Gerald Segal, *The Great Power Triangle* (London: Macmillan, 1982); and Donald S. Zagoria, ed., *Soviet Policy in East Asia* (New Haven: Yale University Press, 1982).

6. See the China section of the annual survey, *Thee Military Balance* (London: International Institute for Strategic Studies).

7. Quoted in *Economist*, July 23, 1983, p. 44.

8. See, for example, Robert H. Donaldson, ed., *The Soviet Union and the Developing Nations* (Baltimore: Johns Hopkins University Press, 1974), and Jonathan Steele, *The Limits of Soviet Power* (Harmondsworth, U.K.: Penguin, 1985).

9. This was evident to empirical observers at the time. See, for example, the contributions in part II of Michael MccGwire, Ken Booth, and John M. Donnell, eds., *Soviet Naval Policy: Objectives and Constraints* (New York: Praeger, 1975).

10. See, for example, David E. Albright, "East-West Tensions in Africa," in Marshall D. Shulman, ed., *East-West Tensions in the Third World* (New York: Norton, 1986), 116–57, Edward N. Luttwak, *The Grand Strategy of the Soviet Union* (London: Weidenfeld and Nicolson, 1983); and Bruce D. Porter, *The USSR in Third World Conflicts* (Cambridge: Cambridge University Press, 1984).

11. See M. El Azhary, "The Attitudes of the Superpowers towards the Gulf War," *International Affairs* 59 (Autumn 1983): 609–20; Galia Golan, "The Soviet Union and the Israeli Action in Lebanon," *International Affairs* 59 (Winter 1982): 7–16; Mark N. Katz, *Russia and Arabia: Soviet Foreign Policy toward the Arabian Peninsula* (Baltimore: Johns Hopkins University Press, 1986); Dina Spechler, "The USSR and Third World Conflicts: Domestic Debate and Soviet Policy in the Middle East, 1967–1973," *World Politics* 38 (April 1986): 435–61; and Aryeh Yodfat, *The Soviet Union and the Arabian Peninsula* (London: Croom Helm, 1983).

12. See, for example, Anthony Arnold, *Afghanistan: The Soviet Invasion in Perspective* (Stanford, Calif.: Hoover Institute Press, 1981); Henry S. Bradsher, *Afghanistan and the Soviet Union* (Durham, N.C.: Duke University Press, 1983); Garthoff, *Detente and Confrontation*, chap. 26; and Thomas T. Hammond, *Ref Flag over Afghanistan* (Boulder, Colo.: Westview, 1984).

13. On the incidents discussed below, see Stephen T. Hosmer and Thomas W. Wolfe, *Soviet Policy and Practicce towards Third World Conflicts* (Lexington, Mass.: Lexington Books, 1983); Mark N. Katz, *The Third World in Soviet Military Thought* (London: Croom Helm, 1982); Arthur Jay Klinghofer, *The Angolan War: A Study of Soviet Foreign Policy in the Third World* (Boulder, Colo.: Westview, 1980); Porter, *USSR in Third World Conflicts*; Shulman, *East-West Tensions*; and Steele, *Limits of Soviet Power*.

14. See, for example, Douglas Pike, "The USSR and Vietnam," in Robert H. Donaldson, ed., *The Soviet Union in the Third World* (Boulder, Colo.: Westview, 1981), 251–66.

15. Edwina Moreton, "The East Europeans and the Cubans in the Middle East: Surrogates or Allies?" in Adeed Dawisha and Karen Dawisha, eds., *The Soviet Union*

in the Middle East: Policies and Perspectives (London: Heinemann, 1982), 62–84; Jorge I. Dominguez, "U.S., Soviet, and Cuban Policies towards Latin America," in Shulman, *East-West Tensions*, 44–77.

16. *Time*, March 23, 1985, p. 13.

17. Santiago Carillo, *Eurocommunism and the State* (Westport, Conn.: Lawrence Hillard, 1978); Rudolf L. Tokes, ed., *Eurocommunism and Detente* (New York: New York University Press, 1978).

18. This even included challenges to the prevailing image of the early postwar years. At that time it was generally assumed without question that the disparity in force levels was such that all the Red Army needed to reach the English Channel were—in the joke of the time—"Boots." See Matthew A. Evangelista, "Stalin's Postwar Army Reappraised," *International Security* 7 (Winter 1982–1983): 110–38.

19. *Economist*, March 13, 1982, p. 16.

20. Neal Ascherson, *The Polish August* (Harmondsworth, U.K.: Penguin, 1981).

21. See Karen Dawisha and Philip Hanson, eds., *Soviet-East European Dilemmas: Coercion, Competition, and Consent* (London: Heinemann, 1981); and Sarah Meiklejohn Terry, ed., *Soviet Policy in Eastern Europe* (New Haven: Yale University Press, 1984).

22. See Robin Remington, *The Warsaw Pact* (Cambridge, Mass.: MIT Press, 1971); Christopher D. Jones, *Soviet Influence in Eastern Europe: Political Autonomy and the Warsaw Pact* (New York: Praeger Special Studies, 1981); and David Holloway and Jane M.O. Sharp, eds., *The Warsaw Pact: Alliance in Transition?* (London: Macmillan, 1984).

23. The phrase is Paul Dibb's, in his *The Soviet Union: The Incomplete Superpower* (London: Macmillan, 1986).

24. See, for example, Zhores Medvedev, *Gorbachev* (Oxford: Blackwell, 1986); and Martin Walker, *The Waking Giant: The Soviet Union under Gorbachev* (London: Michael Joseph, 1986).

25. Thane Gustafson, "Will Soviet Foreign Policy Change under Gorbachev?" *Washington Quarterly* 9 (Fall 1980): 155. See also David Satter, "The Foreign Correspondent in Moscow: On Manipulation and Self-Deception," *Encounter* 68 (May 1987): 58–63.

26. Frederick Painton, "Charm Offensive," *Time*, March 23, 1987.

27. On the ideological debate surrounding this, see Stephen Shenfield, *The Nuclear Predicament: Explorations in Soviet Ideology* (London: Routledge and Kegan Paul, 1987).

28. See, for example, Ken Booth, "Soviet Defense Policy," in John Baylis et al., eds., *Contemporary Strategy*, vol. 2 of *The Nuclear Powers*, 2d ed. (New York: Holmes & Meier, 1987), 56–112.

29. See Matthew Evangelista, "The New Soviet Approach to Security," *World Policy Journal* 3 (Autumn 1986): 561–97.

30. Ibid.; Michael McGwire, *Military Objectives in Soviet Foreign Policy* (Washington, D.C.: Brookings, 1987), chap. 11; Jane M.O. Sharp, "Mikhail Gorbachev's Arms Control Diplomacy" (paper delivered at the annual conference of the British International Studies Association, Aberystwyth, December 1987); Shenfield, *Nuclear Predicament*; Mary C. FitzGerald, "The Strategic Revolution behind Soviet Arms Control," *Arms Control Today* 17 (June 1987): 16–19.

31. Evangelista, "New Soviet Approach to Security."

32. On the 1970s see Garthoff, *Detente and Confrontation,* chaps. 11, 19; and for the views of a central actor, see Henry Kissinger, *White House Years* (Boston: Little, Brown, 1982), passim. On the more recent period, see Robert O. Freedman, "The Superpowers, the Middle East, and Conflict Management" (paper delivered at the conference, The Superpowers and Third World Security, Ford Foundation Research Project, North/South Security Relations, Southampton University, March 1987).

33. Ian Black, "Russian Team Plans Early Visit to Jerusalem," *Guardian,* April 2, 1987.

34. Robin Lustig, "Irangate Scandal Breaks Ice between Saudis and Soviets," *Observer,* March 5, 1987.

35. Martin Walker, "Libya: Shadow of Sarajevo over Moscow," *Guardian* April 16, 1986.

36. I. Clark, "Collective Security in Asia: Towards a Framework for Soviet Diplomacy," *Round Table* 63 (October 1973): 473–81; H.C. Hinton, "The Soviet Campaign for Collective Security in Asia," *Pacific Community* 36 (January 1976): 147–61.

37. Nicholas Cumming-Bruce, "Soviet Foreign Minister in Asia," *Guardian,* March 3, 1987.

38. Edward W. Desmond, "Rivalry in the Pacific," *Time,* November 24, 1986; Patrick Walters, "Hawke Steps Up Defense Role in the South Pacific," *Guardian,* February 21, 1987.

39. Eric Silver, "India Returns to the Arms of Its Soviet Suiter," *Guardian,* November 25, 1986.

40. And this pattern continued: see *Observer,* November 27, 1988, p. 1.

41. The ideological justification given by the Soviet Union for its invasion of Czechoslovakia in 1968 became known in the West as the Brezhnev doctrine. It asserted that "socialist" states had no right to abandon socialism or to leave the socialist bloc.—ED.

42. See, for example, Moscow Correspondent, "Gorbachev Turns Reform Guns on the Military," *Guardian,* March 25, 1987. "New thinking" did not begin with Gorbachev. Under the surface, Brezhnevism was cracking before March 1985: see Shenfield, *Nuclear Predicament*; and Dusko Doder, "Soviets Debating Arms Issues: Nuclear Weapons Policies Edging into the Public Arena," *Tribune* (Oakland, Calif.), January 8, 1985.

43. MccGwire, *Military Objectives,*

44. Ken Booth, "The Soviet Naval Presence in the Third World," *Marineblad* (Dutch Naval Digest) 96 (February 1986): 143–51.

45. Ibid.

46. Marshall D. Shulman, "Towards a Western Philosophy of Coexistence," *Foreign Affairs* 52 (October 1973): 35–58.

47. The formulation is Stanley Hoffmann's; see his *Duties beyond Borders* (Syracuse, N.Y.: Syracuse University Press, 1981), 232.

Part II
Subjective and Objective Determinants

Robert B. Bathurst challenges Western readers in chapter 3 to perform the difficult task of becoming aware of their ethnocentric assumptions, those that seem so logically obvious within Western strategic culture that they are unwittingly projected onto a quite different Soviet strategic culture. Too often those in the West have predicted Soviet naval conduct based on how they think rather than on how the Soviets think about how to employ navies. Admiral Harry D. Train II argues in chapter 4, on the other hand, that there are objective determinants of strategy proceeding from the circumstances of the situation, including the interactive nature of Soviet and Western strategy. From the vantage point of the North Atlantic Treaty Organization's (NATO's) Atlantic Command, Train suggests that, given NATO's strategy and capabilities, any Soviet regime and high command would respond in a largely similar fashion, irrespective of culture, ideology, or planning process.

It is a key task for evaluating our own thinking, not just Soviet thinking, to examine how much our view is molded by the inner subjectivity of the particular strategic culture in which we are bred and how much by the outer objective circumstances in which we find ourselves.

3
The Soviet Navy Through Western Eyes

Robert B. Bathurst

> All measurement is a matter of the frame of reference within which the measurement is made.
> —Albert Einstein

Styles of War and Analysis

All who analyze the Soviet Navy must start from the position that there are conceptual incongruities in how the West, particularly the United States, studies national security problems and how the Soviets study national security problems. For example, in determining strategy, the Soviets operate deductively, while the West works inductively. Consequently, the Soviets begin with an ideology about war in which the navy, as a concept, derives from a larger system of a political-military whole. The United States appears to start with a navy and, partly on the basis of its capabilities, then determines how it is to be used. The Maritime Strategy is an example of this kind of conceptual modeling.[1] The widespread publication of the idea of the strategy—in itself a cultural act—gives us the possibility of analyzing the Maritime Strategy as the manifestation of a specific cultural process. In order to avoid some confusion, it should be emphasized that the overall merits of the Maritime Strategy are not being discussed here; the concept is simply being used to illustrate of the difference between Soviet and U.S. military thinking.

The incongruities in how the two nations understand and build navies create the possibility of speaking of cultural and national patterns of naval analysis. This concept is particularly important at a time like the present when the Soviet Union is undergoing rapid and radical change, for unless we can identify the recurring cultural patterns, we will lose our way in a forest of changing indicators. This is especially true of U.S. analysis, which dwells heavily on the present with almost no vision of the future. Yet while we have traditionally studied the Soviet Navy according to its capabilities and intentions, we have paid little attention to the Soviet Navy as the expression of a culture and a worldview. But just as the Great White Fleet was an expression of American values and the Maritime Strategy is an expression of American military culture, so the Soviet Navy is the expression of Russian-Soviet military culture.

To complicate the problem, we also must consider that truth about the Soviet Navy is influenced by the preconceptions of the viewer. What we have here is a problem in sorting information. Different cultures create different boxes for sorting data, and the boxes do not exactly fit from one culture to another. Thus, in analyzing foreign information, we necessarily take the facts out of their context to file in our boxes. We are always dealing with a series of incongruities. For example, for many years, the late Admiral Sergei Gorshkov was put in the same box as Admiral Elmo R. Zumwalt, Jr, which masked the vast differences in how the Soviet Navy and the U.S. Navy are planned.[2]

This chapter proposes to ask how such incongruities in the ways in which the West thinks about and structures navies affects its analysis of the Soviet Navy. My method is primarily comparative and certainly tentative. Nothing is more difficult than trying to compare national cultures, and yet it must be done, for otherwise we are condemned to thinking in mirror images. We cannot be sure when an idea is our own projection and when it is an authentic statement of someone else's reality.

Comparative naval behavior will be examined through the lenses of four methodologies for cultural study with the hope of gaining some useful insights. Most important are anthropologist Edward Hall's notions of high- and low-context societies, space, time, anger, and the value of life and political scientist Nathan Leites's summary principles of Soviet political behavior in *The Operational Code of the Politburo*, including central control, cultural deception, risk avoidance, and hierarchy of goals.[3] Also contributing to this investigation are physicist Max Planck's observations concerning the effect of separating a part from its whole and historian Edward Keenan's postulates of Russian cultural persistence (for example, in the demand for unity and the strategy of deception.[4]

Soviet-U.S. Conceptual Incongruities

The most serious danger in analysis is that of ethnocentric projection, that is, perceiving the enemy in one's own cultural forms. This is particularly seductive for those with little direct Soviet experience because it is difficult for them to see the world from the Soviet point of view. In the history of our naval analysis, there have been many examples of this: predicting that the Soviets would build an aircraft carrier long before that was possible or useful; expecting a much greater development of the naval infantry than ever took place; expecting that the Yankee nuclear-powered ballistic missile submarines (SSBNs), copies of U.S. Polaris-armed SSBNs, would be used in the same way; expecting that a blue-water Soviet Navy would mean greater and bolder overseas aggression; or predicting that the modern Soviet Navy was being built for fleet-against-fleet operations, although there was little evidence of this.

It is true that there can be arguments about the details of each of these cases, but they are examples of cultural projection. The point that Einstein makes is that all things are relative; that is, they take place within a cont˄xt. This means that it is impossible that any culture so complex and enormous as the Soviet culture would plan to fight the way the United States would fight or would draw the same conclusions that the United States would draw from the same data.

Putting Information in One's Own Boxes

Gregory Bateson points out that intelligence is the perception of differences.[5] But with respect to the Soviet Navy our perception of the differences is extremely difficult. In particular we must avoid the trap of uncritically using ready-made compartments to contain the phenomena we observe. Thus we confront the pervasive problem of form (or structure) and content—of correctly naming the boxes into which we put information.

A prime example of the misconceptions fostered by the difficult problem of form and content is our tendency to look for a Soviet counterpart to the Maritime Strategy. In doing so we fail to perceive how different Soviet military culture is. Because the job of the Soviet General Staff is to solve military problems—that is, to determine the desired outcome and then to shape forces and strategies to achieve this outcome—the Soviet Navy does not perform in the same role as the U.S. Navy, which acts more independently. Although the Soviet Navy exists as an administrative organization in peace and war, in its operational function it loses any separate identity, merging into the combined arms concept as one of a variety of assets for winning the war. But the navy does not win wars and therefore, in Soviet thought, the Soviet Navy does not have a strategy that is identifiably naval.[6] For the Soviet Navy, a concept such as the Maritime Strategy is impossible.

Styles in War

Just as many nations have an identifiable style of war, so they have an identifiable style of perceiving and estimating threats.[7] This must necessarily be so. The history, geography, experience of war, and indeed, the process by which a culture develops a system that ensures its survival combine to create a context that determines how threats are perceived and avoided.

German military planning, for example, has historically emphasized precise theater operations as part of expansive global objectives. The Russians-Soviets, on the other hand, have shown a preference for massed forces against precise military objectives. The U.S. style shows a frequent consideration of bombing as a military solution. Bombing is a recurrent concept in U.S. foreign policy and theory of war, a solution that the United States is apparently culturally inclined to choose. The idea of bombing, then, must fit into some larger context of thinking about war—a context that can reveal information useful for prediction.

The Soviet style of war is different. In World War II the Soviets did not adopt a policy of bombing cities, and they have argued that the U.S. idea of mutual assured destruction (MAD) which derives from the bombing idea, is not a military concept. Thus, we may have identified an incongruity in military thinking that will result in vastly different operations being classified under the same name.

Further, the inclination in the United States to adopt bombing as a military solution should alert us to its mirror image: an overestimation of the threat of being bombed. Indeed that fear has recurred in the United States since World War II at roughly ten-year intervals: with the "bomber gap" of the 1950s, the "missile gap" of the 1960s, and the "window of vulnerability" of the 1970s.[8]

Styles in Threat Analysis

Just as there are styles of war, so there are styles of perceiving the threat. For example, in maritime warfare, the United States has consistently underplayed the role of mines, a historic Soviet naval preference, in conventional as well as unconventional operations. The U.S. preference is obviously for surface/air warfare. It uses carriers as the central force of a naval strategy that is culturally preordained to be a surface/air strategy. The Soviets give greater weight to submarines, to the covert military platforms.

As a result, the United States is programmed to anticipate those kinds of war that exercise this preference, and it underestimates those that do not. The U.S. Navy responds more readily to threats against carriers than against convoys, although convoys may be essential to strategic success. Moreover, in the Maritime Strategy, the United States makes the assumption that the Soviets will respond so overwhelmingly to a carrier threat that they will divert forces from the central front. Soviet doctrine implies that the main axis of a Soviet attack probably would not be on the most highly defended central front; more likely the advance would take place on one of the weaker flanks. In any case, once a Soviet surprise attack were launched, Soviet forces, "scientifically" organized for victory, would not be diverted.

There is also a distinctive mode of threat perception. U.S. planning prefers to focus on one threat at a time and on one phase of that threat. In contrast, the Soviets visualize a multiplicity of threats from a multiplicity of forces. For the United States, war on the central front is the major focus of strategic planning; for the Soviets, such a war could take place only on a global scale—in the Far East as well as in Europe. And the role of the Soviet Navy, as it constantly demonstrates, would be to act not only in the strategic submarine bastions but also in the maritime choke points.

The Relevance of Context for Analysis

Anthropologist Edward Hall's distinction between high-context and low-context cultures illuminates differences in Soviet and U.S. patterns of thinking about naval warfare.[9] Operating in a high context, Soviet planning presupposes the interconnectedness of threats. On the other hand, employing a low-context mode of thought, the United States tends to study naval problems separately. The act of isolation of a problem is, of course, a more rapid and efficient method of solving it and has many advantages. The high-context mode of thought is slow and easily given to paralysis due to the complexities it must consider. (The terms *high-context* and *low-context* are unfortunate in that they suggest that one is good and the other bad. That is not the case. They are simply different ways of dealing with the world.) Context changes meaning and therefore the perception of threats. The same ship gives different signals in different contexts. The *Eisenhower* in the Sea of Okhotsk is not the same as the *Eisenhower* in the Sea of Japan.

The Problem of Wholes

Physicist Max Planck makes a remarkable statement that is useful in the study of the Soviet Navy: "In physics, . . . we regard all complicated processes as combinations of simple elementary processes, . . . that is, we think of the wholes before us as the sums of their parts. But this procedure presupposes that the splitting of a whole does not affect the character of this whole. . . . One cannot understand such processes on the assumption that all properties of a whole may be approached by a study of its parts."[10] The problem Planck raises is that of separating an element, in this case the Soviet Navy, from its context, which is Soviet national security. Clearly the parts must be examined but it must also be recognized that they have a different meaning when separated from the whole. The Soviets customarily discuss military questions in terms of wholes, while the United States discusses them in terms of parts. For example, Soviet naval operations are necessarily conceived of as part of a political concept that has as its objective a victory that transforms a society and does not merely conquer it. Therefore, in a maritime operation, the Soviet Navy acts as one of the combined arms to crush an opponent's military-economic potential and to eliminate its capability of making war.

In Soviet naval operations, it is difficult to identify a part of an exercise that demonstrates this overall objective because the whole operation determines the meaning of the parts. Moreover, approaching the study of the Soviet Navy from this direction leads to a paradox. Since Soviet military strategy is about victory—which determines the operations of the navy—and since victory is achieved on land, the Soviet Navy's operations are, ultimately, about the land.

Maritime Bastions and Strategy: Cultural Contexts

It has been argued that a nation plans its naval strategy and interprets the enemy threat in terms of its own context. If it thinks in a high-context way, the naval element is probably seen as an operation in a global campaign; if it thinks in a low-context mode, then it is likely to see the naval element as solving specific problems. It is characteristic that Soviets pay considerable attention to choke points, while the United States concentrates on high seas operations.

If the Maritime Strategy gives us a useful model of U.S. naval thought, then the idea of the maritime bastions can provide a helpful paradigm of Soviet naval thought.[11] The maritime bastions model has much to recommend it from a cultural point of view. Such a model strengthens command and control by a leadership obsessed with the demand for supremacy at the center; it reduces the danger of individual initiative and command decision by otherwise widely scattered ships; it ensures a large role for secretiveness and deception; and it casts a lure to catch the U.S. naval mind.

A Historical Parallel. Furthermore, the maritime bastions model invites a comparison, in terms of military culture, with the Battle of Borodino in 1812. The Russian field marshal, Prince Mikhail Kutuzov, after a long retreat offered to engage the French armies below Borodino to protect Moscow, the last bastion of Russian power. The battle took place, it should be noted, in the Russian heartland, where Kutuzov's forces were strongest and Napoleon's troops, with overextended supply lines, were weakest. After a bloody battle, Napoleon's army technically achieved the victory but was so weakened by its campaign and Russian attacks from the rear that it lost the war. Napoleon's assumption had been that by taking Moscow, the prize of that battle, he would win the war.

There is something of a parallel between the Maritime Strategy and the Battle of Borodino. Like Napoleon's invasion, the Maritime Strategy takes the battle into the area of the enemy's strength and U.S. weakness; it assumes that achieving a single objective will somehow end the war; and it designates the conditions suitable for its operation while ignoring other issues, such as the problems of the rear.

Some Contextual Incongruities of Strategy. Some of the Maritime Strategy's basic premises assume Soviet mirror images of war. For example, the Maritime Strategy assumes that the Soviets will interpret U.S. intentions correctly; that the United States will agree about the precise levels of violence to be used in case of escalation; that we will agree about what are conventional and unconventional weapons; and that there will be a common understanding about damage assessment and targeting. These assumptions are based on the obviously invalid notion that the Soviet and U.S. contexts are nearly identical.

It will be difficult in terms of Soviet military doctrine for the General Staff to sort the Maritime Strategy into their own boxes. For example, under the Maritime Strategy category "Phase I: Deterrence or the Transition to War," it is stated: "Aggressive forward movement of anti-submarine warfare forces, both submarines and maritime patrol aircraft, will force Soviet submarines to retreat into defensive bastions to protect their ballistic missile submarines."[12] In Soviet military doctrine, such an action would signal the start of nothing short of a global war.

There is also a problem with ending such a war. The Maritime Strategy calls for war termination on favorable terms, not victory. But in Soviet strategic culture there is no counterpart for such a concept. And, the Soviets—in this case mirror imaging on their part—attribute to the United States the desire to destroy utterly the bastion of world socialism. The only likely strategy for the Soviets under such circumstances is to seek to destroy the ability of the United States to make war, which in their case means not a partial victory.

Thus, when we discuss war prosecution and termination on such a scale, we must address these concepts not solely in a low-context mode. These concepts need to be connected to comparable North Atlantic Treaty Organization, U.S. Air Force, and U.S. Army strategies, to some notion of how to deal with the Warsaw Pact, and to some idea of possible alternatives to Soviet power. When the Maritime Strategy fails to make its context clear, we become conceptually stuck. There are no more boxes into which to sort the operation.

Styles in the Understanding of War

By treating the Maritime Strategy as a contextual problem, we can confront the perceptual factor of having to examine how cultures predict how wars begin, are fought, and end. With respect to the Soviets, there are some significant incongruities in the understanding of war. As a consequence, it is very likely that we will find ourselves fighting different wars.

The most significant problem is the difference in approach to how wars begin. Soviet doctrine emphasizes the opening phase. There are precise definitions about the degrees of danger and zones in which action must be taken.

The Soviet shooting down of the Korean airliner in 1983 demonstrated that quite drastic measures are, efficiently or not, necessarily initiated.

The United States does not have such a clear doctrine concerning borders. Instead, in the discussion of a war with the Soviets, it emphasizes the escalation process. The U.S. literature on war clearly reflects a low-context cultural approach involving a series of discrete acts based upon assumptions of national rationality and ethnic congruence about unmistakable signals—a series of warning shots across the bow, as it were. It sometimes seems as if the game is to be played—as in the Maritime Strategy—by one clearly marked team, following its own rules of Hoyle in its own arena, while the opposition is in another field with a ball of a different shape.

The language of military theory is also significant. The Soviet literature, written almost entirely by military officers, reflects its high-context origin. Meant to obfuscate the issues for outsiders while giving a significant line to the informed, it adopts a grandiloquent Aesopian language in which "laws" are issued requiring action far removed from Soviet reality. But the important authors, only recently including some without World War II experience, reflect a concrete understanding of both the horrors and the unpredictability of war. They write about war not only as an event expressing a whole society but also as one marking a colossal historical transformation.

U.S. military literature reflects a compartmented, episodic, and usually narrowly intellectual mind expressing itself in finely drawn distinctions that do not have the smell of war. Like the Maritime Strategy, U.S. concepts tend to be presented with considerable fanfare that masks the apocalyptic nature of the subject. For example, discussions of war termination are almost entirely in terms of rational, legal concepts—more the language of plea bargaining than of the battlefield. The idea of escalation dominance has already been cited as a prime temptation for ethnocentric projection. The language of MAD, counterforce, and countervalue gives us a distance from the events we are describing and helps to make war the abstraction with which we prefer to deal. This introduces a certain vagueness into U.S. military concepts and allows an avoidance of such subjects as the rear (a voluminous subject in the Soviet literature), the control of forces and populations, and the realities of mobilization and supply.

The Power of Either-Or

There is an alternative way of sorting information that is very different from that of the Soviets—a way of sorting information that has brought confusion to our analysis. As a low-context culture, analysts in the United States often structure thought in terms of either-or, especially when they are new to a subject or are explaining a complex idea to those unfamiliar with it. Observe, for example, how our notions of war—as either nuclear or nonnuclear, aggressive or defensive, and strategic or tactical—structure our thought.

There are significant problems in analyzing foreign, especially Soviet, systems taken out of their own context. Taking the most obvious example, we often refer to conventional or unconventional warfare, although the parameters of each are extremely uncertain. Thus we emphasize what weapons are being used, although we do not know how to classify chemical or biological weapons and many other variations. The Soviets place more emphasis on who is using the weapons in question. For them, any kind of armed confrontation with the imperialist bloc is likely to lead to an unconventional form of warfare, and the General Staff will be responsible (to the point of neurosis, one may be sure) for predicting and fortuitously preempting this war.

This tendency to an either-or classification in American thought, when applied to conventional and unconventional warfare, appears to lead to some significant incongruities in predicting Soviet behavior in war. The tendency in American analysis to sort the data into these two boxes appears to have a powerful influence in structuring Soviet strategy into our terms.

Thus the change in Soviet doctrine to recognize that war could begin with a long conventional phase is often interpreted in the United States to mean that the Soviets do not plan to fight a nuclear war. The either-or categories could only be so clear out of the Soviet context. First, the Soviet decision whether to use nuclear weapons will depend on perceptions and estimates of the enemy and on the manipulation of an infinite variety of possibilities. Second, although there is no doubt that the Soviets would prefer not to use nuclear weapons, there is also no doubt that they have fully developed operational plans for doing so and have ensured the readiness of the fleet to execute these plans. That an old Whiskey-class submarine on a delicate espionage mission off Sweden's Karlskrona in 1981 was carrying nuclear weapons—in order, presumably, to be ready to execute its wartime nuclear mission—should not be forgotten.[13] Finally, the literature—unless it is largely deceptive, which is, of course, possible—establishes that military scientists are not prohibited by the leadership from continuing to study the problems of conducting operations under nuclear conditions.[14]

Strategic Boxes

The differences between the Soviet and U.S. response to nuclear war illustrate how different conceptual boxes affect the content of strategy. Because Soviet strategy comes down from the top and focuses on the objectives of war and the possible means of winning it, Soviet strategy necessarily considers all possibilities—nuclear and nonnuclear—simultaneously. The most difficult problem for Soviet planners therefore is how to prepare for the transition from conventional war to nuclear war. Thus for the Soviets the context tends to remain wide, while for the United States the context tends to narrow. In any case, it is inconceivable that Soviet naval theory could ignore the nuclear question, as the Maritime Strategy has done.

The context of Soviet naval thought gives us a considerable benefit, which the Soviets do not have in reverse: we can expect a unified vision from the Soviets. If we understand nuclear doctrine for the Soviet Navy, we can make some very reliable assumptions about decisions of the Soviet General Staff. In the United States—with its individualized, competitive management—we cannot assume that same congruity.

Predicting Behavior with Cultural Concepts

The purpose in presenting these ways of looking at the Soviet Navy is not to prove new facts about it but to determine if a different point of view can produce useful new insights that may help in predicting and understanding Soviet patterns of behavior and decision making. Unlike the historian or the political scientist, however, the military commander must predict behavior. His most critical requirement is to anticipate the decisions of the enemy.

Edward Hall defined several cultural concepts useful in military analysis and prediction. Among them are four that we shall sample for their practical application: the anger chain, the idea of space, the concept of time, and the value of life and/or property.[15]

The Anger Chain

The idea of the anger chain—that nations, like individuals, have ways of signaling stored hostility and resentment—is obviously important in detecting the approach of war. The anger chain is the psychological counterpart to the watch officer's list of indications of hostilities, and, although less well defined, the concept has played a significant historical role. Much of the political settlement in Eastern Europe at the end of World War II, for example, was influenced by the belief that imaginary Russian hordes were about to attack from the East—an enduring nightmare. The uproar across the world when Korean Airlines flight 007 was shot down in 1983 must have astonished the Soviet military leadership, for according to the Soviet anger chain, this was a predictable riposte.

President Jimmy Carter's response to the invasion of Afghanistan was an excellent example of the American pattern in an anger chain. It proceeded from the frustration of expectations (in this case, the end of détente) to moral outrage and was followed by the demand for punishment. Similarly, the euphoric declarations of success by the principal American players at the 1988

Moscow summit may have set the stage for a future triggering of the American anger chain.

Another difference in anger chains affecting U.S.-Soviet summitry concerns the importance of personal relations in diplomacy. Since diplomacy in the American culture tends to be heavily interpreted as a function of personal relations, a Soviet leader's change from a perceived friendly position is usually experienced as personal betrayal. On the other hand, Soviet leaders, actors in a high-context mode, are freed by their historical roles from the need to be liked.

Anger chains are excellent examples of the need for accuracy in cross-cultural perception because the signal of impending violence, given in one culture, must be correctly interpreted in the other. In this case, we can again fault the Maritime Strategy for assuming that the signal it proposes to give—attacking Soviet submarines in their bastions with conventional weapons—will be understood according to low-context rule—that is, a discrete event, not signaling the use of unconventional weapons (whatever that means) outside the designated theater of operations (wherever that is.)

A key difference between the two military cultures is that Soviet military strategy tends to be oriented around the control of people and therefore, once set in motion, involves a variety of moves to seize both psychological and military dominance. U.S. strategy is more equipment oriented and appears to concentrate on events, targets, and objectives.

Soviet writers express their puzzlement about U.S. military thought by frequently charging that it is saturated with emotion, mysticism, and a lack of scientific rigor. (The Soviets, of course, argue that their military thought is scientific, unemotional, and realistic.) Soviet strategic culture does, however, reflect the Russian anger chain in its secretiveness, obsession with control, and demand for sudden elimination of Soviet enemies, including their leadership and means of making war.

Whether or not this is a successful explanation, we are confronted by striking differences in military theories. The Soviets unanimously emphasize the importance of choosing the place and time for an overwhelming surprise blow after carefully determining the weakest link. This decision also will be based on significant espionage activity. The U.S. Navy, on the other hand, in the Maritime Strategy proposes to announce well in advance the place and time of its attack.

The Idea of Space

Edward Hall also stresses the importance of space in understanding a political culture. It is generally true that fear increases the requirement for surrounding space, and as most observers have noted, this has certainly characterized Russian and Soviet politics. Supporting that pattern, the operations of the Soviet Navy have given us considerable insight into the Soviet sense of space, with its successive zones and echelons of defense.

The relative weight of secure space in Soviet strategy is also suggested by the willingness of the Soviet government to give precedence to spatial security over important political goals. The invasions of Czechoslovakia and Afghanistan did much to weaken the political correlation of forces for the Soviet Union. The amphibious landing in the Kurils in the summer naval exercises of 1985 was also a curious act since it came at a time when the Soviet Union was making great efforts to change its relationships in the Far East, particularly with Japan.[16] The same kind of cultural response may have been a part of the continuing incursion of Soviet submarines into Norwegian and Swedish waters, fatally weakening the Soviet case for making the Baltic region a nuclear-free zone.

This response to space is useful in defining some other differences in military thought between the Soviet and U.S. navies. In Soviet thought the seas have been extensions of the land. Soviet maritime strategy, which accomplishes many tasks, seems to begin with securing the heartland by trying to establish strong maritime borders protected by multiple defenses. Although blue-water aspirations are attributed to the Soviet Navy, they are not likely to constitute a powerful Soviet concept. The Soviet concern is with fringes and flanks—notions neglected in the United States—and with the passages between seas as well as with the rear—areas the United States has been able to disregard in the past.

The Soviet response to space is to ensure a tight control and strict fulfillment of hierarchical objectives. The bastion concept—a secretive grouping of controllable submarines, both a lure and a trap—is a more likely Soviet cultural pattern than the idea of a high seas fleet.

The Concept of Time

Of Hall's ideas about how cultures differ, the concept of time is useful. A low-context culture like the United States is preoccupied with the present. Thus, the United States focuses less on the future and the past than does the Soviet Union, a high-context culture. This distinction in responses to time helps to underscore some important differences in national approaches to naval problems.

Because Soviet doctrine is very clear about how the world should look ten years from now, Soviet naval planners have an advantage in how to shape their forces. The lack of such a stable vision in U.S. doctrine makes it difficult to justify such concepts as the need for a 600-ship navy and weakens such ideas as the Maritime Strategy, which is not a response to a perceptible threat. This preoccupation with the present is, perhaps, a factor explaining why the

United States periodically abandons the idea of a balanced navy, rediscovers the convoy, and reconstitutes the riverine forces. As the focus is in the present, so are U.S. priorities.

The Soviets, however, appear to focus more heavily on the future and the past. Past wars, past invasions, and past hostile acts are very much a part of the threat perception of the present. The Baltic was a strategic sea in the past, and it could become so again; therefore, the aged Golf submarines remain there.

Time is also politically confusing for the Soviets. Since the future is already determined, it exists to some extent in the present. Soviet leaders have characteristically misinformed the world about future capabilities, treating them as if they were already a present reality. First Secretary Nikita Khrushchev, for example, frequently confused the plans for Soviet missiles with current realities. Thus he boasted that Soviet missiles could hit a fly in space, had enabled the Soviet Union to burst out of containment, and could destroy a variety of countries. With similar exaggeration Admiral Gorshkov claimed in the 1960s—as General Secretary Mikhail Gorbachev did again in Paris in the 1980s—that the Soviets could locate and destroy a submarine anywhere in the world's oceans.

The reason that Soviet naval tacticians dwell so heavily on the past in creating theories for contemporary warfare is not simply for self-stimulation. They write of past wars because history is a laboratory for the study of patterns of human behavior. In the Russian past, one of the main questions studied was how an inferior power defeats a superior one. While this question remains a part of current naval science, it is no longer so crucial. Nevertheless, history is replete with instructive examples of how the correlation of forces was suddenly changed. Consequently, study of the past teaches the military strategist to expect change and, as a result, to have little confidence in the future of parity.

This connection with the future is important. It means that the Soviets are constantly aware of the need to occupy strategic positions already during peace. A possible future war always has a present reality. The Soviet concept is of a social and political development (they call it a dialectic) in which forms are stable but content changes.

Their conceptual pattern differs from that of the United States, which tends to view the world as performing in discrete, often unrelated, events. The United States lacks the benefit of a cohesive vision—such as the transformation of colonial empires—to rationalize its international conduct. Its pattern is expressed in the way it fashions forces and thinks about armed forces: to prevent war, not to end it, and to maintain the status quo, not to correct it. Thus, the Soviets—who are nearly always dissatisfied with the present—focus aggressively on future planning in an ambiguous world. For the United States that is a problem.

The Value of Life

Finally, in Edward Hall's keys to analysis, it is important to include a culture's attitude toward human life and property, since this element is essential for estimating military risks, as well as the extent to which a threat might be tolerated. In Eastern Europe the Czechs have been, for example, much less militarily daring than the Poles. And in Western Europe the French have made great accommodations for self-preservation, whereas the Germans submitted to a modern Götterdämerung.

There is little ambiguity about the United States in this respect. It has officially established—and since abandoned—the MAD doctrine that the loss of one-third of a city's population is a sufficient deterrent; however, beyond MAD, the cultural pattern has been to adopt extreme measures for the protection and safety of its own armed forces while showing a curious indifference to enemy civilian populations.

The Soviets, on the other hand, have demonstrated a different attitude toward civilian populations. Unlike the United States, in wartime they have chosen a policy of reckless use of their men, population, and arms. Their profligate waste of human life was legendary in both world wars, and indicators of this cultural attitude are present today.

Soviet naval construction and deployments of the 1960s and 1970s made almost inhuman requirements of the crews. Long voyages and patrols were made in southern seas in un-air-conditioned ships with inadequate provisioning. The ships themselves were planned for operations and were constructed for survival only through the first salvo. Improper shielding of Soviet naval nuclear plants—similar to the pitiful shielding of Soviet civilian nuclear plants (as revealed in 1986 during the catastrophic release of radiation at Chernobyl)—made the submarine service a notoriously dangerous assignment.

The Maritime Strategy, then, viewed against this cultural dimension, makes some assumptions about relative risks that are culturally dubious. First, U.S. culture does not appear to tolerate such large-scale expenditures of life and equipment as the Maritime Strategy requires. Second, the Maritime Strategy assumes that the Soviets would divert sufficient forces from the central front to make a decisive difference in that theater of military actions (TVD); however, Soviet military science emphasizes picking the main axis of attack and then driving with maximum force and maximum speed. The notion of redeployment and flexible response—whatever the realities—is American, not Soviet. And finally, the Soviets have—at least since naval exercise Okean in 1970—been perfecting and demonstrating their theories of how to deal with a threatened carrier attack. In order to do so, they would not divert forces from the central front, but would attack in advance with air and submarine forces designed for that purpose. And if such an attack were to fail, Soviet military theory instructs that forces would not be transferred for the rescue of an unsuccessful operation. In Soviet theory, one pursues victory, not defeat.

Predicting Behavior with the Operational Code

Another valuable tool for making estimates on the basis of political culture is the late Nathan Leites's *Operational Code of the Politburo*.[17] First published in 1951, the operational code has been a consistently useful model for analyzing and predicting Soviet behavior. It is remarkable that although this paradigm was formulated on the basis of a content analysis of largely Stalinist literature, the operational code remains a useful guide. That, surely, contributes some support to the notion of stable and predictable patterns of political culture in military behavior. This model is also of enormous importance during periods, like the present, of apparent radical change. Although the U.S. tendency will be to assume that Soviet restructuring is irreversible, Leites reminds us of the Soviet structural continuity with the past.

Leites studied patterns of Soviet behavior and identified, among many others, the following patterns: centralized control, secretiveness and deception, risk avoidance, and a hierarchy of goals. It is interesting that these characteristics were also identified by Edward Keenan in his historical study of Muscovite folkways and are being named by the general secretary as objects for change under *perestroika, glasnost',* and the new thinking.

Control at the Center

One of the most consistent characteristics of Russian and Soviet political practice is to maintain absolute control at the center. This is in stark contrast to the U.S. system of military control, where each service aggressively and openly lobbies for its own interest. In any case, the Russian cultural need to concentrate power gives us a powerful indicator for predicting Soviet behavior.

Centralized control makes it easier to understand the Soviet Navy because, unlike the U.S. armed forces, the navy must reflect the same doctrine as the other military services. Because of the Soviet demand for absolute command authority, provisions for maintaining control are given the highest priority.

Understanding this Soviet characteristic, we can predict Soviet wartime priorities through a kind of law of mirror imaging. As culture necessarily responds to the reality it sees—or (following Gregory Bateson) creates—so the Soviet Union will tend to interpret its adversary in its own image.[18] Thus we can expect that the destruction of the U.S. command authority would also be one of the highest priorities of Soviet planning and that the Soviets would not expect U.S. command authority to be exercised at lower levels. Such lower-level authority and initiative would be unlikely in the Soviet system, where initiative is exercised only by the central command authority and at the General Staff and the theater levels. (When the Soviets discuss initiative at lower levels, they are calling for leaders to fulfill their orders—not change them, no matter what the personal or unit sacrifice.)[19]

Whereas the Soviet lower commands are obliged to fulfill a detailed hierarchy of goals, the General Staff reserves for itself a variety of options. Thus, while we can expect to see in exercises patterned behavior with a rigid execution of prescribed maneuvers, we should not be fooled that this is the only option available to the staffs. For example, in solving antisubmarine warfare (ASW) problems, the Soviets can be expected to engage—in addition to normal hunter-killer operations—in destruction of command and control capabilities, including space communications, and to employ espionage, sabotage, *Spetsnaz* (special forces), and port bombardment. Furthermore, because of centralized authority, unity of views, and strict command hierarchy, the staffs can move with great rapidity and cohesion, as they did in World War II.

Cultural Deception

For centuries before *glasnost'* (visibility) there was *neglasnost'* (invisibility), and an understanding of cultural cycles gives us confidence that *neglasnost'* will recur. Of course, there was a reason for *neglasnost'*, for *neglasnost'* gave Russia a strategic advantage over the enemy.[20]

In today's Soviet culture the control of information and disinformation is taken very seriously. Foreknowledge—as Stalin said, in referring to spies— is the equivalent of combat arms. The exposure of the John Walker naval spy ring in 1985 and the revelation that U.S. operational secrets had been relayed to the Soviets since the 1960s disclosed also a weakness in the somewhat rationalized naval analysis of the United States: its underestimation of the role of espionage, subversion, and disinformation in Soviet military operations. The Soviets have methods for solving military problems for which the United States seems to have no comparable cultural boxes.

The secretive aspect of Soviet culture combined with the need for centralized control suggests that the Soviets will emphasize wartime methods that the United States tends to underemphasize. Thus, mines and submarines are preeminent Soviet naval-cultural weapons—weapons with uses the United States has tended to underestimate. Nor does the United States have anything quite comparable to the *Spetsnaz*—with its missions of political assassination and dirty tricks—involving, undoubtedly, men trained for years in foreign languages and cultures.

Risk Avoidance and Hierarchy of Goals

The characteristic of risk avoiding is consistent with the modern history of the Soviet Navy. Much is written about the contrast between the Soviet view of war as an event that, once started, develops a momentum of its own and that of the United States, in which war is treated as a rational process with accepted and defined stages. For the Soviets, this has meant devising multiple systems, employing intermediate stages, and avoiding uncertainty. It is possible that the Soviet Navy's minimal forward deployment is influenced by this cultural caution against unnecessary risk. The U.S. Navy's forward deployment under the Maritime Strategy underscores this contrast.

Because of the importance of centralized authority in Soviet planning, much greater weight is put on the experience and wisdom of the leader, and consequently, much greater confusion results when he disappears. It is important to pay attention to what the political and party leaders say as setting the parameters within which the military leaders are permitted to plan. A safe assumption is that, given the extreme concentration of power, the military leaders will be allowed to diverge very little from the central doctrine, and it is a strategic advantage to keep that a secret.

Thus, the Soviets do not speak of military use unconnected with political objectives or of armed struggle without reference to the advancement of economic stages. If they are building large ships, we must interpret these ships not only as military signs but also as political and economic indicators, as Norman Friedman suggests. For example, is the building of larger, more efficient ships in part a reflection of the growing shortage of appropriate naval recruits, that is, recruits from of the great Slavic nationalities? Are big submarines required because of their more efficient use of manpower—a significant goal considering the drastic decline in the draftable greater Slavic population? Are large ships an indication that the Soviets are at last preparing to engage in distant naval battles and/or a signal that deterrence, interposition, and intimidation require much more formidable weapons platforms than before in view of the revolution in military technology?[21]

Predicting Behavior from the Demand for Unanimity

The demand for unanimity in the Supreme Soviet, the Politburo, and the Central Committee is not incidental. It comes from both an ancient tradition of organizing for survival in a hostile land and from a high-context cultural mode of achieving greater stability through integration of differences. The demand for uniformity means that the Soviet Navy—for reasons beyond the imperatives imposed by geography and enemy forces—will operate in some culturally distinctive ways.

First, we can be certain that the Soviet Navy will fulfill, as its highest priority, combined arms operations in defense. Since its missions and functions will be approved from above, its operations will necessarily reflect the mentality of the General Staff. Therefore, we should look for exercises paralleling such ground force concepts as the operational maneuver group (OMG), the echeloning of forces, the use of reserves, plans for massing and dispersal connected with nuclear use, and so on. In addition, there will be operations for strategic defense, partial defense, and, of course, diversion from the massing of forces for attack on the main axis.

In U.S. naval operations, the main axis of attack will be obviously marked by the aircraft carrier. Comparable Soviet operations will not be so easily identified. Perhaps this difference is a useful metaphor for thinking about the cultural relativity of the two navies.

The point is that the Soviet pattern—dictating as it does strict hierarchical controls and plans, a unanimity of views, and consensus in doctrine— enforces mirror-image concepts within its organizations. In Max Planck's terms, the whole dictates the nature and cohesiveness of its parts.[22]

Avoiding Fallacious Images

A fundamental problem in understanding the Soviet system of thought and military doctrine and in predicting Soviet behavior has been that Soviet political culture promotes a feature that is very confusing to the West and, in particular, to the United States: not only are the Soviets unwilling to share with the outside world the rules of the game, but also they consciously encourage misinformation. Edward Keenan, one of the foremost scholars of Russian political culture, puts it this way:

> Until the very threshold of modern times there seems to have been no attempt—nor, presumably, any felt need—to articulate or to codify the operative principles and "rules" that governed political relations; as in other traditional systems, those who needed to know such rules knew them, and those who had no need to know were kept in ignorance. Further, to the extent that political statements for the consumption of outsiders were made at all, such were intended to serve the purpose of the system, that is to decorate and to conceal the system's essential features.[23]

Under such conditions the possibilities for misinterpretation are enormous. The temptation for a culture that thinks of itself as rational is to fill the gaps in information with what it judges to be reasonable. That leads, of course, to the trap of mirror imaging.

Keenan also makes the point that the Soviet system, like its Russian predecessor, could not function effectively without unanimity at the center and autocratic control. This assertion comes from noting the continuity of these factors in the cycles of Russian history. Obviously the Soviet Navy, to the extent that it is also an expression of that culture, must be congruent with those norms. By studying the factors of congruence, we can at least identify some of the areas of mirror imaging and develop a greater resonance in predicting Soviet naval behavior.

Escaping the Cultural Prison

It is very difficult for a low-context culture to understand a high-context culture. Americans want to look at one box at a time. The Soviets start with the big picture, while the United States wants to look at a small picture. That game was played at the Reykjavik summit in 1987 when General Secretary Gorbachev caught President Ronald Reagan off-guard with his vast proposal for nuclear disarmament.

Simply in the process of picking one aspect of Soviet military strategy for scrutiny, such as the navy (which ranks last of the five Soviet armed forces), we are placed in the danger of exaggerating the Soviet Navy's role by taking it out of context. A more serious aspect is that, in the need to make the Soviet Navy's operations fit its own boxes, the United States may not develop sufficiently its ability to prepare for the war the Soviets expect to fight. The commander's problem is to predict the enemy's behavior, and to do that, he must surmount his cultural barriers to think of the options that otherwise would not occur to him.

The rational approach cannot reliably yield correct answers, for rationality is culturally relative. Given the same set of circumstances, those who have grown up in the Soviet culture will usually come up with a different analysis from those socialized in the American culture.[24] For the high-context Soviet culture, as Planck says, there is an interaction of the whole that is not the sum of the parts.[25] And a naval battle inevitably reflects larger cultures, like the Maritime Strategy and the defense of the homeland. Only by surmounting one's cultural prison can one intelligently plan for such a cross-cultural interaction. The point here is that the Soviet Navy through Western eyes is probably that—the Soviet Navy through Western eyes. There are, it must be so, other Soviet Navies.

Notes

1. I shall be referring to the Maritime Strategy frequently entirely as a cultural concept—a model of U.S. thinking about war at sea in contrast to Soviet thinking about war at sea. For reference, I use James D. Watkins, "The Maritime Strategy," U.S. Naval Institute *Proceedings* Supplement 112 (January 1986): 2–17.

2. Admiral Sergei G. Gorshkov (1910–1988), known as the builder of the modern Soviet Navy, served as commander in chief of the Soviet Navy from 1956 to 1985. Admiral Elmo R. Zumwalt, Jr., served as U.S. chief of naval operations from 1970 to 1974.

3. Edward Hall, *Beyond Culture* (New York: Bantam Books, 1979); Nathan Leites, *Operational Code of the Politburo* (Santa Monica: RAND Corporation, 1951).

4. Max Planck, lecture in New York, 1909, quoted in Wolfgang Kohler, *The Task of Gestalt Psychology* (Princeton, N.J.: Princeton University Press, 1969); Edward L. Keenan, "Muscovite Political Folkways," *Russian Review* 45 (April 1986): 115–81.

5. See Gregory Bateson, *Mind and Nature: A Necessary Unity* (New York: Bantam Books, 1980), 250, and elsewhere for a discussion of the mind's problem in distinguishing differences and its proclivity for imposing its own images on the data of the senses.

6. There is an excellent discussion of the organization and operation of the Soviet armed forces that makes this point about misconceptions about the Soviet Navy particularly well. See Tomas Ries and Johnny Skorve, *Investigating Kola: A Study of Military Bases Using Satellite Photos,* Norwegian Foreign Policy Studies 57 (Oslo: Norsk Utenrikspolitisk Institutt, 1986), 4–20.

7. This is a convincingly argued theme in Barbara Tuchman's work but especially in *The Guns of August* (New York: Macmillan, 1962).

8. The U.S. Joint Chiefs of Staff (JCS) predicted that the Soviet Union could deliver one hundred bombs against the United States by 1954, and the secretary of the air forcce warned that U.S. cities were vulnerable to attack. Meanwhile, the JCS had estimated that there could be a major war by 1950 with Soviet air and sea attacks launched against lines of communications, cities, and nations. Such capabilities did not then exist. See Samuel F. Wells, Jr., "Sound the Tocsin: NSC 68 and the Soviet Threat," *International Security* 4 (Fall 1979): 132–33.

9. Hall, *Beyond Culture.* The terms *high context* and *low context* carry no qualitative connotations. Instead, they refer to a culture's pattern of treating information as part of a whole, in context, or isolating it from the context for simpler analysis. All cultures contain both elements, and there are advantages in each. The problem in cross-cultural analysis is that high- and low-context cultures sort information in different ways, which is a barrier to understanding. As it applies to navies, a low-context culture will translate foreign naval strategies into its own terms and then respond to these. In other words, a low-context culture will mirror image of necessity. A high-context culture, on the other hand, is not so prone to mirror image since it does not study phenomena out of context.

10. Planck, lecture.

11. The idea of the maritime bastions is, briefly, that in wartime, the Soviets, needing to protect their ballistic missile submarines for a possible second strike, will locate them in confined geographical areas where they can be protected by surface ships and naval air forces until the moment of truth.

12. Watkins, "Maritime Strategy," 9.

13. I am referring to the Whiskey that went aground off the Swedish naval base at Karlskrona in October 1981.

14. Discussions of tacticcs and operations using nuclear weapons continue in the literature in addition to discussions of war fighting using conventional weapons. For example, see V.G. Reznichenko, *Taktik* (Moscow: Voenizdat, 1984), 60. Also, see M.A. Gareev, *M. V. Frunze—Voennyi teoretik* (Moscow: Voenizdat, 1985), 236–46.

15. Hall, *Beyond Culture.*

16. Gorbachev's Vladivostok speech of July 28, 1986, confirmed a policy of change in East Asia that had long been expected.

17. Leites, *Operational Code.*

18. Bateson, *Mind and Nature.*

19. The literature on this subject is quite consistent. See, for example, P.N. Lashchenko, *Iskusstvo voenachal'nika* (Moscow: Voenizdat, 1986), 168.

20. For the term *neglasnost'*, see Keenan, "Muscovite Political Folkways," 119–20.

21. Norman Friedman discusses this problem in "The Soviet Fleet in Transition," U.S. Naval Institute *Proceedings* 109 (May 1983): 173.

22. Planck, lecture.

23. Keenan, "Muscovite Political Folkways," 145. In this article Professor Keenan gives convincing guidelines for interpreting the political culture of Russia, particularly in respect to leadership selection and Kremlin behavior.

24. This hypothesis was tested in a series of seminars at the Esalen Institute in which seven different groups composed of Americans with university eductions and recent Soviet émigrés from major cities in the Soviet Union with higher education met to negotiate, bargain, mirror image, and solve problems. Each time in the bargaining game, the ex-Soviets designated one of their members for espionage, and each time without hesitation they created "legal" documents to support their case. Furthermore, the ex-Soviets always used a technique characteristic of Russian diplomacy and war: manipulating the opponent into confusion, anger, or indecisiveness by overwhelming him with contradictory information and events. What was repeatedly demonstrated was that those socialized in the Soviet culture routinely operate in ways that Americans do not predict.

25. Planck, lecture.

4
The Objective Dynamics of U.S.-Soviet Strategy

Harry D. Train II

T he dynamics of interactive U.S. and Soviet strategy may be illustrated by investigating what might occur in the case of an actual North Atlantic Treaty Organization (NATO)–Warsaw Pact war. The starting point for such an exercise is the perspective of the U.S. Atlantic Command and how it interfaces with the Soviet armed forces. (The Atlantic Command is the theater that starts at the North Pole, goes down to the South Pole, and extends east and west from the Pacific coast of South America to the east coast of Europe and Africa, covering 144 million square miles.)

The commander in chief of the Atlantic Command (CINCLANT) is given a rather comprehensive set of guidance. From that guidance he derives his strategy and all subsets of that strategy.

This guidance boils down to a set of chores, a word no one would recognize in the academic world. *Chores* has no relationship to the correct terminology that we employ in talking about strategy. CINCLANT has four basic chores:

1. To maintain a secure strategic sea-based deterrent. That is a euphemism for nuclear-powered ballistic missile submarines (SSBNs) on patrol.

2. If deterrence fails and NATO becomes involved in conflict with the Warsaw Pact, to create, sustain, and protect a sea bridge across the Atlantic over which will flow the reinforcement and resupply material that U.S. forces and those of allies in Western Europe depend upon, not only to survive but also to fight for any length of time.

3. To sustain and protect the economic arc around Africa over which flow the energy supplies and the essential resources that the industrial machinery and the war-fighting machinery in both Western Europe and North America depend upon.

4. To support the adjacent unified commands. In the case of the Atlantic Commander, that means the U.S. European Command, the U.S. Southern Command, and the U.S. Pacific Command.

As for Soviet strategic planning, let us say that a large country colored salmon on a map—and located considerably to the east of Germany and bordering on Finland, Turkey, Afghanistan, and China—is named country X—not the Soviet Union, just country X. And its government is not necessarily a communist form of government. We might assume that country X has a Latin American junta in charge. Given its geostrategic position, what does country X need to do in order to defend its interests and to use its military power in support of its political objectives?

Country X needs to use its navy to support its own secure sea-based strategic systems, to anchor the flanks of the army and support the land war in Europe, to defend the approaches to its landmass (its homeland), and to deny to its adversary the ability to support its military operations in Europe. Thus we have country X's set of chores. It does not matter whether it is the Soviet Union that has this complex strategic planning to accomplish. Whoever is in charge of Country X must have that family of strategic chores.

Sea-Based Deterrence

Let us discuss the simplest of all dynamics—those involving the sea-based strategic systems—before taking up some of the more complex dynamics, and let us begin some years ago. Specifically, why did the United States develop the Trident submarine? The reason was that the United States needed to create a hedge against an antisubmarine warfare (ASW) breakthrough on the part of the Soviet Union—the nature of which the United States could only dimly perceive but could predict with some certainty would occur in the next decade or two. In the process of creating this hedge, it would develop a missile with double the range of the Polaris-Poseidon missile. And by doubling the range it would make the laws of probability work in its favor. It reached this conclusion by looking at the sea space between the east coast of the United States and West Africa—that is, the sea space in which this longer-range missile-firing submarine could operate. The United States would increase the sea space in which its missile submarines could operate by a factor of five, therefore making the laws of probability work in its favor.

Shortly after, the Soviets—by whatever thought process they might have used (admitting that they think differently from the way the United States does—woke up in the morning and said: "By George, our Yankee submarines are right in the middle of the ASW battleground. That doesn't seem like too good an idea. So let's get those submarines out of the ASW battleground and move them away from the coast of the United States." The Soviets then developed the Delta/SS-N-18 system, which permitted their submarines to back away from their targets.

What is interesting is what happened to those submarines: instead of ending up with additional sea space, they found themselves jammed up at the top of the Norwegian Sea and in the Barents Sea—like worms in the bottom of a bucket. This created a vulnerability for the Soviets, and the United States started thinking about that vulnerability. It started licking its chops over the possibility of going in to that small amount of sea space and digging Soviet SSBNs out of this bucket.

Consequently the United States decided that—if it could force the Soviets to become sufficiently concerned about the survival of their SSBNs—the Soviets would invest a considerable amount of their attack assets, attack submarines, and conventional fighting assets in the task of protecting that force. If the Soviets did that, fewer Soviet submarines and surface ships would be available to accomplish the chore of interdicting our vital sea bridge. That leads us to another part of the dynamic.

The Atlantic Sea Bridge

Let us explore the interactive strategy underlying the second chore: creating, sustaining, and defending the Atlantic sea bridge. Recall the sea bridge that sustained U.S. forces and its allies in Western Europe during World War II. That convoy route followed a path close to the coast of the United States, up past Nova Scotia, up past Greenland, close to Iceland, and down into the United Kingdom or Western European ports. The United States chose this route because it was the shortest (it followed the great circle route) and because it kept the convoys under the protection of land-based air.

Land-based air was crucial in World War II. It was the most effective Nazi submarine killer because the submarines in the war were essentially surface ships that could submerge. And although the United States lost 2,603 merchant ships in the course of the battle of the Atlantic, it did a fairly credible job of disposing of the Nazi German submarine threat; it sank 784 German submarines.[1]

Nevertheless, the sea bridge had one vulnerability: land-based air—operating from either Narsarssauk (Greenland) or Gander (Newfoundland)—could not reach an area in mid-Atlantic that became known as the black hole. German submarines concentrated their activity in the black hole and therefore had to resort to wolf-pack tactics, designed to help the German submarines avoid mutual interference.

Today the United States still has to get merchant ships across the Atlantic, but the route laid down in World War has been changed for good tactical reasons. The United States plans to get merchant ships across the Atlantic in a way that will make the laws of probability work in its favor. It has bent that sea bridge as far south as possible. Now these ships, most of which originate in the Gulf of Mexico, cross the Atlantic along the Tropic of Cancer and then turn north in the vicinity of the Madeira Islands and head up toward the southwest approaches to the English Channel. The United States moved the route for one reason: it wants Soviet submarines based in the Kola Peninsula to travel as far as possible to reach the merchant ships in the sea bridge so that they will have a minimal number of days on station. Moreover, a submarine is most prone to detection when it is in transit.

In addition, the United States has taken the sea bridge out of the range of Soviet land-based air or has forced the Soviets to make a decision to base their land-based air forward in North Africa. There is nothing that the United States hopes more to happen in the event of conflict than for the Soviets to forward base their land-based air. Soviet land-based air cannot be reached where it is today. If the United States could lure the Soviets into such a forward basing, it would be a much easier task to attack, bomb, and dispose of the Soviet land-based air threat. This is another piece of the dynamic of interactive strategy.

The Norwegian Sea Campaign

Let us turn to the Maritime Strategy. If the United States is to carry out this concept, then it will have to deploy early, fight as far forward as possible (and certainly not in its own backyard in the Straits of Florida), and place the enemy's forces at risk. On that basis, the Norwegian Sea becomes crucial. The Soviets are at the edge of that maritime stage, and the United States is at its center. The Soviets will have to fight their way in; the United States is there already. If the Soviets are going to interdict the sea bridge, the Soviets will have to use the Norwegian Sea. Hence one can deduce, without much fear of contradiction, that in the event of another world war in the Atlantic, the first maritime campaign will be fought over control of the Norwegian Sea. That is, if the Soviets initiate a war, the battle for the Norwegian Sea will be its first campaign.

The United States will not have to initiate this battle if the Soviets do not choose to challenge for control of the Norwegian Sea to gain access to the North Atlantic. If they behave as Admiral Sergei Gorshkov would have us believe and therefore express disinterest in interdicting the sea bridge (if one believes that, one can believe anything), then the United States will not have to fight for control of the Norwegian Sea because it already will have won the battle of the Atlantic. If the Soviets do challenge, however, the United States will have to engage, and the Norwegian Sea will be the site of the first maritime campaign of the war. Thus, the Norwegian Sea will be the site of the first campaign because by denying the Soviet Navy access into the North

Atlantic, the United States is in effect defending, in the most secure way possible, the security of the sea bridge. This is another piece of the interactive strategy.

The Soviets, on the other hand, must decide what vulnerabilities they can exploit in keeping the United States from seizing control of the Norwegian Sea. One of the vulnerabilities that must loom large in their minds has to be the fact that the United States can conduct an ASW campaign only if it can fly its maritime patrol air in secure airspace. The United States can do the submarine component of the ASW campaign, but it cannot use its maritime patrol air (the P-3s) unless it controls the airspace. And it can control the airspace if it can fly out of the bases in the Norwegian littoral. The P-3s could then fly out of Iceland and out of the Norwegian littoral, as well as out of the bases in the Azores and Bermuda.

The Soviets have to perceive that one of NATO's vulnerabilities is the Norwegian littoral and Iceland. That being the case, they must place— whether they are Soviets or Latin Americans occupying country X—the neutralization of the Norwegian littoral and Iceland high on their priority list. If the Soviets can proceed one step further and take possession of the bases in the Norwegian littoral and take possession of a base in Iceland from which to project power, they can wreak havoc with the sea bridge with their land-based air. And that land-based air would be a bit more difficult to cope with than land-based air in North Africa—but that is a judgment call. Once again, this is an element of the interactive strategy.

If one believes that the Soviets have a rigidity in the strategic planning process and cannot react to developments, then the dynamic is not going to occur. But can one really choose to believe that the Soviets will be unable to identify an opportunity and exploit it?

The South Atlantic Scenario

Author Tom Clancy in his *Red Storm Rising* suggests other possible strategic dynamics in a war at sea between the Soviet Union and the United States. One of Clancy's compelling scenarios concerns the South Atlantic.[2] According to this dynamic, the Soviets may realize that putting their ballistic missile submarines in the role of worms in the bottom of a small bucket may not be to their advantage and that if they moved those submarines, they could still be within range of their targets in the United States. Moving the SSBNs and attack submarines could accomplish two goals for the Soviets. First, it could reduce the vulnerability of their SSBNs and take some of the demands off their attack submarines in the protection mode and, in addition, create a second threat-axis for the United States and NATO. Second, it could threaten the economic arc around Africa, a route the Soviets do not have the ability to threaten today and a route that the United States lacks the ability to protect today.

If the Soviets were to move—Tom Clancy style—their SSBNs and their attack submarines into the narrows between Recife (Brazil) and Dakar (Senegal), they would create an enormous problem for the United States: first in the form of an unexpected development, second in the form of a second threat-axis, and third in the form of a much expanded sea space in which they could operate, making the strategic ASW mission against ballistic missile submarines much more difficult. Were the Soviets to do this, all the rationale that prompted the United States to move the sea bridge south to get it away from Soviet land-based air and to make it difficult for the Soviet submarines to reach the sea bridge would be gone. The United States would have to do something else.

Are the Soviets agile enough to do that? I think so. It is difficult to subscribe to the notion that the Soviets are so rigid in their strategic thinking that they could not exploit the type of opportunity Tom Clancy suggests. Supporting the possibility that they may intend to move into the South Atlantic is the fact that they spent four years surveying these waters with hydrographic and oceanographic ships in exactly the same way in which they surveyed the waters in the rest of the Atlantic where their submarines actually operated. One can spend sleepless nights thinking about this.[3]

A War in the Middle East

Another part of the dynamic is that—as crucial as the Norwegian Sea is to the United States in denying access for the Soviet northern fleet into the Atlantic—the United States may not be able to do anything about the Norwegian Sea because the war may start someplace else. If it should start in the Middle East—for example, the oil-bearing regions of the Middle East—and in the course of the rising international tension that led to war the United States had placed the majority of its carrier battle groups at that scene, they obviously would not be available to fight an early campaign for control of the Norwegian Sea. Would the United States interrupt the formation of the sea bridge until it could get its carriers in the right position? Not likely. The war might be short, just as the short-war theorists postulate. The United States must get the reinforcement and resupply moving because that is the only way to get lots of things onto the continent in the time required.

Thus, at the outset of a world war, the United States might have all or most of its carriers in the eastern Mediterranean engaged in fighting a very short, but fierce, maritime campaign. After this campaign had concluded, the United States could move the carriers out into the Atlantic and embark upon that which has become identified as the essence of the Maritime Strategy, the fight for control of the Norwegian Sea.

The Cuban Contingency

Another conceivable dynamic would have U.S. carriers involved in other areas of the world while hostile submarines deploy out of Cuba into the Gulf of Mexico to plant mines. Certainly that scenario is something that the United States has agonized over in the past. And this dynamic becomes more difficult to deal with because the United States takes great pains not to make any Cuban contingency plans. The U.S. government does not update any of the Cuban contingency plans for fear that it will become known that it is doing this. Some U.S. congressmen and senators have large Cuban contingents in their districts. Since it might look as though the United States was going in to bomb those congressmen's or senators' constituents' relatives, the United States tries to avoid at all costs even thinking about updating Cuban contingency plans.

But the United States recognizes an imperative. If a U.S- Soviet—or a Warsaw Pact—NATO—war begins, the United States will have to make Cuba commit one way or another fairly early. This is because the United States has no forces programmed for or committed to the Cuban or the Caribbean threat. To the extent that the United States is constrained to hedge against Cuban exploitation of a NATO–Warsaw Pact war, the United States must hold forces back. The United States would probably hold back with late deployers: ships like the *Lexington,* replacement air groups, late-deploying air force squadrons, and perhaps a late-deploying carrier battle group if one was just coming out of overhaul and was training up. But forces that are withheld cannot be applied where they are committed—that is, in the North Atlantic or toward the coast of Europe. The longer the Cubans fail to commit, the longer the United States must keep forces tied down to hedge. The pressures would get enormous after about thirty days to do something: to force the Cubans to commit one way or another—for example, throw the Soviets out and firmly come down on the U.S. side rather than just choosing neutrality—or to go in and neutralize their power projection capabilities. Certainly the United States would not invade Cuba.

When one recognizes that half of all the reinforcement and resupply material comes out of the Gulf of Mexico and has to go through the 90-mile-wide Straits of Florida and the 105-mile-wide Yucatan Channel, and that virtually all of the petroleum, oils, and lubricants that heads to Europe comes out of the Gulf of Mexico, that becomes quite a vulnerability, one so painful that one does not like to think about it.

The Maritime Strategy

Some people believe that United States strategy has evolved into a focus on the Kola Peninsula. That is not true. The basic concept of the Maritime Strategy, which is a restatement in modern terms of solid strategic concepts, is that the United States deploys early wherever it must deploy, it takes the fight to the enemy, it does not fight the enemy in its own backyard, and it does not count on having to fight its way through the Straits of Florida or the Yucatan Channel. Rather, the United States takes the fight forward, makes the enemy feel that its own forces are at risk, and fights in the enemy's backyard. It is difficult to fault that concept.

The Maritime Strategy, despite all the debate, is a solid concept. It helps the United States get out the mode of viewing techniques as strategy. In the past, the U.S. Navy would say to those who did not understand it very well: "Well, we know you don't understand what we're all about, but essentially all we do is project power ashore—Korea, Vietnam-style, with aircraft carriers—and we use all the other assets to circle the wagons around convoys, and we route those convoys with a system known as naval control of shipping, and that's all you need to know about a navy. Give us a lot of it."

But the navy was guilty of taking techniques and marketing them as strategy. Thus the great benefit of the strategy was coherence. It has been identified with the name of navy secretary John F. Lehman, Jr, but it is actually more the product of Commodore William T. Pendley than any other person; it was then developed and marketed by Vice-Admiral Henry C. Mustin. The strategy is not only a solid one, also it is quite consistent with its NATO maritime counterpart, the Tri-MNC Maritime Concept of Operations.[4] In fact, it is totally consistent with its NATO counterpart.

Nuclear War at Sea

Another interactive strategy concerns the possibility that the war at sea may go nuclear. In that case, some analysts fear the United States would lose. Therefore a vital question is, What will keep the war from going nuclear? If the Soviets can win simply by going nuclear at sea, why would they not do it? Because the United States believes almost at the 100-percent confidence level that the Soviets believe at the 100-percent confidence level that if the Soviets were to strike the U.S. fleet at sea with nuclear weapons, the United States would retaliate against the base in the Kola Peninsula from which that attack was launched.

Then the question is, Would not the Soviets view that as an intercontinental strike? The answer is probably yes: they would believe it was an intercontinental strike, particularly if it was conducted with Poseidon missile rather than a Tomahawk land attack missile-nuclear. And if the Soviets believe it is an intercontinental strike, would they not retaliate against the continental United States? Again, the answer is yes, they would. So why would the Soviets, no matter how rigid their thinking, want to go through the intervening step of attacking the U.S. fleet at sea with nuclear weapons knowing that they would get attacked in the Kola Peninsula with nuclear weapons and knowing that their reaction to that would be a strike against the United States? In that case, would the Soviets not strike the United States first? Of course not. For why would the Soviets alert the U.S. systems to the fact that they were going to be striking the United States?

Therefore one hears more and more words to the effect that the Soviets would probably not resort to first use at sea. Now the question that troubles me is if General Bernard Rogers or General John Galvin, his successor as NATO's Supreme Allied Commander Europe (SACEUR), really act as they speak and would indeed resort to first use of tactical nuclear weapons ashore on the central front, would the Soviets not then resort to the use of nuclear weapons at sea? I do not know. I do not think anybody knows. Would the same deterrent reasoning apply? That is harder to judge. But that is another piece of the dynamics.

Soviet Large-Deck Aircraft Carriers

One question that frequently arises is, What will the future Soviet aircraft carriers do to the dynamic? The Soviets are building aircraft carriers roughly the size, shape, and theoretical capability of the *Kitty Hawk*. They are building large-deck aircraft carriers, and with those carriers they will achieve the ability to take tactical aircraft to sea. The lack of this capability almost caused the British to lose in the Falkland Islands. If the British had had one large-deck aircraft carrier instead of the little imitation carriers they used there, they would have been in and out in a week.

Perhaps the Falkland conflict is the best example to use in addressing this issue. That is the type of action that the Soviets will be able to take in various areas of the world when they develop enough critical mass with their sea-based tactical air capability. Until they get five to seven aircraft carriers, however, they will never be able to employ their sea-based tactical air in exactly the way the United States does.

Soviet Submarines and SLOC Interdiction

Another frequently posed question focuses on the Soviet sea-lines of communication (SLOC) interdiction mission. If SLOC interdiction is one of the vital missions of the Soviet Navy, why do the Soviets not appear to be building a submarine force aimed toward that mission? Since they have been building very expensive submarines up to now, one might indeed wonder whether instead they should be building cheaper submarines in larger numbers. Yet if

I were in their position, I would not suggest such a direction. If I were to trade places with Fleet Admiral Vladimir Chernavin, that is certainly not a route that I would follow.

That is why I have consistently taken the position, for example, that the United States should not pour money down a rat hole by buying diesel submarines, which are mines with only a little more mobility than actual mines here. A nuclear submarine gives the ability to travel great distances to station and stay there for a reasonable length of time. The fact that the Soviets are building submarines that are quieter than they have ever built before and therefore more expensive reflects their intelligence efforts to find out how the United States has been able to track them so well. Obviously they were astounded to find out that their submarines are noisy and therefore capable of being tracked. Cheapness also equals noisiness; noisiness equals vulnerability; and vulnerability is always to the advantage of one's adversary.

So to the extent that the Soviets might want to achieve numbers by building cheaper submarines, I doubt that they would go below a certain threshold of capability to achieve those numbers. And I am not at all sure that they have the same concept of cheap versus expensive platform that the United States has. They probably are careful to ration man-days devoted to building something. I doubt if they are worried about rubles or how much their defense budget might be. But the Soviets probably do have a good mix of lesser capability and higher capability submarines. They could really devastate merchant shipping if they chose to do so with some of their missile-carrying submarines. The Charlie-class submarine is not optimized to apply against the carrier task force. You can kill them just by trolling for them and making them go fast, and then you kill them. But the Charlie would be a very effective antimerchant ship platform, and it would be a very effective platform to use against an amphibious objective area where the United States had concentrated its amphibious ships. I just could not agree that the Soviets would ever start building cheaper submarines.

Attack the Sea Bridge at the European Ports

I am frequently queried on the vulnerability of the sea bridge and whether the Soviet Navy is an optimum force for sea bridge interdiction. There are some who believe that their forces are optimized for protecting their assets. The fact that they have not built a follow-on to the Charlie, a good submarine for attacking merchant ships, may indicate that they have something else in mind—particularly attacking the terminus of SLOCs. The point is often made that if you can eliminate the ability to off-load the merchant ships, then the fact that they can go back and forth across the Atlantic does not make that much difference. This is another important piece of the dynamic.

If you were to look at the sea bridge as a whole and identify the most vulnerable points along it, those points are the pedestals at each end. The second most vulnerable point is that part of the route between the Madeira Islands and the southwest approaches to the English Channel. I have often heard it discussed in fairly high places that it will do little good to have 100 percent confidence that all of the merchant ships can cross the Atlantic only to find out that the Benelux ports they are headed for are not mine free and not free from air attack. That is a serious problem that has to be dealt with. I do not know what U.S. reaction to that will be other than to ensure that it retains the capability to keep at least one of those Benelux ports open or to ensure that the Soviets cannot get in to mine them. The Soviets have between 250,000 and 400,000 mines; they are going to do something with them.

Conclusion

If I have jumped around a lot, it is because the subject of interactive dynamics involves jumping about. The most important point, however, is that regardless of ideology—and regardless of the type of planning process that a nation goes through—there are certain things that country X has to do whatever type of government it might have. And I would be hard pressed to be persuaded by anyone that the Soviet maritime missions are other than those I have described. No matter how the Soviets arrived at them, those must be their maritime objectives. It is of valid military interest to get there, and therefore they will get there. I cannot think of a more valid way of assessing what might happen.

Notes

1. David Mason, *U-Boat: The Secret Menace* (London: Pan Books, 1972).
2. Tom Clancy, *Red Star Rising* (New York: Putnam's, 1986).
3. The Soviet surveying of the bottom of the South Atlantic took place from 1978 to 1982 and was designed to enable Soviet submarines to navigate using contour-type navigation.
4. Tri-MNC refers to the major NATO commanders (SACEUR, SACLANT, and CINCHAN).

Part III
Historical Proclivities

A reciprocal tendency has long operated in Russian and Soviet naval thinking—a recurring proclivity toward major oceanic ambitions, with such dreams brought back to a more modest reality by troublesome facts of geography, technical and economic weaknesses, and real or perceived continental threats.

In chapter 5, Jürgen Rohwer underlines the competition over the centuries within the Russian and Soviet navies between an assertive *classical* or *old school* with oceanic pretensions and a *young school* favoring light naval forces integrated into a combined-arms strategy for continental defense. Rohwer describes the tension between such polar tendencies after World War II producing a *new young school* (or *Soviet school* in the language of Robert Herrick) that combined elements of both of the older schools. This Soviet school has been further elaborated as naval policy became dominated by the global strategic-nuclear issue and more recently as Mikhail Gorbachev has initiated sweeping reforms. This process of elaboration continues.

Jacob Kipp in chapter 6 demonstrates the Russian and Soviet combined-arms approacch to warfare, in which the navy is a valued but restricted *second arm* to the army. As Robert Herrick points out in chapter 7, however, the soviet Navy in the post-war years vigorously pushed against the constraints of being only a "faithful handmaiden" to the army. In its arguments for a *limited command-of-the-sea* strategy, the navy pressed for wider missions and the force capabilities to carry them out.

These chapters raise the issue of whether it is likely that the tension between these historic reciprocal tendencies would become significantly altered in an age of new reciprocal tendencies characterized by increasingly capable Soviet naval forces on one hand and the requirements of *perestroika* and "new thinking" on the other.

5

Alternating Russian and Soviet Naval Strategies

Jürgen Rohwer

The historical literature concerning the development of the Russian and Soviet navies contains a great number of errors resulting from a superficial analysis of the performance of these navies during the several wars of the twentieth century. The defeats and reversals the Russian Navy experienced in the Russo-Japanese War and World War I and the Soviet Navy in World War II led some authors, especially in the English-speaking world, to overlook the achievements of Russian sailors and to neglect the conditions under which the Russians had to operate. These conditions were different from those most other navies were facing, and they must be considered when evaluating the performance of the Russian and Soviet navies.[1]

First are geographic conditions. The main harbors and shipbuilding centers are located at the innermost shores of landlocked seas and are separated from the oceans by narrows or barriers dominated by probably hostile nations. The Russians therefore had to assign their resources to three and later four different fleets. Even in peacetime, much time was needed to transfer ships over great distances from the main industrial and shipbuilding areas in the Baltic and Black seas to the Far East or the Arctic, where, up to World War II, only limited maintenance and repair facilities existed. Notwithstanding the fact that since World War II the Arctic (or Northern) and Pacific fleets have replaced the Baltic and Black Sea fleets as those with the most important roles, most surface vessels are still built in the yards at Leningrad in the Baltic and Nikolaev in the Black Sea. The bulk of the submarines come from the building yards at Severodvinsk in the Arctic or Komsomolsk in the Pacific. In wartime, only limited possibilities exist for exchanges of vessels between fleets, using rail transport for disassembled small vessels or inland waterways for vessels up to 3,000 or 5,000 tons. In addition, most of the contiguous seas are ice bound to a great extent during the winter, preventing training cruises of ships during this time.

Second, an important constraint influencing the development of the Russian and Soviet navies and their strategic thinking has been the dominance of the army in the organization of the armed forces. The greatest danger to the defense of the homeland up to the end of World War II was seen as coming across the long, open continental borders and since then from the airspace around the huge continental landmass. To improve the security of the borders, the acquisition of glacis areas was possible only by using ground forces to gain control of neighboring countries. The navy had to play a secondary role in support of the coastal flanks of the army. The experiences of World Wars I and II apparently underlined this role of the navy and smokescreened the fact that there were several periods in Russian and Soviet history when the navy started to play a more independent and prominent role as an instrument of a global state policy and grand strategy.

Because these global ideas and intentions were checked before they could unfold by the adverse developments of the wars of 1904–1905, 1914–1918, and 1941–1945, a distorted picture of Russian naval history developed in the West, leading many authors to assert that only in our time, under the efficient leadership of Admiral of the Fleet of the Soviet Union Sergei G. Gorshkov, have the Russians tried to build a high seas fleet as an instrument of the power policy of the state.

It is almost forgotten that the Imperial Russian Navy for most of the nineteenth century was the third naval power behind Great Britain and France and that the Russian Navy during this period not only produced some important explorers, inventors, engineers, and naval strategists but used its ships for power projection, as did all the other great navies of this high time of imperialism. Few historians tell us anything about the big naval shipbuilding programs of Stalin before and after World War II, which make sense only in a concept of global strategy beyond the continental borders of the Soviet Union.

In contrast to most other major navies, Russian and Soviet naval history displays a disproportionately high number of clear conceptual breaks, that mark basic changes in the strategic concepts governing the navy. As was the case in France under the Third Republic before 1914, the history of the Russian and Soviet naval policy shows periods with a dominating *classical school* standing in contrast to other times when a *young school* had the upper hand. The classical school was bent on winning control of the seas, whether regionally or globally, by building a seagoing battle fleet superior to the probable opponent. The best-known prophet of this school of thought was the American captain, Alfred Thayer Mahan, but there were many like-minded advocates in other navies.[2]

The *jeune école* ("young school"), on the other hand, followed the ideas of the French admiral Théophile Aube, who wanted to undermine the superior opponent's control of the seas through mercantile warfare and to thwart its control by means of blockades or attacks on land targets through the employment of modern technology aboard inexpensive, small fighting craft.

This was a conscious renunciation of the expensive battle fleet for naval supremacy.[3]

It is of interest that the ideas of the French *jeune école,* which developed to counter the overwhelming superiority of the British Royal Navy and the decline of the once-strong French fleet after the defeat of France in the Franco-Prussian War of 1870–1871, were already practiced in Russia after the humiliating defeat of Russia in the Crimean War of 1853–1856.[4] During the reorganization and reform period in the 1860s, interest in mercantile warfare was foremost. It found its greatest advocate in Admiral Grigorii I. Butakov, the driving force behind the development of steamships in the Russian Navy, who was to make a name for himself with his worldwide travels to train officers and sailors and his *New Foundations for Steamship Tactics* (1863).[5]

After the American Civil War (1861–1865) the Union Navy's experiences in combat with its monitors along the coast and in the river mouths exerted a similar formative influence. The Russians, after beginning the construction of a few armored frigates in the early 1860s as most other navies were then doing, quickly shifted their energies to the construction of shallow-draft monitors for coastal defense, which they hoped would be able to block the entrances of the Gulf of Finland and hence the capital of St. Petersburg against even superior battle fleets. One of the driving forces of this period was Vice-Admiral Aleksandr A. Popov, known not only as a drillmaster but also as an inventor. He designed the curious Popovka circular floating batteries for harbor defense in the Black Sea. He also designed the turret battleship *Pëtr Velikii,* which was laid down a little earlier than the similar British *Devastation,* whose revolutionary design was said to have laid the basic pattern for all future battleships. But Popov's most forward-looking construction was the world's first armored cruiser, *General Admiral,* a vessel well suited for commerce raiding.[6]

At the same time in the late 1860s and early 1870s, experiments were started with the new technologies introduced during the American Civil War: the torpedo, the submarine, and the mine. During the Russo-Turkish War of 1877–1878, the Russians for the first time successfully used spar, towed, and self-propelled torpedoes against Turkish ships.[7] This led to the construction of more than a hundred small torpedo boats and the first torpedo-steamship, *Vzryv,* of 160 tons with two torpedo tubes. Other experiments were carried out with the first hand-powered and then steam-driven submersibles invented by I.F. Aleksandrovskii and S.K. Dzhevetskii. In 1874, the first minelayer, *Galvaner,* was built.[8]

During the reign of the new czar, Alexander III (1881–1893), diverse paths were simultaneously followed in naval construction, reflecting the uncertainties that the many new inventions and technologies had brought to strategic and tactical thinking in most navies.[9] No fewer than eight different and unique designs of seagoing and coast defense battleships appeared in the Baltic and the Black Sea. Emphasis was also laid on the construction of different types of commerce raiders in the form of armored or protected cruisers. Their employment was projected in a book entitled *Russia's Hope,* which appeared in the mid-1880s. According to this work, it would be possible to cripple England's maritime commerce with some eighteen cruisers of the 5,000-ton *Admiral Kornilov* type, the prototype of which was then under construction in France for delivery to Russia.[10] At the same time, the construction of great numbers of torpedo boats continued, incorporating British, French, and German designs.

When in the 1880s colonial imperialism began to envelop all of the European great powers, and even many lesser states, most sea powers changed their naval strategy to follow the lines set by the Royal Navy. Experiences during maneuvers or operations to project Great Britain's power around the world demonstrated that only squadrons of steam-driven battleships of equal characteristics could use their capabilities to the fullest advantage. This was already envisaged during the 1870s by the now almost forgotten professor at the Austrian Naval Academy at Pola, Ferdinand Attlmayr.[11] Because such homogeneous squadrons of battleships were to be built only within programs running over many years, most navies started in the 1890s to regulate their battleship construction with long-term fleet programs, formulated as legal acts or laws decided upon by parliaments, following the example of the British Naval Defense Act of 1889.[12]

This period of navalism from 1890 to 1914 found its theoretical foundation in the writings of such authors of the classical school as Alfred Thayer Mahan (1890–1892),[13] the British Philip Howard Colomb (1891),[14] as well as in Alfred von Tirpitz's "Denkschrift" of 1891 to Emperor Wilhelm II.[15] In Russia this thinking found interpreters in no less a person than Admiral Stepan O. Makarov in his book *Considerations on Problems of Naval Tactics* (1895–1896)[16] and the teachings of Captain Nikolai Klado at the Naval Academy at Kronstadt.[17]

After Great Britain had started to build homogeneous battleship squadrons of eight ships each in 1889 and 1893, Germany and France attempted to regulate their battle fleet construction with long-term naval acts promulgated in 1898 and 1900. The Russians had begun three-ship battleship divisions for the Baltic Fleet already in 1892 and 1895, while they started a new five-year program in 1898, projecting eight new battleships and six heavy and ten light cruisers to be built partly in yards in France, the United States, and Germany. This was followed in 1903 by a new five-year program for the Baltic Fleet alone with a similar number of ships.

The new battleships and cruisers of the Baltic Fleet sailed immediately upon their completion to the Mediterranean or the Far East, an indication of the far-ranging naval goals the new czar Nicholas II (1893–1917), nourished, as did his cousin, Wilhelm II, in Germany.[18] Their competition in sending naval and ground forces to the Far East during the Boxer Rebellion in China in 1900 marked the zenith of worldwide European colonial imperialism, in which Russia participated, as did all the great powers of the time.[19]

This first great upsurge of a worldwide Russian naval policy came to an end in the Russo-Japanese War of 1904–1905 with the fall of Port Arthur and the Battle of Tsushima.[20] The catastrophic outcome of the war against Japan and the mutinies of 1905–1906, which shook the navy to its core, compelled a fresh start.[21] This start was also to a great extent influenced by changes in the European power balance and the alliances of the time and by the shift of the center of gravity of Russian policy from the Far East and Southern Asia to Europe and the Balkans, where "panslavists" hoped to liberate their "brothers" from Austrian and Ottoman rule. The settlement of conflicts with Great Britain along the southern border of Russia allowed the British-French Entente Cordiale of 1904 to develop into an alliance including Russia from 1907 onward. Although during the whole nineteenth century the Russian Navy looked at the Royal Navy as its most probable enemy, the view now became more and more directed against the German Navy in the Baltic and against the Turkish and Austrian navies in the Black Sea or the Mediterranean.

The reconstruction of the Russian fleet was accompanied by serious conflicts over the proper strategy and building policy in the new surroundings. As is often the case when a fleet is in a state of material weakness, ideas of the *jeune école* again came to prevail for some time with the Naval Main Staff, and the thoughts of Captain Klado, who had become known through his many writings as the Russian Mahan, lost currency.

Under the circumstances, the primary objective of the weakened Baltic Fleet, consisting mostly of over-age ships, could only be defensively to protect the seaward flanks of the army and to deny enemy entry into the Gulf of Finland and the power center around St. Petersburg by means of mine fields covered by long-range coastal batteries and supported by the remaining ships of the fleet. In the Black Sea, after the restoration of discipline, the material superiority against the outdated Turkish fleet seemed to allow a more offensive thinking, supporting an army drive in the direction of the Bosporus.[22]

But before long a new planning body, the Naval General Staff (Genmor), founded by young officers with the support of the czar in 1906, started to formulate plans for big shipbuilding programs, including modern battleships, along more offensive lines. Although the first naval minister, A.A. Birilev, was overthrown, and although the struggle between the Main Naval Staff (Glavmorshtab) and the Genmor remained undecided, the new minister, Ivan M. Dikov, in 1908 was able to overcome the resistance of the Duma to a reduced Genmor building plan, and Professor Klado reappeared.

In 1909, the first four dreadnought battleships for the Baltic Fleet were laid down together with some destroyers and submarines for the Baltic and Black Sea. When the Turkish Navy acquired two old battleships from Germany and ordered two modern dreadnoughts in Great Britain, the Russians in 1911 began to construct three dreadnoughts for the Black Sea Fleet. Yet it was not until 1912 that an especially skillful naval minister, Vice-Admiral Ivan K. Grigorovich, who had taken office only the year before, succeeded in getting a new long-term naval act through the duma. This act called for the construction by 1930 of three squadrons for the Baltic Fleet, each consisting of eight battleships, four battle cruisers, eight light cruisers, thirty-six destroyers, and twelve submarines. The first squadron was to be ready in 1916. Construction began in 1912–1913 on four battle cruisers of the *Borodino* class (32,500 tons), four cruisers of the *Svetlana* class (6,800 tons), and thirty-six destroyers of the *Grom* class (1,280 tons), as well as twelve submarines of the *Bars* class (650 tons). Because of bottlenecks in industrial capacity, some of the machinery had to be ordered from Germany, as were two more light cruisers for the Pacific.[23]

After efforts to buy some Latin American dreadnoughts failed, one more dreadnought, four cruisers, eight destroyers, and some submarines were ordered for the Black Sea, and plans envisaged additional 32,000-ton battleships with nine 406-mm guns.[24] The new ships put under construction were clearly superior to the possible opponents in firepower and speed but at the cost of endurance. There were also some new ideas and inventions, like the first special minelaying submarine *Krab* and the first built-for-the-purpose minesweepers. But of all the ships in the new construction plans, only the large destroyer *Novik*, built from German plans, had been completed when World War I broke out. Several of the ships came into commission in 1914–1915 and 1916–1917, but plans for the future had to be put back in the drawer.[25]

The Baltic Fleet was greatly inferior to the German High Seas Fleet. Even when the main German force was concentrated in the North Sea, the Russian naval staffs had to count on the possibility of a rapid German redeployment into the Baltic.[26] The first task of the Baltic Fleet was to cover and block the entrances to the gulfs of Bothnia and Finland, with the capital St. Petersburg (renamed Petrograd), and to the Gulf of Riga protected by extensive mine fields covered by heavy coastal batteries.[27] But when it became clear that the Germans had concentrated, aside from old vessels, only a few modern ships in the Baltic, the Russians became more enterprising. During the dark nights of the winters of 1914–1915 and 1915–1916, cruisers and destroyers were sent into the southern part of the Baltic to lay many offensive mine barriers, which caused some losses of German armored cruisers, light cruisers, minesweepers, and merchant vessels. Submarines, especially some British craft that had entered the Baltic through the Danish straits, also achieved successes against German shipping.[28]

When the German Army started to attack to the northeast in the direction of Riga in the summer of 1915, the main task of the Baltic Fleet was to defend the Baltic Islands and the Strait of Irben to prevent the Germans from entering the Gulf of Riga, a task in which the Russians were mainly successful up to 1917. As the revolutionary movement rose, however, the fighting value of the fleet declined, and so there was only limited resistance when the Germans landed in the Baltic Islands in October 1917.

While the sailors of the Baltic Fleet played a decisive role in the great October Revolution in Petrograd, the Germans found almost no resistance when they occupied the Aland Islands in early 1918. But the Soviet naval command was able to evacuate the fleet in time by its legendary ice march from Helsinki to Kronstadt to prevent its capture by the Germans in support of the White Finns.[29]

In the Black Sea, the Russian Navy was superior to the Turkish Navy, and after the first surprise attack of the German-Turkish force, the Russian Black Sea Fleet exercised control of the greatest part of the Black Sea and laid many offensive mine fields off the Bosporus, but there was no coordination with Anglo-French attacks against the Dardanelles or with the landings at Gallipoli in 1915. Later, the fleet supported several amphibious operations behind the land front in Anatolia, using for the first time landing ships built for the purpose and passenger ships rebuilt into seaplane carriers.[30]

The losses during World War I and the following civil war reduced the fleets in the Baltic and the Black Sea to a few obsolete remnants. The achievement of independence by Finland and the Baltic states shrank Russian sea access to the innermost shores of the Gulf of Finland. Finally, the March 1921 uprising of the sailors of Kronstadt, once held in high esteem because of their part in the revolution and now bloodily suppressed, greatly reduced the willingness of Lenin and the Soviet leadership to do anything for the navy. In consequence of the subsequent purges, the navy had to start from a nascent state—not only from the material side but also with its personnel.[31]

By recruiting candidates from the Komsomol youth organization, the navy tried to close the gaps in its cadres. Probably the deficiencies in the higher ranks were one reason for the discrepancies one can observe between the real situation and the astonishing continuity of the strategic thinking concerning the long-term goals of the Russian Navy from the period 1911–1912 up to 1925–1927. While young officers aboard the few decrepit ships had to come to terms with insufficient material, financial, and personnel conditions, even revolutionary war commissar Leon Trotsky was opposed to a reinterpretation of the fundamentals of military and naval strategy, and instruction at the Naval War College and the Naval Academy continued along classical school lines.[32]

Not only was the czarist professor Klado, the "Russian Mahan," retained as a rear admiral in command of the Naval Academy until his death in 1919, but until the late 1920s, the two foremost representatives of the classical school, professors B. Gervais and to a lesser degree M. Petrov,[33] were allowed to continue their teaching unopposed at the central training institutions for candidates for higher leadership positions. However, the chief of the naval Forces, V.I. Zof, in an address at the Naval War College in 1925, reminded the audience of the few real possibilities to follow such theories, some of which even asked for aircraft carriers.[34] The idea of control of the seas maintained by battleship squadrons was quite alive not only in theory but also in practice. From 1921 through 1925, the repair of the three battleships remaining in the Baltic was carried on with particular vigor. Attempts were made to get the French government to return to the Black Sea Fleet the battleship *General Alekseev,* taken by the White Russians to Bizerte. Plans were even made for the completion of the *Izmail,* the last remaining battle cruiser. One of the ambitious construction plans of this period foresaw by 1930 the construction of eight battleships, sixteen cruisers, and over sixty destroyers. A conference of sea powers not represented at the 1921–1922 Washington Conference was held in Rome in February 1924 to discuss armaments limitations. The Soviet delegate, Berens, demanded a battleship tonnage of 491,000 tons for the Soviet Union, a little less than the 525,000 tons Great Britain and the United States each were allowed at Washington.[35]

With some of the younger officers coming into the higher positions from 1925–1926 onward, a change in strategic thinking started to gain prominence, with the vastly superior British fleet seen as the most probable enemy. Given the existing situation, the Red Fleet wanted to fulfill its mission of protecting the territory of the Soviet Union against the threat of "counterrevolutionary or interventionary" landings of which the officers, fighting in the civil war, had become so painfully conscious, it had to look to an active coastal defense carried out with simple naval weapons that could be produced without great industrial expense.[36]

Apparently now a new young school began to prevail not only in the fleet but also in the high command and the academies. Between 1926 and 1928, its supporters won the backing from high-ranking commanders of the Red Army, especially its chief of staff, M.N. Tukhachevskii.[37] They proposed to use scarce resources mainly to develop artillery, tanks, and the air force in their theory of mobile deep mass strikes into the territory of the enemy. Following the replacement of V.I. Zof by R.A. Muklevich as chief of the naval forces on August 23, 1926, the preponderance of views in the dispute between the two schools inside the navy tilted toward the young school, which preached the massive employment of mines, small submarines, torpedo boats, and aircraft. Its most important propagandist was Professor A.P. Aleksandrov, who silenced his colleagues Gervais and Petrov, among others, with his article, "A Critical Analysis of the Theory of Naval Supremacy," which appeared in *Morskoi sbornik* and closed with the exclamation: "Down with the idea of naval supremacy!"[38]

In 1926, the strategic ideas of the young school resulted in the first new construction program that went beyond the stage of paper plans. In keeping with the capabilities of the shipbuilding industry, which had been damaged badly during the revolution and civil war, it provided for the construction within the next six years of twelve submarines, eighteen coastal patrol ships (vessels similar to destroyers but much smaller), and thirty-six motor torpedo boats. Two years later, this program was integrated into the First Five-Year Plan, that of 1928–1932.[39] At first this plan provided for the completion, repair, or restoration of five cruisers, seventeen destroyers and fifteen submarines, as well as the modernization of the three remaining battleships. This was completed in early 1932.

Since there were not enough ships available in the Black Sea, a battleship and a cruiser were reassigned from the Baltic in 1929–1930. The construction program was increased during the term of the plan and continued during the Second Five-Year Plan, spanning the years 1933–1937. The new plan, approved on July 11, 1933, put the heaviest emphasis on submarine and motor torpedo boat construction. This program exceeded the possibilities of reality, with no fewer than 369 submarines (69 large, 200 medium, and 100 small) to be completed by the end of 1937.[40]

In April 1932, the naval forces of the Far East were assembled in Vladivostok, and in 1935 they became the Pacific Fleet. Since construction of shipyards in Vladivostok and Komsomolsk had just begun, the ships of the new fleet (particularly the submarines) had to be prefabricated at Leningrad or Nikolayev and transported, partly disassembled, by rail to the Far East for reassembly and completion.[41] Similarly, in August 1933, the Northern Flotilla was formed, and in 1937 became the Northern Fleet. Its destroyers, guard ships, and submarines were transferred by way of the new White Sea Canal.[42]

The concept of active coastal defense that found expression in the first two Five-Year Plans for naval rearmament did not retain its currency for long. In the discussion of the 1930s, one side proceeded on the premise that, given the existing and foreseeable circumstances, the outcome of a war would be decided on land. Therefore the navy must be assigned tasks that were rooted in the army's mission. The other side did not wish to exclude the possibility that the fleet "could itself fulfill the main objectives during some phases of the war in one theater or in another."[43]

The latter took the view that the Soviet fleet was already capable of carrying out operations beyond the limits of its own coastal waters and relied again on a revised theory of naval supremacy. Especially the commander of the Pacific Flotilla/Fleet, M.V. Viktorov, after 1934 put this idea forward to the Council of Labor and Defense, presided over by V.M. Molotov. In a session Stalin held with the fleet commanders at the end of 1936, Viktorov was opposed by the commander of the Black Sea Fleet, I.K. Kozhanov, who argued for a small-ship navy, as had done the commander of the naval forces,

V.M. Orlov, his deputy, I.M. Ludrii, and his predecessor and now chief of the Construction Department, R.A. Muklevich.[44]

During these years, Stalin was increasingly influenced by far-reaching ideas on the subject of sea power. Possibly the experiences of the Spanish Civil War played a role; for example, the sinking of Soviet merchant ships carrying arms to the Spanish Loyalists by Spanish Nationalist or Italian surface ships or submarines made suddenly clear that the Soviet Union, with its coast defense navy, was not in a position to supply the side it supported in the civil war. Meanwhile, Italy and Germany sent weapons and munitions to Spain by sea unimpeded by any hostile naval forces. Stalin drew the conclusion that if the Soviet Union wanted to play the part of a major power, it must have a navy that could give credibility to its demands.

In January 1937, Stalin started a thorough reorganization of the naval command, eliminating step by step the supporters of a small-ship navy. First, Ludrii was sent to the Naval Academy and half a year later was dismissed. He was replaced by L.M. Galler, the commander of the Baltic Fleet, who as a "big-ship man" had already commanded a battleship at the end of World War I as a captain in the Imperial Navy. His successor became A.K. Sivkov, aided by another "big-ship man," I.S. Isakov, also a graduate of the Imperial Naval Academy where Captain Klado was teaching.[45] Isakov soon replaced Sivkov for a few months before he took over as head of the Construction Department, replacing Muklevich, who was arrested in May. The most prominent members of the small-ship navy group were arrested: Commander in Chief Orlov in July, Kozhanov in October, and their teachers at the academy led by Aleksandrov. At the same time, the Red Army high command was purged, and one of the charges against Marshal Tukhachevskii was that he had prevented new surface ships from being added to the navy.[46]

Then Stalin's delusion about sabotage everywhere reached even the successors and the remaining fleet commanders. In January 1938, Viktorov's successor in the Pacific Fleet, G.I. Kireyev, Kozhanov's successor in the Black Sea Fleet, P.I. Smirnov, and Viktorov himself, who had first succeeded Orlov, were arrested, followed in March by I.N. Kadatskii-Rudnev of the Amur Flotilla and in June by K.I. Dushenov of the Northern Fleet.[47] All of these officers were liquidated from 1938 to 1940. In March 1938, Stalin organized the War Council of the Naval Forces, headed by the now independent people's commissar of the navy, P.A. Smirnov, a former army commissar 1st Rank, and composed of the party secretary of Leningrad A.A. Zhdanov, L.M. Galler, I.S. Isakov, N.G. Kuznetsov, the new commander of the Pacific Fleet, and G.I. Levchenko, new commander of the Baltic Fleet, all members of the big-ship navy group.

Now Stalin could assign naval buildup a very high, if not the highest, priority in the Third Five-Year Plan. In 1938, he inaugurated a shipbuilding program that not only put Adolf Hitler's ambitious Z-Plan in the shade but was comparable in scope to President Franklin Roosevelt's enormous 1940 naval program. The proposals for this program were made mainly by Admirals Galler and Isakov, who were two of the few high-ranking officers to survive the purges.

But even People's Commissar of the Navy P.A. Smirnov did not evade Stalin's obsessions. He was replaced by the terrible People's Commissariat of Internal Affairs (NKVD) Corps commander M.P. Frinovskii, one of the primary assistants of the bloodthirsty head of the NKVD, N.I. Yezhov. Smirnov disappeared, while Frinovskii shared the fate of his former chief; both were shot. On April 28, 1939, Stalin finally called the young admiral Nikolai G. Kuznetsov to Moscow to become the new people's commissar of the navy and commander in chief of the naval forces.[48] He was only a captain in 1937 when he returned as the chief adviser of the Spanish Republican Navy and became for fifteen months the new commander in chief of the Pacific Fleet. This energetic man was to guide the Soviet Navy through its phase of massive expansion, made much more difficult by the great gaps in the cadres caused by the purges of Stalin.

Even with the vast expansion of shipyards and supporting industries started during the Second Five-Year Plan, this new plan could hardly have been carried out by the target date of January 1, 1943. Foreign assistance had to be asked for. After earlier Italian support with plans for destroyers and cruisers, the prototype flotilla leader *Tashkent* was laid down in Italy in 1937, while battleship plans were developed by the Ansaldo yard in Genoa. At the same time, the U.S. firm Gibbs & Cox was asked for plans of big hybrid battleship-carriers and superbattleships, and in 1939 Admiral Isakov was sent over to negotiate orders for battleships and heavy guns. These negotiations were finally called off by the United States after the Soviet occupation of eastern Poland but were then continued with Germany after the German-Soviet treaties of August 1939.[49]

Including the ships yet to be completed from the Second Five-Year Plan, the program of 1937–1942 called for the construction of sixteen battleships of the *Sovetskii Soiuz* class (59,150 tons standard displacement) and battle cruisers of the *Kronstadt* class (34,240 tons),[50] fourteen cruisers, among them ten of the *Chapaev* class (11,500 tons), twelve flotilla leaders of the *Kiev* class (3,000 tons), ninety-six destroyers of the *Ognevoi* class (2,240 tons), and at least twenty-four fast steam-driven minesweepers of the *Polukhin* class (700 tons). The construction of an additional twenty-seven large, eighty-nine medium, and eighty small submarines was planned along with two experimental boats with rotary drive.[51]

By the end of the plan on January 1, 1943, the Soviet fleets were to consist of 19 battleships, 20 cruisers, 18 flotilla leaders, 145 destroyers, 341 submarines, and 44 river monitors. In addition a great number of guard ships, minelayers, minesweepers, and other vessels were to be built. Major shipyards were erected in Molotovsk on the White Sea and in Komsomolsk on the Amur River, as well as a big submarine yard in Gorky on the Volga River, to augment the existing yards in Leningrad and Nikolaev.[52]

In the fall of 1939, Stalin obviously hoped that this fleet construction program, which provided for a yearly production rate of about 250,000 tons, could be continued in spite of the war started by Hitler in Europe. In the context of the German-Soviet treaties, the Soviets asked for the plans of the German battleships of the *Bismarck* class, tried to purchase up to three heavy cruisers, and placed orders for heavy gun turrets and machinery. Hitler finally agreed to sell the unfinished cruiser *Lützow*, to be completed as the *Petropavlovsk* in Leningrad with German assistance.[53]

With Hitler's successes in the first year of the war and the resulting grave dislocation in the power structure of the major powers, Stalin seems by the summer of 1940 to have harbored some doubts. Although the construction of large ships in particular continued, his altered assessment of Hitler's intentions demanded a renewed emphasis on the buildup of the army. So on October 19, 1940, the construction of all large ships was halted while the building of destroyers, submarines, and small combatants was accelerated. The shift in emphasis had scarcely taken effect when the Germans attacked on June 22, 1941. By this time, the number of ships laid down since 1927 was as follows: 3 battleships, 2 battle cruisers, 14 cruisers, 11 flotilla leaders, 71 destroyers, 36 patrol ships, 55 minesweepers, 2 net layers, 10 river monitors, 9 river gunboats, 17 large submarine chasers, and 297 submarines. Of those, 4 cruisers, 7 flotilla leaders, 30 destroyers, 22 patrol ships, 38 minesweepers, and 8 monitors, as well as 206 submarines and 477 small combatants, had entered service.[54]

Neither Germany nor the Western Allies were aware of Stalin's plans for the creation of a high seas fleet to be effective in global politics. The Soviet Union was considered a land power with strictly continental aspirations.

The picture of the Soviet Union and its opponents that the Western experts have assembled from the events of World War II seems to reflect negatively on Soviet naval capabilities. The Soviet Navy is reproached for not using its capabilities because it was not employed in its most important strategic mission, the interruption of enemy sea traffic or for offensive naval missions. It was used instead only for secondary missions in support of the land campaign. But this purely naval view overlooks the problems of matériel and personnel arising from the fast buildup of the navy, the conditions that influenced the training program, and especially the war situation ashore, which forced the Soviet leaders to put aside any plans for an independent naval campaign in favor of using naval forces to meet the demands of the war.

When one considers Soviet fleet employment during the war against this background of the necessities imposed by the overall strategy, which were determined by the events in the land theaters of war and postwar political considerations, it is hardly possible to argue with Admiral Gorshkov when he says: "This employment of naval forces was the only correct one and it was in every way appropriate to the situation.[55]

In the Baltic, the Soviet fleet started with operational plans similar to those of 1914.[56] This time the German Navy disrupted Soviet operations through its offensive minelaying campaign in cooperation with the Finnish Navy far into the Finnish Gulf, and the attack of the German Army in the direction of Leningrad forced the Soviet Baltic Fleet to evacuate its new bases in Libau, Riga, and Tallin and to retreat into the inner part of the Finnish Gulf to Kronstadt and Leningrad. The Baltic Fleet was able to evacuate back to Kronstadt most of the defenders of Tallin, and later of Hanko, sustaining heavy losses from the German-Finnish mine barriers, and then to participate effectively in the defense of Leningrad. Submarines in 1942–1943 had to start their operational cruises without any training at sea. In 1942, many of them, also sustaining heavy losses, forced their way through the strong mine barriers in the Finnish Gulf and sank some ships in the open Baltic. In 1943 a net barrier stopped all efforts, but in 1944–1945 they again came out and caused some heavy shipping losses. From the breakout from the Leningrad pocket in February 1944 to the fight in the Bay of Danzig at the end of the war, Soviet light naval forces supported the sea flanks of the advancing Red Army with fire support, small tactical landings, and a few attacks against German supply routes.

In the Arctic, the Northern Fleet's main task was to cover and support the sea flank of the 14th Army defending the Murmansk area.[57] Second, the Northern Fleet and the subordinated White Sea Flotilla had to secure the summer shipping route along the Northern Passage, which proved to be difficult against German surface incursions in 1942 and U-boat operations in 1943 and 1944. But most important was the participation in the escort of the Allied Murmansk convoys in the last easternmost part of the voyage against German surface, air, and U-boat attacks. The many very critical Western accounts of the Soviet efforts in this field tend to overlook the small number of available destroyers for such a task and their insufficient range and sea-keeping qualities (these ships had been built from Italian designs for Mediterranean conditions, not for the heavy seas of the Arctic). Also the Soviet naval air force was equipped with outdated planes of limited range. Only when the critical time was over in late 1943 did the Lend-Lease deliveries of ships and aircraft ease the situation. Finally, the submarines of the Northern Fleet achieved some successes off northern Norway against German supply traffic but suffered heavy losses mainly from German flanking mine fields.

In the Black Sea, the Soviet fleet was greatly superior to all the other navies there, and especially the navy of the German satellite Rumania, but there even more than in the Baltic the operations were dependent on developments on land.[58] Only a few weeks after the start of the war, Odessa was surrounded by German and Rumanian forces and had to be supplied and, later in October 1941 to be evacuated, by sea. In this the Soviet Black Sea Fleet was successful, evacuating without great loss four divisions during the last night to the endangered main base of Sevastopol. Then for almost seven months, surface ships and later submarines had to supply Sevastopol, which was under heavy attack by the German Army. All this had to be done without the support of the normal naval yards in the occupied territory. Sevastopol was lost in early July 1942, but there was no time for rest because by then the German Army was already attacking from the land side the last bases on the Caucasian coast of the Black Sea. Only with the transport efforts of the surviving ships of the Black Sea Fleet was it possible for the Soviets to hold on to these places and prevent the Germans from capturing an access to the port of Novorossisk. During all those retreat operations, the Soviet Navy effected several amphibious assaults behind the German-Rumanian front and a great number of fire-support missions. Those operations were dictated by the developments on land; there was no possibility for fighting a naval war according to the theories of a naval strategy. The navy had to support the coastal flanks of the army, incurring heavy losses during this lengthy effort. Only when the German pressure was relieved after the Battle of Stalingrad, did the Black Sea Fleet change to a naval strategy, trying to interrupt the German-Rumanian supply routes. The distance from Caucasian bases prevented any great effect. In October 1943, the fleet lost three of its seven surviving modern destroyers during an unsuccessful raid against a German evacuation transport, and Stalin ordered the navy not to risk the surface ships.[59] At the end of 1943, when the final victory over the Axis powers was no longer in doubt, Stalin renewed the plan for building a powerful high seas fleet, and so now he had to conserve the remaining big ships and destroyers for training purposes after the war. Because the personnel then in training for manning the ships of the First Five-Year Plan had to be sent to the marine infantry brigades during the crisis of 1941–1942, a completely new training program of new recruits had to be started.

Stalin's program of 1944 provided for the construction of 4 or 8 battle cruisers, probably some aircraft carriers, 24 cruisers, 175 destroyers, and 1,200 submarines, as well as a great number of minor combatants and auxiliaries, all to be built within the next twenty years.[60] However, pressing needs at war's end contended against such a long-range naval buildup for an oceanic fleet. The reconstruction of industry and the demands of the developing cold war forced an uneven distribution of research and production capacity in the postwar armament programs. The execution of the new program apparently proceeded less smoothly, particularly in the naval sector, than Soviet authors tell us now. There were numerous conflicting reorganizations. All those administrative events reflected controversies that must have been taking place among the Soviet leaders concerning the role of naval forces. This impression is strengthened by the ups and downs in the status in the people's commissar appointed by Stalin in 1939. Promoted to fleet admiral of the Soviet Union in May 1945, Kuznetsov was replaced in January 1947 and demoted to vice-admiral. The official reason was the accusation that he gave away some secrets of German acoustic torpedoes to the British. The real reason was probably his opposition to the division of the Baltic and the Pacific fleets into two commands each, and especially his opposition to slowing down the building program. In February 1950, however, he was reappointed to command the 2d Pacific Fleet, and in July 1951 Stalin reinstalled him as supreme commander in chief of the navy, certainly an indication that the original oceanic concept had finally triumphed, although in a graduated form.[61] In this plan, the construction of an antiamphibious fleet, which seemed to be urgently necessary from a military point of view, took precedence over the construction of a world-power oceanic fleet, whose largest ships were to be the battle cruisers of the *Stalingrad* class (38,420 tons) so dear to Stalin. Two of these ships were laid down in 1949–1950, but their construction did not advance very far.[62] In contrast, in the United States the years 1945–1950 were characterized by a comprehensive disarmament, based on the confidence that political conflicts would be solved through the instrument of the United Nations, while the U.S. monopoly of atomic weapons seemed to offer backup security in case of an emergency. The initial absence of a U.S. delivery system of adequate range placed the credibility of this deterrent in such doubt, however, that the Soviet Union was able to eliminate domestic opposition in those territories controlled by its vast army and to push forward with a vigorous expansion of communism through material and political support of revolutionary movements and warring civil factions, through blockades such as at Berlin, and through military aggressions by its satellites as in Korea. The Kremlin's hope was that the coming threat posed by the U.S. nuclear-armed intercontinental bombers could be met by the construction of a great number of jet interceptors and by an accelerated production of a Soviet atomic bomb. Plainly the powerful amphibious potential of the Anglo-U.S. sea powers, whose capabilities had been put to the test in the great landing operations in Europe and the Pacific, was also considered a most serious military threat.[63]

Regarding these capabilities, personal memories of Anglo-American landings during the Russian civil war may have prevented many Soviet leaders from seeing that such intentions were now entirely lacking on the Western side, as a reduction of about 93 percent in precisely this potential by the U.S. Navy demonstrated. Emphasis was first on ships for countering an amphibious threat before the building program of conventional submarines, destroyers, and cruisers gained momentum with the rehabilitation of Admiral Kuznetsov. The development of the next generation of such types, as well as the construction of the first nuclear-powered submarines, were begun at the same time.[64]

After Stalin's death in March 1953, it became clear to the new leadership that the Soviet Union, with its still inadequate industrial capacity, could not cope with the threat now assumed to be most dangerous (nuclear-armed long-range aircraft coming from bases around the Soviet Union and from carriers at sea) without dropping the expensive antiamphibious program, directed against a threat that was no longer relevant, and the ocean fleet program, designed for a far distant future. After stopping new construction in 1954, the new leader, Nikita Khrushchev, supported by Minister of Defense Marshal G.K. Zhukov and other army leaders, fired Admiral Kuznetsov, who had opposed the cuts. Khrushchev ordered his successor, Admiral S.G. Gorshkov, to concentrate on acute needs. To free resources, the new naval program was cut to about half its former building capacity. The first priority was now directed toward ships, submarines, and aircraft armed with standoff cruise missiles against the nuclear-armed aircraft carriers.[65]

As a second priority, Gorshkov had to develop a sea-based strategic nuclear weapon system. In contrast to the Americans, the Soviets started with a two-way approach. In 1955, an adapted army ballistic missile was launched from a surfaced submarine, and the Soviets started to build two parallel classes of diesel- or nuclear-powered submarines with ballistic missiles. At the same time a large program was started to build conventional and nuclear submarines equipped with long-range cruise missiles against shore targets, while long-range bombers were equipped with standoff missiles.[66]

When, as in the United States in the late 1950s, it seemed possible for the Soviets to build ballistic missile–armed submarines, there simultaneously arose a danger to Soviet territory from the new nuclear-powered U.S. carriers carrying supersonic long-range bombers. Therefore the Soviets replaced the cruise missiles against land targets aboard the new submarines with antiship missiles.

Before the anticarrier program for surface ships and submarines came into full swing, a new evaluation in 1959–1960 produced evidence that the most dangerous threat to the Soviet Union from the sea had shifted from carriers to the new U.S. Polaris-armed nuclear-powered ballistic missile submarines (SSBNs). The emphasis in Soviet naval armament then shifted to antisubmarine warfare in a new anti-Polaris program. Surface ships designed for fighting against sea and air targets were first renamed "large antisubmarine ships" before new types of ships equipped with modern antisubmarine warfare (ASW) systems, including helicopters, entered the fleet.[67]

At the same time, the development of Soviet strategic offensive potential received higher priority. This was when First Secretary Khrushchev tried to transform the seeming lead in ballistic missile development demonstrated by space successes into political advantages. He not only forced the development of land-based strategic missiles but also ordered the navy to produce as fast as possible an effective sea-based strategic system. The resulting program absorbed the greater part of the remaining naval-building capacity, but in Admiral Gorshkov's eyes it had a great weakness.

With their insufficient missile range, the Yankee SSBNs had to pass the dangerous North Atlantic Treaty Organization (NATO) ASW barriers to come close enough to the U.S. coasts to launch their missiles. Oceangoing surface warships, attack submarines, and long-range airplanes were necessary to fight the missile submarines through the barriers and to cover their return. Even then, it remained doubtful that the submarines could reach their launching areas against the strong ASW capabilities of the Western navies. A much better solution seemed to be to develop submarine-launched ballistic missiles of a range allowing the submarines to stay in areas off their own bases and to block those areas against the entry of enemy ships and submarines by establishing barrier forces to defend bastions such as the Barents or Arctic seas or the Sea of Okhotsk.

This was accomplished in the 1970s by the construction of SS-N-8, SS-N-18, and later missiles on the nuclear submarines of the Delta classes on the one hand, and by providing multipurpose surface ships with good sea-keeping qualities and endurance that could hold on against attacks by carrier aircraft or submarines on the other hand.[68]

It seems difficult to associate these efforts only with the ideas of the classical school or with the young school, because since World War II, military or strategic concepts no longer can be attributed to purely land, sea, or air warfare. The efforts described now belong to the global nuclear-strategic confrontation of the superpowers and their allies, the dominating new element of military strategy being the use of strategic air forces of intercontinental range, land-based and sea-based intercontinental ballistic missiles, and defenses against all these weapon systems.[69]

In the Soviet Union for the last thirty years, the sea-based nuclear strategic offensive and defensive components absorbed more than half the naval building capacities. Only by combining the elements of the defense of the Soviet homeland against any dangers coming from the sea by using the possibilities of new weapon systems against the sea powers, the several "anti" programs up to the mid-1960s can be subsumed under a label *new young school.*

In this context, the Soviet Navy always had to provide in addition to the described "anti" programs the light forces necessary to defend the Soviet coast and sea transport routes or to support the sea flanks of the army. Great numbers of light combatants with guns, torpedoes, and antiship missiles, minelayers and minesweepers, and amphibious vessels for tactical landings during front or theater operations had to be built.

Since the mid-1960s, there were increasing signs that Gorshkov tried to get the Soviet leadership again into a more classical school mode of thinking. After Khrushchev's rocket-backed bluff policy failed with the Cuban crisis, Gorshkov in 1964 introduced a new role for his surface ships. Besides sending ships to visit ports of many countries of the Third World as ambassadors of goodwill, he began a forward deployment of his surface ships and submarines, first to spy on NATO carrier task groups, then to provide a standing presence in the North Atlantic, the Mediterranean, then off West Africa, in the Indian Ocean, and especially in the Persian Gulf, and finally also in the Caribbean, the South Atlantic, and the Pacific. The nervous reaction of Western experts to his worldwide maneuvers Okean in 1970 and 1975 gave evidence of Gorshkov's claims of the possibilities that a powerful high seas fleet offered in world politics. This was underlined by the cautious behavior of the U.S. task forces in conflict areas when there was a Soviet naval presence, as in the Six-Day War of 1967, the Indo-Pakistan War of 1971, and especially during the Angolan Civil War of 1975.[70]

In his many publications of the 1970s and early 1980s, Gorshkov made it clear that his idea of sea power is not circumscribed only by the categories of a classical sea power theory or strategy alone, which deal with winning control of the sea and the struggle for sea-lines of communication (SLOCs). To him, the participation of the navy in a nuclear confrontation in an offensive and a defensive way is only one element, albeit an important one. Given the growing North-South tension between the industrial states and the developing lands, the growing ideological enmities, as well as the importance that the riches of the sea will have as a source of sustenance and raw materials for the whole world, Gorshkov obviously anticipated more conflicts in the Third World in which the great powers could not remain neutral. In the words of Gorshkov, "For the Soviet Union, the main goal of whose policy is the building of communism and a steady rise in the welfare of its builders, sea power emerges as one of the important factors for strengthening its economy, accelerating scientific and technical development and consolidating the economic, political, cultural and scientific links of the Soviet people with the peoples and countries friendly to it." To this end, he needed large warships of great endurance and power, and also, to project sea power globally, the cooperation of the other services, the commercial fleet, the fishing fleet, the fleet of research ships, and also the various branches of oceanography and ocean technology, which are all considered to be important factors of modern sea power.[71]

The question now is whether this concept of sea power as an instrument of global policy of the Soviet leadership has changed with the unannounced retirement of Gorshkov in November 1985 and his death in May 1988. There are some important forebodings indeed for a fundamental change in the priorities of the Soviet policy. In his policy of *glasnost'* and *perestroika*, the new general secretary, Mikhail S. Gorbachev, vigorously pushed administrative reforms and demanded more efficiency in the bureaucracy at all levels and in the economy. In his foreign and defense policy, he appeared to be trying to reduce existing tensions and to come to agreements for extensive arms reductions.[72]

Gorbachev also began to break up the old establishment of civilian and military functionaries *nomenklatura* whose strategic thinking was fixed on the idea of gaining more security by building up a strong military superiority in all fields of weapon systems on land, in the air or in space, and at sea. The group of younger and more flexible manager-type leaders around Gorbachev may want to gain a broader spectrum of political options beyond the long-cherished pure military strategy in order to master the challenges of the future.

The Soviets must save financial resources to modernize their economy and to adapt the structures of their society for the new tasks. This they can achieve only by avoiding a new round in the big arms race and by reducing the high rates of military expenditures.

In this context, the diverse proposals for extensive arms reductions make additional sense. Probably the young military leaders have realized, or they had to accept, that benefits in worldwide public opinion coming from achievements in arms reduction efforts outweigh by far the advantages to be gained from one or another new weapon system for the security of the Soviet Union. This is especially true when a system of great international publicity, like the SS-20 ballistic missile, is made replaceable by another system of low public awareness. So the targets of the SS-20 can be covered by the old Yankee nuclear-powered submarines with their old SS-N-6 missiles or by the new submarine-launched, land-targeted cruise missiles, the SS-N-21 or SS-N-24, on a lower but sufficient level, especially when this leads in exchange to the abolition of systems on the other side that can reach Soviet territory, such as the U.S. Pershing II or land-based cruise missiles.

If the intermediate nuclear forces treaty to this end is to be followed by new treaties for a drastic reduction of strategic nuclear weapons, several steps seem possible in the direction of the Soviet goal of reducing or abolishing tactical nuclear weapons in exchange for the Western goal of a balanced relation of conventional forces especially in Europe.

It remains to be seen what all this means for the Soviet Navy. Gorshkov's successor, Admiral of the Fleet V.N. Chernavin, coming from the rocket nuclear submarine force, has, like Gorbachev, initially directed his energies into internal reforms to bring personnel and matériel toward more efficiency at lower expenditures. Admiral Chernavin may in the future put more emphasis on the integration of all naval forces into the theater- and task-oriented organization of the five Soviet military services and as a consequence may have to reduce worldwide commitments.[73] In this context, operations for the interruption of enemy SLOCs will gain a higher priority than they have had in the past. To sever the SLOCs between the New World and Europe or East Asia, big surface ships may not be so useful as they were for Gorshkov's global concept, and their building rates may be slowed. At the same time, nuclear submarines with cruise missiles may gain more importance, as may be seen by an accelerated building program in this field.

To avoid the spillover of the naval arms race to new areas, we have to find ways for both sides to test the truth and reliability of the publicly announced policies and strategies. Only with the establishment of confidence can we hope to start a reversal toward a world with fewer weapons but sufficient security to both sides. We have to depart from our hitherto purely military strategic thinking and counting of weapon systems and must find the means for a peaceful containment of unavoidable conflicts by new political ideas. To trust the announced political goals, we must be wary of our own perceptions and prejudices and correctly interpret the real intentions of the other side. Both sides have to allow their opponent on the other side to get a true picture of their decision-making processes.

Notes

1. There were many books and articles on the Russian and soviet navies published in the first twenty years after World War II before the Soviet historians started to publish detailed descriptions of operations and events of the war, so the publications in the Western countries could count on only Western sources. Some examples are: Mairin Mitchell, *The Maritime History of Russia, 1848–1948* (London: Sidgwick & Jackson, 1949; reprint, New York: Books for Library Press, 1969); Jurg Meister, *Der Seekrieg in den osteuropäischen Gewässern 1941–1945* (Munich: Lehmanns, 1958); M.G. Saunders, ed., *The Soviet Navy*, (London: Weidenfeld & Nicolson, 1958), including an essay of a former British liaison officer written from a pure naval point of view: R.C.S. Garwood, "The Russians as Naval Allies, 1941–45," 75–83; *Das deutsche Bild der russischen und sowjetischen Marine* (Beiheft 7/8, Marine-Rundschau, Frankfurt/Main: Mittler, 1962); David Woodward, *The Russians at Sea* (London: Kimber, 1965). Russian publications include: *Boevaia lepotis' russkogo flota. Khronika vazhneishikh sobytii voennoi istorii* (Moscow: Voenizdat, 1948); *Istoriia voenno-morskogo iskusstva*, ed. Glavnyi Shtab Voenno-Morskogo Flota, Admiral S.E. Zakharov (Moscow: Voenizdat, 1969); Sergei G. Gorshkov, *Morskaia moshch' gosudarstva* (Moscow: Voenizdat, 1969); Sergei G. Gorshkov, *Morskaia moshch' gosudarstva* (Moscow: Voenizdat, 1976, 2d ed., 1979); trans. as *The Sea Power of the State* (Annapolis: Naval Institute, 1979); Pavel A. Zhilin, ed., *Russkaia voennaia mysl': Konets XIX—nachalo XX*, (Moscow: Nauka, 1982). Later Western publications include: Donald W. Mitchell, *A History of Russian and Soviet Sea Power* (London: Deutsch, 1974); Harald Fock, *Vom Zarenadler zum Roten Stern. Die Geschichte der russischen-sowjetischen Marine* (Herford: Mittler, 1985).

2. Alfred Thayer Mahan, *The Influence of Sea Power Upon History, 1660–1783* (London: Sampson Low, Marston, 1890), and *The Influence of Sea Power upon*

the French Revolution and Empire, 1793–1812 (London: Sampson Low, Marston, 1892); Sir Julian Corbett, *Some Principles of Maritime Strategy* (London: Longmans, 1911); Raoul Castex, *Théories stratégiques,* 5 vols., vol. 1, new ed. (Paris: Sociéte d'éditions géographiques, maritimes et coloniales, 1930–1937); Júurgen Rohwer, "Technical Progress, Naval Acts and the Building of Warships, 1845–1918," *Acta,* Athens, August 24–31, 1987 (Athens: Commission Internationale d'Histoire Militaire, 1988).

3. J.-H. Paixhans, *Nouvelle force maritime* (Paris: Bachelier, 1821); Paul Dislère, *Les Croiseurs: La guerre de course* (Paris: Dupont, 1876); Théophile Aube, *La Guerre maritime et les ports français* (Paris, 1882), and *De la Guerre navale* (Paris, 1885); Gabriel Charmes, *Le Réforme de la marine* (Paris: Calman Levy, 1886); Chaband-Arnault, *Histoire des flottes militaires* (Paris, 1889); Theodore Ropp, *The Development of a Modern Navy: French Naval Policy, 1871–1904* (Annapolis: U.S. Naval Institute, 1987); Volkmar Bueb, *Die "Junge Schule" der französischen Marine. Strategie und Politik, 1875–1900* (Boppard/Rhein: Boldt, 1971).

4. Hans Busk, *The Navies of the World: Their Present State and Future Capabilities* (London: Routledge, 1859; reprint, Richmond, 1971); Yevgenii V. Tarle, *Krymskaia voina,* 2d ed. (Moscow, 1950).

5. Grigorii I. Butakov, *Novye osnovaniia parokhodnoi taktiki* (St. Petersburg, 1863); A. Luré and A. Marinin, *Admiral Grigorii Ivanovich Butakov (1820–1882)* (Moscow: Voenizdat, 1954).

6. Paul Dislère, *La Guerre d'escadre et al guerre des côtes: Les Nouveaux navires de combat* (Paris, 1876); J.W. King, *Warships and Navies of the World* (Boston: Williams & Co., 1881); J.F. von Kronenfels, *Das schwimmende Flottenmaterial der Seemächte* (Vienna: Hartleben, 1881); Jacob W. Kipp, "Das russische Marineministerium und die Einführung der Panzerschiffe," *Marine-Rundschau* 78 (1981): 210–14.

7. *Illiustrirovannaia khronika voiny 1877–78* (St. Petersburg: Goppe, 1877–1878); N. Monasterev and Sergey Terestchenko, *Histoire de la marine russe,* trans. Jean Pereau (Paris: Payot, 1932); Vasilii I. Achkasov, "Russkii flot v voine 1877–78," *Morskoi sbornik,* no. 3 (1978) 71–75.

8. C. Sleeman, *Torpedoes and Torpedo Warfare,* 2d ed. (Portsmouth: Griffin, 1889); d'Armor [Alfred M. Laubeuf], *Les Sous-Marins et al guerre contre l'Angleterre* (Paris, 1899); Grigorii M. Trusov, *Podvodnye lodki v russkom i sovetskom flote,* 2d ed. (Leningrad: Gosudizdat, 1963).

9. Philippe Masson, *La Révolution maritime des XIXe siecle* (Paris: Lauvauzelle, for the Service historique de la marine, 1987).

10. Fred T. Jane, *The Imperial Russian Navy* (London: Thacker, 1899; 2d ed., 1904), 244.

11. Ferdinand Attlmayr, *Über Seetaktik* (Pola: Gerold's, 1875) and *Über den Seekrieg: Reihe Studien über Seetaktik und den Seekrieg mit den Kriegsschiffen der Neuzeit* (Pola: Gerold's, 1878).

12. Oscar Parkes, *British Battleships: "Warrior" to "Vanguard," 1860 to 1950: A History of Design, Construction and Armament* (London: Seeley, 1956), 349–66.

13. See note 2.

14. Philip H. Colomb, *Naval Warfare: Its Ruling Principles and Practice Historically Treated* (London: Allen, 1891); H.W. Wilson, *Ironclads in Action: A Sketch of Naval Warfare from 1855 to 1895* (London: Sampson Low, Marston, 1896).

15. Alfred von Tirpitz, Denkschrift "Unsere maritim-militärische Fortentwick-lung" (presented to the emperor, April 6, 1891), and Denkschrift "Über die Neuor-ganisation unserer Panzerflotte," 1891, Bundesarchiv-Militärarchiv, Freiburg i.B.

16. Stepan O. Makarov, *Rassuzhdeniia po voprosam morskoi taktiki* (St. Petersburg: Tipogr. Morskogo Ministerstva, 1895–1896; 2d ed., 1916); B.G. Ostriv-skii, *Stepan Osipovich Makarov (1848–1904)* (Leningrad: Izd. Molodaia Gvardiia, 1951, 2d ed., 1972).

17. Nikolai L. Klado, *Osnovy sovremennogo voenno-morskogo dela* (St. Petersburg, 1901).

18. Kornelii F. Shatsillo, *Russkii imperializm i razvitie flota nakanune pervoi mirovoi voiny (1906–1914 gg.)* (Moscow: Nauka, 1968); Dieteer Matthei, "Russische Seemachtbestrebungen in der Epoche des Navalismus," *Marine-Rund-schau* 75 (1978): 17–25; H.J.M. Campbell, "Russia," in *Conway's All the World's Fighting Ships, 1860–1905,* ed. Robert Gardiner (London: Conway, 1979), 170–215.

19. Jürgen Rohwer, "International Naval Co-operation during the "Boxer"-Rebellion in China, 1900–01," *Revue internationale d'histoire militaire,* no. 70 (1988): 79–96.

20. Nikolai L. Klado, *Posle ukhoda vtoroi eskadry Tikhogo okeana (1904)* (St. Petersburg: Suvorin, 1905), Engl. transl. L.J.H. Dickinsin, *The Russian Navy in the Russo-Japanese War* (London: Hurst & Blackett, 1905), and *The Battle of the Sea of Japan* (London: Hodder & Stoughton, 1906); Vladimir I. Semenov, *Boi pri Tsushime* (St. Petersburg: Vol'f, 1906); Nikolai N. Beklemishev, *V russko-iaponskoi voine na more* (St. Petersburg: Impr. Russ. Techn. O-vo., 1907); *Russko-iapanoskaia voina. 1904–1905,* vols. 1-9 (St. Petersburg: Suvorin, 1910).

21. Jürgen Rohwer and Walther Hubatsch, "Politik und Flottenbau," in *Seemacht,* ed. E.B. Potter, C.W. Nimitz, and J. Rohwer (Munich: Bernard & Graefe, 1974), 315–42.

22. Charles E. Adams, "Der Wiederaufstieg der russischen Kriegsmarine in den Jahren, 1905–1914," *Marine-Rundschau* 61 (1964): 12–21; René Greger, *The Russian Fleet, 1914–1917* (London: Ian Allan, 1971), 11–14.

23. Przemyslaw Budzbon, "Russia," in *Conway's All the World's Fighting Ships 1906–1921,* ed. Robert Gardiner (London: Conway, 1985).

24. René Greger, "Russische Schlachtschiff-Projekte von 1914 bis 1916", *Marine-Rundschau* 73 (1976): 165–69; and "Imperator Nikolai I.' Das letzte in Russ-land gebaute Schlachtschiff," *Marine-Rundschau* 73 (1976): 582–90.

25. Greger, *Russian Fleet.*

26. N.B. Pavlovich, ed., *Flot v pervoi mirovoi voine,* 2 vols. (Moscow: Voenizdat, 1964).

27. Nikolai L. Klado, *Ocherki mirovoi voiny* (Petrograd, 1915).

28. H. Graf, *The Russian Navy in War and Revolution from 1914 to 1918 (Munich: Oldenbourg, 1923); Greger, chronology in Russian Fleet;* Jürgen Rohwer and Jurg Meister, "Der Seekrieg in der Ostsee und im Schwarzen Meer," *Seemacht,* 400–25.

29. N. Monasterev, *Vom Untergang der Zarenflotte,* trans. M. Zimmerman (Berlin: Mittler, 1930).

30. René Greger, "Russische Landungsschiffe von 1916: Die "El'pidifor"-Fahrzeuge, *Marine-Rundschau* 71 1974): 163–68; "Geschichte des russischen und sowjetischen Bordflugwesens," *Marine-Rundschau* 76 (1979): 761–70.

31. A.S. Bubnov, S.S. Kamenev, and R.P. Eideman, *Grazhdanskaia voina 1918–1921 gg.*, 3 vols. (Moscow, 1928); Arkadii K. Selianichev, *V.I. Lenin i stanovlenie sovetskogo voienno-morskogo flota* (Moscow: Nauka, 1979); A. Zakharov, "Pervyi komanduiushchii morskami silami respubliki V.M. Al'tfater," *Voenno-istoricheskii zhurnal*, no. 12 (1983): 80–82.

32. Leon Trotsky, *The Revolution Betrayed* (New York: Doubleday, 1937); *Boevoi put' sovetskogo voenno-morskogo flota*, ed. N.A. Piterskii (Moscow: Voenizdat, 1964, 2d ed., 1967).

33. B. Gervais, "Flot segodniashnego dnia: Boevye sredstva," *Krasnyi flot* (February 1922): 18–30; M.A. Petrov, "Zametki o taktiki malogo flota," *Morskoi sbornik* (September 1923): 45–61; I. Gordeev, *Krasnyi morskoi flot* (Moscow: Voenizdat, 1925).

34. V.I. Zof, "Mezhdunarodnoe polozhenie i zadachi morskoi oboroni SSSR," *Morskoi sbornik* (May 1925): 3–16; M.A. Petrov, *Podgotovka rossii k mirovoi voine na more* (Moscow: Voenizdat, 1926), and *Obzor glavneishikh kampanii i srazhenii parovogo flota v sviazi s evoliutsiei voenno-morskogo iskusstva* (Leningrad: Gosvoenizdat, 1927); B. Gervais, "Piat' let raboty voenno-morskogo akademii RKKA," *Morskoi sbornik* (March 1927): 3–12.

35. League of Nations, *Official Journal*, February 21, 1924, 708–10.

36. John Erickson, *The Soviet High Command. A Military Political History, 1918–1941* (London: Macmillan, 1962); Robert W. Herrick, *Soviet Naval Strategy: Fifty Years of Theory and Practice* (Annapolis: U.S. Naval Institute, 1968); Sergei G. Gorshkov, *Die Rolle der Flotten in Krieg und Frieden* 2 (Munich: Lehmanns, 1975), 2:77–105; I.A. Korotkov, *Istoriia sovetskoi voennoi mysl'. Kratkii ocherk 1917-iiun 1941 gg.* (Moscow: Nauka, 1980).

37. A.V. Basov, "Bau der Seekriegsflotte der UdSSR vor dem Zweiten Weltkrieg, 1921–1941," *Revue internationale d'histoire militaire*, forthcoming.

38. R.A. Muklevich, "Desiatiletie oktiabrskoi revoliutsii i morskoi flot," *Morskoi sbornik* (October 1927); Ivan Ludri, "Desiat' let bor'by i stroitel'stvo," *Morskoi sbornik* (February 1928): 28–36, "Krasnyi flot v sostave vooruzhënnykh sil respubliki," *Morskoi sbornik* (October 1927): 23–28, and "Morskie operatsii," *Voennaia mysl'* (February 1937): 75–86; V.M. Orlov, "Na strazhe morskikh granits SSSR," *Morskoi sbornik* (March 1937): 11–21.

39. Claude Huan and Jürgen Rohwer, "La marine soviétique," *Documentation française*, October 3, 1978; Siegried Breyer, *Enzyklopädie des sowjetischen Kriegsschiffbaus*, vol. 1: *Oktoberrevolution und maritimes Erbe* (Herford: Koehler, 1987).

40. Jurg Meister, *Soviet Warships of the Second World War* (London: Macdonald, 1977); Przemyslaw Budzbon, "Soviet Union," in *Conway's All the World's Fighting Ships, 1922–1946*, ed. Robert Gardiner (London: Conway, 1980).

41. S.E. Zakharov et al., *Krasnoznamennyi tikhookeanskii flot*, 2d ed. (Moscow: Voenizdat, 1973).

42. I.A. Kozlov and V.S. Shlomin, *Severnyi flot* (Moscow: Voenizdat, 1966).

43. Sergei G. Gorshkov, *Red Star Rising at Sea*, ed. Herbert Preston (Annapolis: U.S. Naval Institute, 1974), 71.

44. John Erickson, *The Soviet High Command* (London: Macmillan, 1962); Basov, "Bau der Seekriegsflotte"; Viacheslav Molotov, "Likovanie naradov Sovet-

skogo Soiuza," *Pravda*, December 16, 1937, and "Speech on the Creation of a Strong Navy in the USSR," *Moscow News*, February 5, 1938.

45. Ashot M. Arzumanian, *Admiral flota sovetskogo soiuza I. S. Isakov (1894–1967)* (Yerevan: Izdat-Ajastan, 1973; Moscow: Nauka, 1975); V. Redanskii, "Admiral L.M. Galler," *Voenno-istoricheskii zhurnal*, no. 11 (1983): 92–94.

46. Erickson, *Soviet High Command*, 476.

47. P.I. Mus'iakov, *Flagman Konstantin Dushenov* (Moscow: Voenizdat, 1966).

48. Nikolai G. Kuznetsov, *Nakanune* (Moscow: Voenizdat, 1966), 213–26.

49. René Greger, "Sowjetischer Schlachtschiffbau," *Marine-Rundschau* 71 (1974): 461–79; Siegfried Breyer, "Sowjetischer Schlachtschiffbau," *Marine-Rundschau* 72 (1975): 141–63.

50. William H. Garzke, Jr., and Robert O. Dulin, *Battleships*, vol. 2: *Allied Battleships in World War II* (Annapolis: U.S. Naval Institute, 1980), "The Sovetskiy Soyuz Class," 307–32, "The Soviet Battlecruisers," 333–38; Gorshkov, *Red Star Rising*, 68–69.

51. Budzbon, "Soviet Union," 332–38.

52. Meister, *Soviet Warships*.

53. Siegried Breyer, "Die Kreuzer 'K' and 'L' der deutschen Kriegsmarine ('Seydlitz' und 'Lützow'), *Marine-Rundschau* 63 (1966): 20–28, 99–100; M.J. Whitley, *German Cruisers of World War II* (London: Arms and Armor, 1985), 48–50.

54. Meister, *Soviet Warships*.

55. Gorshkov, *Red Star Rising*, 94, and "Der Aufbau der sowjetischen Flotte," *Seemacht Sowjetunion*, ed. E. Opitz (Hamburg: Hoffman & Campe, 1978), 203–4.

56. There are many Soviet publications about the Soviet Navy in general and about the four fleets and the flotillas in World War II. Some of the general works are: Ivan S. Isakov, *Voyenno-morkoi flot SSSR v velikoi otechestvennoi voine* (Moscow: Voenizdat, 1946), Engl. trans., *The Red Fleet in the Second World War* (London: Hutchinson, 1945); *Boevoi put' sovetskogo voenno-morskogo flota*, ed. N.A. Piterskii (Moscow: Voenizdat, 1964), German trans. N.A. Piterskij, *Die Sowjetflotte im Zweiten Weltkrieg*, ed. Jürgen Rohwer with 100 pages of commentary (Oldenburg: Stalling, 1966), 3d ed., ed. V.I. Achkasov and A.V. Basov (Moscow: Voenizdat, 1974); Nikolai G. Kuznetsov, *Na flotakh boevaia trevoga* (Moscow: Voenizdat, 1971); V.I. Achkasov and N.B. Pavlovich, *Sovetskoe voenno-morskoe iskusstvo v velikoi jotechestvennoi voine* (Moscow: Voenizdat, 1973), English trans. *Soviet Naval Operations in the Great Patriotic War, 1941–1945* (Annapolis: U.S. Naval Institute, 1981); A.V. Basov, *Flot v velikoi otechestvennoi voine 1941–1945: Opyt operativno-strategicheskogo primeneniia* (Moscow: Nauka, 1980). A German account is Friedrich Ruge, *The Soviets as Naval Opponents* (Annapolis: U.S. Naval Institute, 1980). Soviet general works on special ship types include: G.I. Chor'kov, *Sovetskie nadvodnye korabli v velikoi otechestvennoi voine* (Moscow: Voenizdat, 1981); V.I. Dmitriev, *Atakuiut podvodniki* (Moscow: Voenizdat, 1964, 2d ed., 1973). A French account is Claude Huan, *L'Énigme des sous-marins sovietiques* (Paris: Ed. France-Empire, 1959). Special works on the Baltic Fleet include: V.I. Achkasov and B.A. Vainer, *Krasnoznamennyi baltiiskii flot v velikoi otechestvennoi voine* (Moscow: Voenizdat, 1957); *Kraznoznamennyi baltiiskii flot v bitve za Leningrad, 1941–1944 gg.*, ed. V.I. Achkasov (Moscow: Voenizdat, 1973); *Krasnoznamennyi baltiiskii flot v zavershaiushchii period velikoi otechestvennoi voine, 1944–1945 gg.*, ed. V.I. Achkasov

(Moscow: Voenizdat, 1975); *Krasnoznamennyi baltiiskii flot v velikoi otechestvennoi voine, 1941–1945,* ed. A.M. Samsonov (Moscow: Nauka, 1981); V.F. Tributs, *Podvodniki baltiki atakuiut* (Leningrad: Lenizdat, 1963); and V. Grinkevich and M. Korsunskii, *Admiral Tributs* (Tallin: Eesti raamat, 1980).

57. Arseni G. Golovko, *Vmeste s flotom* (Moscow: Voenizdat, 1960); English tans. *With the Red Fleet: The War Memoirs of the Late Admiral,* trans. Peter Broomfield (London: Putnam, 1960); B.A. Vainer, *Severnyi flot v velikoi otechestvennoi voine (Moscow: Voenizdat, 1964); Podvodnye voiny riadovye,* ed. A.A.F.V. Konstantinov and S.S. Shakhov (Murmansk: Murmanskoe Knizdat, 1979); *V studenykh glubinakh,* ed. V.M. Moshcheerna (Moscow: Voenizdat, 1980); M.I. Chametov, *Admiral A.G. Golovko* (Moscow: Voenizdat).

58. G. Kislyi, *Pobeda na iuge* (Moscow: Voenizdat, 1955); N.P. V'iunenko, *Chernomorskii flot v velikoi otechestvennoi voine* (Moscow: Voenizdat, 1957); I.D. Kirin, *Chernomorskii flot v bitve za kavkaz* (Moscow: Voenizdat, 1958); G.F. Godlevskii, N.M. Grechaniuk, and V.M. Kononenko, *Pokhody boevye: Eskadr chernomorskogo flota v velikoi otechestvennoi voine, 1941–1943* Moscow: Voenizdat, 1966); P. Bolgari et al., *Chernomorskii flot: Istoricheskii ocherk* (Moscow: Voenizdat, 1967); G.I. Vaneev, *Chernomortsy v velikoi otechestvennoi voine* (Moscow: Voenizdat, 1978).

59. Godlevskii et al., *Pokhody boevye,* 215–23; Nikolai G. Kuznetsov, *Kursom k pobede* (Moscow: Voenizdat, 1978). Some books on the Pacific Fleet and the flotillas include: Grigorii M. Gel'fond, *Sovetskii flot v voine s iaponiei* (Moscow: Voenizdat, 1958); S.E. Zakharov et al., *Tikhookeanskii flot* (Moscow: Voenizdat, 1966); I.I. Loktionov, *Dunaiskaia flotiliia v velikoi otechestvennoi voine* (Moscow: Voenizdat, 1962), and *Pinskaia i dneprovskaia flotilii v velikoi otechestvennoi voine* (Moscow: Voenizdat, 1958).

60. Siegried Breyer and Norman Polmar (from 3d ed. Norman Polmar), *Guide to the Soviet Navy* (Annapolis: U.S. Naval Institute, 1970, 2d ed. 1977, 3d ed. 1983, 4th ed. 1986); Jürgen Rohwer, "Strategische Konzepte und Schiffbauprogramme der Vereinigten Staaten und der Sowjetunion seit 1945 under Berücksichtigung Grossbritanniens und Frankreichs," in *Seemacht und Aussenpolitik,* ed. Dieter Mahncke and Hans-Peter Schwarz (Frankfurt: Metzner, 1974), 191–259; John E. Moore, *The Soviet Navy Today* (London: Macdonald and Jane's, 1975); Norman Friedman, "Soviet Union," in *Conway's All the World's Fighting Ships, 1947–1982,* ed. Robert Gardiner (London: Conway, 1983), 464–509; Siegfried Breyer und Armin Wetterhahn, *Handbuch der Warschauer Pakt Flotten/Manual of Warsaw Pact Navies* (Koblenz: Bernard & Graefe, 1984ff.).

61. Michael MccGwire, "The Background to Russian Naval Policy," *Brassey's Annual,* 1968.

62. Siegfried Breyer, "Grosskampfschiffbau in der Sowjetunion 1938–1950," in *Grosskampfschiffe 1905-1970: Eine Dokumentation in Bildern,* vol. 3: *Mittelmeeranlieger, Russland/Sowjetunion, Niederlande und ABC Staaten Lateinamerikas* (Munich: Bernard & Graefe, 1979), 139–69.

63. Jean Labayle-Couhat, *La Marine sovietique* (Paris: Editions Ozanne, 1957); Raymond Garthoff, *Soviet Strategy in the Nuclear Age* (New York: Praeger, 1958); V.D. Sokolovskii, *Voennaia strategiia* (Moscow: Voenizdat, 1962, 2d ed. 1963, 3d ed. 1968); *Soviet Nuclear Strategy,* ed. R.D. Crane (Washington, D.C.: Center for Stra-

tegic and International Studies, 1963); Sergei G. Gorshkov, *Morskaia moshch' gosudarstva* (Moscow: Voenizdat, 1976).

64. L.M. Yeremeev and A.P. Shergin, *Podvodnye lodki inostrannykh flotov vo vtoroi mirovoi voine* (Moscow: Voenizdat, 1962); *Blokada i kontrblokada: Bor'ba na okeano-morskikh soobshchenniakh vo vtoroi mirovoi voine*, ed. V.P. Bogolepov (Moscow: Voenizdat, 1966); V.A. Belli and K.V. Pen'zin, *Boevye deistviia v atlantike i na srednezemnon more, 1939–1945* (Moscow: Voenizdat, 1967); I.A. Bykhovskii, *Atomnye podvodnye lodki* (Moscow: Voenizdat, 1959).

65. Norman Polmar, *Soviet Naval Developments* (Washington, D.C.: Nautical & Aviation, 1979).

66. Michael MccGwire, ed., *Soviet Naval Developments: Context and Capability* (New York: Praeger, 1973); Júrgen Rohwer, *Superpower Confrontation on the Seas*, Washington Papers vol. 3, no. 26 (Beverly Hills: Sage, 1975).

67. Michael MccGwire, ed., *Soviet Naval Policy: Objecctions and Constraints* (New York: Praeger, 1976).

68. Bruce W. Watson, *Red Navy at Sea: Soviet Naval Operations on the High Seas, 1956–1980* (Boulder, Colo.: Westview, 1982).

69. Edward Wegener, *Moskaus Offensive zur See* (Bonn: MOV-Verlag, 1972, 2d ed. 1974).

70. Michael MccGwire and John McDonnell, eds., *Soviet Naval Influence: Domestic and Foreign Dimensions* (New York: Praeger, 1977); *Soviet Naval Diplomacy*, ed. Bradford Dismukes and James McConnell (New York: Pergamon, 1979); Hervé Coutau-Bégarie, *La Puissance maritime Soviétique* (Paris: Economica, 1983).

71. Robert G. Weinland, "Die 'Naval Diplomacy' der Supermächte im Yom-Kippur-Krieg Oktober 1973," *Marine-Rundschau* 79 (1982): 422–29, 543–50; Vasilii M. Grishanov, *Vse okeany riadom* (Moscow: Voenizdat, 1984); Jürgen Rohwer, "Das Ende der Ara Gorschkow," *Marine-Rundschau* 83 (1986): 88–97. For the Gorshkov quote, see his *The Sea Power of State*, 1–2.

72. Mikhail Gorbachev, *Perestroika. Die zweite russische Revolution*, trans. Ulrich Mohr (Munich: Droemer-Knaur, 1987).

73. N.V. Ogarkov, *Vsegda v gotovnosti k zashchite otechestva* (Moscow: Voenizdat, 1982); V.N. Chernavin, "Voyenno-morskoi flot. XXVII s"ezdu KPSS," *Morskoi sbornik*, (1986): 3–11; "O nekotorykh kategoriiakh voenno-morskogo iskusstva v sovremennykh usloviiahk," *Morskoi sbornik*, no. 9 (1986): 26–33, "Uchit' tomu, chto neobkhodimo na voinee," *Morskoi sbornik*, no. 1 (1987): 3–11, "Boevoi obespechenie deistvii sil' flota," *Morskoi sbornik*, no. 9 (1987): 16–22, "Vysokaia bditel'nost' i boevaia gotovnost' velenie vremeni," *Morskoi sbornik*, no. 2 (1988): 3–7.

6

The Second Arm and the Problem of Combined Operations: The Russian-Soviet Experience, 1853–1945

Jacob W. Kipp

The joint navy-army combat actions in seas adjacent to and upon the lakes and rivers within Russian and Soviet continental theaters of military actions have had a persistent importance to the development of Russian-Soviet naval art and provide a fundamental continuity during the age of industrial war between naval art as practiced by the czarist navy and that practiced by the Soviet Navy. While the nature of such combined operations (*sovmestnye operatsii*) has evolved with the industrialization of warfare, they have not lost their relevance from the Russian-Soviet perspective even today.[1]

Advocates of Russian naval power have traditionally associated such power with gaining and exploiting access to the sea, the development of maritime trade, the growth of the national economy, and the enlightenment of the nation.[2] However, in the use of naval power, Russian historical experience has placed greater emphasis on the struggle for, and protection of, such access than it has on the protection of national commerce upon the high seas. Cooperation between the army and the navy in the struggle for access became the hallmark of Russian naval history and gave that history a distinctly non-Mahanian cast.[3]

No greater authority than Peter the Great, the founder of Russia's new army and navy, need be cited to make this point. It was Peter in his naval regulations who observed that "a potentate with only an army has but one arm, but he with an army and a navy has both."[4] From a Russian geostrategic perspective these two arms could be employed most effectively when they acted in concert in a given theater of military actions during a given campaign. This implied a mutual connection between the actions of the army and naval units and some level of mutual support and interaction (*vzaimodeistvie*) providing a unified leadership toward a single goal.[5]

This chapter reflects the views and opinions of the author and should not be construed to represent those of the Department of the Army or the Department of Defense.

In his campaigns from the Second Azov Expedition (1696) down to the end of the Northern War (1721), the czar demonstrated a profound ability to employ his army and navy in such ways so that the two arms might best be utilized tactically to achieve decisive results. Under Peter there emerged attention to coastal and green-water forces that provided the organic tie between the sailing fleet of the line, which contested for command of the sea in the Baltic, and the army, which advanced in the Baltic provinces and Finland. Peter's galley fleet was a force configured to provide such linkage between naval and ground forces by conducting campaigns on the maritime flank of a continental theater of military action. Admiral Count Fëdor Aprakhsin's adroit utilization of all three forces (232 galleys, 27 ships of the line and 26,000 troops) made it possible for Russia to project power even to the shores of Sweden itself in 1719.[6]

Russian naval history during the age of sail is replete with episodic examples of successful and unsuccessful joint operations in the White Sea, the Gulf of Finland, the Baltic, Mediterranean, Adriatic, Aegean and Black seas, and the Pacific, where, by either design or necessity, commanders practiced close collaboration between the navy and army. In each theater conditions dictated that combat take place in coastal waters and in support of Russian advances along the adjoining coast or while naval forces were protecting the maritime flank of their army or their base of operations. In a few cases, when the diplomatic constellation permitted the deployment of a naval squadron in the Mediterranean, strategic cooperation developed in the form of two mutually supporting efforts by that squadron and Russian army and naval forces operating in the Balkans and the Black Sea.[7]

The degree of success in such joint actions largely depended on the leadership skills of the army and navy commanders within the theater, the organization of the combined actions of their forces, the integration of the operational plan, and their level of experience in conducting such actions. Because of the locale, the threat, and the forces available, Black Sea and Mediterranean naval commanders—especially Admirals F.F. Ushakov, D.H. Seniavin, A.S. Greig, M.P. Lazarev, and V.A. Kornilov—proved particularly adept at such cooperation. These talented commanders were, however, aware of the dangers to naval professionalism to be found in a fleet tied to Russia's coasts in times of peace and war. They supported the notion that long-range cruises were the best method of developing the skills and attitudes necessary for effective command.

Following the Crimean War, they linked such cruises to a posture of *guerre de course* (destruction of maritime commerce by attacks on merchant shipping), utilizing oceangoing fast frigates, corvettes, and clippers. This force deployed on distant stations in the Pacific, Atlantic, and Mediterranean was designed to deter England from entering into hostilities with Russia. Oceangoing ships had a strategic-diplomatic mission, but there was no explicit linkage between them and the coastal defense gunboats, ironclads, and light forces that were intended to operate in cooperation with the army in Russia's immediate maritime theaters. While recognizing the need for a strategic grand design to link the actions of all naval forces under one war plan, the Naval Ministry and the Main Naval Staff lacked the technical means and an approach that would permit the integration of various naval platforms into a single, unified tactical system. Nor did they possess the means of command and control to link the actions of such forces over great distances and prolonged time.[8]

Combined Actions and the Industrialization of Warfare

With the dawning of the age of steam and steel, the nature of such combat began to change and was the topic of war planning by the army's General Staff and the various naval fleet staffs and the Main Naval Staff.[9] The radical changes in naval tactics associated with weapons, propulsion, and protection led to speculation about shifts in the strategic employment of Russian naval forces.[10]

As the industrialization of war at sea radically reshaped the particulars of naval tactics, so the character of the cooperation between naval and ground forces in each theater also changed. In both the Crimean War (1853–1856) and Russo-Turkish War (1877–1878), ad hoc staff arrangements worked out after the start of hostilities proved adequate. In both cases it can be argued that Russia's strategic situation handicapped the execution of plans by forcing naval forces to operate in a context where the very limited resources of the Black Sea Fleet had to confront the real or threatened intervention of powerful maritime powers with naval forces far more numerous and modern than those that Russia could deploy in that theater.[11] In the face of difficult circumstances, Russian naval forces in both wars demonstrated an ability to improvise to meet theater requirements, whether providing the core of the sea and land defenses of Sevastopol against Allied attacks or denying the Turks the ability to reinforce their forces along the Caucasian frontier by destroying the covering fleet at Sinope. During the Russo-Turkish War, Russian naval officers continued the tradition of innovation and improvisation against a Turkish fleet that had an overwhelming superiority at sea in ships and modern ironclads. The Russian naval officers proved highly competent in three key areas: combined operations along the Danube, the passive defense of Russian ports and waterways, and active defense by merchantmen converted into cruisers carrying mine-torpedo launches.[12]

S.O. Makarov, who commanded the armed merchantman *Velikii Kniaz' Konstantin* in 1877–1878, had played a leading role in developing tactical forms for the employment of contact mines, spar-torpedoes, and self-propelled torpedoes, these being incorporated into the navy's plan for its role in the war with Turkey as the operational concepts of passive defense, active defense, river crossing operations, and the mine-artillery position. Such positions involved close cooperation between naval and ground forces. They were employed to deny an opponent access to a narrow body of water by providing for the combined action of mine fields, shore batteries, and surface ships to defend the barrier. The Russians had experimented with mines in the defense of Kronstadt during the Crimean War, were aggressive in their development of a mine warfare school in the 1870s, and pursued both minelaying and torpedo attacks during the Russo-Turkish War to neutralize the Turkish Black Sea Fleet and Danubian flotilla.[13]

Following the Russo-Turkish War, Makarov was appointed chief of the naval flotilla, which provided logistical support for General M.D. Skobelev's expedition against the Tekintsy in Central Asia. Makarov's own combat experience with advanced weapons technology shaped his own developing views of naval tactics and naval architecture, areas in which he made major contributions during his long and productive career.[14]

The rapid development of naval technology following the Russo-Turkish War and the appearance of new types of warships increased the complexity of combat at sea and required a much more integrated process of staff planning for the conduct of sustained combat. To some officers, this situation required the development of a more integrated staff system similar to that of the army's General Staff to plan and prepare for operations in the event of war. Such efforts were seen as a guarantee of more effective mutual support and interaction (*vzaimodiestvie*) among the emerging combat arms of the fleet, and the fleet as a whole with the ground forces. In 1888 Admiral I.F. Likhachev, one of a generation of reform-minded officers who had overseen the reconstruction of the navy following the Crimean War, advocated the transformation of the Main Naval Staff into a Naval General Staff that would assume all operational-strategic planning. Among its functions Likhachev included "complete knowledge of its own strength as well as its own weakness; timely study and establishment of strategic plans for the conduct of war and military actions; the establishment of programs of cruises and maneuvers."[15] The Naval Ministry, however, was in a period of stagnation and decline and steadfastly refused to address the issue.

More progress had been made in the area of professional education for senior naval officers. Vice-Admiral Makarov applauded the efforts of Admiral N.M. Chikhachov, the director of the naval ministry, to establish in 1895 a special class devoted to topics in naval science for commanders and senior lieutenants at the Nikolaev Naval Academy. For Makarov the explicit model for such a program was the U.S. Naval War College, founded in 1884.[16] In 1902 the Nikolaev Naval Academy conducted a strategic war game under the direction of Lieutenant Colonel N.L. Klado of the academy's faculty. The scenario called for a surprise Russian amphibious assault upon the Bosporus by the Black Sea Fleet and army units from the Odessa military district against Anglo-Turkish defenders. One of the critical weaknesses the umpires identified in their postgame assessment was the absence of a mechanism for strategic planning. They recommended as a solution "to create in the Main Naval Staff an operations section that would work out plans of campaigns, programs of shipbuilding, maneuvers, and deployments of naval forces." This operations section was to be closely tied with the operations sections of the various fleet staffs. Furthermore, they recommended that the staffs of naval expeditions be manned by naval general staff officers, educated along the lines of the Nikolaev Academy of the General Staff.[17]

Just prior to the outbreak of the Russo-Japanese War, the Main Naval Staff, which was an administrative organ of the ministry, did get a "strategic unit" staffed by twelve officers; however, this unit was only in the process of formation when war began and so had no influence on the conduct of naval operations in the Far East.[18]

Admiral Makarov's own speculations on naval tactics during this period underscored his emphasis on the interconnections between naval professionalism and technological innovation. First, he did not accept the idea that professional education could be left to on-the-job training, as had traditionally been the case. Commanders could no longer rely on common sense and estimates by eye. Instead, Makarov recommended intensive professional study of the new technologies and mastery of the art of employing them, a broad familiarity with writings in military and naval sciences, and a systematic study of military history in order to understand the complexity of war and to aid the commander in his most difficult decisions. He was fundamentally hostile to those who sought to find cook-book solutions based on historical cases. In this regard he had grave doubts about the primacy given to command of the sea as the first principle of naval strategy in Mahan and Colomb. At one point he flatly stated: "I personally am not an advocate of slavish adherence to principles." He criticized both Mahan and Colomb for drawing strategic conclusions about the primacy of the struggle for command of the sea on the basis of the experiences of sailing fleets. He warned, "their conclusions, which are based on examples from the age of sail, should not be taken as unconditionally true in our era of machines and electricity."[19]

Makarov's analysis of naval operations during the Sino-Japanese War (1894–1895) focused directly on the relationship between command of the sea and the demands of mutual interaction and support (*vzaimodeistvie*) as conditioned by the new technology of war. He fully supported Admiral Count Ito's decision to commit the Japanese fleet to the protection of the maritime flank of the Japanese Army as it deployed to Korea and moved into Manchuria. The deployment of the Chinese fleet into the ports of northern and southern China and the inability of Japanese naval forces to maintain a close blockade precluded effective execution of a national strategy tied to the immediate seizure of command of the sea. The priority of the theater support mission for Japanese strategy hinged upon the protection of the operational line connecting their supply bases with the campaign's objective, Port Arthur. Furthermore, the limitations of his own forces, which precluded a close blockade of all Chinese ports, and the vulnerability of his heavy forces to torpedo attacks in any close blockade, dictated a mutually interacting and supporting role for the navy. When the Chinese Navy did mount a major threat to the Japanese sea-lines of communication (SLOCs), Ito destroyed that force in the Battle of the Yalu. Ito continued his covering mission until Field Marshal Aritomo Yamagata's army took Port Arthur. Ito then employed his naval forces to protect an amphibious force to the second naval base in the north, where Chinese naval forces had concentrated. In this case, the Japanese threatened the base from the land side, while Ito's fleet attacked the Chinese warships with gunfire and torpedo attacks until the squadron and forts surrendered.[20]

In spite of Makarov's insights regarding the effectiveness of integrated war plans in such maritime theaters of war, little progress had been made by the outbreak of the Russo-Japanese War toward such an integrated effort in any potential theater. Now it was the Russian Army and Navy that had to defend Port Arthur from the Japanese. In 1894 Nicholas II had confirmed the Naval Ministry's recommendation to deploy major naval forces from the Baltic Fleet to the Far East. The Main Naval Staff debated the thorny problem of concentrating Russian naval power under various contingencies: war in the Baltic against a powerful German Navy, war over the Eastern question, and war with Japan in the Far East. Unable to build and sustain a fleet in the Far East, the Main Naval Staff sought a quick fix in the deployment of further forces to the Far East.[21]

Operational planning, however, was still in the hands of the commanders of the various fleets, squadrons, and flotillas. The command and staff system of the 1st Pacific Squadron at Port Arthur proved both inflexible and ineffective in moving from a peacetime to a wartime footing in spite of considerable intelligence that war was imminent. The Russian viceroy did not even think it necessary to inform the squadron commander, Vice-Admiral O.V. Stark, or its chief of staff, Rear Admiral V.K. Vittgeft, of the fact that the Japanese government had broken off diplomatic relations. Thus, Admiral Heihachiro Togo's light forces were able to achieve tactical surprise in their attack on the 1st Pacific Squadron as it lay in the outer harbor of Port Arthur. This initial torpedo attack under cover of darkness (three hits out of sixteen launched) damaged the battleships *Retvizan* and *Tsarevich* and the cruiser *Pallada*. This attack did not cripple the squadron. Admiral Togo had, however, with one blow reduced the 1st Pacific Squadron's immediate ability to contest for operational command of the sea in the theater. The Japanese success had an immediate effect on Vice-Admiral Stark's handling of his forces the next day when he fought an indecisive action with Togo's battle fleet outside Port Arthur. Vice-Admiral Stark's inability to break the Japanese blockade or seize back the initiative at sea from Admiral Togo undermined the squadron's confidence in its commanders and itself.[22]

Vice-Admiral S.O. Makarov shortly replaced Stark but commanded Russia's 1st Pacific Squadron at Port Arthur for less than a month before his death aboard the *Petropavlovsk*. In that short time, however, Makarov had a profound impact on the squadron and left a legacy upon which Russian naval reformers built after the war. One of his first steps was to improvise his own staff to coordinate naval operations, and he included in it a representative of the Russian General Staff to provide coordination with the army at Port Arthur.[23] Even while on his way to the Far East to his new command, Makarov looked to means to reinforce his squadron by ordering the disassembly and dispatch by rail of disassembled small torpedo boats (*minonostsy*) of the *Cyclone* class to Port Arthur. Makarov's approach to naval combat emphasized the role of the fleet in providing an active defense of Port Arthur, including sorties against the Japanese blockading force. Should an amphibious landing threaten, he proposed to deploy his squadron against it and pursue an aggressive program of countermining. Makarov asked to have several hundred copies of his book on naval tactics sent out to the squadron so that his fellow officers might better understand his tactical conceptions and grasp his overall operational plan. He was also very much interested in the employment of A.A. Popov's radio-telegraph for communications among vessels at sea and with their ports. Makarov hoped to draw the Japanese battle fleet into combat off Port Arthur, where fortified heavy artillery might support his squadron. Following Makarov's death, no Russian naval commander in the theater had the skill or initiative to counter Admiral Togo and his fleet.[24]

Vice-Admiral Z.P. Rozhdestvensky, who commanded the 2d Pacific Squadron on its long voyage to the Far East and disaster at Tsushima, improvised his own staff prior to the squadron's departure to the Far East.[25] Among the members of that staff—men who knew the severe combat limitations under which that jumbled collection of ships would have to face Togo's battle fleet—there were grave doubts about their own ability to direct the squadron in combat. One of the admiral's staff observed during the voyage, "At last I find myself at the very heart of that force which is supposed to save the nation's honor at sea, and I have no faith in it. What is to be done?"[26]

In their turn, officers of the Main Naval Staff were critical of the manner in which the Naval Ministry had approached the problems of organizing the squadron, determining its composition, and, finally, deciding on sending it around the world without any operational design. They were critical of Captain 2d Rank N.L. Klado's use of the media to promote the dispatch of both the oceanic capital ships and the coastal defense ironclads to the Far East, lamented the lack of leadership within the Naval Ministry, but sympathized with Admiral Rozhdestvensky's stoic acceptance of an impossible task.[27] The fall of Port Arthur and the subsequent destruction of the 2d Pacific Squadron set the stage for naval reform and reconstruction in the postwar period.

Naval Reform and Cooperation, 1906–1917

Following the Russo-Japanese War, naval planners had to confront a host of problems that defeat and destruction had revealed. Losses in ships and matériel crippled naval defenses in both the Baltic and Far East.[28] One area of reform that naval officers deemed critical was strategic and operational planning. In April 1906 the navy got its own Naval General Staff. Initially the staff was quite small: twenty-four officers, five senior noncommissioned officers, and fifteen enlisted men. It had six sections: three were operational and addressed the Baltic, Black Sea and Far Eastern theaters, and three were statistical, historical, and organizational-technical. The Naval General Staff concentrated in its hands operational planning, the navy's shipbuilding program, naval exercises and maneuvers, and the collection of naval intelligence.[29]

The emergence of new weapons systems and the improvement of older ones encouraged radical changes in naval tactics and forced naval officers to address the problem of sustained combat actions over larger areas, encompassing various types of weapons systems. These innovations included the submarine, self-propelled torpedo, wireless telegraph, and the airplane. During World War I were added four additional sections dealing with submarines, aviation, signal communications and intelligence, and rear services.[30]

In 1906 the Naval General Staff and the General Staff of the army embarked on joint planning for army and navy cooperation in three theaters: the Gulf of Finland and Baltic, the Black Sea, and the Far East. In each case, the two agencies agreed upon the major threat in theater and outlined the role of naval forces in a future conflict.[31] It is particularly noteworthy that the joint planning document underscored close army-navy cooperation in the Baltic (due to the overwhelming threat of German naval power) and in the Far East (due to the absence of effective naval forces in that theater). In the Black Sea, however, a juncture of imperialist ambitions and the ideology of the West's new navalism gave rise to an aggressive program of naval construction and political ambitions that aimed at securing for Russia control of the straits. Initially the Naval General Staff sought leverage in the Mediterranean by building up the capital ships of the Baltic Fleet with the idea of maintaining a portion of that force in the Mediterranean for purposes of presence and suasion. However, after repeated Balkan crises, increased German military influence in Turkey, and the decision of the Turkish government to expand its own naval forces, the naval minister in 1910 recommended and the government confirmed a major naval buildup in the Black Sea.[32]

In the decade separating the Russo-Japanese War and 1914, Russian naval planners addressed the problem of naval reconstruction and expansion. Their naval construction programs of 1908 and 1912 caused serious conflict within the government, pitting the War Ministry, its General Staff, and the Ministry of Finance against the Naval Ministry in a contest for scarce resources. Naval officers justified their construction programs in ideological terms, shaped by the new navalism and linked with the Petrine vision of naval power and national development.[33]

Russia's naval planners, like their contemporaries elsewhere, fell into the trap of mistaking the potential power of the new generation of capital ships, the dreadnoughts, for actual combat power and so created a navy radically out of balance between its potential combat power and its immediate combat missions in the various theaters. A.P. Shcheglov, a founder of the Naval General Staff, justified a navy that could compete with those of England and Germany on the grounds that such a force would provide deterrence (a Russian echo of Admiral Alfred von Tirpitz's "risk theory") and political incentives for other powers to make alliances with Russia.[34] Such arguments were silent about the role of such forces if deterrence failed.

Furthermore, in presenting their claims upon the treasury for scarce resources, the naval advocates competed for funds that the army desperately needed for its own modernization. In a heated competition for funds, army leaders criticized both the pace and extent of the shipbuilding program. The chief of Main Directorate of the General Staff, Lieutenant General A.Z. Myshlaevsky, warned: "The history of Russia teaches us that the fleet plays an auxiliary role in relation to the land army."[35] Naval officers responded that, unlike an army, a fleet and its infrastructure could not be created once war had begun.

After 1912 Russia was in the curious position of funding massive modernization of both its army and navy, creating alarm in the capitals of Central and Eastern Europe, and facing a period of vulnerability before these programs brought about a redressing of the military balance on the continent, which thoughtful Russian officers understood had to be their outcome.[36]

At the same time coordination between the Naval and army General Staffs broke down. After 1907 each staff was subordinated to its respective minister. This cut both chiefs of staff off from direct access to the czar and brought both staffs into the ministries' struggle for funds from the state budget. This rivalry contributed to a marked deterioration of their relations. On the eve of war, the Naval General Staff had not shared its war plans with the army General Staff. The army General Staff in its turn did not specify any missions for the navy under the "A" (primary war effort against Austria) or "G" (primary war effort against Germany) plans confirmed in May 1912. These oversights were especially important because of fundamental shifts in the plans for the conduct of initial operations. Down to 1910 the underlying assumption of war plans had been that Russian forces would stand on the defensive until mobilization could be completed. After 1910, however, on the basis of changes in the military situation and doctrine and in response to French pressures, the Russian Army was committed to the conduct of offensive operations even before mobilization had been completed. The Baltic and Black Sea fleets, however, concentrated their efforts on preventing amphibious landings.[37]

In March 1914, on the eve of hostilities, the naval minister and chief of the Naval General Staff had to admit that in spite of the long-term benefits of the naval construction programs, it would be impossible for the next few years to count on an effective battle squadron to contest for command of the Baltic.[38] Thus, the lack of time for completion of the construction programs, delays caused by reduced funding, and the priority given to capital ships over light forces and auxiliaries meant that Russian naval forces were not balanced at the start of hostilities. In this case, balance refers not to a mechanical relationship expressed by the number of ships in each class but to the correlation of available naval forces to the immediate missions that stood before the Baltic Fleet.[39]

The Naval General Staff, which had proved itself a powerful means of stimulating naval development over the preceding decade, did not, however, provide strategic-operational leadership for the navy once hostilities began. Several crucial factors combined to reduce its role. While charged with drafting war plans for employment of the fleets in case of hostilities, it did not have a role in operational execution because of the dominant assumption that a general European war would be short. Also, as a result of serious command and control problems in the Far East and the need to provide coordinated leadership in a vast theater of military action, the Russian General Staff had promoted a series of reforms culminating in the creation of the post of commander in chief as "the highest commander of all the land and naval armed forces designated for military actions" and a unified headquarters of the commander in chief (*Stavka*) to coordinate all military operations.[40] Below the *Stavka* was the intermediary level of command to coordinate the actions of a group of armies on a single axis within the theater (*front*). This new command arrangement raised the problem of where the Baltic and Black Sea fleets would fit into the structure of the high command.

The weakness of Russian naval forces in the Baltic precluded decisive, independent, strategic-operational actions by that fleet. With the start of hostilities, to the surprise of its commander, Vice-Admiral N.O. Essen, the Baltic Fleet came under the operational direction of the commander of the 6th

Army.[41] Only the day before the German declaration of war, the Naval General Staff had initiated the creation of a Naval Directorate, headed by Captain 2d Rank V.M. Al'tfater, the former chief of the Operations Section of the Naval General Staff, within the staff of the 6th Army. Al'tfater found both the army commander and his staff quite unprepared to undertake the direction of joint army-navy operations.[42] *Stavka* in its turn largely ignored the relations between the 6th Army and Baltic Fleet, confining its intervention during the first year of the war to limiting the freedom of action of Vice-Admiral Essen still further.[43]

At the same time the Black Sea Fleet was subordinated directly to the headquarters (*Stavka*) of the supreme commander, which had its own naval directorate under the command of Rear Admiral D.V. Neniukov, the former deputy chief of the Naval General Staff. The creation of such naval directorates, while necessary for operational coordination, took experienced officers away from the Naval General Staff and so further weakened its ability to provide leadership and coordination.[44]

In 1915, as a result of the deterioration of the situation along the Eastern Front, it became evident that the subordination of the Baltic Fleet to the 6th Army did not provide for an effective defense of the coast. In response to this situation, *Stavka* created a Northern Front and a Naval Directorate within it and subordinated the Baltic Fleet to that front.[45] This arrangement did not resolve the problem of army-navy cooperation in that theater. The commander of the Baltic Fleet, who saw his own role as that of commander in chief (CinC) of a Baltic theater of naval operations, sought to have his own forces placed directly under *Stavka*, as was the case with the Black Sea Fleet. This situation came to a head in January 1916 when *Stavka* created its own Naval Staff to coordinate the actions of both the Baltic and Black Sea Fleets and to guarantee cooperation between naval and ground forces in both theaters. The Naval General Staff was left with no operational-strategic role but concerned itself with the direction of the Caspian, Siberian, and Northern Flotillas.[46]

As Soviet authors have pointed out, the very scale of combat operations during the war, that is, the number of forces involved, the physical dimensions of maritime theaters, and the sustained nature of combat placed severe strains upon these command and control arrangements for the conduct of independent and joint operations. One Soviet writer has described the most typical combat actions at sea as

> destruction of enemy warships, amphibious landings, joint actions on the maritime flank of forces, disruption and defense of sea lines of communications, blockading activities, and mine laying. In those cases when combat actions at sea had operational objectives they grew into naval operations.
>
> The appearance of naval operations in the First World War was condi-

tioned by the quantitative and qualitative changes of the fleet. With the appearance of operations the necessity of working out a special theory of operational art was created. This theory was first created after the First World War.[47]

While the term *operational art* to describe such an intermediary level between tactics and strategy was not coined until the 1920s, problems associated with the command and control of independent and joint operations on both maritime flanks of the Eastern Front during World War I provided the most fertile ground for the development of naval interest in operations. This was particularly true of the Black Sea, where the correlation of forces in the theater permitted "naval operations against the shore."[48]

The series of events leading up to Turkey's entry into World War I in October 1914, including the arrival of the German battle cruiser *Goeben* and the cruiser *Breslau* in theater, complicated the Black Sea Fleet's war plans. As in the case of the Russo-Japanese War, the enemy seized the initiative at the start of hostilities. Enemy naval forces bombarded Sevastopol, attacked Odessa with torpedo boats, and sank the minelayer *Prut* but proved unable to cripple the Black Sea Fleet.[49]

The Black Sea Fleet's responses to war with Turkey were shaped by the nature of the theater, the correlation of forces in it, and the constraints that coal and oil imposed upon naval forces. Russian capital ships were coal fired and when operating from Sevastopol did not have the ability to maintain a sustained presence at the Bosporus to support either a close blockade or a major amphibious assault. Russia's newest destroyers, however, were oil fired and needed the fuel from Baku, which could reach them through the Transcaucasian port of Batumi. This situation had unforeseen consequences for naval operations in the Black Sea.

Independent naval operations took the form of a series of sorties, designed to cut Constantinople off from the coal fields of Anatolia. In the course of three years of war, the fleet carried out five bombardments with capital ships, twenty attacks with light forces, one attempt to close the port of Zunguldak by sinking block ships at its entrance, and several attacks by fleet hydroplanes. In addition, the fleet later engaged in aggressive mining operations at the entrance of the Bosporus and at other points along the SLOCs linking Constantinople and the coal fields. Destroyers, torpedo boats, and submarines carried out frequent raids, sinking merchantmen in the area. The campaign was not a sustained effort, however, and in the interval between each such effort, shipments of coal resumed.[50] The fleet did carry out demonstrations off the Bosporus in support of the Allied assaults upon the Dardanelles but achieved very little.

Although there were repeated proposals from *Stavka* for joint operations against the Bosporus in the form of an amphibious assault and against the

Anatolian coal fields by amphibious raid to wreck the ports and mine shafts, none of these efforts was undertaken. Only after the appointment of Vice-Admiral A.V. Kolchak as CinC Black Sea Fleet in late 1916 did preliminary planning for a Bosporus landing begin, but the February Revolution of 1917 and the deterioration of the fleet's combat power precluded such an effort. Unforeseen developments in joint operations along the Transcaucasian coastline of the Black Sea had set the stage for such planning.

In the Caucasian theater of military actions, in spite of the fact that little thought had been given to joint army-navy operations in the prewar period, the need for cooperation in defense of Batumi drew the commands of the Caucasian Army and the fleet into cooperation. Once hostilities began, both naval and army commands recognized the need for cooperation and the development of Batumi as a base of operations. From this forward base, the Black Sea Fleet could strike most effectively against the Anatolian coast. The fleet dispatched a light squadron and a battalion of naval infantry to strengthen the port's land defenses. However, since the fleet and the Caucasian Army both answered directly to *Stavka*, neither could impose its operational concepts on the other. Most of 1915 was taken up with stabilizing the defense, countering Turkish naval bombardments, and working out effective means of cooperation when the Caucasian Army had the opportunity to go over to the offensive on its maritime flank. This, in turn, depended upon the successful completion of its operation against the Turkish fortress at Erzurum.[51]

In early 1916 the Black Sea Fleet reinforced its Batumi detachment (Captain 1st Rank M.M. Rimsky-Korsakov, commander) with the battleship *Rostislav*, two gunboats, and two destroyers with orders to carry out a series of bombardments in support of the Caucasian Army's coastal detachment (15,000 men). These efforts proved quite successful, and the Turkish defense in this sector was thrown back in disarray. As a result of the lessons learned in the first bombardment, army-fleet cooperation improved substantially during the next bombardment of the Turkish position at the River Abu-Vitse. Shore-based artillery spotters with the coastal detachment provided excellent fire correction, and with its help the ship's heavy guns proved very effective in a counterbattery role. On February 16, 1916, gunfire of the battleship *Rostislav* smashed the Turkish trenches and strong points near the village of Iani-Kei. The destruction of that section of the line and the simultaneous flank attack by the detachment's forces on the Turkish right flank broke the defense. Russian ground forces went over to the pursuit but met no organized resistance for several days.[52]

These successes in joint operations stimulated much greater interest in the use of naval forces on the Turkish flank. General V.N. Liakhov, commander of the coastal detachment, advocated the employment of naval forces for tactical amphibious landings in the rear of the Turkish defense. Liakhov proposed to land 2,100 men and two mountain howitzers with horses after a powerful preliminary bombardment of the Turkish position. To transport the troops, the Black Sea Fleet chose to use the *El'pidifor*-class grain transports because of their shallow draft, maneuverability, and cargo space. Some of these vessels had been mobilized as fleet transports for coastal waters, and now they were pressed into service to transport the landing force from Batumi and land the force at sunrise. Minesweepers and destroyers escorted the transports on the voyage. Finally, reconnaissance of the landing site at Atina on the coast of Lazistan was carried out on March 4, 1916, with senior army and naval commanders taking part. The landing on the morning of the next day took the Turkish troops by complete surprise. Panic ensued among the defenders, and when the coastal detachment began its advance, it faced no organized resistance. Such flanking attacks were repeated five times during the advance across Lazistan between February and April 1916.[53]

The threat of Turkish reinforcements to its army in Turkish Armenia gave rise on the Russian side to consideration of ways of slowing down or stopping the arrival of such forces. The Black Sea Fleet command proposed a major operational amphibious landing against Trebizond. While the Caucasian Army under General N. N. Yudenich supported such an operation, *Stavka* had major reservations, most of them concerning the allocation of ground forces from other theaters to provide the landing force. When reserves did become available and after the successful tactical landings in Lazistan, *Stavka* did agree to some sort of joint operation against Trebizond. However, details of the operational plan were to be worked out by the staffs of the front and fleet. Once again there was no initial agreement. General Liakhov of the coastal detachment proposed three successive operations, each employing tactical landings. Vice-Admiral A.A. Eberhardt, CinC Black Sea Fleet, criticized this proposal on the ground that a succession of tactical blows would invite a Turkish counterstroke. Instead he proposed one short, decisive blow.[54]

In February, the Caucasian Army took the Turkish fortress at Erzurum, putting itself in a position to address the Turkish threat to its maritime flank. An agreement was reached between the Caucasian front and the Black Sea Fleet later in the month. The initial tactical successes gained by the Batumi and coastal detachments drove the overall operational design, in turn raising the issues of reinforcements for the coastal detachment to sustain its advance, and the form and substance of army-navy operational cooperation.[55]

The first step in such operational cooperation, by common agreement, involved sealifting two Cossack infantry brigades (18,000 men) from Novorossisk and landing them successfully at Rize. To protect the convoy of twenty-two transports from Odessa to Novorossisk and then to Rize, the Black Sea Fleet provided a covering force made up of two modern battleships, two cruisers, and six destroyers. Direct convoy protection from enemy submarines and destroyers was provided by the convoy escort composed of cruisers (including two that had been converted into seaplane carriers) and destroyers.[56]

Because of its scale and duration, the Russian command did not expect to achieve surprise during this operation and had to adopt measures to counter anticipated efforts by Turkish surface ships and submarines to disrupt the operation. The initial movement of troops was, however, a success. Having completed the sealift, the transport force and its direct escorts took up the task of landing the two brigades at Rize in late March. Although there were problems in this landing because of lack of training among the transport crews in amphibious landing techniques, the assault force went ashore quickly and in good order. When on the next day it became necessary to reembark one of the brigades without its matériel and land it at Khamurkan to stop a Turkish attack, the fleet was able to do that with dispatch.

The covering force, reinforced by the battleship *Panteleev* and a destroyer from Sevastopol, lent its fire to support the bombardment of Turkish positions along the Karadere River, which covered the eastern approach to Trebizond. There its heavy guns, along with those of *Rostislav*, proved effective against the fortifications. Prior to the bombardment both capital ships had taken on liaison officers from the coastal detachment's artillery to provide coordination. Using their maps and intelligence regarding the Turkish positions, those firing the ships' guns were able to conduct a systematic fire with correction provided by ship spotters and, by radio, army spotters ashore. The bombardment went on for two days.

Due to premature and uncoordinated attacks, the Russian ground forces suffered heavy casualties during the first day's fighting on April 14. However, the combination of shore and naval artillery and infantry assaults disrupted enemy defenses. Russian infantry penetrated the Turkish lines. Resistance broke on the second day. General Liakhov's forces were able to go over to a general pursuit. With the reinforcements provided by sealift, the Caucasian Army was able to renew its drive on Trebizond in cooperation with the fleet. The city fell on April 18.

The navy provided operational lift for two divisions (35,000 men) sent from the Sea of Azov to Trebizond to reinforce the defense and permit the transformation of the port into a secure forward supply base for the entire front.[57] At the same time the seizure of Trebizond denied the 3d Turkish Army a secure forward port linked to Constantinople. Finally, the light forces of the Black Sea Fleet were able to use Trebizond as a secure forward base to strike at Turkish SLOCs along the Anatolian coast.

These joint operations of the Black Sea Fleet and the Caucasian Army stimulated plans for similar amphibious landings in August 1916 in the Gulf of Riga. A force of three infantry divisions and a cavalry brigade (50,000 men) were concentrated in the Baltic ports, transports were dispatched to

Reval, Helsinki, Riga, and the islands of Moon Sound to lift the force, and the Russian squadron in the Gulf Riga made preparations to cover the invasion force, provide fire support to the landings, and block any effort by German naval units to intervene; however, this operation was never executed, in part because Rumania's entry into the war drew off available forces.[58]

The planning and execution of such joint amphibious operations had substantial importance for the development of later Soviet joint operations because they provided case studies for examining the processes of fleet-front cooperation in operations, where Russian forces were able to seize and hold the initiative on land and sea and to bring both arms quickly and decisively to bear according to an operational design that linked a succession of tactical successes into a strategic-operational design. It was also important because it represented a case where *Stavka* served as an honest broker between two coequals, the Black Sea Fleet and the Caucasian Army. Furthermore, the experience of joint operations in the theater suggested that the necessary skills needed for such cooperation could be worked out only over time and with serious effort at mutual training and education regarding operational concepts.

Soviet Naval Power and Combined Operations

The Revolution of 1917 brought a deterioration of Russian naval capabilities and a radicalization of the navy. Initial violence against officers in the Baltic Fleet created substantial distrust between officers and men. At the same time, however, the need to maintain some sort of defense of the Baltic coast to cover Petrograd did lead some naval officers into a cooperative arrangement with the Sailors' Committees and other revolutionary organs of power. This, in turn, set the stage for cooperation between some naval specialists and the new Bolshevik regime once it came to power and found that it had to confront the problem of creating a new military establishment and fight a civil war. Among those officers was Honored Professor of the Naval Academy of the Fleet Major General N.L. Klado, who wrote one of the first texts on strategy published by the Soviet government.[59]

Although most of the Baltic Fleet was brought back to Petrograd in the spring of 1918, the Soviet Republic had little immediate use for such naval power. In the course of the civil war, the combat power of the Baltic Fleet steadily deteriorated. After the Peace of Brest-Litovsk, part of the Black Sea Fleet was scuttled at Novorossisk rather than let it fall into German hands. What remained or was refloated fell into the hands of the Germans, the Allies, and finally the Whites during the civil war.[60]

For the Bolsheviks one of the first problems was the creation of a new military establishment to replace the old one swept away by the revolution.

Between December 1917 and February 1918 they disbanded the old army and navy and set about creating new executive agencies to manage military and naval affairs, replacing the War and Naval Ministries with People's Commissariats for Military Affairs and Naval Affairs. In the spring of 1918 they began actively recruiting former army and naval officers to serve as military specialists with the new Soviet forces, curtailed the committees that had so undermined order and discipline in the old army in 1917, and introduced the system of dual command by officers and commissars to increase military effectiveness and guarantee political reliability.[61]

With the start of the civil war, the Bolsheviks set about creating a new command structure to replace the old *Stavka*. V.I. Lenin and his colleagues created a unified, centralized national command authority, the Revolutionary Military Council of the Republic (RVSR), in September 1918 and the post of CinC of all the army and naval forces of the Republic.[62]

In the field the Bolsheviks subordinated all military force in a given sector to the front commander responsible for the conduct of the war in that area. Thus, during the civil war, naval power took the form of thirteen ad hoc sea, river, and lake flotillas organized around available personnel and hulls and subordinated to the military councils of the fronts where such forces fought. Soviet students of the role of naval forces in the civil war, including P. Stasevich, who became editor of the naval journal *Morskoi sbornik*, stress the improvised and joint character of their actions. Among the eleven missions Stasevich listed, "struggle with the enemy fleet" came last; fire support to ground forces in the attack and on the defense came first, followed by actions against the flanks and rear of the enemy, transport of troops, amphibious landings, and breakthroughs of the enemy front by advances along rivers. The civil war on the rivers, lakes, and seas was a war of small flotillas composed of riverine gunboats, armed launches, minelayers, minesweepers, shallow draught transports, light auxiliaries to carry ammunition, supplies, and fuel, and seaplane tenders to support naval aviation.[63]

In the course of the civil war, the quality of Red naval forces in the riverine war improved, as did the ability of the various front commands to exploit these forces. Front commanders who appreciated the value of army-navy cooperation often found the navy unable to hold up its end of the operation. Thus, in November 1920, when M.V. Frunze planned his final assault on Wrangel's forces in the Crimea, he had initially planned two pincer blows against the Crimea: one via Perekop Isthmus and the other via Chongar and the Arbat Needle. Frunze had planned the latter attack to come two days after the blow at Perekop. The success of the Chongar-Arbat attack hinged upon the ability of the Azov Flotilla to land forces in the rear of General Baron P.N. Wrangel's position via the Arabat Needle. However, because of ice at Taganrog, the Azov Flotilla could not put to sea, and Frunze fell back upon a single blow, which combined a frontal pinning attack at Perekop and a risky advance across the Sivash—a coastal marsh separating the Crimea from northern Tavrida on the Azov—to take the Perekop fortifications from the rear. He relied on favorable winds to keep the marshy waters of the Sivash fordable.[64]

Thus, even in the final year of the civil war, the Red Navy was able to gain command of only the Caspian Sea. The critical need to secure the shipment of oil from the Caucasian oil fields to Soviet Russia led to the decision by the RVSR to strengthen its Caspian Flotilla. In the spring of 1920, Britain's withdrawal as an active supporter of the Whites and revolutionary events ashore, especially an uprising in Baku, forced the sizable White flotilla to seek protection in the Iranian port of Enzeli. That flotilla, although interred by the British garrison at Enzeli, still constituted a "fleet in being" to threaten Baku and the republic's oil supply. Therefore, the Red Navy was given the authority to undertake a raid against the port with the objective of seizing or destroying the enemy flotilla. In spite of inadequate reconnaissance, uncertainties about the nature of the defenses, and inadequate time to organize a raid, the Volga-Caspian Flotilla was able to carry out a surprise tactical landing (2,000 men) supported by naval gunfire. The first salvo from the ships' guns hit the British garrison headquarters, paralyzing the defense and preventing an organized defense against the landing. After two days of intermittent fighting and negotiations, the British commander surrendered the port and the White flotilla, thus ending any threat to the republic's oil supply and giving the Soviet Navy command of the Caspian Sea[65] The civil war thus provided young Soviet officers with a wealth of practical experience in combined operations with the Red army.

Interwar Naval Theory and Cooperation

With the end of the civil war and the suppression of the Kronstadt mutiny in 1921, the fortunes of the Soviet Navy reached an all-time low. The Soviet economy was in ruins; the nation's shipyards were in utter disorder; the remaining capital ships were little more than floating batteries; and the political reliability of the navy was suspect. In this context the Communist party and the Soviet state embarked on Lenin's New Economic Policy (NEP) with its concessions to revive trade and agriculture. National economic recovery depended upon the demobilization of the armed forces and their reorganization to provide a mix of forces that would sustain a credible defense while not imposing a major strain upon an already overtaxed national economy. Hand in hand with demobilization and limited resources went military and naval reform.[66]

As Robert Herrick has pointed out, Soviet naval theory in the interwar period developed around a sharp debate between two schools, the young and the old.[67] The old school included those officers who supported the classical concept of sea power that had guided the Naval General Staff in the prewar period. Former czarist naval theorists in Soviet service remained Mahanian in their emphasis on capital ships and independent missions for the navy. Among them were students of Nikolai Klado, who as a teacher at the Naval Academy from 1895 to 1917 had been one of the most powerful spokesmen for the new navalism in Russia. From 1917 until his death in 1919 he had headed that institution. Klado had a profound impact on both the Naval Academy and the research regarding the naval history of World War I. Among the most outstanding spokesmen was the naval historian M.A. Petrov, whose work on Russia's naval preparations for World War I emphasized the failure of the czarist government to create an oceanic navy.[68] Petrov addressed the problem of cooperation and army-navy combined operations in terms of coastal defense and not offensive operations.[69]

Other naval officers, notably N. Novikov, placed greater stress upon combined operations as one of the most decisive forms of offensive combat and emphasized the need to learn from the problems encountered during World War I. Young Soviet naval commanders who had fought in the civil war were predisposed by their own experiences to support such a concept of *little war*.[70] Limited resources, the nature of probable opponents, problems of naval education and political indoctrination, and combat experience thus combined in the 1920s to place greater emphasis upon coastal defense and joint operations, in which light forces, submarines, and naval aviation had pride of place.[71]. V.I. Zof, chief of the naval forces, made this point in his survey of the international situations, the immediate threat confronting the Soviet Union, and the missions of Soviet naval forces in 1925.[72]

With the interpenetration of Marxism-Leninism into Soviet military writings and education during the NEP, the *young school* mounted a critique of Klado as a philosophical idealist who emphasized "eternal and unchanging principles of war" at the expense of the dialectics of armed conflict that had its base in historical and dialectical materialism. The young school contended that "eternal truths" stripped the observer of the ability to foresee by transforming military thought into aphorisms and abstractions, robbing it of a concrete sense of time and space. In this critique, military science's essential topic was the study of future war (*budushchaia voina*), and a premium was to be placed upon systematic exposition under the slogan "to know is to foresee."[73]

The young school found powerful support for its position among the most talented commanders of the Red Army. Both former czarist military specialists (*voenspetsy*) and young Red commanders agreed that one of the compelling lessons of the arms race before the world war had been the excessive expenditures on naval forces by continental powers, including Russia. These officers argued that the key to military success was the intense study of the possibilities of future war, which included addressing political, social, economic, and technological factors that would shape such a contest. In the late 1920s Soviet military officers argued over whether such a war would be dominated by attrition or decisive maneuver, but they agreed that technological changes now demanded working out a correct correlation among not only the army and navy but now also the "air fleet."[74]

Two of the most telling commentators on this subject were A.A. Svechin and B.M. Shaposhnikov. Svechin wrote the first Soviet work on military strategy and coined the term *operational art*. Shaposhnikov addressed the issue in his three-volume study of the role of the General Staff in war, in which he identified that organ as the "brain of the army." Shaposhnikov was concerned about the costs of naval forces. Naval construction cost "devilish money," and therefore one had to build with economy to meet specific missions. "Luxury can not be tolerated."[75] Shaposhnikov, who became the father of the Soviet General Staff, not only shaped the general approach that military and naval analysts brought to the study of future war but also had a close relationship with Stalin at a time when Stalin had already established his political hegemony within the party and the state apparatus.[76] Shaposhnikov's approach to the question of future war set the context for a general discussion of this issue.

In 1929, as part of a series of articles devoted to all aspects of future war, V. Pereterskii discussed the major trends affecting "navies' combat means in a future war." He assumed that a future war would be a total war, which would require the mobilization of the entire state, population, and economy. He went further to assert that the technological potential of the belligerents would have a decisive impact on the course and outcome of the struggle. He anticipated that such a conflict would be a war to exhaustion. Naval operations would be subordinated to the struggle ashore, which would be decisive:

> Thus the naval front according to our views will be only part of the general front of armed conflict, of the war's front, i.e. a continuation of the land front, so that it must be united with it by a general command, by a common plan of direction, and therefore all operation taking place in it must be co-ordinated and linked with the operations taking place on the land front.[77]

Under the influence of a group of highly talented and thoughtful young commanders, the decade 1926–1936 witnessed the development of a Soviet conception of operations, which, emphasizing both mass and maneuver, stressed successive deep operations by tank and mechanized forces supported by air armies.[78] The center of gravity of Soviet combat power would be its ground-air combination, and the navy was assigned to a supporting role.

It was not an accident that the publication of combat regulations (*boevoi ustav*) for the navy in 1930 and 1937 followed in the wake of the appearance of new field regulations (*Polevoi ustav*) for the Red Army. The 1930 combat regulations (*Bu-30*) stated that "modern combat conditions at sea demand from naval forces . . . the closest operational mutual support and cooperation (*vzaimodeistvie*) with the ground forces of the Red Army" and tactically called for the concentration of all forces on the decisive axis.[79] In these regulations the Soviet Navy appeared as an integral part of the Red Army:

> *The Naval Forces of the RKKA* [Workers' and Peasants' Red Army], being component and indivisible part of the Red Army, defending together with it workers' interests, *must be prepared for the daring and decisive conduct of struggle with the enemy at sea,* directed toward the defense of the coasts of the USSR, by cooperation in the operations of the ground forces of the Red Army and by supporting them from the sea as well as on the river and lake systems.[80]

Even with Stalinist industrialization of the First and Second Five-Year Plans, naval development down to 1938 proceeded more slowly than that of land forces and emphasized the acquisition of modern light forces, submarines, naval aviation, torpedo boats, and destroyers. Between 1927 and 1941, Soviet shipyards laid down the hulls of 533 warships, of which 312 entered service. More than two-thirds of the ships entering service (206) were submarines. By 1941 naval aviation contained over 2,500 aircraft.[81]

In late 1937, at the time of the establishment of the People's Commissariat of the Navy and when the Soviet General Staff was busily preparing its threat estimates to guide the military requirements of the Third Five-Year Plan, the newly appointed People's Commissar of the Navy (NARKOMVMF), P.A. Smirnov, a political commissar with party duties in both the Red Army and Navy, dramatically announced a commitment to create a powerful oceanic navy.[82]

With Stalin's purge of the military in full swing, it appeared that the Soviet Navy was about to shift its emphasis from light forces to a capital ship fleet, as advocated by the old school. Viacheslav Molotov's proclamation of an oceanic navy as a national priority was given prominent play in *Morskoi sbornik*.[83] It seemed for a time as if the navy was in the process of regaining the independent status it had enjoyed under czarism.

German naval attachés in Moscow took note of this new line, described it as a 180 degree turn in Soviet naval strategy, and considered it a victory for classical naval theory. The German naval attaché did note that the polemics between the old and young schools were presented to Soviet naval officers as a competition between two sinister groups, composed of enemies of the people, who were striving to subvert the maritime defenses of the Soviet state.[84] The new position was described as Stalinist and therefore ideologically correct.

German naval analysts were at a loss to explain such charges of betrayal and subversion. They sensed, however, that the harsher criticisms were aimed at the young school. Its members had overemphasized light forces (submarines and naval aviation), had underestimated the value of capital ships, and had stressed attrition as opposed to the single decisive naval engagement as the way to victory.[85] The German naval attachés could not explain the set of circumstances that led to such a radical shift in naval policy in so short a time.

During these years, among the darkest in Soviet history as a result of the purges and the chaotic situation among civilian and military cadres, it is possible to identify certain objective conditions that contributed to the shift to an oceanic navy. By late 1937 the Spanish Civil War was already into its second year. For over a year Soviet naval advisers as "volunteers" had taken part in the struggle on the Republican side. The most important task for the naval forces of the Spanish Republic became the protection of its SLOCs, especially those with the Soviet Union, from which flowed the arms and supplies to sustain the Republican forces in their struggle against Franco's rebels and their Italian and German supporters. N.G. Kuznetsov, one of the Soviet naval advisers to see the limitations of the republic's navy, returned to Moscow in August 1937 with an appreciation of the risks involved in fighting a powerful opponent with the means of a little war and recognized the importance of heavy surface combatants, ship air defense, and naval aviation. Kuznetsov became aware of what might be achieved by their immediate and decisive use.[86]

At the same time the political-military situation in the Far East was becoming tenser. Six years after its conquest of Manchuria, Japan attacked the Chinese Republic. Relations between the Soviet Union and the Japanese empire deteriorated steadily as the Soviet Union increased its military support for Mongolia and the Chinese Republic. In 1932 the Soviet Far Eastern Flotilla had been reorganized as a third fleet, the Pacific Fleet, and by 1937 it was the largest Soviet fleet in terms of personnel.[87] At the same time, however, as both naval and army commanders in the Far East were aware, Soviet naval forces were no match for the Japanese Navy and would have to contest them using submarines and land-based naval aviation.

War not only appeared more likely, but it also clearly had assumed the character of a great war, involving a contest with a coalition of major capitalist powers, particularly Germany and Japan. A viable defense hinged on the ability of the various arms of the navy to cooperate and upon the cooperation between the army and fleet.[88] During the fighting around Lake Khasan in the summer of 1938, Kuznetsov's Pacific Fleet took an active hand in supporting the Soviet ground forces, creating a Naval Detachment of Special Assignment composed of merchantmen, tugs, fishing boats under escort by motor torpedo boats (MTBs), a destroyer, and a coastal defense craft.[89]

Among those forces involved in the escorting of troop convoys were the vessels of the 7th Naval Brigade, commanded by Captain 3d Rank S.G. Gorshkov.

In 1938–1939 it appeared that the Soviet-Japanese rivalry might escalate from minor border clashes into full-scale war. This situation and the menace of German naval power after 1936 created a need for a radical expansion of both the Pacific and Baltic fleets. At the Eighteenth Party Congress in 1939, Kuznetsov, who had assumed the post of CinC Pacific Fleet, stated: "We must build various classes of vessels conforming to our naval theaters and conforming to our probable opponents."[90] As V. Danilov has pointed out, the NARKOMVMF had no independent role in the actual military assessment of the threat; all questions relating to operational and mobilization plans were the province of the General Staff of the RKKA.[91] B.M. Shaposhnikov, its newly appointed chief, reversed his position of the late 1920s opposing naval expansion.

The General Staff's threat assessment for the Third Five-Year Plan addressed the need for an oceanic navy and called for the construction of modern battleships, heavy cruisers, and aircraft carriers as the only means of extending the Soviet state's naval defenses beyond its immediate coastal waters. At the same time the program far exceeded the capacity of Soviet shipyards to meet the demands. Attempts to purchase modern combatants abroad did not meet with great success. This was a long-term program, and what haunted Soviet naval planners most was whether war would come in twenty months rather than twenty years. Kuznetsov observed in his memoirs:

> In such circumstances, as experience showed, to make long-term plans of naval construction was, of course, risky. A great navy is not only ships but also naval bases, docks, ship-repair facilities, warehouses, training institutions, and much more. The creation of all this demands a great deal of time and tremendous resources. The program, of course, could not be laid out even in one five-year plan.[92]

Shortly after the party congress, Kuznetsov was named first deputy commissar and then, in April 1939, commissar of naval affairs. In this post he worked closely with Stalin, Shaposhnikov, and A.A. Zhdanov in bringing to life this naval construction program.[93] Events in Europe and the Far East shortly called this long-term program into question. In October 1940 after the German victory in France and the failure of the Germans to invade England, the Soviet government suspended the construction of all large combatants and concentrated on destroyers, submarines, torpedo boats, and auxiliaries, which could be completed in a short time.[94]

The anticipated creation of an oceanic navy encouraged serious reconsideration of the basic problems of operational cooperation between the army and navy that had been at the heart of the naval theory of the young school. I.S. Isakov, who had taken part in the Enzeli operation of 1920 and rose to prominence in the navy in the interwar period to become chief of staff of the naval forces of the Baltic Sea in 1935, addressed this topic in several essays published in the prewar period. The most important of these was "The Navy in a Future War," published in *Komsomol'skaia pravda* in January 1938. Isakov, who had experience with amphibious operations and had written on the topic, took the German amphibious assault upon the islands of Ezel' and Moon in the Gulf of Riga during the fall of 1917 as the model for such operational amphibious landings. He described them in the following terms:

> One should consider the amphibious operation as one of the more charac-teristic operations in a future war. This type of combat is quite complex since here the cooperation of land units with naval [units] is necessary. In these battles the troops selected for landing, transports to carry them, destroyers and escort vessels to protect the transports at sea from submarine attacks, mine sweepers to clear path through mine fields, and aviation to conduct reconnaissance must take part. Beside this, these operations require the par-ticipation of cruisers, which along with gunboats will provide fire support with their artillery for the landing. The basic maneuver forces, composed of a squadron of capital ships and heavy aviation, must protect the landing from the enemy's decisive counterstroke.[95]

The same description would have fit the operations of the Black Sea Fleet at Lazistan and Trebizond as well. Modern capital ships were thus integrated into one of the most important combined operations. Isakov made no men-tion of specially designed landing craft and so seemed to hark back to the improvisations that had proved successful in the Black Sea. In fact, it re-mained to be seen whether a modern combined-arms force could rely on such wartime conversions for amphibious operations.

Isakov also considered operations to counter enemy amphibious assaults (*protivodesantnaia operatsiia*) as a matter of combined action. But in that case the crucial role fell to submarines, aviation, and the concentration of all means of coastal defense against the enemy during the landing and when ashore. Isakov listed several independent missions for naval forces, especially blockade and protection of SLOCs, but did not emphasize the single decisive naval engagement between battle fleets. Instead Isakov stressed two intercon-nected and mutually affecting forms of naval combat: a succession of episodic operations of high intensity, organized around the theater commander's intent and executed according to his plan and, at the same time, the day-to-day tasks of combat support associated with mine and antimine warfare, submarine and an-tisubmarine warfare, and naval and air reconnaissance.[96] Shortly after the publi-cation of this article, Isakov became deputy NARKOMVMF.

While Isakov's focus was upon operational-tactical combined actions like those of the German Navy in the Baltic or the Russian Navy in the Black Sea, other Soviet naval officers saw in the new oceanic navy the potential for a strategic coup de main. A.V. Nemitts, a graduate of the czarist Naval Academy, Red naval specialist during the civil war, CinC Soviet Navy in 1921–1923, and then professor of naval art at the Military Academy from 1924 to 1940, was more ambitious in his proposals for cooperation between the army and navy. Nemitts identified three strategic missions for the navy to influence the course and outcome of a war: a naval blockade to starve the national economy or cut off the state rear from its fighting army, sealift of an army to destroy the enemy army or to counter such actions by an opponent, and operational-tactical cooperation of units of the fleet with the army when they act on a single field of battle. Whereas Isakov had emphasized the latter form of cooperation, Nemitts called attention to the possibility of a strategic blow.

Reviewing Germany's geostrategic situation in 1914, Nemitts stated that its armed forces were incapable of delivering a decisive blow against either France or Russia. Instead the Soviet naval officer saw a German opportunity in 1914 for a surprise amphibious assault by 200,000 troops on England itself. Nemitts based his case for such an option on British politico-military vulnerability and the existing dispositions of naval forces.

Nemitts, in fact, was proposing a succession of deep operations that culminated not in Paris but in London. The first stage was an advance through Belgium, creation of a defensive line on the Somme, seizure of the French ports on the English Channel, then by a sortie of the High Seas Fleet, and finally the dispatch of the German transport fleet to the Channel ports. The success of such a combined operation hinged upon surprise.

Once the transports and warships were in the channel, Nemitts proposed that the German High Seas Fleet begin laying two powerful mine barriers to the north and south. The German Navy would then take up a defensive position to cover its invasion fleet and invite the Royal Navy to break through such a position. Nemitts expected that the successful landing of the first army would be followed by a second and then a third wave, until Germany had a force of 600,000 in England.[97]

While the Nemitts proposal bordered on the foolhardy, his point for a Soviet naval audience was that there could be strategic-operational circumstances where combined actions of army and fleet went beyond the direct support of the maritime flank of a front. Reduced to basics, Nemitts was arguing two points. First, "for a successful war by a great power a first-class navy is as necessary as a first-class army." Second, he abandoned one of the most fundamental principles of naval strategy: that struggle for command of the sea preceded and was a precondition for any such attempts to use SLOCs for the transport of an invading army to a hostile shore. Against those who saw the chances of success too limited to justify the risks, Nemitts pointed to Peter the Great at Gangut taking a calculated risk and winning.[98]

Nemitts wrote months before the Wehrmacht's (armed forces') victories in Norway, the Low Countries, and France would place on the agenda of the Kriegsmarine (navy) the very problem he had raised in his article. German naval planners, while quite daring in the planning and execution of the Norwegian operation, when confronted with the grave risks involved in such an invasion of England and the real problems of bringing about cooperation among the army, Luftwaffe (air force), and Kriegsmarine, were not so willing to take such a grave risk. The German Navy of 1940 was not the kaiser's navy of 1914, and its heavy losses during the Norwegian campaign had taxed its resources to the very limits. However, Nemitts would have answered that its thinking was dominated by the same "unfounded caution" that had condemned it to inaction in 1914 and so had created the opportunity for England to apply its naval blockade and the steady strangulation of the German economy.[99]

Military operations in 1940 seemed to confirm the importance of joint operations. Norway, even if it lacked the decisiveness of a cross-channel invasion, was the sort of high-risk venture Nemitts had recommended. Soviet naval officers saw in the Dunkirk evacuation confirmation of the need to plan and prepare for joint operations. V.A. Belli informed Soviet naval officers that the lessons of Dunkirk were the need for "close mutual interaction and support (*tesnoe vzaimodeistvie*) of the army, navy, and aviation" in carrying out such an evacuation; the decisiveness of command of the air over the operational area; the critical nature of favorable geostrategic conditions; the exceptional difficulties associated with the evacuation of not only men but also combat matériel and equipment; and the absence of effective mutual interaction and support by German naval, ground, and air forces in countering this evacuation.[100]

The decisive German victories in the first year of the European war and the problems observed in all branches of the Soviet armed forces during the Winter War with Finland set in motion a hasty set of reforms to improve combat capabilities and to prepare for what was recognized at the very top of the Soviet state and military as a decisive confrontation with Hitler's Germany. Both Nazi Germany and the Soviet Union were maneuvering to prepare for a war that seemed only a matter of time.

Cooperation and Combined Action during the Great Patriotic War

In that same period German naval officers began to consider the implications of an attack on the Soviet Union and a wider war. Grossadmiral Erich

Raeder, CinC Kriegsmarine, reports in his memoirs that he was kept unin-formed of the initial planning for an attack on the Soviet Union.[101] However, the chief of the naval war staff, Admiral Otto Schniewind, ordered a study by that staff to address the question in late July 1940, when Operation Sea Lion was still a possibility. The naval war staff viewed England as its primary enemy and saw the need to conclude that war before any operation against the Soviet Union. It acknowledged a fear that German hegemony on the con-tinent would never be secure until the question of the Soviet Union had been resolved.

One of the war aims that the naval war staff emphasized was the trans-formation of the Baltic into a German *mare nostrum*. The military focus of attention was the destruction of the Baltic Fleet. This fleet was seen as aimed directly against Germany, and the staff noted that Soviet territorial gains at the expense of Finland and the Baltic states had made it a more serious threat. The naval war staff proposed to destroy that fleet by an advance up to Lake Ladoga, where German and Finnish troops would meet. Robbed of its bases, the Baltic Fleet would lose its combat power and could be dealt with easily. They were willing to consider a surprise U-boat attack upon Soviet capital ships even before the start of hostilities if responsibility for such an action could be denied.[102]

The naval war staff considered that the navy's contribution to victory in the east would be primarily light forces, while major responsibility for the operation remained with the German ground and air forces.[103] The staff study provided a set of objectives in the Baltic littoral with which these forces would have to deal but offered very little help from the navy. Furthermore, the staff's considerations totally ignored the Soviet Black Sea Fleet, which, although not a threat to Germany proper, was uncomfortably close to a key source of the Reich's oil supply in Rumania. Although a naval mission was sent to Rumania in May 1941, German naval planning did not resolve the problem of dealing with the Black Sea Fleet.[104]

From the first signal sent out by Admiral Kuznetsov placing Soviet naval forces on a high state of alert on the night of June 21–22, questions of co-operation (*vzaimodeistvie*) and combined action figured prominently in the employment of Soviet naval power.[105] While the Baltic and Black Sea fleets were quite evenly matched in their combat power (capital ships, light surface forces, submarines, and aviation), the operational-strategic situation of the Black Sea Fleet was far more favorable, and this permitted it from the first month of the war to engage in both independent and combined operations of greater operational-strategic importance. Unlike the Black Sea Fleet, which had a well-developed network of bases throughout the depth of its theater, the Baltic Fleet had just added a set of forward bases in the Finnish Gulf (Tallinn and Hango) and in the Baltic (Riga, Libau, and on the islands of the Gulf of Riga) to support its permanent bases at Kronstadt and Leningrad.

During this period, the most critical combined operations for the Red Banner Baltic Fleet were the stubborn defense of these bases and, after the evacuation of Tallinn, the employment of fleet personnel and weapons to bolster the land and sea defenses of besieged Leningrad.[106] The Northern Fleet, which had been organized as a fleet only since 1937, was undergoing expansion in the wake of the Soviet-Finnish Winter War, so its combat power and support infrastructure were severely limited at the start of the war.

At the time of the German attack, the Pacific Fleet was the most powerful Soviet naval force in terms of its strike assets. It deployed 1,183 combat aircraft, 91 submarines, and 135 torpedo boats. Only its air assets could be moved quickly and with some ease to reinforce the Soviet forces fighting in European Russia.[107] However, even these could not be redeployed in large numbers until it was clear that Japan did not intend to join in the attack upon the Soviet Union. In the first six months of the war, it appears that over 600 aircraft and crews were transferred from the Pacific Fleet to the front.[108] The Pacific Fleet and Amur Flotilla provided the manpower to staff twelve of the twenty-five naval rifle brigades formed in 1941.[109] Transfer of surface warships and submarines from the Pacific to the Northern Fleet began in 1942. The navy also had four flotillas with limited combat means: the newly formed Danubian, Caspian, Pinsk, and Amur flotillas.

In prewar planning for combined operations involving ground, air, and naval forces, primary leadership was entrusted to the Soviet General Staff, which assumed the role of "brain" of the armed forces and acted as "the highest organ of control of the country's armed forces."[110] In practice this meant that it worked out the strategic war plans and then entrusted to the staffs of the coastal military districts and the staffs of the appropriate fleets the specific plans for the use of covering forces and the combined defense of the coast. Soviet military doctrine assumed that such a defense would incorporate immediate and repeated counterstrokes on the enemy's maritime flank. These actions could be independent actions by fleet units or combined actions involving army and naval units.[111]

With the start of hostilities, the NARKOMVMF, with the concurrence of the Main Naval Council, ordered the initiation of the operations outlined in each fleet's war plans. Mine barriers were laid, unrestricted submarine warfare initiated, a convoy system introduced, and naval direction provided for surface attacks on enemy warships and merchantmen at sea. The individual fleet commands did not have the authority to begin attacks on airfields, ports, and other targets in enemy territory. Once the *Stavka* of the Supreme High Command of the Soviet Armed Forces was organized, it assumed responsibility for such decisions regarding the employment of the fleets.[112]

The surprise, weight, and speed of the German offensive quickly created demands by the ground forces for naval support in stemming the tide. The tempo of these initial operations placed a tremendous strain on centralized decision making. The very scale of warfare made it imperative that front and fleet commanders be given more immediate and timely guidance than *Stavka* could provide. As a partial and only marginally effective solution to this problem, the State Defense Committee created three intermediary instances of command between *Stavka* and the fronts and fleets. These "strategic directions"—northwestern, western, and southwestern—were headed by their own CinCs with a supporting staff. The northwestern strategic direction had under its control the Baltic and Northern fleets, and the southwestern had the Black Sea Fleet. The northwestern CinC, in turn, placed the two fleets under the operational control of the commander of the northern front. When that front was split into the Karelian and Leningrad fronts in late August 1941, the Northern Fleet was subordinated to the former and the Baltic to the latter front.

These arrangements brought some improvement in the conduct of coastal defense, which included fire support for Soviet forces, prevention of enemy amphibious assaults, and defense of naval bases. Neither naval nor army commanders were experienced in such combined actions on such a scale, and as Soviet officers admit, the process of working out the organization of cooperation to support combined actions took time and practice. A crucial step in this process was the appointment of naval representatives to the staffs of the appropriate directions, fronts, and armies.[113]

Such subordination of the fleets to the directions and fronts did not preclude either independent actions by the fleets or proposals for combined actions initiated by naval commands and staffs. Independent operations that were initiated by the Main Naval Staff and had the endorsement of the General Staff and *Stavka* included the decision to send naval heavy bombers from Ezel' and Moon Island airfields against Berlin in August 1941.[114] While hardly a serious threat to Germany's war potential, these strikes provoked the German High Command into assigning Luftwaffe, army, and naval units to attack Moon, Ezel', and Dago islands in September. After a month of fighting, German efforts opened the Gulf of Riga to German shipping but drew away vital air, naval, and ground forces from operations against Leningrad and Kronstadt.[115] It does not appear that these minor raids on Berlin had any impact on the German decision to pause and bomb Moscow while the German High Command shifted its main effort to the Ukraine.

With the start of hostilities, the Black Sea Fleet initiated similar strikes by air, surface, and submarine forces against Rumania, suggesting that such attacks were part of the Soviet war plan; however, initial losses and concern over a German amphibious threat brought those initial efforts to an end.[116] Bomber units from the Black Sea Fleet mounted day and night attacks on the oil facilities at Constanta between June 23 and 25. These unescorted attacks inflicted significant damage on the port facilities, oil farms, cracking plant, and vessels and drew German fighters back to the defense of this high-value target. From June to August Black Sea naval aviation mounted air raids against Constanta, Ploesti, and other targets, including eighteen small-scale raids on the storage tanks and refineries at Ploesti.[117] In late July the State Defense Committee ordered a renewed series of air attacks upon Ploesti and the railroad bridge and pipeline across the Danube at Chernavod during the first half of August. Four separate raids were mounted between August 5 and 18. This offensive, which involved only twenty-five sorties by DB-3 naval bombers and other specialized aircraft, was called off after the fourth raid because of the mounting threat to Odessa and the Crimea.[118]

In the Baltic and Black Sea, independent air, surface, and submarine operations were designed to provoke German counteractions that would influence the development of subsequent operations. Black Sea operations forced the Germans to redeploy fighters and flak guns to increase the protection of the Rumanian oil fields and helped to prod the German High Command into shifting the direction of subsequent operations from the Smolensk-Moscow axis into the Ukraine, where Hitler proclaimed the capture of the Crimea, the Soviet Union's unsinkable aircraft carrier, as an operational objective.[119]

In the desperate fighting of the first period of the Great Patriotic War (June 1941–November 1942), cooperation took the form of naval support for front and army defensive positions and counterattacks. Frequently ground force units were subordinated to naval commanders with the creation of port defense districts as at Odessa, Tallinn, and Sevastopol.[120] Initial combined actions by naval, air, and army units suffered from a lack of understanding by the commanders and staffs of the real capabilities and needs of the other branches of the armed forces. The Black Sea Fleet Command at one point in August 1941 refused to detach its strike aviation to support the troops of the southern front, saying that the aircraft were needed for operations at sea, when, in fact, no direct naval threat existed.[121]

There were, however, successful cases of cooperation and combined action even in the initial period of the war. The Black Sea Fleet supported the garrison defending Odessa, bringing in reserves and needed supplies, providing necessary gunfire, and evacuating the wounded. In September, as the enemy ring around Odessa tightened, *Stavka* asked the Black Sea Fleet to organize the transport of infantry reserves to the Odessa defensive area for an attack and to organize a tactical landing by a regiment of naval infantry at Grigor'evka in the rear of the Rumanian forces.[122] This operation, which included a parachute drop on a Rumanian command post by specially trained naval infantry, disrupted the Rumanian-German siege of the city and permitted the defenders to continue the defense until October 1941.

As Admiral S.G. Gorshkov has pointed out in his memoirs, this was not a flawless operation. Its success hinged on steel nerves and quick decisions, when unexpected events threaded the operations's success. Gorshkov, then commander of the fleet's cruiser brigade, found himself at sea with the 3d

Naval Infantry Regiment aboard his ships when the amphibious assault commander, Rear Admiral L.A. Vladimirskii, and the landing craft failed to make the rendezvous. Gorshkov was informed by radio that Vladimirskii's flagship had sunk, that the fate of the admiral was unknown, and that he was to assume command of the landing. Gorshkov decided to go ahead with the landing using the ships' boats and launches. This was possible because in preparing for the operation, the naval command had studied that variant and ordered extra motor launches placed aboard the cruisers and destroyers. The ships' boats and launches were not able to get as many troops ashore as fast as the operation demanded, but just then the landing craft arrived and got the rest of the naval infantry ashore.[123]

At Odessa and later at Sevastopol the Black Sea Fleet supported a sustained defense. When after seventy-three days it was no longer possible to sustain the defense of Odessa, the Black Sea Fleet provided the protection and the sealift to evacuate 85,000 men of the garrison, much of its equipment, 15,000 civilians, and a portion of the city's industrial plant. More than 150 warships and transports took part in this effort. Many of the troops evacuated from Odessa went directly to Sevastopol to bolster its defenses during the critical October period.[124] Vice-Admiral Friedrich Ruge in his evaluation of Soviet naval operations during World War II judged the support and evacuation of Odessa as a highly successful operation that threw the German timetable back by a year.[125]

In the first period of the war, the *Stavka* employed tactical- and operational-scale amphibious landings as part of an all-arms effort to wrest the initiative from the Germans. As Vice-Admiral K. Stalbo has pointed out, more than one-third of the amphibious landings executed by Soviet forces were carried out during this period when the strategic initiative was in German hands. Such landings took place under inadequate air cover, without specially trained troops, and in the absence of specially designed landing craft. In spite of these handicaps, more than 57,000 troops were put ashore in 1941–1942, with the largest landings at Kerch-Feodosiya in the Crimea, where two armies went ashore. This counterattack was designed to relieve pressure on Sevastopol and tie down Axis forces in the Crimea so they would be unable to render assistance to other sectors of the eastern front.[126]

As the situation along the front stabilized and the Soviet defense slowed or stopped the German advance on the maritime flanks of the eastern front, a division of labor emerged with regard to the control of the fleet's operations. The coastal fronts took on the direction of the employment of naval forces in direct support of the ground forces. The deeper battle against the enemy SLOCs, defense of Soviet SLOCs, minelaying, and blockade and counter-blockade activities came under the direction of NARKOMVMF, later CinC Naval Forces, Kuznetsov, and the main naval staff. With the improved situation along the front, more assets were released for such operations, including naval aviation. *Stavka* itself took on the task of organizing the protection of the Soviet Union's external SLOCs and organizing Soviet cooperation with Allied forces.[127]

Combined operations by the army, air forces, and navy during the second and third periods of the war, when Soviet forces were gaining and then exploiting the strategic initiative (November 1942–May 1945), profited from the abolition of the three intermediary strategic directions and the substitution of *Stavka* representatives to coordinate offensive operations by fronts, air armies, and a fleet and one or more flotillas. Senior naval staff and *Stavka* representatives were often sent to improve the cooperation of naval forces.[128] By keeping a central role in the control process, *Stavka* was able to focus its ground, air, and naval assets on the destruction of the Wehrmacht, which was identified as the German center of gravity. In major offensive operations the quality of the navy's contribution improved with experience.[129] Thus, while the landing of naval infantry and units of the transcaucasian front during the Kerch-Feodosiya operation to relieve Sevastopol (December 1941–February 1942) was marked by serious miscalculations and mistakes regarding beach selections, weather conditions, and the ability of the fleet to transport additional echelons for introduction into the fighting, the process for reviewing past combat experience provided for rapid and wide dissemination of information regarding such problems and a search for solutions.[130]

The contribution of naval forces to combined operations was direct and immediate, as in a host of tactical and operational amphibious assaults and the struggle for air supremacy. These forms came together in the struggle for the Kuban region in the spring of 1943.[131] Because of the command of the air over Novorossisk in September 1943, Soviet forces could mount a simultaneous, broad-front landing with complete surprise, provide close air and naval gunfire support for attack, and deliver timely reinforcements. Threatened with encirclement by both the twin prongs of the landing force and the troops of the northern caucasian front, German forces withdrew towards the Kerch Straits.[132] Vice-Admiral N. Klitnyi has observed: "The experience of conducting amphibious operations confirmed the necessity of their thorough planning, the organization of a close mutual support and cooperation of all forces taking part in the landing, and of a tight control of them."[133]

In the final period of the war (January 1944–May 1945), with Soviet forces holding the strategic initiative, *Stavka* removed the various fleets from subordination to their respective fronts and placed them directly under the NARKOMVMF. The Northern and Black Sea fleets were so placed in March 1944, and the Baltic Fleet followed in November 1944 after the relief of Leningrad.[134] In this new situation NARKOMVMF took a more direct role in *Stavka*'s planning—naval forces taking part in thirteen of the fifteen operational-strategic offensives executed during the final period of the war.

The mass employment of naval forces (attack aviation, motor torpedo boats, and artillery) in support of operations on the axis of the main blow went hand in hand with the employment of other naval forces (bomber, torpedo, and attack aviation, motor torpedo boats, and submarines) in strikes against enemy SLOCs and theater targets. Such was the case with naval aviation, submarines, and motor torpedo boats of the Black Sea Fleet during the liberation of the Crimea in the spring of 1944, when their strikes against the German-Rumanian SLOCs inflicted heavy casualties upon the enemy and reduced the number and caliber of forces available for the defense of the Balkans.[135]

This flexibility in the control of naval forces proved critical to the Soviets' ability to get timely and decisive concentrations of forces and means on the main axis of each operation.

> By the re-subordination of fleets and flotillas to the commands of fronts (directions) and by their return to the direct subordination of the Peoples Commissariat of the Navy, *Stavka* conditioned the basic direction of the actions of the fleets: against enemy ground forces in cooperation with the maritime fronts or against enemy naval communications and shore targets in independent operations.[136]

Far Eastern Finale

What *Stavka* and the General Staff achieved by such coordination was the modernization of Peter's concept of the two arms so that it encompassed the concentrated application of ground, naval, and air power in successive operations within a continental theater of military actions. The major successes of the Soviet armed forces were due in good measure to the system of command and control for ground, air, and naval forces that had been worked out in theory prior to the war and modified by the hard tests of praxis during the struggle. *Stavka's* strict centralized control of strategic-operational planning and reserves and the utilization of *Stavka* representatives to coordinate deep operations, employing several fronts, their air armies, and a fleet and/or flotilla(s) where appropriate, provided a command system adapted to the scale of warfare on the eastern front.[137] The cooperation of the army and navy was a necessary response to the ever-growing complexity of modern warfare at the tactical, operational, and strategic levels. Soviet authors consider a well-developed system of command and control that facilitates cooperation among the various branches of the armed forces to be among the most important contributions of Soviet military and naval art to the development of military science during the Great Patriotic War.

The decision to create a unified command for the entire Far Eastern the-ater of military action in 1945 is considered a mature manifestation of the Soviet approach to the strategic-operational control of all theater forces:

> As the experience of the war has shown, one of the most important condi-tions of the effectiveness of cooperations is a well-organized system of troop control. In strategic offensive operations of the Great Patriotic War the ten-dency of the centralization of the control of large formations of all the branches of the Armed Forces in the hands of the *Stavka* of the Supreme High Command with the enlistment of the services of its representatives to the coordination of the actions of fronts and fleets in each place became self-evident. This insured a unity of will, clarity of objective, exactness of agree-ment of the efforts of large formations in the achievement of common goals, the high level of effectiveness of control, and the sufficiently complete esti-mation of the concrete situation. The creation of such a strategic organ of control as the High Command of Soviet Forces in the Far East also proved completely justified.[138]

In the Far East, *Stavka* created a theater command in June 1945 by nam-ing Marshal A.M. Vasilevskii—former chief of the General Staff, *Stavka* rep-resentative, and commander of the 3d Belorussian Front—to the newly cre-ated post of commander of Soviet forces Far East. Vasilevskii—who had planned the liberation of the Crimea and the destruction of German forces in Courland working closely with the CinC Soviet naval forces, the Main Naval Staff, and the commanders and staffs of both the Black Sea and Baltic Fleets—now had the task of planning and coordinating a theater-strategic offensive involving three fronts, three air armies, the Pacific Fleet with its naval aviation (1,500 planes), the Northern Pacific Flotilla, and the Amur Flotilla. Vasilevskii included on his Military Council and staff senior com-manders to coordinate air, naval, and rear services. Admiral Kuznetsov him-self, the CinC Soviet naval forces, coordinated the naval forces; and Chief Marshal of Aviation A.A. Novikov coordinated the air offensive. Vasilevskii and his staff proposed to strike at the Kwantung army in Manchuria using three simultaneous deep blows directed at central Manchuria and designed to dismember the Japanese forces, isolate them in central and southern Man-churia, and then to destroy them piecemeal while not allowing any units to retreat to their prepared defensive positions or their evacuation by sea. Mar-shal R. Ya. Malinovskii's trans-Baikal front was to execute the main blow from Mongolia, while Marshal K.A. Meretskov's 1st Far Eastern Front was to strike south from the Soviet Far East to cut off any possible retreat into Korea. General M.A. Purkaev's 2d Far Eastern front, supported by the Amur Flotilla, was to execute a fixing attack to pin much of the Kwantung army in northern Manchuria. The Pacific Fleet under Admiral I.S. Yumashev was entrusted with a wide range of independent and combined missions in support of the fighting in Manchuria and Korea and on Sakhalin and the Kurils. These included cutting Japanese SLOCs with Manchuria, destroying enemy naval forces and port facilities in northern Korea through an initial operation by naval aviation, securing Soviet SLOCs in theater, and preventing Japanese amphibious counterstrokes. The scale of the success of the operation in its initial phase, the weakness of enemy coastal defenses, and the rapid collapse of the Japanese defenses made it possible for the Soviet Far Eastern command to order a number of tactical amphibious assaults before Japan surrendered.

The success of this operation hinged on the ability of the Soviets to conceal their strategic intention and operational design so that their forces could achieve operational-strategic surprise. In its scale, tempo, and decisiveness, the Soviet offensive in the Far East was the culmination of the concept of deep, successive operations in a continental theater of military actions in which cooperation and combined actions by ground, air, and naval forces were concentrated according to a unified operational design and directed against the enemy's center of gravity—his available combat power in theater.[139]

Soviet authors see the forms of cooperation between army and navy as worked out during the Great Patriotic War to be uniquely Soviet and especially appropriate to the situation confronting the Soviet military in those theaters and against those adversaries. These authors have grudgingly acknowledged the contribution made by Allied naval power to radical shifts in the correlation of forces in various maritime theaters in the course of the war but remain critical of the Allies' failure to create a unified operational command structure that would institutionalize cooperation among the ground, air, and naval forces. Only Operation Neptune-Overlord seems to have encompassed the centralized, theater-strategic direction that they identify as the most rational form of cooperation. Soviet writers consider the failure of Nazi Germany and Imperial Japan to develop the mechanisms to control theater war and provide effective cooperation among the branches of their armed forces as an Achilles' heel of their military art that contributed to their final defeat.[140]

For Soviet authors, the critical problem facing military art throughout World War II was the application of concentrated combat power against the enemy's center of gravity. Admiral Sergei Gorshkov, who has been depicted by some Western analysts as a Soviet Mahan, has identified that center of gravity as the great mass of the Wehrmacht deployed on the eastern front. Soviet forces defeated the Wehrmacht through a series of successive deep operations in which the combined forces of Soviet fronts, air armies, and fleets were applied to the direct destruction of enemy combat power.[141] As Gorsh-kov observed, close mutual support and cooperation (*vzaimodeistvie*) was itself a combat multiplier on both the defense and the offense:

> The unity of the efforts of the army and navy improved their combat capa-bilities. With the navy's direct support the ground forces radically changed the qualitative and quantitative correlation of forces to their advantage on the coastal axes. The navy supplemented the efforts of the ground forces, gave them new qualities, strengthened the activeness of the defense, raised its flexibility and stability, made it insurmountable for the enemy. The navy's support in the course of an offensive increased the mobility of the troops, the depth and results of the blows, made possible the build-up of the pace of conducting major operations against coastal groupings of enemy forces.[142]

The issue from the Russian and Soviet perspective, then, is not just to have two, three, or more arms but to possess the means and skills necessary to apply these arms decisively in a given operation at a particular time and in a particular place. Rear Admiral V. Belli observed, "*Vzaimodeistvie* of ground forces with air and naval forces is the basis for the modern conduct of war." The mix of forces and the forms of conducting combined actions would differ depending on the nature of the objective and the scale of combat—tactical, operational, or strategic. Belli emphasized, however, that on the basis of So-viet military science and experience, "all operations at sea exist in one form or another of interaction and mutual support with operations ashore."[143]

Notes

1. L.I. Ol'shtynskii, *Vzaimodeistvie armii i flota (Po opytu osnovnykh sovmest-nykh nastupatel'nykh operatsii vtoroi mirovoi voiny)* (Moscow: Voenizdat, 1983), 3.

2. Jacob W. Kipp, "Sergei Gorshkov and Naval Advocacy: The Tsarist Heri-tage," in *Soviet Armed Forces Review Annual*, ed. David Jones (Gulf Breeze, Fla.: Academic International, 1979), 3:225–239.

3. Alfred Thayer Mahan, *The Influence of Seapower upon History* (New York: Hill & Wang, 1957), 22–77. Mahan's presentation of the influence of seapower and its permanent elements upon national power largely condemned great continental states without a maritime tradition to perpetual inferiority. For a recent attempt to examine the role of naval forces in the military systems of maritime empires, conti-nental states, and minor powers, see Clark G. Reynolds, *The History and Strategy of Maritime Empires* (New York: Morrow, 1974), 1–16. Reynolds acknowledges that under favorable conditions, continental powers can use certain forms of naval power in conjunction with their armies or allies to achieve profound successes against mar-itime states and coalitions. For a further examination of the problem of modern sea power in the light of the impact of the industrial revolution see Paul M. Kennedy, *The Rise and Fall of British Maritime Mastery* (Malabar, Fla.: Krieger, 1982), 177–204.

Kennedy argues that Mackinder grasped the major strategic changes wrought by the industrialization of warfare and the shift of relative advantage in theater war from maritime powers to continental powers.

4. P.I. Belavenets, *Znachenie flota v istorii rossii,* 2d ed. (Petrograd: "Iakor,'" 1914), 79.

5. R. Golosov, V. Yasenovenko, and V. Koriavko, "K voprosu o kategorii vzaimodeistviia," *Morskoi sbornik,* no. 4 (1987): 21–22.

6. F. Veselago, *Kratkaia istoriia russkogo flota (s nachala moreplavaniia do 1825 goda),* 2d ed. (Moscow: NKVMF SSSR, 1939), 26–35; Jacob W. Kipp, "Peter the Great and the Birth of the Russian Navy," *International Commission of Military History, Acta No. 7* (Washington, D.C., July 25–30, 1982) (Manhattan, Kans.: Sunflower, 1984), 113–39.

7. F.F. Veselago, *Kratkiia svedenie o morskikh srazheniiakh za dva stoletiia s 1656 po 1856 god* (St. Petersburg: Tipografiia Imperatorskoi Akademii Nauk, 1871). This volume, which combines a listing of naval engagements and an atlas of their locations by theaters, underscores the importance of joint operations in each theater.

8. Jacob W. Kipp, "Russian Naval Reforms and Imperial Expansion," *Soviet Armed Forces Review Annual* 1 (1977): 118–39.

9. B.I. Zverev, "Russkii chernomorskii flot v krymskoi voine 1853–1856 gg" (candidate's dissertation, Institut Istorii, Akademiia Nauk SSSR, 1954); I.I. Arens, *Rol' flota v voine 1877–1878 gg.* (St. Petersburg: Tipografiia Morskogo Ministerstva, 1903); I.I. Rostunov, ed., *Russko-turetskaia voina 1877–1878* (Moscow: Voenizdat, 1977); I.I. Rostunov, *Istoriia russko-iaponskoi voiny 1904–1905 gg.* (Moscow: Nauka, 1977).

10. Jacob W. Kipp, "Tsarist Politics and the Naval Ministry, 1876–1881: Balanced Fleet or Cruiser Navy," *Canadian-American Slavic Studies* 17 (Summer 1983): 151–79.

11. A. Zaionchkovskii, "Sinopskoe srazhenie i chernomorskii flot osen'iu 1853 goda," *Voennyi sbornik,* no. 11 (1903): 1–97; and E. Arens, "Rol' flota v voinu 1877–1878 gg.," *Voennyi sbornik,* no. 7 (1903): 13–41.

12. Kipp, "Tsarist Politics and the Naval Ministry," 151–179; Arens, "Rol' flota v voinu," *Voennyi sbornik,* no. 8 (1912): 12–46, and no. 9:1–24.

13. Arens, "Rol' flota v voinu," *Voennyi sbornik,* no. 7 (1903) 13–41; no. 8: 12–46; no. 9:1–25; no. 10: 1–26.

14. S.O. Makarov, *Rassuzhdeniia po voprosam morskoi taktiki* (Moscow: Voenizdat, 1943). See also Nikolai L. Klado, *S.O. Makarov i voennaia nauka* (St. Petersburg, 1914).

15. "Sluzhba general'nogo shtaba vo flote," *Russkoe sudokhodstvo,* no. 24 (1888): 12–15.

16. S.O. Makarov, *Razsuzhdaniia po voprosam morskoi taktiki* (St. Petersburg: Tipografiia Morskogo Ministerstva, 1897), 4–5.

17. Russia, Nikolaevskaia Morskaia Akademiia, *Voenno-morskaia strategicheskaia igra 1902 g.* (St. Petersburg: Tipografiia Morskogo Ministerstva, 1902), 31–47, 104–5.

18. A. Stal', *Sluzhba shtaba morskikh sil* (Leningrad, 1928), 31–32. See also L.G. Beskrovnyi, *Armiia i flot rossii v nachale XX v.: Ocherki voenno-ekonomicheskogo potentsiala* (Moscow: Nauka, 1986), 220–21.

19. S.O. Makarov, "Rassuzhdeniia po voprosam morskoi taktiki," in *Russkaia voenno-teoreticheskaia mysl' XIX i nachala XX vekov,* ed. L.G. Baksrovnyi (Moscow: Voenizdat, 1960), 409.

20. Ibid., 408–9.

21. M. Petrov, "Zadachi i plany russkogo flota v period, predshestvovavshchii mirovoi voine (1880–1914): Po arkhivnym materialam," *Morskoi sbornik,* no. 8 (1925): 19–30.

22. I.I. Rostunov, ed., *Istoriia russko-iaponskoi voiny 1904–1905 gg.* (Moscow: Nauka, 1977), 110–25.

23. Ibid., 125–144.

24. A.I. Dubravin, "Vitse-admiral Stepan Osipovich Makarov," in *Deiatel'nost' vitse-admirala S.O. Makarova v sudostroenii,* ed. A.I. Dubravin (Leningrad: Sudostroenie, 1977), 37–41.

25. Beskrovnyi, *Armiia i flot rossii v nachale XX v.,* 221.

26. E.V. Sventorzhetsky, "Do Tsushimy," *Krasnyi arkhiv,* no. 67 (1934): 199.

27. V.A. Shringer, "Podgotovka II eskadry k plavaniiu," in *S eskadroi Admirala Rozhestvennskago: Sbornik statei, posviashchennykh dvadtsatipiatiletiiu pokhoda II-i eksadry tikhago okeana,* ed. G. K. Graf et al. (Prague: Izdanie Vladimira Kolesnikova, 1930), 27–59. On Klado's strategic vision and his debt to Mahan, see N.L. Klado (Priboi), *Posle ukhoda vtoroi eskadry tikhago okeana* (St. Petersburg: Tipografiia A.S. Suvorina, 1905), 10ff.

28. K.F. Shatsillo, "O disproportsii v razvitii vooruzhënnykh sil rossii nakanune pervoi mirovoi voiny (1906–1914 gg.)," *Istoricheskie zapiski* 63 (1969): 124.

29. Beskrovnyi, *Armiia i flot rossii v nachale XX v.,* 221–22.

30. Ibid., 222; S.E. Zakharov, ed., *Istoriia voenno-morskogo iskusstva* (Moscow: Voenizdat, 1969), 134.

31. K.F. Shatsillo, *Russkii imperializm i razvitie flota* (Moscow: Nauka, 1968), 318–321.

32. Ibid.; K.F. Shatsillo, "Razvitie chernomorskogo flota nakanune pervoi mirovoi voiny (1907–1914 gg)," *Istoricheskie zapiski* 75 (1965): 86–121. For an excellent assessment of Russian naval involvement in the Mediterranean and its association with imperial expansion and navalism in the two decades before 1906, see Dieter Matthei, "Die Russische Marine im Mittelmeer im Bildfeld Deutscher Seeinteressen" (dissertation, Rheinischen Friedrich-Wilhelms Universität, 1983).

33. E.N. Kvashin-Samarin, *Morskaia ideia v russkoi zemle* (St. Petersburg: Izdanie Morskogo General'nogo Shtaba, 1912), 178–89.

34. Shatsillo, "O disproportsii v razvitii vooruzhennykh sil," 128.

35. Ibid., 132.

36. A. Svechin, "Bol'shaia voennaia programma," *Russkaia mysl'* 34 (August 1913): 19–29.

37. A. Shtal', "Somestnaia rabota vyschego morskogo i verkhovnogo komandovaniia v rossii v mirovuiu voinu," *Voennaia mysl' i revoliutsiia,* no. 4 (1924): 126–36.

38. Ibid., 351–56.

39. In spite of the fact that minelaying was critical to the defense of the Baltic coast and the Gulf of Finland, the Baltic Fleet had only six minelayers in 1914. Only two, the *Enisei* and *Amur,* had been built since 1905. Three others were converted

ironclads built in the 1860s and 1870s. See Russia, Morskoe Ministerstvo, *Sudovoi spisok rossiiskago imperatorskago flota 1914 g.* (St. Petersburg: Izdanie Morskogo General'nago Shtaba, 1914), 136–43.

40. I.I. Rostunov, *Russkii front pervoi mirovoi voiny* (Moscow: Nauka, 1976), 113–15.

41. Beskrovnyi, *Armiia i flot v nachale XX v.*, 222. See also N.V. Pavlovich, ed., *Flot v pervoi mirovoi voine* (Moscow: Voenizdat, 1964), 1: 35–45.

42. V. Simonenko, "Organy upravleniia russkogo flota v pervuiu mirovuiu voinu," *Voenno-isoricheskii zhurnal*, no. 9 (1975): 104.

43. Shtal', "Sovmestnaia rabota vyschego morskogo i verkhovogo komandovaniia," 138–40.

44. Simoneko, "Organy upravleniia rosskogo flota," 104.

45. Ibid., 105–6.

46. Beskrovnyi, *Armiia i flot v nachale XX v.*, 222–23.

47. S.E. Zakharov, ed., *Istoriia voenno-morskogo iskusstva*, 133. See also "Operativnoe iskustvo voenno-morskikh sil," *Bol'shaia sovetskaia entsiklopediia* (Moscow, 1955), 31:54.

48. N. Novikov, *Operatsii flota protiv berega na chërnom more v 1914–1917 gg.*, 3d ed. (Leningrad: Gosvoenizdat, 1937), 3.

49. Ibid., 3–36.

50. Ibid., 37–88.

51. Ibid., 105–26.

52. Ibid., 127–47.

53. Ibid., 148–61.

54. Ibid., 163–79, 250–55.

55. Ibid., 178–79.

56. Ibid., 180–84.

57. Ibid., 161–230.

58. A. Gerua, *Polchishcha* (Sophia: Rossiisko-Bolgarskoe Kniznoizdatel'stvo, 1923), 263–65.

59. N.L. Klado, *Strategiia: Vvedenie* (Petrograd: Tipografiia Morskago Ministerstva, 1918). This book is noteworthy on several grounds. First, Klado treats strategy, not naval strategy, implying that the general category shaped the subcategory. Second, the work was critical of dialectics in military science and cited a host of bourgeois thinkers and critics who were both critics and enemies of the Bolsheviks. Finally, Klado provides a capital guide to the relationship between military science and art and their application to a strategy.

60. P. Stasevich, "Rechnye flotilii i morskoi flot v grazhdannskuiu voinu," in *Grazhdannskaia voina 1918–1921*, ed. A.S. Bubnov et al. (Moscow: Voennyi Vestnik, 1928), 2:182–213.

61. On the navy and the Russian revolution, see Evan Mawdsley, *The Russian Revolution and the Baltic Fleet: War and Politics, February 1917–April 1918* (New York: Barnes & Noble, 1978).

62. B.I. Zverev, *V.I. Lenin i flot (1918–1920)* (Moscow: Voenizdat, 1978), 99–107.

63. Stasevich, "Rechnye flotilii i morskoi flot," 185–87. See also A. Sobelev, "Krasnyi flot v voine 1918–1921 gg.," *Morskoi sbornik*, no. 12 (1922): 30–55; and

A. Selianichev, "Boevye deistviia rechnykh i osernyhk flotilii v grazhdanskoi voine," *Voenno-istoricheskii zhurnal*, no. 6 (1978): 82–86.

64. *Direktivy komandovaniia frontov krasnoi armii (1917–1922)* (Moscow: Voenizdat, 1974), 501–2, 505–6.

65. N. Yu. Ozarovsky, "Enzeliiskaia operatsiia 18 Maia 1920 g.," *Morskoi sbornik*, no. 2 (1941): 96–122; I. S. Isakov, *Izbrannye trudy: Okeanologiia, geografiia i voennaia istoriia* (Moscow: Voenizdat, 1984), 122–77.

66. I.B. Berkhin, *Voennaia reforma v SSSR (1924–1925 gg.)* (Moscow: Voenizdat, 1958), 226–39; and K.F. Skorobogatkin et al., *50 let vooruzhënnykh sil SSSR* (Moscow: Voenizdat, 1968), 172–76.

67. Robert Waring Herrick, *Soviet Naval Strategy: Fifty Years of Theory and Practice* (Annapolis: Naval Institute Press, 1968), 9–27.

68. M.A. Petrov, *Podgotovka rossii k mirovoi voine na more* (Moscow: Gosvoenizdat, 1926), 3–15. Petrov was a prolific author with a substantial interest in technological innovation and its impact on naval campaigns and engagements. See his *Obzor glavneishikh kampanii i srazhenii parovogo flota v sviazi s evoliutsiei voenno-morskogo iskusstva* (Leningrad: Gosvoenizdat, 1927) and *Boevoe primenenie vozdushnykh sil v morskoi voine: Posobie dlia komandnogo sostava RKKA* (Moscow: Gosvoenizdat, 1925).

69. M.A. Petrov, *Oborony beregov: Kriticheskii ocherk zadach i vziamodeistvii razlichnykh rodov vooruzhënnykh sil pri oborone beregov* (Moscow: Gosvoenizdat, 1926), 7–9, 203–5.

70. I. Zabelin, "Iz istorii nachal'nogo perioda razvitiia sovetskogo voenno-morskogo iskusstva," *Voenno-istoricheskii zhurnal*, no. 7 (1959): 70–75.

71. Critical to all Soviet work on military doctrine and force development during this period was the concept of future war, which was specifically linked with operational art, technological development, the political-class nature of the society of potential adversaries, and the socioeconomic and economic-technical potentials of the opposing sides as they applied to military potential. See V.K. Triandafillov, *Kharakter operatsii sovremennykh armii* (Moscow: Gosvoenizdat, 1929); and *Sovetskaia voennaia entsiklopediia* (Moscow: Gosudarstvennoe Slovarno-Entsiklopicheskoe Izdatel'stvo, 1933), 2:834–44

72. V. Zof, "Mezhdunarodnoe polozhenie i zadachi morskoi oborony SSSR," *Morskoi sbornik*, no. 5 (1925): 1–17

73. "Voennaia nauka i dialektika," *Morskoi sbornik*, no. 1 (1925): 17–27.

74. As elsewhere, the Soviet Union had witnessed an intense debate in the early 1920s over the question of whether the air fleet would replace the navy. However, by the mid-1920s the issue had become one of defining the nature of naval aviation. See V. Vasil'ev, "Nekotorye mysli o primenenii morskoi aviatstii v voennoe vremia," *Morskoi sbornik*, no. 6 (1924): 60–69; V. Svobodin, "O morskom vozdushnom flote," *Morskoi sbornik*, no. 4 (1925): 56–57; D. Sokolov, "Primenenie aviatsii dlia bor'by s podvodnymi lodkami," *Morskoi sbornik*, no. 5 (1925): 80–90; A. Algazin, "Sovremennye tendentsii morskoi aviatsii," *Morskoi sbornik*, no. 11 (1925): 89–104; and P.I. Smirnov, "K itogam spora o morskom i vozdushnom flote," *Morskoi sbornik*, no. 6 (1926): 16–23.

75. B.M. Shaposhnikov, *Mozg armii* (Moscow: Voennyi Vestnik, 1927–1929), 1:255.

76. A.M. Vasilevskii and M.V. Zakharov, "Predislovie," in *Vospominaniia. voenno-nauchnye trudy,* ed. B.M. Shaposhnikov (Moscow: Voenizdat, 1974), 9–23. In his memoirs on the prewar years Admiral Kuznetsov makes the telling comment that the only person in Stalin's entire entourage whom the dictator addressed by his first name and patronymic (a sign of deep respect in Russia) was Boris Mikhailovich Shaposhnikov. No other senior military commander or party official was addressed in this fashion. See N.G. Kuznetsov, *Nakanune* (Moscow: Voenizdat, 1966), 280.

77. V. Pereterskii, "Boevye sredstva flotov v voine budushchego (Kak sledstvie razvitiia voenno-morskoi tekhniki za dva poslednie desiatiletiia)," *Voina i revoliutsiia* 2 (1929): 119–20.

78. Jacob W. Kipp, "Mass, Mobility, and the Red Army's Road to Operational Art, 1918–1936," in *Transformation in Russian and Soviet Military History,* ed. Carl Reddel (Washington, D.C.: Government Printing Office, forthcoming).

79. USSR, Narodnyi komissariat po voennym i morskim delam, *Boevoi ustav voennomorskikh sil RKKA* (Moscow: Gosizdat, Otdel Voennoi Literatury, 1930), 7.

80. Ibid., 9.

81. A.B. Kalishev, ed., *Voprosy taktiki v sovetskikh voennykh trudakh (1917– 1941 gg.)* (Moscow: Voenizdat, 1970), 424–25.

82. P.A. Smirnov, "Moguchii morskoi i okeanskii flot," *Pravda,* February 3, 1938. See also P. Golubev, "Meropriiatiia kommunisticheskoi partii po razvitiiu i ukrepleniiu VMF SSSR nakanune velikoi otechestvennoi voiny (1937–1941 gg.)," *Voenno-istoricheskii zhurnal,* no. 9 (1983): 65–72.

83. A. Pukhov, "Partiino-politicheskaia rabota v voenno-morskom flote za 20 let," *Morskoi sbornik,* no. 2 (1938): 56. At the time Molotov was chairman of the Council of People's Commissars.

84. "Strategische Theorien der Sowjetmarine," pp. 2–4, RM 6/66 Bundesarchiv-Militärarchiv, Freiburg i. Br. (hereafter cited as BA-MA).

85. Ibid., 3–6.

86. N.G. Kuznetsov, *Na dalekom meridiane: Vospominaniia uchastnika natsional'no-revoliutsionnoi voiny v ispanii,* 2d ed. (Moscow: Nauka, 1971), 251–52; Kuznetsov, *Nakanune,* 172, 257.

87. Kuznetsov, *Nakanune,* 195.

88. Ibid., 209–10.

89. V. Sologub, "Tikhookeanskii flot v period boev u ozera Khasan," *Voennoistoricheskii zhurnal,* no. 8 (1978): 121–22.

90. A.V. Basov, *Flot v velikoi otechestvennoi voine 1941–1945: Opyt operativnostrategicheskogo primeneniia* (Moscow: Nauka, 1980), 30.

91. Danilov, "General'nyi shtab RKKA v predvoennye gody (1936–iiun' 1941 g.)," *Voenno-istoricheskii zhurnal,* no. 3 (1980): 71.

92. Kuznetsov, *Nakanune,* 214.

93. Ibid., 218–61.

94. Basov, *Flot v velikoi otechestvennoi voine 1941–1945,* 33.

95. Isakov, *Izbrannye trudy,* 185.

96. Ibid., 185–86.

97. A.V. Nemitts, "Vzaimodeistvie armii i flota," *Voennaia mysl',* no. 9 (1939): 37–55.

98. Ibid., 58–59.

99. Ibid., 59.

100. V.A. Belli, "Uroki diunkerkskoi operatsii," *Morskoi sbornik,* no. 3 (1941): 13–14.

101. Erich Raeder, *My Life* (Annapolis: Naval Institute Press, 1960), 332–37.

102. "Betrachtungen über Russland," pp. 38–41, RM 6/66, BA-MA.

103. Ibid., 42.

104. "Kriegstagebuch der deutschen Marinemission Rumänien (1 Mai 1941 - 30 November 1941), M/698/45605 BA-MA. See also "Fuehrer Conferences on Naval Affairs," in *Brassey's Naval Annual 1948* (New York: Macmillan, 1948), 245, 262.

105. Kuznetsov, *Nakanune,* 314–39.

106. V.F. Tributs, "Rol' krasnoznamennogo baltiiskogo flota v voine," in *Krasnoznamennyi baltiiskii flot v velikoi otechestvennoi voine,* ed. A.M. Samsonov et al. (Moscow: Nauka, 1981), 10–12.

107. Basov, *Flot v velikoi otechestvennoi voine,* 33–38.

108. Ibid., 37; S.E. Zakharov et al., *Krasnoznamennyi tikhookeanskii flot* (Moscow: Voenizdat, 1973), 147. Basov puts the air strength of the Pacific Fleet at 1,183 aircraft on June 22, 1941, while Zakharov says that during 1941 the fleet had almost 500 aircraft. The difference in these figures suggests a strategic-operational redeployment of Pacific Fleet naval aviation of around 700 planes in 1941. The operational regrouping of naval air units proved to be one of the most flexible forms of operational-strategic regrouping of forces and means available within and between theaters of military action available to *Stavka* and NARKOMVMF during the war. Thus, between the end of the war against Germany and the initiation of hostilities against Japan, the Soviet Navy was able to augment the aviation of the Pacific Fleet and Amur Flotilla to 1,500 aircraft.

109. Zakharov, *Krasnoznamennyi tikhookeanskii flot,* 152–53.

110. Ibid., 215.

111. Ibid., 216.

112. Ibid., 216–17.

113. Ibid., 217–18.

114. N.G. Kuznetsov, *Na flotakh boevaia trevoga* (Moscow: Voenizdat, 1971), 36–40.

115. "Der Einsatz der Luftwaffe bei der Besetzung der Baltischen Inseln," pp. 1–11, RL 2 IV/34, BA-MA.

116. Basov, *Flot v velikoi otechestvennoi voine,* 135–36.

117. N.F. Zotkin et al., *Krasnoznamennyi chernomorskii flot,* 2d ed. (Moscow: Voenizdat, 1979), 133–34.

118. N. Grechaniuk, "Udary chernomorskogo flota po ob'ektam protivnika v 1941 godu," *Voenno-istoricheskii zhurnal,* no. 12 (1975): 26–33.

119. Hans-Adolf Jacobsen, ed., *Kriegstagebuch des Oberkommandos der Wehrmacht (Wehrmachtführungsstab), 1 August 1940–31 December 1941,* in *Kriegstagebuch des Oberkommandos der Wehrmacht,* ed. Helmuth Greiner and Percy Ernst Schramm (Frankfurt/Main, 1961–1965), 1:1066–68.

120. G. Egorov, "Sovershenstvovanie upravleniia silami VMF v pervom periode voiny," *Voenno-istoricheskii zhurnal,* no. 5 (1979): 26–28.

121. Basov, *Flot v velikoi otechestvennoi voine,* 219.

122. I.I. Azarov, *Osazhdennaia Odessa,* 2d ed. (Moscow: Voenizdat, 1966), 120–63.

123. S.G. Gorshkov, "Vo flotskom stroiu," *Morskoi sbornik*, no. 3 (1987): 52–56.

124. Basov, *Flot v velikoi otechestvennoi voine*, 143, 153. The navy evacuated 462 artillery pieces, 14 tanks, 36 armored cars, 1,156 vehicles, 163 tractors, 3,625 horses, and 25,000 tons of cargo.

125. Friedrich Ruge, *The Soviets as Naval Opponents, 1941–1945* (Annapolis: Naval Institute Press, 1979), 189–90.

126. K.A. Stalbo, "Ob iskusstve primeneniia morskikh desantov," *Voennoistoricheskii zhurnal*, no. 8 (1977): 37–38.

127. Ibid., 221–22.

128. Ibid., 230.

129. N. Klitnyi, "Sodeistvie chernomorskogo flota voiskam sovetskoi armii na primorskom napravlenii v nastupatel'nykh operatsiiakh 1943–1944 gg.," *Voenno-istoricheskii zhurnal*, no. 7 (1983): 65–71.

130. Kh. Kh. Kamalov, *Morskaia pekhota v boiakh za rodinu* (Moscow: Voenizdat, 1966), 145–46.

131. A.A. Grechko, *Bitva za Kavkaz* (Moscow: Voenizdat, 1967), 325–27. During the Kuban fighting of 1943, Black Sea naval aviation received substantial enough reinforces to allow elements of its force (seventy planes) to join in the air operations conducted by the Northern Caucasian Front under the direction of *Stavka* representatives Marshals G.K. Zhukov and A.A. Novikov, while sustaining deeper air strikes against the ports in the Crimea and other targets at sea. Marshal Novikov was able to coordinate the application of air units from the 4th and 5th Air Armies, Black Sea Naval Air Forces, and Long Range Aviation in this contest for air supremacy. In this fashion the Soviet command was able to shift the correlation of forces in the air over that sector of the front in the spring of 1943. See M.N. Kozhevnikov, *Komandovanie i shtab VVS sovetskoi armii v velikoi otechestvennoi voine 1941–1945 gg.* (Moscow: Nauka, 1977), 121–30.

132. Klitnyi, "Sodeistvie chernomorskogo flota," 65–66.

133. Ibid., 67.

134. V. Chernavin, "Sovetskoe voenno-morskoe iskusstvo v tretii period velikoi otechestvennoi voiny," *Morskoi sbornik*, no. 5 (1985): 15.

135. K.A. Stalbo, "Chernomorskii flot v nastupatel'nykh operatsiiakh 1944 goda," *Morskoi sbornik*, no. 5 (1974): 23–25.

136. Ibid., 231.

137. V.I. Achkasov and N.B. Pavlovich, *Sovetskoe voenno-morskoe iskusstvo v velikoi otechestvennoi voine* (Moscow: Voenizdat, 1973), 399.

138. Ol'shtynskii, *Vzaimodeistvie armii i flota*, 313.

139. Ibid., 288–97.

140. Ibid., 311.

141. S.G. Gorshkov, *Morskaia moshch' gosudarstva*, 2d ed. (Moscow: Voenizdat, 1979), 222–23.

142. S. Gorshkov, "Vzaimodeistvie voenno-morskogo flota s sukhoputnymi voiskami," *Voenno-istoricheskii zhurnal*, no. 11 (1978): 25.

143. V. Belli, "Vzaimodeistvie flota s sukhputnymi voiskami," *Voennaia mysl'*, no. 9 (1946): 37.

7

Soviet Naval Strategy and Missions, 1946–1960

Robert W. Herrick

T hroughout World War II the Soviet Navy was little more than a faithful handmaiden to the army. A half-million sailors fought ashore as naval infantry. Naval aviators and their unsuitable aircraft were diverted to afford what support they could to the fighting on the ground fronts. Many large naval guns were dismounted and taken ashore for the land war. The remaining naval forces were largely employed to provide gunfire support to the ground forces operating in coastal sectors, to ensure the coastal transport of military supplies for the ground forces, and to support ground operations with tactical-scale amphibious operations. Not until May 1944 was the navy able to begin to undertake any significant naval operations against the enemy's merchant shipping and naval forces. Since this subordinate role for the navy had served the army's needs in winning the Great Patriotic War, senior army officers in the early postwar years saw no reason to change the navy's role.

The senior naval officers saw the matter quite differently. Keenly aware of the vast gulf between their coastal forces and the large and powerful, fast aircraft carrier task forces of the Western naval powers, they lobbied with the army and party for a decade before winning acceptance for a command-of-the-sea strategy limited in area and duration that would serve expediently for the time and yet be expandable for the future to entire sea theaters and vital ocean areas as Soviet naval strength could be increased. This limited command-of-the-sea strategy had been conceived in 1938 by a Soviet Naval War College professor, Rear Admiral V.A. Belli. It envisioned a gradual expansion of the navy's zone of command from immediate offshore areas eventually to embrace the contiguous seas in which the four fleets were based. This *Soviet school* strategy, which had developed as an expedient amalgam of the former *old school* (full command of the sea gained with battleships) and *young school* (fleet-in-being deterrence with mosquito-fleet forces) was adapted to the zonal defense concept of the Army in order to give it a semblance of fitting into the Soviet Union's unified military doctrine.

This chapter concentrates on an analysis of Soviet writings and speeches rather than construction programs and naval employments. Soviet naval theory leads practice by five to twenty years and, more important, provides the basic framework that makes other developments comprehensible. Thus the construct of naval strategic theory and its resulting naval mission assignments form a fundamental basis for evaluating Soviet naval conduct.)

Writing in August 1946 in *Military Thought*, the restricted distribution journal of the Armed Forces' General Staff, a wartime chief of the Main Naval Staff, Admiral V. A. Alafuzov, revealed the Soviet Union's doctrinal concept for a war at sea to be an application to naval warfare of the doctrinal tenet for land warfare of several zones of defense: "The sea is found to be divided into zones in which . . . the power of the navy varies. It has the greatest power close to its bases and coasts but has increasingly less power as it moves further away from the coast."[2] Alafuzov also showed the flip side of this zonal defense coin, one that then, and still today, constitutes the basis for Soviet military doctrine for defense of the homeland against seaborne attack: "Even a stronger navy may lose its superiority when it is operating close to the coasts of an enemy and find it impossible to carry out its missions."[3]

It is the fond hope of Soviet military strategists that in a general war, the weaker Soviet Navy's sea control capabilities are greatest just offshore, which will enable it to deal successfully with any U.S.–North Atlantic Treaty Organization (NATO) aircraft carriers sent on missions into Soviet home waters. For this reason the Soviet Union has made a large investment in what to big-navy minds seems like a nineteenth-century anachronism—coastal defense batteries—modernized, to be sure, with antiship missiles with over-the-horizon radar and emplaced in mobile launchers.

Noting that aviation had come to "play a decisive role in warfare for maintaining and expanding a given fleet's zone of command, Alafuzov pointed out the inadequacy of land-based aviation for fleet air cover and as the main striking force at sea because it could be employed only "relatively close to the shore and, in any case, at considerably less distance from it than that at which the major surface combatants and submarines operate."[4] "In the final analysis," he noted, "the essence of naval warfare lies in striving to expand one's own zone of established command so that it eventually embraces the entire theater."

Alafuzov also implied quite clearly that the advent of aircraft carriers made it possible to compensate for the wholly inadequate flight radius of land-based fighter aviation.[5] His advocacy of aircraft carriers for the Soviet Navy seems unmistakable:

> The assignment of particular missions to the various kinds of naval forces . . . depends on the conditions of the theater. In small sea theaters the

role of coastal artillery and especially of shore-based aviation increases. In oceanic theaters the roles of the surface-ship and submarine forces increase— and particularly those of the heavy surface combatant ships and of aircraft carriers.[6]

Fleet Admiral I.S. Isakov, another wartime chief of the Main Naval Staff, has been cited as having become convinced by 1945 that aircraft carriers were the key ship type for successful naval warfare and, consequently, their de- struction became the Soviet Navy's top-priority mission.[7] This view was to persist and to be explicitly stated in the first edition of *Military Strategy,* edited by Marshal V.D. Sokolovskii, when it made its appearance in 1962.

There is abundant evidence that Soviet military and naval leaders had been mightily impressed by the U.S. amphibious landings in the Pacific in World War II and particularly by the amphibious invasion of Normandy in 1944. In early 1945 an article in *Military Thought,* "Strategic Amphibious Landing Operations," implied that concern over the eventuality of a similar amphibious invasion of the Soviet Union—as unrealistic as such concern was under postwar conditions—had made the naval mission of countering any such amphibious invasion rank in importance with that for countering the aircraft carriers of the Soviet Union's recent U.S. and British allies.[8]

The defensive countercarrier and counterinvasion missions, and that of protecting the Soviet Union's coastal military shipping (which had been found to be of vital importance during the Great Patriotic War for supporting army ground operations in coastal sectors), were dictated by the Soviet Union's lack of an oceanic navy based on attack aircraft carriers. The resultant lack of any capability to contest for sea control in key ocean areas also meant that any offensive operations in those areas, whether against shipping or against naval combatant ships at sea or in their bases, would have to be conducted largely by submarines. Alafuzov explained this situation well in a *Naval Digest* ar- ticle in the spring of 1946:

> The submarine forces are a branch of the [naval] service whose basic special capability is that they are able to penetrate an enemy's zone of command. This capability makes submarines the main arm for attacking enemy sea communications in zones not accessible to our surface forces . . .
>
> In accomplishment of the mission of supporting an invasion of enemy territory from the sea, submarines can help by supporting surface forces in establishing command of the area by denying enemy naval forces access to the area.[9]

In a third major article published in November–December 1946, Alafu- zov set out the navy's view on the utility of the coastal defensive "naval ['mine-artillery'] positions" of World Wars I and II and noted the special value of "straits and narrows" with respect to "naval positions":

> Infrastructuring and support of naval positions have in view the creation of such conditions in which the relatively small forces of the navy operating on these positions could bar a strong enemy from the approach to naval bases, to the coastal flank of the Ground Forces; and, if there are favorable geographic conditions [narrows and straits], [such conditions] could bar him from the entire region of a theater.[10]

Alafuzov asserted that naval positions had proved their viability in both world wars, though the first was positional warfare and the second maneuver warfare, and that they continued to be important due to the "low penetrability of these positions from the sea."[11]

Just as the wartime commander in chief of the navy, Admiral N.G. Kuznetsov, had foreseen a future for the navy to play a more extensive role than merely supporting the coastal flank of the ground forces, so too did Admiral Alafuzov in 1946 foresee the day when the navy would be capable of and assigned wider missions than an offshore zonal defense role in protection of the homeland from seaborne carrier strikes or amphibious invasion. Concluding a conference held in March 1946 at the Naval War College, which he then headed, on the subject of "The Development and Modernization of the Theory of War at Sea from Mahan and Colomb to Our Day," Alafuzov looked into the future:

> The experience of the present war, as the freshest and richest one, must occupy the leading place in our research. Yet, it is necessary to foresee other forms of warfare which may be realistic, among them those when the navy, too, can perform wider missions. Only taking this into account can we have a navy worthy of our country.[12]

In his August 1946 *Military Thought* article, Alafuzov had argued that it was not only feasible to gain command of the sea in an individual region of a theater but also that it was realistic and achievable to gain the command in an entire theater. This would be a gradual process, he maintained, and could require years of warfare for one or the other side to achieve. The fact that the advance of technology was causing the various types of naval forces to become more specialized and task specific, Alafuzov predicted, would lead to an ever greater utilization of the zonal defense method—an apparent reference mainly to the greater endurance of larger ships that allowed their use in the open seas and oceans while smaller ships and craft could be employed only in coastal regions not far from their bases.[13]

Less than six months later in January 1947, an article in *Red Star*, "The Struggle for Command of the Sea," by Vice-Admiral Yu. A. Panteleev returned to the accepted view of the extent of command of the sea that could be feasibly gained by the navy as limited to just that of "a given region of a theater." Panteleev went on to make several points relevant to the limited command-of-the-sea concept:

> In modern warfare, command of the sea is not gained by the destruction of the whole fleet of an enemy or by blockading it in port [as Mahan and Colomb had specified] but by gaining command of the sea in a given region of a theater and [just] for the time required by a fleet [or task force of a fleet] to carry out the missions assigned it. Such command is practicable. It does not distract the fleet [from the direct conduct of its assigned missions]. Rather, it . . . gives it direction.
>
> Command of the sea is to be gained now by the conduct of successive, systematic operations. Experience from the [Second World] war shows that these operations must be directed not only against the "platform" for one or another weapon—combatant ships at sea or aircraft in the air. It also becomes absolutely necessary to destroy the bases of the enemy navy and its airfields.
>
> Finally, to position the navy closer to the area of operations, it is essential to . . . seize enemy bases and airfields for setting up maneuvering [advanced] bases. The struggle for bases and airfields constitutes an integral part of the struggle for command of the sea. . . . Command of the sea is necessary above all in a given area of a theater and [just] for the time required by a fleet to carry out an assigned mission.[14]

In the July 1948 issue of *Military Thought,* Captain V. Andreev argued for a command of the sea so restricted in space and time as only to support army coastal flank operations. Consequently the missions that could be performed would be limited to the following:

1. Anti-SLOC (sea lines of communications) (in European coastal waters to prevent supply and troop reinforcements from reaching the enemy ground forces).
2. Gunfire support for the ground forces.
3. Mine warfare.
4. Amphibious landings (only of a tactical or operational scale, not on the strategic scale that would open a new ground front).
5. Protection of coastal shipping (mainly to ensure the delivery of supplies and troop reinforcements to own ground forces).[15]

Andreev also acknowledged implicitly that the navy would have no missions independent of the army such as fighting the enemy navy (to gain a "full" command of the sea) or conducting an antishipping campaign. Andreev's underlying aim seemed to be to reassure the army leaders, who, then as now, dominated the military establishment, that the navy accepted its main role as continuing to be that of supporting the ground forces.[16]

Andreev also seemed to be currying favor with the army leadership—to whom the idea of building the large force of aircraft carriers that would be necessary to contest for a full command of the sea was anathema—by asserting that it would be "simply impossible" for any navy to gain "permanent command of the oceanic theaters" inasmuch as a strong but weaker navy (like the Soviet Union's) could "compensate" for its lack of carrier forces "to a considerable degree by aviation and other means," presumably submarines and mines. The inclusion of the "considerable degree" phrase suggests that Andreev was really saying that there was no completely adequate substitute for the navy's having its own force of attack carriers. This interpretation gains support from a subsequent remark by Andreev that such ships remained the "main striking force" of the U.S. and British navies.[17] Consistent with his call for the minimum of sea control required for the support of the coastal flanks of the ground forces, Andreev also reduced gaining command of the sea from a mission to merely "one of the methods of preliminary support" for the ground forces.[18]

A seeming dissent from Andreev's view that the navy's main role would be support of the coastal flanks of the ground forces in the event of another war appeared in a *Red Star* article six months later in January 1949. Signed by Captain 2nd Rank V. Kulakov, the article pointed out that the navy would have to contend with the full striking power of NATO naval forces. These forces would be kept "concentrated in a single strike force assigned the mission of gaining command of the sea" in pursuit of a goal of gaining a dominant position in the world. In effect, the article seemed to be arguing, the defense of the homeland against strikes from aircraft carriers was the role that should be the proper focus of priority concern for the navy.[19]

The same theme was echoed in *Military Thought* six months later in July 1949 in an article by Admiral N.A. Piterskii. The United States was portrayed as bent on utilizing its carrier task forces to gain a "full" command of the sea and of the "world itself." Piterskii also repeated Andreev's comforting view of just a year earlier and in the same journal that it would be "absolutely impossible" for the United States to gain a full command of the sea as long as its adversary had submarines and aircraft. Piterskii outdid Andreev in making the carrier strike threat explicit: the U.S. Navy, he asserted, aimed at nothing less than the destruction of the Soviet Navy in order to gain "undivided command of the world."[20] As with the Kulakov article of six months earlier, the implication was that the Soviet Navy must face up to the seaborne threat. Specifically, it should be devising stratagems and tactics and building the forces needed to cope with U.S. attack carriers.

An established naval historian, Captain 1st Rank N.N. Mil'gram, wrote an article in an early August 1949 issue of *Red Star* deriding the view of Sir Julian Corbett, the most prominent successor to Mahan and Colomb, that the ultimate aim of a war at sea must be to gain full and permanent command of the sea. Mil'gram took the standard navy position that it was incorrect strategy to concentrate on destroying or blockading the main naval forces of the enemy so as to gain such command when to do so meant to sacrifice the prosecution of "all other missions, for example, cooperation with the ground forces, protection for the transit and debarkation of amphibious landing forces, protection of communications, and so on." Instead, Mil'gram argued, command of the sea should be viewed only as the means to the end of supporting the coastal flanks of the ground forces. He notably failed to address the matter of the threat of destruction of the navy by U.S. attack carriers as Rear Admiral Piterskii had done a month earlier. But then Piterskii had been writing for the restricted distribution armed forces' General Staff journal while Mil'gram's article had been published openly in the newspaper of the armed forces. And, as has often been noted, the Soviets are usually disinclined to talk publicly about threats for which they have not yet been able to develop sufficient countermeasures or an analogous response.[21]

The navy's roles and missions, as the navy would have liked them to have been, were stated in surrogate form in the third volume of *History of the Naval Art*, appearing in 1953.[22] Missions of support of the army's coastal flank were listed after "independent" fleet-against-fleet missions for the destruction of the enemy's naval forces, including convoys and their screening and covering forces. The priority order was as follows:

1. Destruction of the forces of the enemy at sea.
2. Cutting off of an adversary's sea communications.
3. Protection of one's own sea communications.
4. Making amphibious landings.
5. Providing gunfire and air support to coastal ground forces.
6. Laying mine fields and conducting minesweeping.[23]

The *History* tendentiously interpreted Mahan and Colomb's sea power theory as only having prescribed the limited command of the sea that Soviet naval theory was advocating rather than a full or general command through the destruction or blockade of the enemy's main naval forces. This Naval War College textbook falsely alleged that the two founders of classical sea power theory advocated gaining the command only "in a sea or in a particular region of one" and glossed over the fact that it is usually necessary to fight a strong naval opponent to gain even such limited sea control.[24]

The *History* generally avoided the term *command of the sea* since it was then in disrepute with the army and party and even made pro forma efforts to discredit command-of-the-sea theory on obviously superficial grounds. Nevertheless, the textbook did reveal the navy's underlying appreciation for a basic requirement to gain and maintain sea control at least in Soviet coastal waters. It did so by noting the need to conduct preliminary strikes sufficient to weaken an enemy's main naval forces in an intended area of combat operations before attempting to carry out any of its assigned missions. This requirement for preliminary strikes or preliminary operations before conducting any mission-oriented operations has been restated periodically since the 1920s in Soviet writings—and always in a context that made clear that the aim was to gain command of the sea in a limited sea area just long enough to carry out a hit-and-run strike against enemy naval bases or against a weaker detachment of the enemy's naval forces. This had to be accomplished, it was usually specified, before the enemy had time to send in superior forces and frustrate the Soviet mission.[25]

No explicit mention was made of how to deal with the carrier threat. However, the priority given the mission for destruction of the enemy's naval forces was enough to indicate that the navy was according top priority to that mission. In addition, two passages in the *History* implicitly advocated Soviet construction of attack carriers.[26]

The navy's lack of attack carriers and consequent inability to fight fire with fire found theoretical expression in the denial contained in the opening pages of the *History* that a decisive general engagement battle between large surface fleets could ever again occur.[27] Instead the textbook praised as progressive the czarist Russian coastal defensive concept of World War I of a zonal "defense in depth in a naval theater comprised of fortified regions [offshore from the main ports and naval bases] and of mine-artillery positions [as in the Gulf of Riga and across the mouth of the Gulf of Finland to protect Riga and Petrograd (Leningrad) respectively]."[28] It was explained that this zonal defense method "served as the basis for a theory of battle in previously prepared [infrastructured] positions in coastal regions with the mutual cooperation of heterogeneous forces and means of the navy." It was made clear that zonal defense was the basic method for implementing a fleet-in-being strategy along the lines formulated by Corbett for an inferior navy of conducting only "minor, active operations."[29] Such operations were to be limited to the confines of mine-artillery positions in an effort to hold the command in Soviet coastal waters in dispute and so to prevent the stronger adversary from being free to carry out strike or amphibious operations. For this purpose, the navy would employ only mines and auxiliary forces of light, fast torpedo craft and submarines. This fleet-in-being strategy to hold coastal waters in dispute meant that even Soviet support of the ground forces— whether by providing gunfire and air support, tactical landings, or convoying coastal military shipping—would be subject at any time to the risk of interruption by superior enemy forces.

The precarious situation of weak Soviet naval forces likely had much to do with the *History*'s insistence that the main striking force must be fully supported by all other available and usable forces. The naval requirement was stated that combat support should be rendered in "every kind of combat action at sea" and particularly for operations, defined as military activity at sea requiring special planning and additional forces to those normally in a region of a theater for conducting the patrol and other routine "daily combat activity."[30]

An article implying that gaining command of the sea in an intended area of combat operations was a prerequisite to conducting any mission-oriented operations in that area appeared in the October 1953 issue of *Military Thought*.[31] Written by Captain 2nd Rank N.P. V'iunenko, who subsequently was to become one of a handful of top naval theoreticians under Admiral S.G. Gorshkov and to be promoted to rear admiral, the article dealt with joint operations and the role of naval forces. The implication that gaining sea control in an intended area of combat operations was a prerequisite to the conduct of any mission-oriented operations was made with specific reference to the conduct of army coastal-flank-support operations. V'iunenko seemed to be advocating that the navy be given a free hand for strategic-scale offensive operations throughout any given naval theater of military action (TVD). In effect, he appeared to be taking issue with the navy's being limited to strategically defensive operations in offshore defensive zones. This was a sore point with the navy in having the military doctrinal tenet of zones of defense applicable to land warfare imposed on naval operations, one that was to surface again in 1966 when the defense minister, Marshal R.Ya. Malinovskii, indicated at the Twenty-third Party Congress that the zones of defense concept had been operationalized for the navy in the so-called blue belt of defense.

V'iunenko spelled out in detail the then-current rationale of the navy for successfully supporting army coastal flank operations against the far superior naval forces of NATO. A key point, in accord with the economy-of-force principle of Soviet military doctrine, was that by destroying or weakening enemy naval forces first in their bases and then at sea, substantial forces could be freed from zonal defense of the coasts to engage and beat off major enemy strikes against the coastal flanks of the ground forces:

> For creating an advantageous correlation of forces and favorable conditions for the conduct of joint operations, the navy normally will conduct independent operations for the destruction or weakening of the forces of an adversary. The aim of such operations consists of weakening the fleet of the adversary, to put his surface ships and submarines out of action and so create

conditions which exclude the possibility of any obstacles being placed in the way of the actions of our ground forces as well as of our naval forces. For the accomplishment of this mission there are normally employed surface ships [capital ships, cruisers, destroyers, and others], submarines, aviation and, in some cases, coastal artillery. These forces can destroy or put out of action by joint strikes the ships of the basic forces of the adversary in their bases and at sea and so deprive them of the possibility of being employed for combat missions. The achievement of this aim creates favorable conditions for the conduct of subsequent operations by the forces of the navy and moreover decreases the threat of an attack by the enemy on the coastal flanks of our ground forces. This has the effect of permitting the employment of larger forces in the main direction [of counterattack by the enemy's naval reinforcements] while insuring with fewer forces the defense of the coast and of the coastal flanks of the ground forces.[32]

In addition to the application of the economy-of-force principle, two further points need to be made. First, V'iunenko's listing of destroying ships at their bases ahead of at sea reflects the inescapable necessity of continuing to rely on surprise hit-and-run raids against the enemy's basic forces (specifically attack carriers) while at their bases rather to fight them at sea. Second, it is clear that the navy desired that the scope of the authorized operations include striking the enemy in his bases and wherever they could be engaged at sea rather than passively awaiting his appearance in superior force in the prescribed offshore zones of Soviet naval operations.

Like the third volume of the *History of the Naval Art,* which had just been released by the censors for publication, the V'iunenko article made no favorable mention of command of the sea. Nevertheless, his repeated resort to the "favorable-conditions" euphemism for it and the requirement for "preliminary attacks" prior to mission-oriented operations makes it clear that the point of his discussion of operations in Soviet home waters was to gain the limited sea control that Soviet naval theorists prefer to call command of the sea.

A 1954 Navy Day newspaper article by Rear Admiral A.I. Rodionov appeared to make use of historical experience to convey optimism that the navy would be able to maintain sea control in its coastal waters against any attempted penetrations by NATO naval forces, even by attack carrier forces. The article claimed that Germany had failed in World War I "to gain command of the sea along our coasts" despite having sent "a great number of her surface combatant ships and submarines against the Russian Navy."[33]

It indicated at least that the czarist Russian Navy had managed to avoid giving the superior German forces a free hand in Soviet coastal waters by successfully holding the command of those waters in dispute. This implied that the czarist navy had employed a fleet-in-being strategy to good effect and at the very least established a favorable precedent for using the same strategy in the early 1950s when the Soviet Navy, like its czarist predecessor, found itself confronted by a far superior coalition of naval powers.

An article of exceptional value by Captain 1st Rank D.S. Shavtsov,[34] permitting us an understanding of the Soviet Navy's limited command-of-the-sea concept, appeared in the July 1955 issue of *Military Thought*.[35] In particular, it affords us an appreciation of the great constraints that the military doctrinal principle of requiring sea control only in the main directions or sectors of army coastal flank operations placed on naval missions. It also provides the theory to operationalize the limited command concept for the nuclear era.

In essence Shavtsov described three different types of limited command of the sea—strategic, operational, and tactical—and specified the zones each would include, which were, respectively, the entire TVD involved, just a region of the TVD, or only the area of operation or battle within a region of a TVD. He portrayed the potentially dire consequences of not holding the strategic command throughout a key TVD, particularly in terms of the high risk of the enemy's sending in superior reinforcements to frustrate any given operation or of not being able to undertake most operations because of that risk. At the same time, the inestimable value of holding the strategic command was delineated in terms that seemed calculated to persuade the military and party leadership to accept the necessity of building the bigger, better naval forces that would be required to contest for the command of entire TVDs of key importance for defense of the homeland from seaborne attack.

Almost surely realizing the extreme unlikelihood of persuading the army marshals to adopt a course of action likely to threaten to reduce the ground forces' share of the military budget, Shavtsov made a point of acknowledging that having only the operational command would not condemn the navy to passivity and gave evidence that the navy would have been more than satisfied to have won doctrinal acceptance and the substantially larger forces to enable it to seek operational command in the key regions of active naval TVDs. Still, however, the article made clear that even operational command would not make it feasible to undertake many of the missions possible under strategic command of the entire TVD in question.

Without explicitly equating the definition of tactical command to the main direction of army coastal-flank support operations in which the navy must exercise sea control in limited areas of a region of a naval TVD, the article made it clear that the doctrinal requirement was equivalent to tactical command. The total inadequacy and great risks involved in settling for just tactical command under the then-current doctrinal dispensation were spelled out in convincing detail in an exposition that should have given even the most parochial senior army officer pause for thought, particularly since the unreliability of having just tactical command for support of army coastal flank support operations was made explicitly clear.

The seminal importance of the 1955 Shavtsov article and its valuable clarifications on several key aspects of the limited-command concept, recommend the inclusion here of the following quotations:

The term strategic command of the sea designates a favorable situation which permits the forces of the side enjoying this situation to carry out successfully their strategic missions over either the entire extent of the naval theater or in one of the strategic zones of the theater and for the time necessary for the accomplishment of one or more missions.

Warfare for the strategic command of the sea is aimed at making possible strategic naval and ground operations. This warfare therefore must be undertaken before these [mission-oriented] operations take place. In a number of cases, the beginning of the strategic operations will be timed in dependence on the success of this [preliminary] warfare [for sea control]. It should be noted that gaining and retaining of the strategic command of the sea is a very difficult task. One must, therefore, be prepared to fight at sea even when such command is lacking. As a matter of fact, experience has shown that the lack of strategic command of the sea does not make impossible naval operations of tactical or even operational scale. However, in such a case, it will be necessary to gain and maintain operational command of the sea.

The term operational command of the sea designates a favorable situation within the limits of an operational zone which permits the side enjoying it to successfully carry out a naval operation aimed at accomplishing some operational goal and which makes it impossible for the other side to effectively oppose this operation and bring it to naught. Basically, operational command of the sea is expressed by one side having a decisive superiority in forces and means in the zone of the main effort. The possession of such superiority permits the main forces of the side having it to overcome the enemy's opposition successfully and ensures the effectiveness of the main effort.

In warfare for the operational command of the sea, success is achieved as a rule . . . by a preliminary weakening of the main enemy forces involved.

Especially when the strategic command is held by the enemy, skillful camouflaging of one's own operations, their proper timing, and the maximum possible reduction of their duration are . . . very important for gaining operational command of the sea.

It must be kept in mind that the enemy, despite all our efforts to gain and maintain operational command, will always be able eventually to concentrate forces superior to our own in the zone of the planned operation. Therefore, if the strategic command is held by the enemy, the planned operation must be prepared and carried out in the shortest possible period of time.

It is also necessary to note that if the strategic command is held by the enemy, the operational command cannot always be gained in any desired zone. When the strategic command of the sea is held by the enemy, our own operational command can only be established as a rule within our own coastal regions wherein our naval and ground forces can be employed and where the theater of naval operations can be properly prepared [infrastructured] in the approaches to our own littoral. Offensive operations far from our coasts can be carried out only by submarines and aircraft.

If, however, the strategic command of the sea is in our hands, the gaining of the operational command and, consequently, the carrying out of any kind of mission becomes possible over the entire extent of the theater.

Tactical command of the sea must be understood as a favorable situation in the area of a battle and finds its expression in the creation of a superiority of one's own forces over the main forces of the enemy which it is planned to fight in the case of offensive operations. In the case of defensive actions, the contest for the tactical command of the sea consists essentially of the use of man-made defenses [e.g., mine fields and coastal artillery] already existing in the area of the battle with a view to creating favorable conditions for our own numerically inferior forces.

World War II has shown that warfare for command of the sea involves warfare against both the naval and air forces of an enemy. Such warfare must aim at the destruction of these forces or at hampering their activities [which would at least hold the "command" "in dispute"], with the purpose of creating favorable conditions for the carrying out of one's own naval missions and of the missions of one's own ground forces operating in coastal zones.

The armed forces of a country which has gained command of the sea can cut the sea communications of an enemy and make secure its own. It can conduct overseas invasions of territories held by the enemy and prevent enemy landing on one's own littoral. It can act systematically against enemy troops and targets on the coast by fire from the sea and make similar operations by the enemy impossible. Command of the sea can be gained only by sequence of systematic actions [instead of a winner-take-all "general engagement" of classical sea power theory as per advocated by Mahan and Colomb].

The measures to be taken for gaining command of the sea must be harmonized in their nature and scale with the missions which [the other services of] one's own armed forces have to accomplish in a given theater of naval warfare. Consequently, as the nature of the [mission-execution] problem facing a given military service varies and may be either strategic, operational, or tactical, so the solution of these problems will require command of the sea of the different types: strategic, operational, or tactical.

The advent of nuclear weapons has created additional capabilities for gaining the operational command of the sea when the strategic command is held by an enemy. Nuclear weapons, if exploited properly, make it possible to immediately weaken enemy forces that are deployed into the zone of operations. Such weapons make it possible to create a favorable balance of forces and to accomplish operational goals before the enemy has time to restore the correlation of forces by bringing in reinforcements from other operational zones.

The advent of nuclear weapons, as far as aviation is concerned, has considerably increased its capabilities with respect to the contest for command of the sea. Aircraft have become still more dangerous for surface ships, both those at sea and those lying at their naval bases. Planes can now be employed very effectively for disrupting the system of naval bases of an enemy and for annihilating the centers of his shipbuilding industry [which, in the contest for command of the sea, is one of the most important prerequisites for success]. A nuclear weapon, delivered by a long-range missile, augments aviation's capability for destroying enemy airfields as well as the aircraft based on those airfields. This can be a vitally important step in the contest for air supremacy—and achieving air supremacy, in turn, is one of the basic prerequisites for gaining command of the sea.

It is presumed that special preliminary operations will assume increased importance in future combat operations at sea. For an offensive, these special operations ... must precede any large-scale coastal naval operations planned to achieve the goals set for the Armed Forces as a whole. As for the defensive, the enhanced operational and tactical capabilities of the various arms and branches of the Armed Forces permit the assertion that a skillful employment of nuclear weapons and the aid of aviation and of the Ground Forces will enable the navy, despite its inferiority to the adversary in large surface-ship forces, to weaken an enemy in a timely fashion and, once having gained the command along our costs, to rout him completely.[36]

Finally, Shavtsov's article remarked that submarines are very effective against large surface ships, "even when the command of the sea is held by the enemy."[37] One may reasonably conclude that it was this normal situation of NATO naval forces' being able to exercise sea control wherever desired that resulted in the creation of a Soviet Navy whose main striking force was pronounced by First Secretary Nikita S. Khrushchev and Minister of Defense Marshal G.K. Zhukov in 1955 to be submarines—and which has remained unchanged for the subsequent three decades although missile-strike and antisubmarine aircraft have been given a substantial role.

An indication that the navy finally was facing up to the need to develop capabilities to carry out the anticarrier mission to a significant degree appeared in a Navy Day 1955 article by Admiral L.A. Vladimirskii. His solution for a defense against the NATO carrier threat by the carrierless Soviet Navy was the cruise missile: "The counter to surface ships is the cruise missile launched from an aircraft, a submarine, or from a small, fast surface ship."[38] The fact that Vladimirskii did not mention the navy's coastal missile forces among those that were to conduct the anticarrier mission bespoke a recognition of the fact that successful conduct of that mission required that the NATO strike carriers be intercepted far beyond the range of coastal missile batteries, even ones having over-the-horizon radar.

Vladimirskii did not even esoterically advocate the construction of the attack carriers the navy so ardently desired. However, this restraint may have been due to the fact that he was writing in the Komsomol Youth periodical, scarcely an appropriate vehicle for such advocacy as compared with *Military Thought, Red Star,* or even the *Naval Digest.* Probably more important was that the navy was undergoing a difficult period in which Khrushchev and Zhukov had convinced themselves that, if indeed any naval forces at all were required, submarines alone would suffice—and these primarily as a deterrent anti-SLOC threat to NATO's Atlantic shipping.

Gorshkov was to reveal in a 1967 *Naval Digest* article two and a half years after Khrushchev's ouster in October 1964 that the "very influential authorities" of the mid-1950s had decided that the advent of nuclear weapons had deprived the navy of its value as a military force. Gorshkov went on to describe Khrushchev's rationale for his belief that the navy was dispensable:

> According to their views, all of the basic missions in a future war allegedly could be fully carried out without the participation of the navy—even in those situations when to do so would require the conduct of combat operations on the broad expanses of the seas and oceans. At the same time it was frequently asserted that only missiles emplaced in ground launching sites were required for the destruction of surface striking forces and even submarines.[39]

In an antinavy political atmosphere such as this, it is small wonder that the navy's collective wish for aircraft carriers was not finding expression in public advocacy in mid-1955. This hostile political attitude toward maintaining the navy may also account for the fact that Vladimirskii's revelation that the cruise missile on aircraft, submarine, and surface ship platforms constituted the navy's recommended way for carrying out the anticarrier mission appeared in such a minor publication as the newspaper of the Komsomol Youth organization.

In a December 1955 *Red Star* article, "Aircraft Carriers," however, Captain N.I. Makeev noted that attack carriers constituted the main striking force of the NATO naval forces.[40] While dutifully following the party-army line that aircraft carriers were vulnerable to nuclear weapons, Makeev noted the carriers' relative invulnerability to conventional weapons. Probably realizing that the construction of such costly and complicated ships would be far too expensive and take too many years to answer the immediate threat, the article limited its implicit advocacy to the construction of a substantial number of light-tonnage aircraft carriers. Although such light carriers would not be capable of fighting for sea control in the oceans, they would at least be capable of employing the active (offensive) tactics prescribed by military doctrine for all military operations against any NATO carrier forces bent on attacking the Soviet homeland. We know from Khrushchev's memoirs that it was only the high price tag on aircraft carriers that had prevented him from authorizing construction of some of them. It is moot whether he appreciated the fact that the submarines he favored as a "much more formidable and effective weapon" than aircraft carriers were such for the navy precisely because it lacked the carrier forces to contest for command of the sea and hence was forced to depend on submarines and their stealth to operate at all in the open oceans. Khrushchev's well-documented missile mania combined with his own remark that submarines were cheaper suggest that he did not appreciate the real situation. His words are revealing:

> Gone were the days when the heavy cruiser and the battleship were the backbone of a navy.
>
> This was a painful realization for some of our high-ranking naval commanders who were still very much in favor of keeping a strong surface fleet. They couldn't stop thinking of submarines as auxiliary vessels rather than as the most important element in a modern navy.
>
> We made a decision to convert our navy primarily to submarines. We concentrated on the development of nuclear-powered submarines and soon began turning them out virtually on an assembly line.
>
> Thus we fundamentally changed the strategy and composition of our navy. I take full responsibility on my own shoulders. I have no desire to conceal that I threw my weight to the side of the younger cadres in the navy and helped them overcome the resistance of the older officers who couldn't bring themselves to admit that not only was the submarine much cheaper to build and operate—it was also a much more formidable and effective weapon.
>
> Aircraft carriers, of course, are the second most effective weapon in a modern navy. The Americans had a mighty carrier fleet—no one could deny that. I'll admit that I felt a nagging desire to have some in our own navy but we couldn't afford to build them. They were simply beyond our means. Besides, with a strong submarine force, we felt able to sink the American carriers if it came to war. In other words, submarines represented an effective defense capability as well as a reliable means of launching a missile counterattack.
>
> So we relegated our surface fleet to an auxiliary function, primarily for coastal defense.[41]

In early September 1955, the navy's own newspaper at the time, *Soviet Fleet,* carried an article, "British Aircraft Carrier Aviation," that presented a fairly obvious surrogate listing of the tasks that the navy would expect attack carriers to perform for it—should the army and party eventually acquiesce again, as Stalin had twice done, in 1938 and 1950, to building aircraft carriers. The article listed "the most important tasks of aircraft carriers" as (1) striking at coastal installations, including naval bases and ports; (2) destroying surface combatants and submarines at sea and their bases; and also (*also* is frequently used to signify low ranking) providing support to protect sea communications from attacks by submarines, surface ships, and aircraft.[42]

Marshal Zhukov fully supported Khrushchev in making the submarine the "main striking force" of the navy, reporting to the Twentieth Party Congress in February 1956 that the navy would have "immeasurably greater importance" for the Soviet Union in a future world war than it had had during the Great Patriotic War. Of particular interest was his statement implying that the real value of the navy would be in helping to bring such a war "to a successful conclusion."[43] While this possibly may have implied a broken-back war in which conventional forces would be decisive, it seems more likely to suggest the withholding of ballistic missile submarines in reserve to help ensure satisfactory war termination negotiations.

The force of the antinavy campaign appeared to have spent itself by mid-1957 when an unsigned article in *Soviet Fleet* announced that "the Party and Government have defined with utmost clarity the navy's place and role in the general system of the armed forces."[44] Although the navy's role was said to have been defined—which much other evidence indicates was nothing more specific than defense of the homeland against seaborne attack—the statement notably did not say that the navy's specific missions to fulfill its role had been defined as well.

Even by July 1960, when Rear Admiral V.A. Lizarskii revealed in an obscure Central Asian newspaper in a Navy Day article that the Fourth Session of the Supreme Soviet held in mid-January 1960 had defined "a number of missions for the armed forces and set the direction for their further development," it appeared clear that those general missions for the armed forces overall had not yet been broken down into mission assignments for the five individual military services (the strategic missile forces having been established less than three weeks earlier in addition to the already existing army, air force, national air defense forces, and the navy). The article in question implied rather clearly that the navy's specific missions still had not been determined and assigned:

These instructions [which Khrushchev reportedly had stated himself] defined the new nature of warfare and the role and importance [that is, "place" with respect to the other four services] of the services of the armed forces to gain victory over an adversary. In the defense of our state, a big role is assigned the navy.[45]

It was not to be until the appearance in the spring of 1962 of the first edition of *Military Strategy,* written by a group of army officers on the armed forces' General Staff and edited by Marshal V.D. Sokolovskii, that evidence was placed on the public record that the navy had at least been assigned its three top-priority missions: anticarrier; antiballistic missile nuclear submarine, and anti-SLOC.

In the absence of clear mission assignments, different views on the navy's mission were expressed. In his report as defense minister to the Twentieth Party Congress in February 1956, Zhukov not only acknowledged the need for a navy but also confirmed that the navy's role, aided by the army and air forces, was that of defending the "maritime borders" of the Soviet Union.[46] That the navy required the help of the other services in its defense-of-the-homeland-from-seaward role, including defense against amphibious invasion as Zhukov implicitly noted, was stated to the top military leadership in presumed confidentiality in the July 1957 issue of *Military Thought:*

> It must be noted that, as in the case of warfare for [control of] sea and oceanic communications, carrying out the mission of repelling enemy attacks from seaward . . . is not at present the prerogative of the navy alone. Not one of these missions could the navy carry out by itself.[47]

On the other hand, Admiral Gorshkov took a divergent tack in a *Pravda* article for Navy Day in July 1956. Gorshkov implied that the two main missions of the navy for protecting the Soviet Union from seaborne attack were countering any NATO attempt at amphibious invasion of the Soviet Union and preventing any NATO carrier strikes against the homeland or its ground forces. This implication is derived from statements by Gorshkov that the United States was giving "basic attention to creating the means for supporting long-range amphibious landings" and the more accurate claim that the United States was also developing carrier aviation.[48] The title of Gorshkov's article, "On Guard over the Maritime Perimeters," used the Russian word *rubezhei* (which translates as "barrier" or "perimeter") in place of the word much used earlier for "borders" or "frontiers," implying the forward perimeters of a zonal defense system. Gorshkov found the title so appropriate that he used it for several *Pravda* articles on Navy Days and in a number of other cases. It is one of the few titles he used more than once and the only one he employed so often.

Confirmation that the navy had not yet been assigned explicit missions for its role of protecting the homeland from seaborne attack came in the spring of 1957 from a *Soviet Fleet* article: "No doubt under modern conditions there will be a number of new . . . missions related to repelling the attempts by aggressive forces to employ their navy to penetrate to the shores of the Soviet Union."[49] While the use of the wording "to penetrate to Soviet shores" could have been intended to include both the threat of amphibious invasion and that of carrier strikes, the phrase smacks strongest of concern that the NATO attack carriers would be sent into harm's way to strike at both coastal targets (ground forces, naval bases, airfields, and nuclear storage facilities, for example) and at targets deep inside the Soviet Union from close-in offshore areas.

That the mission structure of the navy, like that of the other military services, was being subjected to a radical revision to bring it into accord with nuclear age requirements emerges from a book entitled *The Navy of Our Homeland,* which passed the censors for publication in September 1957. The relevant passage reads:

> The development of aviation, submarines, and the appearance of supersonic cruise missiles and nuclear weapons have . . . exerted an enormous effect on the operational art and tactics of all services and service arms of the Armed Forces. Such [mission-related] matters have been raised anew as:
>
> 1. Combat operations in the open sea [anticarrier, antisubmarine warfare];
> 2. Warfare on communications [anti-SLOC and pro-SLOC];
> 3. Defense of naval bases;
> 4. Conduct of amphibious landings and counterlandings; . . .
> 5. Providing support for the coastal flanks of the Army; and
> 6. Others [including the provision of "combat support" to all submarines while at sea, especially to strategic submarines].[50]

Evidence supporting a conclusion that this restructuring of the navy's missions was being conducted in conformity with the limited command-of-the-sea concept was evident in a *Red Star* article by Captain 1st Rank N. Gordeev that appeared in May 1957 a week before the *Soviet Fleet* article was published.[51] This article referred to gaining "command of the sea in a given region of a theater," the phrasing of a limited command-of-the-sea concept. With zonal defense imposed on the naval mission structure, missions such as those listed in *The Navy of Our Homeland* would be subjected to great restrictions as to the areas in which they could be performed. The anticarrier, antisubmarine warfare, and anti-SLOC missions, for example, would all have to be performed in the offshore defense zones.

The Soviet concern for NATO naval capabilities for carrier strikes at the homeland and even for a strategic-scale amphibious invasion (defined as one that opens up a new ground front) was reflected in a party guidance for 1957

Navy Day publicity: "The importance of the navy for the country is evidenced by the historical experience of many centuries. Enemies have repeatedly carried out attacks on the country from the sea."[52]

In late May 1957, Marshal Zhukov was quoted as having said that aircraft carriers, due to their (alleged) great vulnerability, would be useful in a general nuclear war only for first-strike missions. This indicated that the navy's anticarrier mission would have to be accomplished in the opening moments of any world war—or at least the forces to accomplish it would already be forward deployed before the start of the war and be maintained in a high condition of readiness on a forward perimeter just beyond the maximum strike range of the carriers' nuclear strike aircraft. Just such a strategy was to be explicitly stated in the first edition of *Military Strategy* in 1962.

An unprecedented claim that the navy was protecting the "state interests" of the Soviet Union at sea was made by Admiral Gorshkov in a February 1958 article in *Red Star*.[53] The navy commander in chief was to repeat this claim on innumerable occasions from that second year of his long incumbency and with varying meanings indicated by the context. On this first occasion, however, it appeared that he had in mind primarily preventing carrier air strikes at the Soviet Union and its ground forces. Unlike subsequent references to the state-interest-protection role that do not impose limits on the sea and oceanic areas involved, on this first occasion he specified that the navy's role was to be played out within the Soviet Union's naval theaters, which probably did not then extend any farther from Soviet coasts than the maximum strike range of carrier aircraft.

An article by Captain 3d Rank Yu. Schvarev, "How the Role of a Navy Is Viewed in the West," published in *Soviet Fleet* in April 1958, made patently obvious surrogate use of its ostensible subject to present the view that support of the army's coastal flanks was "the most important task of the navy."[54] Next after this top-priority role, the article mentioned the conduct of amphibious landings, a key mission Soviet naval practitioners and theoreticians normally include in the army flank support role. Schvarev also listed as a main mission of the navy the protection of one's own SLOCs, which at the time was also usually presented in Soviet writings as primarily a matter of protecting coastal military shipping, and hence also a mission normally included in the army coastal flank support role. The limited command-of-the-sea concept was indicated by a statement that "freedom of action at sea," defined as "a situation in which an enemy cannot constitute an obstacle to the conduct of one's own operations," could be achieved by the maximum destruction of the enemy's forces and by barring him from the region of operations.

Schvarev claimed that "military specialists know that the enemy's submarines will reach the ocean" and so the United States allegedly had "recently reorganized the antisubmarine forces of the Atlantic Fleet." This allegation followed the observation that "a large number" of recent NATO exercises had involved establishing blockades of the Danish and Turkish straits and of the Sea of Japan, with all such blockades aimed "primarily at preventing submarines from exiting to sea."

Schvarev's 1958 article also contained an unprecedented assertion—one that Gorshkov was to repeat in the 1960s—that attack aircraft carriers were viewed as still constituting the main force for a war at sea, at least for "the near future" (usually no more than five years in Soviet usage). The reason for this, according to Schvarev, was that aircraft carriers were "less vulnerable than land bases." The article also gave credit to attack carriers for having good defenses against cruise missiles and downgraded even nuclear-powered submarines as being only second in importance to aircraft carriers. Schvarev noted further that both carriers and their aircraft were equipped with cruise missiles. While such bouquets for aircraft carriers were not an everyday occasion, they were consistent at the time with the navy's efforts to gain increased acceptance for surface ships in Khrushchev's submarine navy.

Finally of note was an apparent surrogate reference to the forward perimeter of the naval zonal defense system. Antisubmarine submarines, Schvarev stated, would be employed on such a perimeter along with other antisubmarine surface ships and aircraft.

The continuing top-priority Soviet concern over NATO's capabilities to stage a 1944 Normandy-style landing on Soviet shores was voiced at the Extraordinary Twenty-first Party Congress in January 1959 by Marshal Malinovskii, successor as defense minister to the temporarily disgraced Marshal Zhukov. Malinovskii expressed the Soviet concern with a bravado worthy of Khrushchev: "Across the ocean it is frequently stated and written that the U.S. Navy is capable of making an attack and carrying out amphibious landings at any point on our coastline. However, as it is said, 'Easy to boast, easier to be discredited.'"[55] In view of the fact that Malinovskii's wording spoke of both "making an attack" and of "carrying out amphibious landings," it is likely that the first was a reference to attack carrier strikes but expressed with a vagueness suitable when counters to a threat are lacking.

The 1959 party line for Navy Day "reports and discussions" spoke for the first time of the navy's role in defending the Soviet Union against seaborne attack for the defense (*oborona*) rather than for protection (*zashchita*) of the homeland. This was a significant change in that it elevated the countering of amphibious landings and carrier strikes from the ordinary war-fighting missions of the armed forces to the status of deterrence missions for the preservation of the state.[56] As the party guidance put it, the navy was said to be undergoing strengthening in order to "create a powerful defense (*oborona*) at sea."[57]

A 1959 Navy Day article in *Izvestia* by Admiral V.F. Tributs, Gorshkov's senior deputy CinC at the time, seems at first reading to constitute a navy renunciation of its long-standing desire for aircraft carriers and a capitulation to the Khrushchev policy that the navy should be basically comprised of submarines:

> After World War II aircraft carriers became the basic nucleus of the strongest navies [those of the United States and United Kingdom]. *Such a situation still exists today* . . . but aircraft carriers too, like battleships and cruisers, *are beginning gradually to lose their importance* in connection with the development of missile weapons. . . . As the replacement for the aircraft carrier must come the fast, nuclear-powered submarine armed with missiles.[58] (emphasis added)

On second reading, however, the emphasized statement that aircraft carriers still remained the "basic nucleus of the strongest navies" and also that the carriers were only just "beginning gradually" to lose their importance (in a dialectical decline that could take decades or longer according to Marxist theory) suggests that the intended message was not what it was to seem at first glance. Rather it seemed carefully worded to give the impression to the casual reader that the navy was resigned to never getting any attack carriers and remaining basically a submarine navy. In actuality, its real message was that carriers would be around for a long time and would continue to constitute the basic nucleus of the strongest navies.

Khrushchev made one of his several statements ridiculing surface ships during his state visit to the United States in September 1959:

> Combatant ships are good only for making state visits. From a military point of view they have outlived their era. Outlived it! *Now they are only good targets for missiles.* This year we are sending even our nearly completed cruisers to be scrapped.[59]

The lie was soon given to Khrushchev's statement. Although six uncompleted *Sverdlov*-class cruisers actually were scrapped, the sixteen completed ones and four older ones were kept in commission, obviously exceeding any requirements for taking Khrushchev on state visits. The real intent of Khrushchev's statement, particularly of the emphasized sentence, appears to have been to make a contribution to a major Soviet propaganda campaign being conducted at the time to convince the United States to scrap its aircraft carriers as too vulnerable for nuclear war—and thus resolve at no cost the anti-carrier mission requirements and thereby nullify the U.S. Navy's inestimably valuable capability to gain and maintain sea control in any region or regions of the world it finds advantageous.

In his address to the Fourth Session of the Supreme Soviet on January 14, 1960, the date on which this chapter ends, Khrushchev let the navy and its surface ships off relatively lightly compared to the air forces, which he said were to be entirely replaced by missiles, "In the navy, the submarine fleet is assuming great importance while surface ships can no longer play the role they once did."[60] The same speech contained a sentence reflecting the kind of thinking that was to support holding a substantial share of the Soviet Union's ballistic missiles as a reserve force to the strategic missile forces in the contingency that the latter would be unable to destroy all of its assigned targets in any initial nuclear exchange. Speaking of a possible U.S. surprise nuclear attack (which he characterized as unlikely in view of the Soviet Union's retaliatory capability), Khrushchev asserted: "It always will be possible to bring reserve means into operation and strike targets from reserve positions."[61] Thus Khrushchev foreshadowed a later phase of Soviet naval strategy, the advent of nuclear-armed ballistic missile submarines (SSBNs) as a strategic reserve. Their protection was to require a further development of the limited sea control concept.

The foregoing account has essentially set out the preferred postwar strategic theory of the Soviet school of the navy's leadership, the acceptance by the mid-1950s of that theory as the naval part of the Soviet Union's unified military doctrine, and the naval missions derived from that doctrine. In the first quarter of a century following World War II, a group of innovative naval practitioners and theoreticians and several of their detractors worked out a unity of views on the most expedient strategy for gaining local sea control in intended areas of operations for just long enough to conduct a raid on a weaker enemy force or its bases before the enemy could concentrate enough naval forces to overwhelm the Soviet force.

The limited command-of-the-sea doctrine accommodates all but one of the desirable missions for defense of the Soviet Union against seaborne attack: anti-SSBN warfare. The decision was taken to make only nominal efforts in that area (until and unless a technological breakthrough should make the oceans acoustically transparent) and to redress the unfavorable correlation of strategic nuclear forces created for the Soviet Union by the U.S. Polaris-armed SSBN force by constructing a comparable and countervailing force of Yankee and Delta classes of SSBNs. Otherwise the new naval doctrine comfortably accommodates the key missions for protecting Soviet submarines (particularly the SSBNs), for anticarrier warfare (ACW), for protection of the vitally important wartime coastal military shipping, and for any anti-SLOC campaign that might be found expedient. In the case of the ACW mission (which the 1962 *Military Strategy* by the armed forces' General Staff stated authoritatively was the navy's top-priority mission), the limited command-of-the-sea doctrine allowed extension of the zone of command, or at least a zone for contesting command, out to the maximum range from which carrier-based bombers could deliver strikes into Soviet territory. Should an anti-SLOC campaign be ordered, the doctrine was elaborated to provide feasible methods for a sea blockade of European waters and strikes at the European termini of enemy shipping.

Among the many sources of Soviet thinking on naval warfare, the following three have loomed large:

1. Constant concern for security against seaborne attack—the Soviet Union's being faced with powerful Western naval powers perceived as intrinsically hostile and intent on encircling its long and exposed maritime borders and eventually deposing the country's communist regime.

2. Unfavorable maritime geography, which not only divides the navy into five segments (counting the Mediterranean battle force) but also crucially restricts the access of each of these parts to the world ocean.

3. Technological disadvantage, a virtually insurmountable lag in construction of attack aircraft carriers with the consequent inability to contest for oceanic sea control to permit conduct of anti-SSBN warfare except by tactical submarines, which the Soviets themselves have acknowledged is inadequate, a team effort of aircraft, surface ships, and submarines being vastly superior for ASW.

At least three interesting deductions about Soviet decision making on naval matters can be drawn. First, that decision making has been quite realistic in designing forces to counter perceived threats from seaward. Among the examples noted were building counterforces of defense, as Admiral Gorshkov described the Soviet counter to the Polaris-armed SSBN force of Yankees and Deltas, in lieu of seriously tackling the anti-SSBN mission, optimizing the navy for ACW by arming planes, submarines, and surface ships with antiship cruise missiles.

A second noteworthy fact about Soviet decision making on naval matters is the fundamental importance for that process of having a well-developed and convincing strategic theory from which to proceed. Unlike the much more pragmatic industrialized states of the noncommunist world, in Soviet decision making, a fully elaborated theory serves as the basis for discussion rather than the practical aspects of implementation. And only after all theoretical hairs have been split can the discussion be ended and movement be made for implementing the theory.

Third, although such discussions of the theoretical underpinnings of a strategy may last only for months, they can drag on for years. For example, discussions over command of the sea continued sporadically for nearly fifty years—from the early 1920s until the late 1960s. The most interesting aspect of such discussions is that the arrival of a decision is marked by a cessation of the debate in the press—and sometimes by a definitive article closing off the debate.

Notes

1. For an example of an effort to reconcile naval theory with the practical manifestations of Soviet military theory for the naval side of any future general war, see my *Soviet Naval Strategy: Fifty Years of Theory and Practice* (Annapolis: U.S. Naval Institute, 1968).

2. Admiral V.A. Alafuzov, "O sushchnosti morskikh operatsii" (On the essence of naval operations), *Voennaia mysl'*, no. 8 (1946) 16. An article in the military newspaper *Red Star* in early 1946 stated that it was a principle of military doctrine binding on all of the military services always to establish and maintain "several echelons of defense in depth." F. Isaev, "Strategicheskoe iskusstvo krasnoi armii v velikoi otechestvennoi voine" (Strategic art of the Red Army in the Great Patriotic War), *Krasnaia zvezda* 20 (February 1946).

3. Ibid., 16.

4. Ibid., 28.

5. Ibid., 16.

6. Ibid., 28.

7. Ashot Arzumian, *Admiral* (Admiral) (Moscow: Voenizdat, 1979), 158.

8. Rear Admiral V. Belli, "Strategicheskie desantnye operatsii" (Strategic amphibious landing operations), *Voennaia mysl'*, nos. 1–2 (1945): 30–39. As a professor at the Naval War College in the late 1930s, Belli had been Gorshkov's mentor as a student and was to serve the latter as his leading "official theoretician" for the first decade of Gorshkov's long tenure as CinC Navy.

9. Admiral V.A. Alafuzov, "O sushchnosti morskikh operatsii" (On the essence of naval operations), *Morskoi sbornik* nos. 4–5 (1946): 6. Note the title is identical with that in note 2 above, which was a revised reprint of the *Naval Digest* article but with the addition of several pages on the zonal defense concept.

10. Admiral V. Alafuzov, "Razvitie povsednevnoi operatsionnoi deiatel'nosti flota" (The development of the daily operational activity of a navy), *Morskoi sbornik*, nos. 11–12 (1946): 11–18.

11. Ibid., 20.

12. "Nauchnaia konferentsiia v voenno-morskoi akademii K.E. Voroshilova" (Scientific conference at the K.E. Voroshilov Naval War College), Lieutenant K.V. Penzin, rapporteur, *Morskoi sbornik*, no. 3 (1946): 111–113.

13. Alafuzov, "O suchnosti morskikh operatsii," 15–16.

14. Vice-Admiral Yu. Panteleev, "Bor'ba za gospodstva na more" (The struggle for command of the sea), *Krasnaia zvezda*, January 16, 1947.

15. Captain 1st Rank V. Andreev, "Psevdonauchnaia teoriia Admirala Kolomba" (The antiscientific theory of Admiral Colomb) *Voennaia mysl'*, no. 7 (1948): 58.

16. Ibid., 49–64.

17. Ibid., 57.

18. Ibid., 58.

19. Captain 2nd Rank V. Kulakov, "Reaktsionnaia sushchnost' amerikanskoi voenno-morskoi doktriny" (The reactionary essence of american naval doctrine), *Krasnaia zvezda*, January 13, 1949.

20. Rear Admiral N.A. Piterskii, "Amerikanskie vzgliady na rol' i zadachi flota v voine" (American views on the roles and missions of a navy in war), *Voennaia mysl'*, no. 7 (1949): 72–81.

21. Captain 1st Rank N. Mil'gram, "Nesostoiatel'nost' i reaktsionnaia sushchnost' angliiskoi voenno-morskoi teorii" (The bankruptcy and reactionary essence of British naval theory), *Krasnaia zvezda*, August 5, 1949.

22. *Istoriia voenno-morskogo iskusstva* (History of the naval art), ed. Rear Admiral N. Piterskii (Moscow: Voenizdat, 1953), vol. 3.

23. Ibid., 316.

24. Ibid., 7.

25. Ibid., 317.

26. Ibid., 314–15.

27. Ibid., 8.

28. Ibid., 124.

29. Ibid., 121.

30. Ibid., 316.

31. Captain 2nd Rank N. V'iunenko, "Sovmestnye operatsii i rol' v nikh voenno-morskikh sil" (Joint operations and the role of naval forces), *Voennaia mysl'*, no. 10, (1953).

32. Ibid., 23.

33. Rear Admiral A. Rodionov, "Na strazhe morskikh rubezhei" (On guard over the maritime perimeters), *Vodnyi transport*, July 4, 1954.

34. Shavtsov's career is so little known that speculation has arisen that the name is a pseudonym. He is described, however, as participating in the defense of Leningrad during the Great Patriotic War. See I.A. Kozlov and V.S. Shlomin, *Krasnoznamennyi baltiiskii flot v geroicheskoi oborone Leningrada* [Red banner Baltic Fleet in the heroic defense of Leningrad], (Leningrad: Lenizdat, 1976), 147 --Ed.

35. Captain 1st Rank D. Shavtsov, "O gospodstve na more" (On command of the sea), *Voennaia mysl'*, no. 7 (1955): 3–17.

36. Ibid., successive quotes: 12, 12, 13, 13, 13, 14, 14, 14, 9, 4, 11, 14, 16, 17.

37. Ibid., 5.

38. Admiral L. Vladimirskii, "Novaia tekhnika na korabliakh" (New technology on surface combatant ships), *Komsomol'skaia pravda*, July 23, 1955.

39. Fleet Admiral S.G. Gorshkov, "Razvitie sovetskogo voenno-morskogo iskusstva" (Development of the Soviet naval art), *Morskoi sbornik*, no. 2 (1967): 19–20.

40. N.I. Makeev, "Avianosnye korabli" (Aircraft carriers), *Krasnaia zvezda*, December 15, 1955.

41. Nikita Khrushchev, *Khrushchev Remembers: The Last Testament*, trans. and ed. Strobe Talbott (Boston: Little, Brown, 1974), 30–31.

42. Lieutenant Colonel I. Kudanov, "Angliiskaia avianosnaia aviatsiia" British aircraft carrier aviation), *Sovietskii flot*, September 7, 1955

43. "XX ss"ezd KPSS, rech' tovarishcha Zhukova" (The Twentieth Party Congress of the CPSU, speech of Comrade Zhukov), *Krasnaia zvezda*, February 21, 1956.

44. Unsigned editorial, *Sovetskii flot*, July 5, 1957.

45. Rear Admiral V. Lizarskii, "Na strazhe mirnogo truda" (On guard over peaceful labor), *Turkmenskaia iskra*, July 31, 1960.

46. "XX s"ezd KPSS, rech' tovarishcha Zhukova."

47. Yu. Ladinskii, "O teorii voenno-morskogo iskusstva" (On the theory of the naval art), *Voennaia mysl'*, no. 7 (1957): 31.

48. Admiral S. Gorshkov, "Na strazhe morskikh rubezhei" (On guard over the maritime perimeters), *Pravda*, July 29, 1956.

49. Captain 1st Rank N. Nikolaev, "Voenno-morskoi flot v sisteme vooruzhnnykh sil SSSR" (The navy in the system of the armed forces of the USSR), *Sovetskii flot*, May 29, 1957.

50. D.I. Kornienko, *Flot nashei rodiny* (The navy of our homeland) (Moscow: Voenizdat, 1957) [signed to press September 11, 1957], 48–49.

51. Captain 1st Rank N. Gordeev, "Oborona voenno-morskogo baz v sovremnnykh usloviiakh" (The defense of naval bases in modern conditions) *Krasnaia zvezda*, May 22, 1957.

52. "Materialy dlia dokladov i besed" (Materials for reports and discussions), *Sovetskii flot*, May 2, 1957.

53. Gorshkov, "Na strazhe morskikh rubezhei."

54. Captain 3rd Rank Yu. Schvarev, "Kak predstavliaiut na zapade rol' flota v sovremennoi voine" (How the role of a navy is viewed in the West), *Sovetskii flot*, April 13, 1958.

55. "Vneocherednoi XXI s"ezd Kommunisticheskoi partii sovetskogo soiuza, rech' Marshala Sovetskogo Soiuza R. Ya. Malinovskogo" (The Extraordinary Twenty-first Congress of the Communist party of the Soviet Union, speech of Marshal of the Soviet Union R. Ya. Malinovskii), *Izvestiia*, February 4, 1959.

56. For the original analysis of the distinction between "defense" and "protection," see James M. McConnell, "Military-Political Tasks of the Soviet Navy in War and Peace," in *Soviet Oceans Development*, Senate Committee on Commerce print (Washington D.C.: Government Printing Office, 1976), 183–209, esp. 208.

57. "Den' voenno-morskogo flota SSSR. Materialy dlia dokladov i besed" (Navy Day of the USSR, materials for reports and discussions), *Sovetskii flot*, July 11, 1959.

58. Admiral V. Tributs, "Na strazhe morskikh rubezhei" (On guard over the maritime perimeters), *Izvestiia*, July 26, 1959.

59. Cited as a statement by Khrushchev in William J. Jorden, "Premier Strolls through the City," *New York Times*, September 22, 1959, 22.

60. N.S. Khrushchev, "Razoruzhenie—put' k uprocheniiu mira i obespecheniiu druzhby mezhdunarodnoi" (Disarmament—the way to peace and friendship among peoples), *Izvestia*, January 15, 1960.

61. Ibid.

Part IV
Soviet Thinking about Navies and War

In chapter 8 MccGwire views Soviet military strategy, and thus naval roles and missions, as developing slowly but changing dramatically in key decision periods, like water turning into ice. Three main decision periods—1957–1959, 1967–1968, and 1976–1977—produced nuclear or conventional strategies for the conduct of a world war and, thus, naval construction programs for the subsequent period. By the mid-1980s Soviet policy had shifted away from preparing for world war and toward the construction with the West of a mutual security regime. The current Soviet fleet is the product of the earlier decision periods; the fleet of the future will be shaped by the requirements for perimeter defense of the homeland, as well as the worst-case requirement of not losing a world war.

Donald C. Daniel in chapter 9 outlines the arguments current in the West over many years for and against the strategic offensive and strategic defensive models of Soviet naval behavior and concludes that the Soviets are likely to retain a strategic defensive posture, with a fleet structured for perimeter defense.

Proceeding from different methodoligies and evidence, MccGwire and Daniel converge to agree on the shape of the future Soviet Navy. They also agreed that the 1988 book by N.P. V'iunenko et al., *The Navy: Its Role, Prospects for Future Development, and Employment,* is one of naval advocacy. Published in the midst of Gorbachev's attempts to demilitarize East-West relations, and yet with its powerful future scenarios for a war-fighting navy, this book has stirred much debate in the West. It is an element in an interservice debate or a product of a politico-military consensus on naval policy? Is it intended as a war-fighting book, or does it lay the groundwork for a naval arms control agenda? Is it a product of "old thinking" about war or future thinking about the relationship between advances in technology, economic restructuring, and emerging requirements for homeland defense? The question has yet to be resolved.

8
The Soviet Navy and World War

Michael MccGwire

The Naval Background

Russia and Sea Power

For two hundred years and more the Russian navy has generally been among the three or four largest in the world.[1] In the eighteenth century Russia used naval forces to support its army in gaining control of its Baltic and Black Sea coasts. Four times between 1768 and 1827 it deployed sizable squadrons to the Mediterranean; three of those deployments took place during wars with the Ottoman Empire, ships being drawn from the Baltic Fleet to operate against the southern side of the Turkish Straits. In 1987, when the United States was celebrating the two hundredth anniversary of its Constitution, the Russian Navy was nearing its three hundredth birthday.

In other words, Russia has always understood the significance of sea power. It used sea power in the past to its own advantage but has more often seen that long arm used against it—most notably in the Black Sea in 1854–1856 and 1878 and the Far East in 1905–1906. Over the years Russia and the Soviet Union have committed substantial resources to naval construction. The major warship program initiated in 1945 was the fourth attempt in sixty-five years to build up a strong fleet. But national strategy involves setting priorities and balancing competing claims for scarce resources. Russia was predominantly a land power; the only threats to its territorial existence had come by land; and the army was the basis of security at home and influence abroad. Naval forces were required to counter the capability of maritime powers to dictate the outcome of events in adjacent sea areas, but the Russians saw their naval forces as an expensive necessity and not (as did the maritime powers) a preferred instrument of policy for peacetime use as much as war.

Evolving Military Doctrine

This ordering of priorities exists today, and Soviet naval developments must be analyzed within the context of the development of the armed forces as a whole to meet the contingency of world war. From 1917 through the 1950s the Soviets lived with war or the expectation that war must come to their territory. Although in 1956 it was ruled that war between capitalists and socialists was no longer fatalistically inevitable, the possibility of such conflict remained inherent in the antagonisms between the two social systems. And by the end of the 1950s it was clear to the Soviets that such a war, if it came, would be a nuclear world war.

Soviet forces were therefore structured for the contingency of world war—a war the Soviets absolutely wanted to avoid but could not afford to lose. This force structure has, nevertheless, varied over the years as Soviet military doctrine about the likely nature of such a war has evolved, with consequent changes in objectives, strategy, and hence military requirements.

Because it takes time to translate new requirements into military hardware, the actual structure of Soviet forces has lagged significantly behind the adoption of the preferred strategy. This is particularly true of the navy, where new programs have a lead time of ten to fifteen years, and major modifications to existing programs have lead times of three to eight years. As a consequence, the evidence of naval developments in hardware is likely to be confusing, particularly when a second change in military doctrine occurs before the first has become manifest.

The West has no real equivalent to Soviet military doctrine, a continuously evolving system of officially accepted views on basic questions about war. Authorized at the highest political level, military doctrine provides the framework for decisions on strategic and operational concepts, the structure and deployment of forces, and the development and procurement of weapons. At the core of Soviet military doctrine is an assessment of the likely nature of a future war. This assessment determines the way the war will be fought, the range of possible objectives, and the peacetime force posture required to cover this contingency.

Turning Points in Naval Policy

To appreciate the changing roles of the navy—when it may or may not simultaneously possess forces appropriate to these roles—a clear understanding of the evolution of Soviet wartime objectives, strategy, and concepts of operation is essential. One must identify and date the decision periods when key doctrinal decisions take place. From these doctrinal decisions flow the series of implementing decisions that result in the production of new types of ships and aircraft and the new patterns of deployment required by new concepts of operation.[2]

The current structure of the Soviet Navy derives from three main decision periods: (1) that of 1957–1959, with a major naval adjustment in 1961–1962, producing the "1960s" objectives and fleet, (2) that of 1967–1968, producing the "1970s" objectives and fleet, and (3) the modifications of 1976–1977, producing the "1980s" navy. The first part of this chapter focuses on the naval developments that stemmed from these decision periods in order to understand the rationale for the Soviet Navy as it exists today. In the mid-1980s, however, the Soviet Union entered a new period of major military change. The nature of this change and what it might imply for the Soviet Navy is discussed in the final part of this chapter.

Doctrinal Evolution from World War II to the Mid-1970s

The Period after World War II

As World War II drew to a close, the Soviet view of the future threat environment was reasonably optimistic. Notwithstanding Marxist dogma that war between the two systems was inevitable, the Soviets did not consider that such a conflict was likely in the immediate future. This sanguine assessment could not be sustained for long, and by 1948 the Soviets had concluded that they faced the more immediate and more serious threat of premeditated attack by 1953 by a capitalist coalition led by the English-speaking powers.[3]

Affirming the reality of this threat was the speed with which U.S. policy toward its erstwhile enemies (the Axis powers) had moved from hostility to friendship. The United States had insisted on Italy's being a founding member of the United Nations, and by 1948 U.S. policy had altered from exacting reparations to rehabilitating Germany and Japan. This development was particularly disturbing because it seemed to confirm the Marxist prognosis of history and involved the key members of the 1936 Anti-Comintern Pact, two of them traditional enemies of Russia.

As a result of World War II, the Soviet Union had established its military perimeter across the narrower part of Europe, but its maritime flanks were very vulnerable. The Baltic coast exposed the lines of communications to Soviet forces in Germany. The Black Sea gave direct access to the Soviet Union's industrial hinterland (outflanking the defense of distance), and its rivers became avenues for Western advance rather than natural defensive barriers.

In such circumstances defense against seaborne invasion assumed a new importance, and the Soviets planned to discharge this traditional naval task with cruiser/destroyer surface-attack groups, torpedo-armed aircraft, fast patrol boats, and submarines deployed in depth. In 1948 the Soviets projected a force of 1,200 submarines, all but 180 of which would be deployed in the area defense role in the four fleet areas.

The failure of the North Atlantic Treaty Organization (NATO) to meet its publicized force goals and advances in Soviet military capability combined to make a conventional invasion of Eastern Europe increasingly implausible. Following Stalin's death in 1953, the Soviets reassessed the threat and the nature of their military requirements. The threat of invasion by land and sea was downgraded, and national priority was given to the threat of nuclear strikes by the U.S. Strategic Air Command, whose force would top 1,750 aircraft in 1959.

The navy was given the more limited task of countering conventional strikes by Western carrier-borne aircraft against naval bases and other coastal targets. It was assumed that Western attack carriers would have to close within range of Soviet shore-based air support, and the decision was taken to rely on coordinated attacks by long-range cruise missiles launched by medium-sized surface ships, diesel submarines, and aircraft. This innovative response was prompted in large part by economic considerations, since this response justified the cancellation of warship building programs then in progress or projected. This represented a 60 percent cut in annual production tonnage and enabled substantial resources to be released to the civilian economy.[4]

By the end of the 1950s a sharp improvement in the capability of carrier-borne aircraft allowed U.S. carriers to strike at the Soviet Union with nuclear weapons from the eastern Mediterranean and the southern reaches of the Norwegian Sea. To meet this new threat from distant sea areas, the Soviets decided in 1957–1958 to place primary naval emphasis on nuclear submarines, which would be able to operate in the face of Western surface and air superiority. This decision necessitated further major changes in the naval building programs, including the cancellation or curtailment of submarine and surface programs that had only been projected in 1954.

The overall Soviet concept of operations in the 1950s was essentially a projection of World War II experience. The basic principles, strategies, and tactics that had proved so successful in driving the Germans back across the eastern half of Europe could be used to repulse and drive a future aggressor back across the other half of Europe.

The emerging implications of long-range guided missiles and nuclear weapons prompted a major reassessment in the 1957–1959 period. It had already been ruled in 1956 that war between the two social systems was no longer fatalistically inevitable, a doctrinal adjustment that reflected the military-industrial rehabilitation of the Soviet Union and the emergence of a powerful communist bloc. And by 1960 the likelihood of a deliberate U.S. attack had been largely discounted, however, the possibility of war between the two systems remained inherent in the prevailing structure of the international system, and the Soviet military continued to plan for this contingency.

Doctrinal Developments in Two Decision Periods: The 1960s and 1970s

By 1959 a doctrinal decision had been taken that any world war inevitably would be nuclear and involve massive nuclear strikes on the Soviet Union. This implied that such a war would be the decisive encounter between the capitalist and socialist systems—an encounter where survival was all that could be expected of victory and where defeat would be synonymous with extinction. In order not to lose such a war, the Soviets would have to "preserve the socialist system" and "destroy the capitalist system." These were the primary wartime objectives.

The impossibility of defending against nuclear-armed ballistic missiles placed a premium on getting in the first blow. This was the only way to reduce the weight of enemy attack and thereby help to preserve the socialist system. The Soviets therefore adopted a strategy predicated on successful nuclear preemption. This meant that (at least in theory) a decision that war with the West was inescapable would be synonymous with a decision to launch nuclear strikes on North America and against military installations located around the periphery of the Soviet Union. The difficulty of making such a determination and the political constraints on launching such strikes were obvious, but an offensive, damage-limiting strategy was the least of all evils—particularly in the face of their opponent's overwhelming superiority.

In late 1966, however, the Soviets ruled that a world war would not inevitably be nuclear, and, even if it were, the war would not necessarily involve massive strikes on them. This seemingly modest adjustment to Soviet military doctrine had immense consequences. The new 1966 doctrine decreed that such nuclear strikes were no longer inevitable; hence it was not only possible to adopt the objective of avoiding the nuclear devastation of the Soviet Union, it was necessary to do so in order to support the overarching objective of "promoting the well-being of the Soviet state."

Once the primary objective of preserving the socialist system was replaced in 1966 by the more ambitious one of avoiding nuclear devastation, the Soviets also had to replace the other primary objective of destroying the capitalist system, an objective that could be achieved only by launching nuclear strikes on the United States, which would inevitably result in retaliation against the Soviet Union. Therefore North America would have to be spared nuclear attack, and a less ambitious objective would have to be adopted, such as "gravely weakening the capitalist system." Under such circumstances, a world war would not necessarily be the decisive encounter between the two systems; it could be seen as a critical campaign in the ongoing struggle.

For ease of exposition, these two different sets of objectives and their associated strategic concepts will be labeled "1960s," deriving from the 1957–1959 decision period, and "1970s," deriving from the 1967–1968 decision period (table 8–1). In practice, 1967–1975 was a period of change during which some policies (such as arms control) were adjusted early on, while other policies had to await the restructuring of forces and operational concepts that would allow the Soviets to adopt fully the new hierarchy of strategic objectives. The evidence from this period, which was also one of considerable internal debate, is therefore confusing. It is all the more confusing because the new concepts that took effect in 1967–1975 did not replace the previous strategy that was designed to wage global nuclear war but meshed with it to produce a flexible strategy that could respond to changing nuclear circumstances. In the event of war, the Soviets would have preferred to stay within the 1970s hierarchy of objectives, but they remain prepared for the full range of contingencies, including global nuclear war.

The 1970s Strategy

The Overall Concept

An important implication of the 1970s objectives was that the North American military-industrial base would be spared. The Soviet Union could not therefore afford to allow the United States to retain a bridgehead on the European continent; otherwise it would be only a matter of time before the United States had amassed sufficient military strength to launch a land offensive designed to destroy the socialist system and overthrow the Soviet state. It would also be necessary to establish an extended defense perimeter that could thwart any attempt to establish a relevant bridgehead in northern Africa or Southwest and South Asia.

The eviction of the United States from Europe was not simply a question of mass and maneuver. The problem was how to defeat NATO without the conflict's escalating to an intercontinental nuclear exchange. Western defense of NATO Europe was predicated on the ultimate resort to nuclear weapons, and this could escalate out of control. And even if nuclear weapons could be limited to the theater, there would be strong pressures on the United States to launch nuclear strikes on the Soviet Union in a last attempt to prevent U.S. forces from going down to defeat in Europe.

The Soviet response to this second problem was wartime deterrence: the threat of nuclear retaliation should the United States strike at the Soviet

Table 8–1
Soviet Doctrine on the Nature of World War

Aspect	The 1960s	The 1970s
	Nature of World War	
Military	Inevitably nuclear, including nuclear strikes on the Soviet Union	May not be nuclear. Strikes on the Soviet Union are not inevitable
Political	A fight to the finish between two social systems	A critical campaign in the ongoing struggle between the two systems
	Primary Military Objectives	
Own survival	Preserve the socialist system	Avoid the nuclear devastation of the Soviet Union
Enemy's defeat	Destroy the capitalist system	Gravely weaken the capitalist system

Source: MccGwire, *Military Objectives,* 45.

Union. A corollary to this response was a shift in Soviet arms control policy. During the 1960s, strategic arms limitations had not been in the Soviet Union's interests. The Soviet Union still lagged behind the United States in intercontinental capability, and the ultimate Soviet objective was nuclear superiority. This changed with the 1970s strategy.

Now Soviet interests would be best served by strategic parity at as low a level as possible. Should deterrence fail, the smaller the U.S. strategic arsenal, the less would be the nuclear devastation of the Soviet Union. Strategic arms negotiations were the only way to get the United States to reduce its inventory of nuclear weapons. Agreement to limit strategic nuclear weapons therefore became an end in itself, justifying major adjustments to future weapons programs and curtailing current production.

The Soviets did not, however, declare these concessions, partly because old habits die hard. But they also needed to conceal their new-found interest in arms control lest it weaken their negotiating position, as well as reveal the major reorientation of wartime strategy, which was then just getting underway. The perception therefore persisted that the Soviet Union was a reluctant partner who had to be dragged to the negotiating table.

The less tractable problem was the danger that NATO's resort to nuclear weapons in the theater would escalate out of control. The Soviet response was to try to prevent the initial resort to nuclear weapons in the theater and, if that were not possible, to limit its extent. The approach was to exploit the NATO concept of flexible response (which foresaw a conventional phase at the start of war in Europe) in order to launch preventive attacks against NATO's nuclear delivery systems, command, control, and communications (C^3) nodes, and higher command structure, and (at the same time) to mount a massive blitzkrieg offensive striking deep to NATOs rear—all of this using conventional means only. It was to be hoped that the ensuing disruption would paralyze NATO's decision-making processes and that the synergism of the combined assaults would encourage the European members to accept defeat without resort to nuclear weapons. If, nevertheless, NATO did go nuclear, its capability would have been considerably diminished.

By the late 1970s the force structure required to carry out this concept of operations was largely in place. This did not mean that the Soviets had a high confidence that their offensive in NATO Europe would succeed or that they thought that the chances of avoiding the resort to nuclear weapons in the theater were very great. But the objective of avoiding the nuclear devastation of the Soviet Union was so important that it justified the costs of restructuring Soviet forces in order to increase the possibility of achieving that objective in the event that war itself could not be avoided (table 8–2).

The 1970s strategy envisaged a two-phase war. In the first phase, initially intense operations would lead to the defeat of NATO forces in Europe, which would be followed (if possible) by some kind of peace agreement. If peace were not possible, the war would then move into a second phase involving a protracted struggle on a global scale whose course would be hard to predict.

In phase I, the main theater would be Europe, and the Western theater of military action (TVD) would be the main TVD in that theater. One can visualize phase I being divided for planning purposes into three stages. The first stage (phase I/1, which might last twelve to twenty days) would cover the period of the offensive into Western Europe, when Soviet operations would be designed to knock NATO out of the war. The second stage (phase I/2, which might last twenty to thirty days) would cover the redeployment of forces, the completion of offensive operations on the secondary axes of advance, and the occupation of territories to the rear of the defeated enemy's main forces. The third stage (phase I/3, another two or three months) would cover the establishment of an extended defensive perimeter.

In the event of a world war, a primary Soviet objective would be to avoid simultaneous campaigns in Europe and the Far East. During Phase I, therefore, the primary objective in the Far Eastern TVD would be to deter the Chinese from any aggressive actions using conventional means only. To the extent that the Soviet Union planned offensive operations in the area (for example, against Manchuria or South Korea), these would be delayed until phase I/3 at the earliest and more probably until phase II.

The Navy in the 1970s Strategy

The 1970s strategy had significant implications for war at sea. The most far reaching in its effects was the new contribution that Soviet nuclear-powered ballistic missile submarines (SSBNs) would be required to make to wartime

Table 8–2
A Comparison of the 1960s and 1970s Strategic Hierarchies

1960s Hierarchy	*1970s Hierarchy*
Objectives	
Preserve the socialist system	Avoid the nuclear devastation of the Soviet
Protect the physical structure of government and secure its capacity for effective operation throughout the Soviet state	Hamper NATO's resort to nuclear weapons
Guarantee the survival of a proportion of the nation's industrial base and working population	Deter nuclear strikes on the Soviet Union
Secure an alternative economic base to contribute to the rebuilding of a socialist society in the Soviet Union	Ensure against the fixed-silo deterrent's being rendered impotent
Destroy the capitalist system	Gravely weaken the capitalist system
Destroy enemy forces in being	Establish physical control of Europe
Destroy the enemy's war-making potential	Deny U.S. access to the western parts of Eurasia
Destroy the system's structure of governmental and social control	Establish hegemony over Japan and South Korea
Type of War	
Short, all-out nuclear war, including intercontinental nuclear exchange	Two-phase war, no intercontinental exchange I: Short, high-intensity offensive operations in Europe, preferably nonnuclear II: Long-drawn-out, primarily defensive; course unpredictable

Source: Ibid., 47.

deterrence. The most controversial implication was the potential role of Soviet naval forces in phase II of a global war against a coalition of maritime powers.

SSBN Development and Roles. Today's Soviet SSBN force is not just the result of incremental product improvement. Rather, the force reflects three distinct developmental periods: 1947–1958, 1961–1967, and 1968 through the 1980s. In each of these periods, the submarine's capability for intercontinental delivery of nuclear warheads was intended to serve a significantly different strategic purpose.

First, in seeking to break the U.S. atomic monopoly in the immediate postwar years, developing a means of delivery was as important to the Soviet Union as building the atomic warhead. To ensure success, the Soviets adopted three lines of attack: the land-based intercontinental ballistic missile (ICBM), the long-range bomber, and the submarine (the submarine-launched torpedo was the only delivery system where Soviet technology and experience were already in place).

Submarine development burgeoned into a four-track program that permuted two different weapons (the torpedo and the ballistic missile) with two different platforms (diesel and nuclear powered), to produce the Foxtrot SS, Golf SSB, November SSN, and Hotel SSBN all of them programmed to start delivery in 1958.[5] By 1958, however, the ICBM had already been declared the winner of the strategic delivery competition. Consequently by 1959 the navy had lost the mission of strategic strike, and nuclear-powered submarines had been reassigned to the countercarrier role.

Second, the strategic strike mission was restored to the Soviet Navy in 1961 in response to the rapid buildup of Polaris submarines initiated by the Kennedy administration. This coincided with the entry into service of the U.S. strategic strike carriers that had been programmed during the Korean War, which meant that one-third of the U.S. strategic nuclear capability would be seaborne and would therefore survive the initial exchanges. This capability had to be matched or balanced; otherwise the United States would have been able to dictate the outcome of the war.

The Soviet response was the Yankee SSBN, with seventy units programmed for delivery in the ten years 1968–1977. Except for a few forward-deployed units that would cover such aircraft carriers and Polaris submarines as were in port at the outbreak of war, the Yankee force would be held back in home waters, available to the Supreme High Command for use in the post-exchange phase.

This new requirement to produce a large number of much bigger hull propulsion units caused considerable turbulence in the submarine-building programs—for example, the need to assemble the Victor SSN in a floating dock. Constraints on the annual availability of naval reactors meant that the production of the torpedo-armed Victor SSN and Charlie SSGN[6] armed with submerged-launched surface-to-surface missiles (SSMs)—planned for the 1968–1972 period—had to be stretched out over ten years; and production planned for the second five years of the original ten-year program was deferred until 1978–1982. Meanwhile the Charlie SSGN had to make do with a single reactor.[7]

Third, further changes in the submarine-building programs were generated by the 1967–1968 decision period.[8] The 1970s strategy introduced a new and demanding requirement: to deter the United States from resorting to nuclear strikes on the Soviet Union when faced by the defeat of its forces in NATO Europe. The primary means of wartime deterrence would be the ICBM force, but the Soviets had to guard against the possibility that U.S. technical ingenuity might find some way of rendering these land-based missiles impotent (thus outflanking the deterrent). Soviet development of a land-mobile ICBM had been unsuccessful; hence the Soviets turned to the SSBN as the means of ensuring against the possibility of such technological out-flanking (see Table 8–3).

The specifications for a 1970s insurance force were more demanding than for a 1960s matching force, reflecting the different operational concepts. In both cases, an unambiguous attack on a Soviet SSBN would be seen as an act of war. But whereas an attack on a matcher would trigger a nuclear strike on North America (as the Soviets sought the advantage of strategic preemption under the 1960s strategy), there could be no such response if an insurer were attacked. This was because the primary Soviet objective under the 1970s strategy was to avoid the nuclear devastation of the Soviet Union (which a nuclear strike on North America would bring about).

The 1970s concept of operations was predicated on avoiding escalation to an intercontinental exchange. Therefore, during such a war the Soviet insurance force would have to be held secure against determined attempts by the United States to draw down its numbers. This requirement—and the requirement for effective command and control—meant that the insurance force would need to be deployed close to Soviet bases (where such a defense could most easily be mounted) and would need missiles with the range to strike at North America from Soviet home waters.

In providing for the security of the insurance force, the Soviets turned to a well-established concept. In order to ensure their exclusive use of the Black Sea and Baltic, they had developed the capability to seize the exits in the initial stages of a war. From this concept it was a short step to envisaging the Arctic as a semienclosed sea that could be sealed off from Western intrusion.

Viewed from the pole, the Arctic Ocean comprises a roughly circular area with a mean radius of about 1,000 nautical miles. Ninety percent of the perimeter is land. There are three ways in by sea. Two of these—the Bering Strait and the straits through the Canadian archipelago—are relatively narrow and/or shallow and lend themselves to being blocked. The third route is the Norwegian Sea, an area some 900 nautical miles square with depths down to 12,000 feet. In order to close off this access, the Soviets would need to gain and maintain command of the Norwegian Sea. This in turn would require them to control the adjacent coastlines.

Establishing command of the Norwegian Sea was a force-consuming requirement. But the new concept of operations also had fundamental implications for the design criteria of major combatants. Under the 1960s concept, war would inevitably escalate to an intercontinental exchange, and nuclear weapons were to be used at sea from the start. The navy's primary mission was to counter Western sea-based strategic delivery systems, and warships only had to be able to survive long enough to discharge that mission. The 1970s concept, however, required a force that could sustain operations in a conventional mode for an extended period but still be able to resort to nuclear weapons should wartime deterrence fail.

Table 8–3
Planned and Actual Delivery of Nuclear-Powered Warships, 1968–1982

Classes of Warship	1957–1958 Decision Period: Delivery Planned for:		1961–1962 Decision Period: Delivery Planned for:			1967–1968 Decision Period: Actual Deliveries			
	1968–1972	1973–1977	1968–1972	1973–1977	1978–1982	1968–1972	1973–1977	(1973–1982)	1978–1982
Tac-Yankee	10	10	—	—	—	0	0	—	—
Yankee I, II	—	—	35	35	—	34	0	—	—
Successor SSBN[a]	—	—	—	—	10	—	—	—	0
Delta (Yankee II)[b]	—	—	—	—	—	—	—	35	—
Typhoon[a,b]	—	—	—	—	—	—	—	—	6[c]
Victor I, II	20	—	10	10	—	10	13	—	—
Victor III	—	20	—	—	20	—	0	—	18
Charlie (½)	20	—	10	10	—	10	—	7	—
Charlie	—	—	—	—	—	0	—	—	—
Papa[a]	—	20	—	—	15[d]	—	1	—	0
Alpha[a]	—	—	—	—	5[d]	—	—	6	—
Oscar[a,b]	—	—	—	—	—	—	—	—	9[c]
Kirov[a,b]	—	—	—	—	—	—	—	—	2
Addenda: Number of reactors[e]									
1968 model	100	60	100	100	40	100	—	139	—
1973 model	—	40	—	—	60	—	—	60	—
Total	100	100	100	100	100	100	—	199	—

Source: Ibid., 428, corrected.

Note: It is assumed that the navy was allocated twenty nuclear reactors a year during this period.

[a] These units have 1973 model reactors.

[b] Because of their size, the date of launch is used for Typhoon, Oscar, and Kirov rather than the date of delivery.

[c] Only three Typhoons and three Oscars were actually launched in this period as the result of decisions made in 1976–1977.

[d] Lead units of Papa and Alpha were built in the preceding delivery period.

[e] All units have two reactors except for Typhoon, which has four, and Charlie (½), which has one.

The Soviet response was to scale up the size of all types of major combatants so as to provide them with greater endurance and larger weapon loads. There was also an increase in the number of different types. These new classes were programmed to start delivery at the beginning of the 1980s.

The Navy's Role in Phase II of a World War. The 1970s concept of a two-phase war in which the superpowers' military-industrial bases would remain untouched opened up questions about the nature of phase II and how it would best be fought. Four such questions had major implications for the Soviet Navy.

First, having evicted U.S. forces from NATO Europe, the Soviets would have to establish a defense perimeter to prevent their return. The need to economize force by exploiting natural defensive barriers suggests the Sahara Desert as the southern boundary of the defense perimeter, which would then angle down to meet the Indian Ocean at the Horn of Africa. To the west, there could be some kind of "Atlantic wall"—this time to include Iceland and the British Isles. To the east, the defense perimeter would run north past the inhospitable shores of the Arabian Peninsula, up through Baluchistan to Afghanistan, and then along the Chinese border to the Pacific. In the Far East the alignment is less obvious, but it would probably be sufficient for the defense perimeter to run along the Kurils chain of islands, Japan, South Korea and the southern border of Manchuria—with Japan remaining unoccupied but subservient.

Second, accepting the requirement for a defense perimeter, there remained the question of how best to defend it. There were two main approaches, which were not mutually exclusive. One approach would be to rely primarily on close defense using all arms (including a land-based capability for long-range strike against groupings of ships at sea). The other would be to attack invading forces at their source and to harass them from the time they began to assemble until they came within range of the perimeter defense forces. This second approach would draw largely on naval assets.

Third, assuming that a defense perimeter could be established and defended, there was the further question of whether the Soviets could afford to remain ensconced behind it or would need to carry the war to the enemy. The idea that Western capitalism would wither on the vine if it were denied access to most of the Eastern Hemisphere was not entirely persuasive. Indeed, the denial of such access might inject new vigor into the capitalist system and allow the United States to forge a powerful coalition from the nations of its own hemisphere plus Australia, New Zealand, and South Africa. In either case there would be an important role for Soviet naval forces in preventing the supply of essential raw materials and in reinforcing political-economic instruments of policy designed to isolate physically the Western Hemisphere.

A fourth and more mundane implication of the 1970s concept of operations was the requirement to be able to supply the Soviet Far East by sea should the need arise. Within the 1960s concept, China was to be struck with nuclear weapons at the same time as the main intercontinental exchange, lest it emerge the winner of a Soviet-U.S. war. Ground operations against China would probably be limited to seizing Manchuria for use as an alternative socioeconomic base from which to rebuild the socialist system, and these military operations would rely on stockpiles in the Far East.

In contrast, the 1970s concept required the Soviets to assume a defensive posture in the Far Eastern TVD until phase I/3 at least, but the Soviet Union would also have to cover the possibility that China might seek to profit from war in Europe. As a separate consideration, there was the possibility of war with China outside the circumstances of a world war. In either case it had to be assumed that China would seek to disrupt the railroad link with the western Soviet Union. In such a situation the Far Eastern TVD would have to be supplied by the southern sea route, preferably out of the Black Sea and through Suez, but if necessary across Iran (either to the head of the Persian Gulf or from Afghanistan through Chah Bahar). In all cases the sea-line of communication (SLOC) across the Indian Ocean and through Southeast Asia would need to be secured.

Disagreement over Naval Missions and Resources. In 1969 it would have been clear that the restructuring of Soviet ground-air forces in the European theater would be sufficiently advanced to permit the full adoption of the 1970s concept of operations in 1976. By the end of 1975 about fifteen Delta-class SSBNs capable of striking at North America from Soviet home waters would have been delivered to the navy; however, the new classes of ships and submarines that were intended to secure their defense were not programmed to start delivery until the 1980s. In the interim, therefore, the mission of securing the SSBN force would have to be discharged at the expense of those naval missions whose relative priority had been downgraded with the adoption of the 1970s hierarchy of objectives.

This reordering of priorities would severely affect the peacetime mission of posing a permanent counter to Western sea-based strategic delivery systems in distant sea areas. A primary objective of the 1970s hierarchy was to avoid a nuclear exchange; therefore, missions that were mainly relevant to the postexchange phase of war had to yield precedence to those that contributed to deterring escalation to such an exchange. Forward-deployed units would not be able to launch their nuclear weapons unless escalation was seen to be inevitable. Meanwhile they would be subjected to sustained attack by greatly superior Western forces, and it was not clear how they could survive to discharge the counterforce mission if the need should arise.

The naval forces originally deployed forward in strategic defense had gradually acquired the additional peacetime role of promoting and protecting Soviet interests in these distant sea areas. The emergence of this role in the late 1960s coincided with a new Soviet interest in the potential role of a military presence as an instrument of policy in the Third World, an interest that stemmed from the restructuring of strategic objectives following the December 1966 doctrinal shift. It was in these circumstances that the navy was able to initiate a broader debate on the implications of the 1970s objectives for war at sea.

The public vehicle for the navy's challenge was the series of eleven articles published in 1972–1973, that are commonly known as the "Gorshkov Series." Eighty percent of the series covered the period prior to 1945, and its central thrust was the importance of navies as a means of influencing the course and outcome of wars. Three major themes can be identified. Taken together, these added up to a powerful argument for a larger and better balanced fleet.[9]

One theme concerned forward deployment in peacetime, which was defended on two scores. The "blunting of nuclear attacks" from the sea was described as a basic naval mission: defending the homeland against such attacks was accorded the same importance as the mission of strategic strike. Second, the navy's presence in distant sea areas served to counter imperialist aggression in those areas while demonstrating Soviet economic and military might.

A second theme concerned the requirements for ensuring the security of the SSBN force. It was not an argument about the desirability or the nature of the navy's contribution to strategic nuclear strikes, a topic Gorshkov all but ignored. Gorshkov's discussion of SSBN protection can be grouped under two main headings.[10] One concerned the kinds of forces needed to protect the SSBNs—specifically emphasizing the need for surface ships and aircraft to support submarines. And the other heading concerned the importance of establishing command of the Norwegian Sea in order to protect the SSBNs and what would be involved in operations to achieve this objective.

The third theme concerned the navy's role in phase II of a global war. Using an analysis of naval operations in the two world wars, Gorshkov argued in support of two missions in phase II. One was to counter Western attempts to reestablish themselves on the Eurasian continent by attacking the invading forces while en route to the disembarkation areas. The other was to deny the United States access to essential raw materials by attacking its SLOCs.

It is generally considered that the initial result of this internal debate was an increase in the navy's political clout, and there are indications that additional resources were allocated to naval construction, including (perhaps) a 50 percent increase in naval reactors for the warship programs that would start delivery in 1983. As part of the compromise the navy had to acknowledge that the traditional fleet-against-fleet mission had yielded priority to fleet against shore, a formulation that included the support of ground-air operations in the continental TVDs as well as the role of the SSBN insurance force. Furthermore, the navy was authorized to produce Gorshkov's book, *Sea Power of the State* (1976), which was favorably received.

The 1976–1977 Decision Period: Military Adjustments during the Late 1970s and Early 1980s

The reviews of *Sea Power of the State* stressed the book's contribution to military science and noted that the role of maritime power had been given a scientific formulation for the first time. The impression that the navy's political clout had increased seemed to be reinforced by the appearance of a second edition in 1979. However, the trend toward greater naval autonomy had already peaked by 1976, and the army-dominated establishment had managed to reassert its authority in the field of military thought and the formulation of Soviet defense policy.

The 1976–77 Decision Period's New Military Requirements

Dmitri Ustinov took over as minister of defense after Marshal Grechko's death in 1976, and Nikolai Ogarkov became chief of the General Staff in January 1977. This was some nine years after the 1967–1968 decision period that had initiated the process of restructuring the Soviet armed forces to conform with the 1970s concept of operations. The change of leadership would have presented an appropriate opportunity to evaluate how those long-range projections had worked out in practice.

It seems likely that this 1976–1977 review resulted in the decisions to reintroduce the Operational Maneuver Group in the Western TVD, to set up a high command for the Far Eastern TVD, to develop the Blackjack bomber, and to design a new type of highly survivable and easily retargetable medium-range missile for use against military targets in the event of escalation to nuclear war in the theater. But the most far-reaching decisions concerned the role of the Arctic Ocean as a secure area for the deployment of SSBNs.

Changing Roles for the Arctic Ocean and the Sea of Okhotsk after 1976–1977

The 1970s concept of operations required that access to the Arctic be closed off by establishing command of the Norwegian Sea. This required in turn that the Soviets gain control of key islands in the area and much of the surrounding coastline. Even if deferred to phase I/2, this ancillary requirement would involve major military operations, and in phase II it would be necessary to occupy large parts of Norway, whose geography favored resistance movements.

All in all, the requirement to gain and maintain command of the Norwegian Sea was extremely costly in terms of scaling up all types of major naval combatants and in terms of the need for additional ground-air capabilities and occupation forces. And while it might be possible to establish command of the surface of and the air over the Norwegian Sea, there would have been considerable doubts about the feasibility of excluding U.S. submarines from the Arctic Ocean. By 1976–1977 the Soviets would have assessed the capability of the U.S. SSN-637 class to penetrate their antisubmarine defenses and would have taken into account the SSN-688 class that would shortly enter service and (according to congressional testimony) had been designed with anti-SSBN operations specifically in mind.

Other developments in this period were relevant. It seemed as if the United States intended to stabilize its navy at some 475 ships, with only 12 carrier battle groups. East-West détente appeared secure and the likelihood of war low. The problems that had previously prevented the deployment of Soviet mobile land-based ICBMs had been largely overcome, and the demands of the Soviet domestic economy were becoming increasingly pressing.

It was in these circumstances that the Soviets appear to have decided to downgrade the relative importance of the Arctic Ocean as an area for the deployment of SSBN and to give priority to making the Sea of Okhotsk secure by improving the military and physical defenses of the Kurils' island chain and reinforcing the Pacific Fleet.[11] The requirement to establish command of the Norwegian Sea appears to have been relaxed, which did not, however, imply conceding command to NATO. The Norwegian Sea probably reverted to being an outer defense zone of the Northern Fleet area, whose defense perimeter would run north from North Cape, through Bear Island and Svalbard, and across to Greenland.[12]

This significantly reduced requirement allowed the cancellation, curtailment, or amendment of naval programs that had been designed to support the original concept of closing off the Arctic Ocean.[13] Only the lead ship of the *Berezina* class of underway-replenishment ship was built and the lead ship of the *Ivan Rogov* class of high-speed long-range lift was followed by a five-year hiatus before a solitary second unit finally appeared. Plans for building an aircraft carrier may have been adjusted at this time, and both the Oscar SSGN and the Typhoon SSBN programs were probably curtailed.[14] The availability of reactors suggests that Oscar had originally been programmed to build at three a year and Typhoon at two a year—both for ten years.[15] As would have been expected, both began delivery in the early 1980s but at only one unit a year. Given the changed concept of operations, both programs are likely to have been cancelled, with the smaller Delta IV SSBN taking the place of the much more ambitious Typhoon.[16]

The untypically slow rate of delivery of the next generation of attack submarine could be accounted for by a decision in 1976–1977 to rescind a 50 percent increase in the allocation of naval reactors that would have been authorized in 1973–1974 in the wake of the Gorshkov series—for submarine deliveries beginning in 1983.[17] Meanwhile it is still too early to be certain that the 1976–1977 decision period did not affect other surface programs (besides *Berezina* and *Ivan Rogov*).

Downgrading the importance of the Arctic Ocean implied increasing the importance of the Far East, and the late 1970s saw the beginning of a new buildup of the Pacific Fleet and a progressive shift in the disposition of SSBNs. Whereas formerly some 70 percent of SSBNs had been in the North and 30 percent in the Pacific, by 1984 the proportion was closer to 55:45.

The 1976–1977 Naval Reversals in Perspective

The effect of the 1976–1977 decision period on Soviet naval building programs has still to be fully discerned;[18] but it is relevant that this same period saw a cutback in the forward deployment of naval units (most notably in the Mediterranean)[19] and a general decline in the political use of the Soviet Navy in the Third World (a role Gorshkov had argued strongly for in his earlier series). In 1979 the discontinuance of a separate doctorate in naval science (as distinct from military science) was a further blow to naval aspirations,[20] and the impression of a decline in the navy's political clout was reinforced by the structured debate on "The Theory of Navies" in 1981–1983, which was wrapped up by Gorshkov himself.[21] These articles can be construed as an attempt to mark out the navy's legitimate turf within a unified system of military science and strategy while setting up a theoretically legitimate vehicle for arguing the naval case within that system.

Whatever gains came to the navy from its demarche in 1971–1973 were largely lost as a result of the 1976–1977 decision period, but the reversal should be kept in perspective. The army-dominated military leadership had consistently acknowledged that the navy had an important role to play in the event of world war. The disagreement was about how best to allocate resources that were scarce relative to the demanding requirements.

A major consideration was that a significant part of the navy's more ambitious requirements was related to phase II of the 1970s strategy. However, unless Soviet ground-air operations in the Western TVD were successful in phase I/1, there would be no phase II of the kind the navy envisaged. This argument applied as much to the Arctic Ocean as to defending the extended perimeter and carrying the war to the enemy. The strategic advantages of sealing off the Arctic from Western intrusion were obvious, but it would take time to establish command of the Norwegian Sea (assuming it could be done at all), and those advantages would not be available during the initial stages of the war when they were most urgently needed. It would seem that in 1967–1968 the feasibility of the plan was oversold, and the full cost in operational and economic resources was underestimated.

The Navy's Missions in Phase I of a World War after the 1976–1977 Setback

Despite the setback in 1976–1977, the navy's role in phase I of a world war continued to be important. Naval support of ground-air operations in the continental TVDs could extend to launching strikes against NATO's C³ and nuclear delivery facilities using conventionally armed land-attack cruise missiles. These would substitute for scarce land-based means of attack and be able to outflank NATO's air defenses.[22] If, however, Soviet operations in phase I/1 ran to plan, there would be little point in deploying naval forces to attack the Atlantic SLOCs. Instead, such NATO reinforcements as could be brought to battle in time to affect the outcome in the Western TVD would be best dealt with by Soviet Frontal Aviation.

This calculation would change if Soviet operations in the Western TVD bogged down. In those circumstances, disrupting the flow of NATO supplies would take precedence over the mission of protecting Northern Fleet SSBNs from Western incursions because an intact SSBN force would have little strategic relevance if the Soviets failed to achieve their objectives in Western Europe. Northern fleet attack submarines (SSNs and SSGNs) would therefore be redeployed in the antishipping role, denuding the SSBNs of this element of their protection and increasing their reliance on concealment, evasion, and various means of self-defense. This is one example of how the relative priority of wartime missions can change with time and circumstance.

SSBN Roles in a World War

Another example is provided by the Soviet SSBN force, which has two different roles: a present role that supports the 1970s strategy and a potential role that supports the 1960s strategy. The present "insurance" role is most critical in peacetime and during phase I of a world war, particularly the first stage. After that it would become less important as the likelihood of escalation waned, but if the war dragged on, so would the insurance role become increasingly important as a hedge against a U.S. technological breakthrough against ICBMs.

On the other hand, the potential role of the SSBNs (stemming from the 1960s strategy) lies in their ability largely to survive an intercontinental exchange. Should the Soviets be unsuccessful in deterring escalation, the SSBN force would constitute an important part of the nation's nuclear war-fighting arsenal to be used as and when the Supreme High Command saw fit. Because the platform can be redeployed and is potentially survivable, the SSBN offers more options than most other strategic delivery systems, including the option of being held back to influence negotiations on terminating the war.

It is, however, a mistake to assume that the West would necessarily acquire strategic leverage by drawing down the Soviet SSBN force. The primary purpose of the SSBNs is to ensure against the possibility that the land-based deterrent might be rendered impotent. Until such time as the United States develops the capability to outflank the ICBM force, there is no predetermined limit to the number of SSBNs the Soviets can afford to lose—as long as the objective of deterring intercontinental escalation is still being achieved. The SSBNs' contribution to the strategic correlation of forces would become relevant only if the Soviets failed to deter escalation, and the importance of that contribution would then depend on operational circumstances.

While recognizing that major changes in the structure of strategic forces are currently under negotiation, it seems likely that the SSBN's role of ensuring against the ICBM force's being technologically outflanked will persist for the time being. The relative significance of this role may diminish if and when truly mobile land-based systems become available. The relative importance of the Sea of Okhotsk as a safe haven for SSBNs is likely to increase, but SSBNs will continue to be deployed on the Barents Sea for reasons of dispersion, the availability of support facilities, and in order to divide U.S. naval strength.

Naval Roles and the V'iunenko Book

The scope of the Soviet Navy's role in world war was reaffirmed in *The Navy: Its Role, Prospects for Development, and Employment*, a book edited by Rear Admiral N.P. V'iunenko and others that became available in 1988.[23] The book discusses the full range of tasks and missions that navies in general might have to discharge in the worst case of world war, providing a listing of what navies could do rather than what the Soviet Navy would do.

The book gives no reason to suppose that the navy's mission structure has changed,[24] although the strategic antisubmarine warfare (ASW) mission is made more explicit than hitherto and there is reference to a space-based means of detecting U.S. SSBNs.[25] On the other hand, a new feature is the navy's emerging role as a sea-based component of national air defense.[26]

The Navy was written for "naval personnel and a wide range of readers" interested in naval matters, and it should be viewed in the context of the debate about naval strength and missions that was underway in the 1970s. The book is said to have been in preparation since at least 1984.[27] This, and the fact that the book was produced under the editorship of Admiral Gorshkov (who also wrote the foreword), suggests that *The Navy* may be an out-growth of the structured debate on "The Theory of the Navies" that Gorsh-kov had organized in 1981–1983. It reflects the 1984 decision about a defensive posture, but it does not reflect the sweeping doctrinal changes adopted in early 1987.

The New Thinking of the Mid-1980s

To this point the chapter has focused on the past: on why the Soviets built the navy they did and how they planned to use those forces in the event of world war. Beginning in the mid-1980s, however, fundamental changes got underway in the Soviet Union. In 1983–1984 the Soviets came to acknowl-edge that in preparing for world war, they had made such a war more likely. By the end of 1986, they appear to have accepted the logic of that conclusion and to have set about the difficult process of re-centering their plans on the less-demanding contingency of limited war on the Soviet-bloc periphery. The radical shift in Soviet political-military objectives has occasioned an internal debate that is now in full swing about the scale and nature of the new military requirements.

The 1983–1984 Reevaluation of International Relations

Although the shifts begun during the mid-1980s were largely a result of gen-erational change in the Kremlin leadership, they were enabled by develop-ments in military doctrine that, if successfully carried to conclusion, will re-move what has previously been an insurmountable obstacle to change: the worst-case contingency of world war. The open-ended objective of not losing such a war had levied heavy costs, imposing an economic burden that af-fected all sectors of the Soviet economy. And the need for military superiority and an offensive posture facing Europe was immensely damaging to the So-viet Union's world image and to its relations with the nations of the Western alliance.

How were the Soviets able to get around the uncomfortable fact that war with the United States (and hence world war) not only remained an inherent possibility but had become significantly more likely (in Soviet eyes) during the first administration of President Ronald Reagan? No new leadership, however dynamic, could cast aside the assumptions underlying established military doctrine, particularly if (as in this case) those assumptions stemmed from ideological theory. Some justification that went beyond political and economic expediency was required. The essential first step in reformulating Soviet military doctrine emerged from the major reevaluation of international relations that took place in 1983 and 1984.

Despite the mounting evidence of foreign policy failures in the late 1970s, the aged pre-Gorbachev Soviet leadership had been extremely reluctant to challenge the underlying tenets of a foreign policy that had achieved relative success in the first half of the 1970s. The leadership had been able to persuade itself that the problem lay in an aberrant deviation of U.S. policy and that "realism" would force the Reagan administration to moderate its confrontational stance and return to more cooperative policies.

It was probably the 1983 Strategic Defense Initiative (SDI) that finally jolted the Soviet leadership out of its complacency. Reagan announced the SDI on March 23, two weeks after he had described the Soviet bloc as an "evil empire," called its leadership the "focus of all evil in the world," and implied that the Soviet Union was comparable to Nazi Germany. By the end of March the official Soviet depiction of the danger of war became sharply more pessimistic, and the very high level of East-West confrontation was explicitly acknowledged at the Central Committee plenum in June 1983.

The evidence suggests that this plenum sanctioned a formal review of the foreign policy line established at the party congress in ·1971 and reaffirmed in 1976 and 1981. This review would have had to acknowledge that developments 1978 and 1983 challenged key Soviet assumptions about the structure of international relations. In particular, doubts would have surfaced about the trend in the correlation of forces, the immutability of détente, and the nature of the superpower relationship.[28]

The tone of the review's conclusions can be inferred from the unprecedented declaration by General Secretary Yuri Andropov issued at the end of September 1983 that asserted that the United States had launched a new crusade against socialism and was bent on military domination. Six weeks later the Soviet minister of defense reaffirmed this charge, asserting that the United States was determined to "eliminate socialism as a sociopolitical system."[29]

This pattern of events argues that Andropov's declaration signaled a decision in-principle concerning the continuing validity of the assumptions that had supported the policies of the 1970s. Past practice suggests that the implications of that decision and the consequential policies would be argued out and the main implementing decisions would be made during the next two years. One aspect of that debate was how to avert the catastrophe of world war.

The Soviets Reach an Impasse

In practical terms the Soviets found themselves at an impasse. A first-order national objective under the 1970s concepts was to avoid world war. Should world war be inescapable, the Soviet objective was not to lose. By definition, the capitalist objective in such a war would be to overthrow the Soviet system, but the Soviets could not respond by seeking to destroy the capitalist system. To attempt the latter would require a nuclear attack on North America—which would provoke retaliatory strikes and the nuclear devastation of Soviet Union. The U.S. military-industrial base had to be spared, and this was a central element of the 1970s strategy. That strategy had implied that NATO must be defeated in Europe and U.S. forces must be evicted from the continent so as to deny the United States a bridgehead from which to mount a land offensive against the Soviet Union. To defeat NATO without NATO's resorting to nuclear weapons, Soviet forces had to be structured for conventional offensive operations and be provided with the necessary superiority.

In restructuring their forces in the 1970s to meet this new requirement, however, the Soviets had caused the West to reaffirm its reliance on nuclear weapons, justified U.S. investment in new weapons systems that exploited emerging technologies, and prompted the U.S. concept of limited nuclear options—all of which increased the probability that war would escalate to an intercontinental exchange. The Soviets' threatening military posture facing Europe reinforced the belief that communists sought military world domination and encouraged the United States to ensure its military superiority—this time through weapons in space. East-West tension steadily increased.

The Soviets were caught in a vicious circle. Between 1971 and 1973 they thought war was highly unlikely; ten years later, they considered it a distinct possibility. In preparing for the theoretical contingency of a war they could not afford to lose, the Soviets had in practice made world war more likely. Despite the restructuring of Soviet forces, the chances of avoiding escalation to a nuclear exchange were slim. And even if NATO did not resort to nuclear weapons, the Soviets could not be certain that their offensive in Europe would be successful. If it failed, the Soviet Union would face protracted conventional war against the industrial might of the United States and its allies.

The 1986 Doctrinal Decision Not to Prepare for World War

The only way out of this cul-de-sac was to redefine Soviet military objectives. The traditional objective to avoid defeat in a world war had become an increasingly onerous burden that skewed the size, shape, and posture of the Soviet armed forces. If the military objectives were restated in less demanding terms, such as ensuring the territorial integrity and internal cohesion of the Soviet bloc, an offensive concept of operations would no longer be needed. That would obviate the requirement for a measure of superiority over opposing forces and would provide new opportunities for confidence-building verification. Secrecy was much less important in defensive operations than in offensive operations, where the role of surprise is crucial.

To redefine Soviet military objectives in this way was an audacious concept—one that the leadership was not yet prepared to contemplate in 1983–

1984. Furthermore, there was an ideological objection to such a redefinition of military objectives. Communist theory asserted that the danger of war was inherent in capitalism and that only the victory of socialism would bring peace to the world. The transition from capitalism to world socialism was seen as a continuous process that divided into stages, each having a different level of war danger. But while the achievement of rough strategic parity and the move to détente in the early 1970s had been an important step in the right direction, there was common acceptance that socialism was still far from being the predominant system in the world.[30] On what basis could military doctrine exclude the possibility of war with the West?

The way out of this ideological impasse was to distinguish between world war and other forms of war and between the danger of world war and the possibility of neutralizing that danger.[31] Renouncing a Soviet capability to invade Western Europe should automatically reduce East-West tension and make world war less likely. More important, the change in Soviet requirements would allow new ways of actively neutralizing the danger of world war. The most important would be comprehensive arms control measures in Europe leading to a new kind of mutual security regime extending from the Atlantic to the Urals. Less tangible, but still important, would be the increased political significance of Western antiwar movements, whose influence had formerly been undercut by the Soviet Union's obsessive secrecy and its offensive posture.

By the fall of 1984 the possibility of neutralizing the danger of world war appears to have been accepted by most of the Soviet leadership, and in the first half of 1985 it was adopted by the party as an official Soviet objective.[32] At this date it seems that the Soviets believed that the danger of world war could be neutralized by relaxing their offensive posture facing NATO and by mutual force reductions. Work was already in progress on "developing military doctrine with a defensive orientation,"[33] and it was at this period that the Soviets decreed that the focus of military doctrine and strategy was to solve the problem of averting war.[34]

There remained the question of how the United States would respond given what the Soviets saw as the U.S. administration's flippant attitude to the issue of war and peace.[35] The practicality of the new approach had to wait until Gorbachev had taken the measure of President Reagan at the summit in November 1985; the new policy appears to have been legitimated at the Twenty-seventh Party Congress in February–March 1986. It was not until April 18, 1986, that Gorbachev provided the first evidence of the shift in policy regarding Soviet military requirements in Europe.

In his speech to the East German Party Congress, Gorbachev proposed substantial reductions in ground and air forces, accepted the need for dependable verification, and acknowledged that the European security problem extended from the Atlantic to the Urals. In the wake of this speech, the Soviets withdrew their objections to intrusive verification. In June 1986 the Warsaw Pact proposed that each side reduce forces within Europe by up to 150,000 troops in two years, with a further reduction of 500,000 to come in the early 1990s, which would represent a cut of about 25 percent.

The final stage in the intellectual process of recentering Soviet military requirements on ensuring the territorial integrity and internal cohesion of the Soviet bloc—rather than on the open-ended objective of not losing a world war—appears to have taken place in late 1986 and early 1987. During the summer of 1986, Gorbachev reached the conclusion that the attempt to restructure the economy would fail unless the energies of Soviet workers were directly engaged. Economic *perestroika* could not work without a political *perestroika* that provided for democratic participation by the people. This controversial new policy was adopted by the Central Committee plenum in January 1987, a date that also marked the emergence of outspoken opposition to the way *perestroika* was developing.

There were obvious dangers, political and economic, in trying to move from an authoritarian political system and command economy to something more democratic, and it was at this stage that the relationship between domestic *perestroika* and the "new political thinking" about international relations became truly symbiotic. Gorbachev was proposing to re-rig the ship of state on the high seas—to restep the masts in mid-ocean—and if this hazardous endeavor was to be successful, calm seas were essential.

It was in these circumstances that the political leadership pushed doctrinal developments to their logical conclusion. If by preparing for world war such a war became more likely, if the chance of avoiding the use of nuclear weapons in a world war was very slim, and if it was accepted that a nuclear war could not be won and must not be fought, then the logical conclusion was not to prepare to fight a world war.

As a means of promoting the objective of neutralizing the danger of world war, not preparing to fight a world war would be more effective than merely adopting a defensive posture facing NATO. More important, only by accepting that conclusion could the Soviet Union dramatically reduce the scale of its military requirements and reap the economic benefits thereof.

Evidence that the Soviet leadership had accepted that conclusion appeared in May 1987 when the Political Consultative Committee of the Warsaw Pact proposed even more substantial cuts in force levels and defense spending through the year 2000 and recognized the need for asymmetrical reductions. The committee issued a formal statement on military doctrine, and among the pact's objectives was the reduction of conventional forces in Europe "to the level where neither side, in ensuring its defense, would have the means for a surprise attack on the other side or for mounting general offensive operations."[36]

In adopting these objectives the Soviet leadership was indicating its readiness to forgo the capability for a successful offensive into Western Europe. Since the defeat of NATO in Europe is central to the Soviet strategy for not losing a world war, the leadership was also implicitly renouncing that open-ended objective and adopting the lesser one of ensuring the territorial integrity and internal cohesion of the Soviet bloc.

"Defensive Sufficiency" versus "Reasonable Sufficiency"

These decisions mainly affected the sociopolitical level of military doctrine. As the debate moved down to the military-technical level and the question of what the new objective implied in terms of forces and hardware, the room for professional disagreement increased sharply. The professional debate gathered momentum in mid-1987, the argument being couched in terms of "defensive sufficiency" as opposed to "reasonable sufficiency"—concepts that can best be distinguished by postulating the underlying approaches.

Defensive sufficiency reflects a traditional military approach that is reluctant to categorize weapons as offensive or defensive and that allows for the possibility of a deliberate attack. Reasonable sufficiency reflects an innovative approach that believes it is possible to distinguish clearly between offense and defense, favors both sides having a defensive capability that significantly exceeds the offensive capability of the other, and assumes that an enemy attack would be the result of local events getting out of control rather than premeditated aggression.

Implicit in the opposing approaches are very different projections of the political and military dimensions of the future threat environment. Those who favor defensive sufficiency see little change in the underlying confrontation—apart from reduced force levels and a defensive posture (which are themselves unsettling). Those favoring reasonable sufficiency assume that major changes are possible, starting with the political dimension. In terms of future requirements, the crucial dimension of the debate concerns the need for a counteroffensive capability. Only a minority place their trust in nonoffensive means of defense. The majority, including many who advocate reasonable sufficiency, consider that some counteroffensive capability is needed, although opinions differ on what is essential. Requirements range from being able to rebuff an aggressor and restore the status quo ante to being able to advance into the aggressor's territory and at least punish him, if not defeat him utterly.

The argument over sufficiency is really about the balance between political and military means in ensuring the security of the Soviet Union. What are the chances of negotiating a mutual security regime extending from the Atlantic to the Urals, and how effective would it be in protecting Soviet interests? In mid-1989 the appropriate balance had still to be decided. It is, however, noteworthy that the concept of sufficiency rather than parity or superiority is being used as the criterion for sizing forces. It is equally note-worthy that the forces need only be sufficient to provide for the secure defense of the Soviet bloc rather than ensure that the Soviet Union is not defeated in a world war.

The Navy in the 1990s

Soviet domestic, foreign, and military policies are in a state of flux as the new Soviet leadership embarks on the difficult task of redefining military require-ments. If this redefinition can be put into practice, it will be a major step toward neutralizing the danger of world war and will yield large benefits to the domestic economy and relations with other states. Significant elements of the Soviet military are doubtful that this is a practical proposition. Mean-while, success is heavily dependent on cooperative involvement by a skeptical Western alliance.

This difficult endeavor reflects in part the new political thinking about international relations that the Gorbachev leadership claims is required by the realities of the nuclear age. The age-old dictum, "if you seek peace, pre-pare for war," no longer holds; preparing for world war makes such a war more likely. Furthermore, the capability of modern weapons means that phys-ical security can no longer be ensured by military-technical means. National security can be achieved only by cooperating with other states to provide mutual or universal security. Although these ideas are hardly original, it is the first time that they have been proposed as government policy by a major state, let alone one of the superpowers.

Evidence of the developing situation will inevitably be confusing. On the one hand, the Soviets are seeking to establish a mutual security regime that will take ten to fifteen years to achieve and will depend on successful nego-tiations with the West about complex force reductions and restructuring. On the other hand, the Soviets have to guard against the threat inherent in the West's military capability and to deal with the realities of the continuing su-perpower competition. There is little indication that political-military estab-lishments in the West accept the Soviet analysis of the new realities or the need for new political thinking.

Meanwhile the Soviet military is bound to hedge against the worst-case contingency of world war, however inappropriate the emerging structure of its forces. This poses a particularly intractable problem for the navy, as can be seen by comparing its situation with that of the ground forces. The latter would have to forgo the optimal strategy of an offensive into Western Europe, but in other respects both NATO and Warsaw Treaty Organization (WTO) forces would be equally handicapped by the mutual reduction and restruc-turing process. Not so the navy, where the scale and structure of forces required to cope with limited conflict on the Soviet periphery are quite different from those required for world war. This is partly because of the gross asymmetry in the opposing force structures and partly because requirements are determined as much by geography as by the enemy's capabilities.

On the evidence of his 3,000-word foreword to *The Navy*, Admiral Gorshkov was clearly among those not believing that it would be wise or practical to recenter military requirements on a contingency other than world war. He was also not convinced that the capitalist leopard could change its spots. He clearly believed that the central tendency in U.S. policy was exemplified by the policies and rhetoric of the first Reagan administration and not by those of the second. Gorshkov noted that *The Navy* had been designed to appeal to a broad audience and should also be useful in "military-patriotic" youth education. Thus, the focus of the book diverged markedly from the new political thinking of the Gorbachev leadership and the new emphasis on a reasonable sufficiency.

Given the fluid context, there is little point in speculating on broader naval developments, except to stress the potentially far-reaching implications of the latest stage in doctrinal evolution. There are, however, four areas where past experience does provide a basis for discussing future developments.

The SSBN Force in the 1990s

First, the future of the SSBN force is not dependent on the new thinking about international relations but will continue to reflect the logic of the 1970s strategy and the progress in negotiating strategic arms reductions. The Soviet objective since the late 1960s has been parity in strategic weapons at as low a level as possible; and if less is better, none is best. There is every reason to believe that Soviet proposals in 1986 to eliminate nuclear weapons were genuine, notwithstanding the obvious problems of implementation. It would serve the Soviet Union's strategic interests in the event of world war and would eliminate the possibility of nuclear war.

The Soviets are wholeheartedly committed to strategic force reductions, but their military will naturally seek to maximize the Soviet capability within whatever limits have been agreed. In deciding the mix of land- and sea-based systems, the question of survivability is likely to predominate. Because of their mobility and capacity for concealment, Soviet SSBNs would likely survive a nuclear exchange. However, because they lack the physical and political protection of sovereign territory, SSBNs are vulnerable to conventional attack prior to a nuclear exchange. There are the further drawbacks that SSBNs carry many eggs in one basket, and it is also harder to ensure effective command and control. For these reasons, if land-based ICBMs could be made truly mobile and achieve the same invulnerability to nuclear attack, they would be preferable to SSBNs.

Force Projection in the Third World in the 1990s

Second, there is reason to speculate about the potential role of Soviet naval forces in the Third World. Soviet policy toward the Third World used to be based on the assumption that history was clearly on the side of socialism. This meant that the Soviets could afford to "win some, lose some" and would be sensitive to the danger that local conflicts would get out of control and precipitate global war. When the utility of Soviet military intervention was debated in the 1969–1974 period, the limited Soviet experience of how the United States would respond to confrontations in the Third World was not reassuring. It was concluded that the dangers of escalation outweighed any potential benefits, particularly since the favorable trend in the correlation of forces appeared to be accelerating.

By the time of the policy review in 1983–1984 the situation was very different. The trend in the correlation of forces was no longer favorable, and the United States was becoming increasingly intolerant of the emergence of Marxist regimes and had shown it was ready to use military force to protect perceived U.S. interests. By that date evidence had accumulated of the United States's extreme reluctance to risk escalation, and the Soviets had a better idea of how the United States was likely to react to their intervention in distant parts of the globe. It could therefore be argued that the Soviet Union should respond to U.S. military intervention with countervailing force. Inaction could result in a setback to the Soviet position in the Third World and in the competition for world influence.

If, however, the Soviets did decide in 1983–1984 that naval interposition would be necessary in the years ahead, it is unlikely that such a policy would have lasted through 1986. The paramount importance of a tranquil international environment is one important reason. Another is that there was probably a shift in the assessment of the place of the United States in Soviet foreign policy.

In the bitter atmosphere of 1983–1984, it seems likely that the Soviets concluded that a sustained collaborative relationship with the United States was not possible and that past attempts to achieve such a relationship had worked to Soviet disadvantage. Good relations with the United States should not, therefore, be the top Soviet priority. In key areas like arms control and the Middle East, collaboration would remain essential, but this did not mean that Soviet interests should be sacrificed in other foreign policy areas.

By the end of 1986, the argument that the first Reagan administration had been an aberration in the trend of Soviet-U.S. relations appeared to have been right after all. The second Reagan administration was clearly committed to a process of summit diplomacy, and, despite subsequent backpeddling, the Reykjavik meeting in October had placed an ambitious program of nuclear arms reductions on the public agenda. Quite separately the Soviets had acknowledged that political democratization was essential if *perestroika* was to be successful, a decision fraught with dangers that sharply increased the importance of new political thinking about international relations.

By 1987 good relations with the United States had not only reassumed a position of central importance, but the theoretical justification for such a relationship had moved beyond the need for peaceful coexistence between the two social systems—to criticism of class analysis as the basis of Soviet foreign policy and to advocacy of an expanding-sum approach to international relations rather than the zero sum implicit in the concept of the correlation of forces.

These latest developments argue against a new and more assertive role for Soviet naval forces in distant sea areas, an argument reinforced by the way the Soviets have actually used the military instrument during the past thirty years. With one insignificant exception in 1969,[37] the Soviet Union has not used actual or latent military force to coerce a Third World state lying outside its contiguous national security zone. The Soviets have exercised this restraint even when base rights were at stake and when they had significant forces on the ground and control of air terminals in the country concerned. This reflected the nature of Soviet interests in the Third World and political judgments about the costs and benefits of using coercive force to protect and promote those interests.

For thirty years Soviet interests in the Third World have been of two kinds. One set of interests is war related: the need to establish the political, physical, and operational infrastructure required by Soviet contingency plans for world war. The 1970s strategy and the concept of a two-phase war increased the scope of these requirements, but the establishment of such infrastructure also became less time critical, which reduced the political priority of this requirement in peacetime. The other type of Third World interest comes under the rubric of intersystem competition—a catchall category whose primary impulse is the Soviet struggle for world influence and that extends to cover Sino-Soviet rivalry in the Third World and the Soviets' need for access to certain raw materials.

Since the Soviet objective has been to gain influence, the military instrument has been used to persuade rather than coerce client states. It has mainly taken the form of supplying arms and training military personnel. The Soviets have also tried to increase the client's ability to defend itself against external intervention, thus raising the costs to the West of using military force to rectify unfavorable political developments. In a few cases, this kind of arms supply has also had the unstated objective of complicating the West's strategic situation by introducing threats that drew Western capability away from the Soviet Union.[38]

To the extent that the military instrument has involved the application of force, either directly or through proxies, such military intervention has always been supportive. Similarly, supportive intervention has been protective of the client rather than punitive of his opponent, it being counterproductive to generate unnecessary hostility. The provision of air defense has been the most typical form of supportive intervention, although Soviet-supplied Cuban forces were used in Ethiopia to repel the Somali invasion and again in Angola against South African forces and UNITA.

This pattern of behavior indicates that the Soviet Union has a very different perception of the utility of naval intervention from that held by the Western maritime powers. Furthermore, if the Gorbachev leadership is successful in writing the contingency of world war out of Soviet plans, their war-related interests in the Third World will lapse. The intersystem competition type of interests will, however, persist, although perhaps in modified form.

Unless they are ready to renounce socialism as a world ideology, the Soviets will have to continue supporting key client states, despite the economic and political costs. The extent to which this Soviet support will have a military dimension will depend largely on the need to use countervailing force "defending the gains of socialism." That will depend in part on Western readiness to view the Third World as an expanding-sum rather than a zero-sum problem.

Naval Arms Reductions in the 1990s

Third, there is little doubt that the Soviets would welcome a far-reaching arms control agreement that effectively neutralized a threat from the maritime axes of attack. Such an agreement is, however, unlikely since the universal problems of negotiating arms agreements are accentuated by the differing requirements in war of a continental and a maritime alliance and by the U.S. Navy's importance in peacetime as an instrument of foreign policy.[39]
The more immediate question is the relevance of NATO's naval preponderance to negotiations on arms reductions in Europe. With some justification, the West has pointed to the Soviet advantage in ground forces facing NATO and demanded disproportionate reductions in those forces. Since 1986, the Soviets have been willing to admit these disparities and to acknowledge the need for asymmetrical reductions until the two sides' ground forces are in balance. They also claim, however, that there are comparable disparities in air forces that favor NATO, and in 1988 they began to stress the West's naval predominance. What can experience tell us about the Soviet commitment to their proposal that their advantage in ground forces be traded for NATO's advantage in naval forces?

A notable feature of past negotiations on strategic arms has been the way the United States was able to exclude whole categories of weapons in which it held a unilateral advantage. Bombers were excluded from the 1972 Strategic Arms Limitation Treaty (SALT I), as were multiple independently targeted reentry vehicles (MIRV), which the United States was about to deploy aboard the Minuteman III, while the Soviets had yet to flight test. The un-ratified SALT II did include bombers and MIRVed missiles but effectively excluded land- and sea-based long-range cruise missiles. In both sets of ne-gotiations, the United States refused to count either its forward-based systems capable of striking at the Soviet Union or the British and French nuclear arsenals. Both agreements required the curtailment of Soviet ICBM programs then in progress or planned, and further cuts were implicit in the Soviet pro-posals at the Strategic Arms Reduction Talks (START) in 1982–1983.[40] The United States made no comparable concessions. Neither SALT agreement had any effect on existing U.S. plans for modernizing its strategic forces, and the weapon limits did not begin to bite until 1985, when the U.S. Navy had to remove a twenty-year-old sixteen-tube Poseidon SSBN to bring a twenty-four-tube Trident on line.

From this behavior it can be inferred that the Soviets are willing to make one-sided concessions as long as the concessions further the long-range ne-gotiating objective, which in this case was to achieve parity in nuclear weap-ons at as low a level as possible. This principle was reaffirmed in the 1987 intermediate nuclear forces (INF) agreement, where the Soviets again agreed to give up many more missiles than the United States. The agreement served the Soviet purpose of reducing the likelihood of uncontrolled escalation in Europe and of resuscitating the arms control process. Arms control now has a twenty-year track record, with the process firmly established and still mov-ing ahead.

The Soviets will not make concessions if, on balance, they would work against Soviet security interests. This was most evident in the case of negoti-ations on mutual and balanced force reductions (MBFR) in Europe in the 1970s. At this period the Soviets were restructuring their forces to implement the 1970s strategy, which was predicated on a measure of conventional su-periority; asymmetrical cuts were therefore ruled out. This principle can also be seen in the Soviets' adamant opposition to SDI and their refusal to con-clude a START agreement unless they are convinced that the United States will abide by the strict interpretation of the antiballistic missile (ABM) treaty and will not seek to emplace strike weapons in space.

This principle can be applied to the asymmetries in naval forces, the most significant being the U.S. aircraft carrier capability. Three factors have to be balanced: the importance to the Soviet Union of achieving major force re-ductions in the European theater, the relative importance to the United States of its navy's role in war and peace, and the threat posed to Soviet interests by U.S. carrier forces. It has already been argued that force reductions in Europe are of paramount importance to the Soviet Union for political and economic reasons and as a way of reducing the danger of world war. Meanwhile, the United States sees its navy as a primary instrument of foreign policy, and the navy's peacetime role is a major consideration in sizing the carrier force. Yet it seems unlikely that the U.S. Navy's peacetime role ranks high among the concerns of the Soviet political leadership.

The carriers' wartime role has to be assessed in three different scenarios. First, under the 1970s strategy for the contingency of world war, the U.S. Navy's contribution becomes crucial only if the Soviet offensive into Western Europe bogs down. This would mean protracted war in Europe (when the seaborne supply of NATO would become a critical factor), and in such circumstances the U.S. carrier force would have an important role to play. In the second and lesser contingency of limited conventional war on the periphery of the Soviet bloc, U.S. carrier battle groups could bring firepower to bear, but their aircraft would usually be operating at extreme range against land-based defenses. The Kurils chain of islands in the Pacific—an exposed salient, parts of it vulnerable to amphibious seizure—is an exception to this unflattering assessment. The carriers' potentially most dangerous role is in the third scenario, where the United States resorts to nuclear weapons in a limited war on the Soviet periphery. In such circumstances U.S. carriers could be the major arsenals of escalation.

Unquestionably the U.S. carrier force poses a threat to Soviet interests in war and perhaps also in peace. But the Soviets have been developing various means of countering that threat for some thirty-five years. The geography of limited war on the Soviet periphery means that carriers would be subject to attack by land-based forces, and if U.S. naval units were used to launch a nuclear strike against Soviet territory, the carriers would themselves become subject to nuclear attack. In a world war, carriers might provide the means for shifting the center of strategic gravity. But the purpose of mutual force reductions in Europe is to neutralize the danger of world war, in which case that threat becomes moot.

Undoubtedly the Soviets would prefer a world without carriers—but not sufficiently to hazard an agreement on ground-force reductions in Europe. This does not exclude other forms of trade-off. For example, if the United States reverted to the idea that it needs (or could afford) only twelve carrier battle groups rather than fifteen, this might be parlayed for an accelerated reduction in Soviet tanks. And the Soviets will certainly persist in their effort to negotiate away the carriers' nuclear capability. It may also be possible to trade asymmetries between naval forces; for example, the Soviets have an advantage in the number of nuclear-powered attack submarines. But limiting naval arms is not only a different kind of problem from limiting theater and strategic nuclear forces; it is also less important than the process of neutralizing the danger of world war.

Naval Force Structure in the 1990s

Fourth, the future size and shape of the Soviet Navy depends on political decisions about the nature and scope of the worst-case contingency that should be used to formulate Soviet military requirements. There is ample evidence concerning the kinds of forces the Soviets have thought necessary to achieve the open-ended objective of not losing a world war. Yet how would these requirements be affected if the Soviets adopted the objective of ensuring the territorial integrity and internal cohesion of the Soviet bloc in the lesser contingency of a war that was limited to its periphery? The answer to what adjustments would be required for perimeter defense comes in two parts: the intercontinental or strategic nuclear component of existing requirements and the conventional component.

Intercontinental-Strategic Naval Requirements for Perimeter Defense. The intercontinental dimension of this problem consists of both offensive and defensive aspects. The Soviets are addressing the offensive aspect of the strategic problem through the START talks—their stated aim being to eliminate offensive nuclear forces through successive reductions in strength that would be designed to ensure continuing parity. Naval forces will meanwhile be needed to defend Soviet SSBNs against Western attack submarines, since no agreement is foreseeable on ways of neutralizing the SSN's inherent capability to penetrate Soviet waters. However, if there are significant reductions in their SSBN force, the Soviets may develop deployment modes that reduce the requirement for general purpose forces intended primarily for SSBN protection.

There is also the defensive aspect of the intercontinental requirements problem: Soviet attempts to counter the Western capability to launch nuclear attacks from maritime axes. As long as SSBNs form part of the Soviet strategic arsenal and remain vulnerable to Western attack, the Soviets will need to persist in their efforts to develop the means of locating and incapacitating Western SSBNs. If, however, the Soviets were able to rely on land-based offensive systems at some future date, this requirement might lapse, as long as ways can be devised and agreed of ensuring that the United States does not develop some means of rendering land-based missiles impotent. Similarly the requirement for naval forces to provide off shore early warning and defense against air- and sea-launched long-range cruise missiles will persist until agreement is reached on eliminating these strategic nuclear weapons.

Changes in the intercontinental component of existing naval requirements therefore will depend on two factors: the kind of agreements reached at START and on Soviet choices between land- and sea-basing of missiles.

Conventional Naval Requirements for Perimeter Defense. Several types of operations (many of them combined arms) that are required by the 1970s strategy would be unnecessary in a more limited contingency. The most obvious are those that apply to phase II of a world war. They include: operations to establish the extended defense perimeter, such as occupying various Atlantic islands, seizing key ports and straits on the Horn of Africa, and evicting NATO naval forces from the Mediterranean; contributing to the defense of the perimeter once established by attacking invasion forces; and interrupting the flow of raw materials and other essential seaborne supplies to the United States. There are also those operations that would be carried out during the first two stages of phase I of a world war. These include helping to seize the Baltic and Black Sea exits, providing flank support to the armies advancing in the western and southwestern TVDs and into Arctic Norway, and launching conventional missile strikes against NATO's nuclear facilities.

This cursory listing suggests that a significant cut in requirements would be possible, although the actual saving in naval forces would be less because some of these operations would be carried out seriatim by the same units. But such a listing also highlights the difficulty of defining the parameters of the limited contingency. For example, can it be assumed that, in the event of a limited conflict in Europe, NATO would refrain from building up its forces by sea? If not, would the Soviets be able to attack the supply terminals, or would they be limited to attacking ships at sea? And if it would no longer be possible to exclude enemy forces from the Black Sea and Baltic by seizing the exits, what would be needed to guard against an overwhelming concentration of NATO naval forces in one or another fleet area?

Problems of Transition from World War to Perimeter Defense. These kinds of questions suggest that for the Soviets, there is no halfway house between preparing for world war and falling back on the perimeter defense of the Soviet bloc. The move is, however, necessitated by both security and economic considerations. Gorbachev asserts that national security can now be achieved only by political means (mutual accommodation and arms control agreements), with military capability becoming the backup rather than the primary means of defense. This is also the only way of releasing substantial intellectual and material resources for use in the domestic economy.

The navy, meanwhile, has the continuing problem of the strategic nuclear threat—a consideration that does not affect the ground-air forces deployed in Europe and along the rest of the Soviet periphery. The problem could be eased if the Soviets were to concentrate their intercontinental offensive capability in land-based missiles, lifting the requirement to protect the SSBNs and to deploy strategic ASW systems. The air-breathing threat from U.S. cruise missiles and carrier-borne aircraft would remain, but the naval requirement would be more manageable, and it might be reduced by agreements to limit U.S. forward-based systems, a category that includes the carriers' nuclear capability.

The Possibility of Naval Cutbacks in the 1990s. The future size and shape of Soviet naval forces will depend as much on negotiations with the United States on strategic forces as on the effects of recentering Soviet military requirements on a less demanding contingency than world war. If this complex process does result in reduced naval requirements, experience suggests that the Soviets will not hesitate to halt or curtail current construction and cancel projected programs if appropriate. An extreme example is provided by the wholesale cuts in the mid-1950s, but repeated manifestations of this policy can be identified through into the 1980s. The 1950s cutbacks are also a good example of resources being switched from defense to the civilian sector, with naval construction facilities being used to build merchant and fishing vessels, and bomber production lines being used to build passenger aircraft.

Comparable cuts should not be expected in research and development unless specific agreements on this score are reached. The Soviets are sensitive to the fact that they are a tortoise matched against an American hare. Only by relentlessly plodding on can the Soviets hope to remain within reach of U.S. technological developments.

Despite its advantages, however, the United States has never been able to achieve the kind of decisive military superiority it has repeatedly sought through technological innovation. The Soviets have been consistent in their readiness to build or embark on the development of whatever had been seen as necessary to the security of the Soviet Union. Their unwillingness to dismiss an operational requirement as too difficult and their willingness to adopt suboptimal measures on the way to some final solution are demonstrated by the early ABM defenses around Moscow and by the attempt to develop the means of countering U.S. SSBNs that has been underway since the first half of the 1960s.[41]

After forty-five years of trying unsuccessfully to achieve a decisive technological advantage—and before it carries the arms race into space—the United States might want to weigh the alternative of seeking agreement on ways to control the application of emerging technologies. This is a daunting endeavor but probably even more important than negotiating agreements on nuclear weapons.

The Soviet Navy—An Expensive Necessity

As the Soviet Union approaches the three hundreth anniversary of the founding of its fleet, the navy continues to be an expensive necessity rather than a preferred instrument of policy. To build the navy requires a disproportionate share of the nation's high-technology production capacity, and even the hulls are no longer simple containers but themselves require expensive specialized metals and advanced assembly techniques. The navy needs highly qualified people to construct, operate, and maintain its ships, submarines, and aircraft. To power them, the navy has needed twenty nuclear reactors a year for the last twenty-odd years (besides countless diesel engines, gas turbines, and steam power plants). The navy's hulls are stuffed with complex weapons and equipment incorporating the latest technological developments—all of which have to meet the rigorous demands of a maritime operating environment.

There is little doubt that the new Soviet leadership would welcome the opportunity to reduce the economic burden of the navy, but there are limits to what is possible. Even if the Soviet Union is successful in recentering its contingency plans and in negotiating major strategic force reductions, the Soviets will continue to face the problem their czarist predecessors first faced more than 150 years ago: the maritime powers' capability to project force by sea.

For the foreseeable future—irrespective of what agreements are reached on limiting strategic weapons and reducing the military confrontation in Europe—the United States will continue to view its navy as a primary instrument of peacetime foreign policy. In such circumstances the Soviets must retain the capability to defend their four fleet areas against a concentration of naval force. While land-based missiles and aircraft can meet part of this requirement, naval forces will continue to play a predominant role. Defense of the homeland (in its most traditional sense) will remain the core mission of the Soviet Navy.

Notes

1. This chapter draws on the analysis in Michael MccGwire, *Military Objectives in Soviet Foreign Policy* (Washington, D.C.: Brookings, 1987), and Michael MccGwire, *Perestroika and Soviet National Security* (Brookings, forthcoming).

2. For a demonstration of this analytical process, see Michael MccGwire, "Identifying the December 1966 Decision," appendix in MccGwire, *Military Objectives*, 381–405.

3. See Michael MccGwire, *The Genesis of Soviet Threat Perceptions* (Washington, D.C.: Brookings, forthcoming).

4. Michael MccGwire, "Soviet Naval Procurement," in *The Soviet Union in Europe and the Near East: Her Capabilities and Intention* (London: Royal United Service Institution, 1970), 74–87.

5. SS: attack conventionally powered submarine; SSB:balistic missile conventionally powered submarine; SSN:attack nuclear-powered submarine; SSBN: ballistic missile nuclear-powered submarine.—ED.

6. SSGN: guided [cruise] missile nuclear-powered submarine.—ED.

7. For reactor allocation and planned submarine delivery rates, see MccGwire, *Military Objectives*, 426–38.

8. The new concept of operations changed the requirement for SSGNs armed with nuclear missiles. The first five years of the revised 1968–1977 delivery period was allowed to run its course with equal numbers of SSns and SSGns, but the mix was changed for the second five years, yielding a total of twenty-three Victors and

seventeen Charlies over the ten-year period. For the same reasons, the Papa program (Charlie's successor) was cancelled, its reactors being used by new-design Oscars and Typhoons, and in *Kirov* and an extra Alpha (the lead Alpha was cannibalized). Meanwhile, the increase in the number of two-reactor Victors at the expense of one-reactor Charlies priduced a deficit in that reactor account, which meant that only eighteen Victor IIIs could be built for delivery in the 1978–1982 period.

9. Ibid., 464–70.

10. A fundamental misreading of the Gorshkov series gave birth to the notion that rather than being an exercise in naval advocacy, the articles were being used to announce some new "withholding strategy" for SSBNs. One might wonder why the Soviet leadership would have thought it either appropriate or necessary to inform the navy at large of such a decision, particularly when the option was inherent in the characteristics of the weapon system. One might also wonder why Gorshkov would need to write 54,000 words in order to convey this rather simple information and why he would then choose to express the message in such cryptic terms that its purport was hidden from the average reader. For the empirical and textual evidence, see ibid., 448–64.

11. Ibid., 174–75.

12. Ibid., 146–52.

13. Ibid., 438–46.

14. Soviet carrier development can be explained in the following terms. The *Moskva* stemmed from the 1957–1958 decision period, which identified the requirement to respond to the perceived threat from Polaris missiles by extending the range of existing land-based helicopter ASW cover, particularly in the Arctic. The *Moskva* could not, however, carry enough aircraft to support ASW operations in the Eastern Mediterranean and South Norwegian Sea, as required by the 1961–1962 decisions; hence the program was cancelled (its weapon outfits being used by Kresta II) and the *Kiev* (twice as large) was projected. In 1967, the *Kiev* project was taken over as the interim response to the new requirement for sea-based air to contribute to establishing command of the Norwegian Sea. It was a "universal" ship, with a long-range anti-surface, antisubmarine and air defense capability, plus vertical/short takeoff and landing, aircraft, which could shoot down maritime patrol and surveillance aircraft at a greater distance from the ship. The argument in the early 1970s is likely to have centered on whether the final response to the new requirement to gain command of the Norwegian Sea should be a scaled-up version of the universal ship (embodying in a single hull the characteristics of the *Kirov* battle-cruiser and the *Kiev*) or a task-specific air superiority carrier, comparable to a U.S. attack carrier. It is possible that the navy's demarche in 1972–1973 resulted in approval for the construction of this air superiority carrier at Severodvinsk. However, the 1976–1977 decision to relax the requirement for command of the Norwegian Sea would have removed the prime argument for such a carrier. This, perhaps coupled with shipyard difficulties in the north, led to the construction of a "universal" ship at Nikolaev. Curtailment of the Oscar SSGN program would have been an important reason for going ahead with this program, despite the change in requirements. See ibid., 439–42, 467–68.

15. These annual production rates are based on the availability of nuclear reactors and the size of the submarine construction halls as depicted in the annual *Soviet Military Power,* published by the U.S. Department of Defense. The class totals are

based on the pattern of submarine construction over the previous twenty years; also, in the case of Oscar, the requirement to counter Western carrier forces, and in the case of Typhoon, the Soviet proposal at the START talks in 1982–1983. See Mcc-Gwire, *Military Objectives,* 432–36.

16. In 1982 the Soviets made a formal proposal to limit the production of Trident and Typhoon submarines to 4 to 6 units. At that date, 6 Tridents and about 4 Typhoons had been laid down or completed. Meanwhile the Soviet proposals at the START negotiations (1982–1983) give an insight to their requirements at that period. They provided for an implicit ceiling of 400 MIRVed submarine-launched ballistic missiles. Starting with the existing 14 Delta IIIs (224 SLBMs), the addition of 4 Typhoons (80 SLBMs) and 6 Delta IVs (96 SLBMs) would bring the total number of SLBMs exactly to that number. It would also allow 17 Tridents. If the agreement were struck at 20 Tridents (480 SLBMs), this could be matched by building additional Delta IVs and/or Typhoons.

17. If this explanation is correct, it implies that the partial hiatus in the delivery of attack submarines after 1982 was intended to be temporary. It also implies that it was planned to backfill this hiatus and to increase the annual delivery of attack submarines in the 1988–1992 period. See ibid., 442–46.

18. Ship-days deployed climbed steadily from 1964 and leveled out during 1972–1976 at an average of 19,400, with a peak of 20,600 in 1973 (the Arab-Israeli war). In 1977, ship-days fell back to about 16,500 and remained at about that level, which had first been achieved in 1970. See Robert G. Weinland, *Soviet Strategy and the Objectives of their Naval Presence in the Mediterranean,* Professional Paper 410 (Alexandria, Va.: Center for Naval Analyses, 1982), 33.

19. This did not include operations directed at China, which is not a Third World country in the political sense of the term. See N. Bradford Dismukes and Kenneth G. Weiss, *Mare Mosso: The Mediterranean Theater,* Professional Paper 423 (Alexandria, Va.: Center for Naval Analyses, 1984), 2.

20. First noted by Charles Petersen.

21. These ten articles appeared in *Morskoi sbornik* as follows (issue no./pages): 1981, – 4/20–28, 5/17–27, 11/24–29; 1982, 1/20–24, 4/27–31, 7/18–24, 11/26–31; 1983, 3/18–23, 7/27–38.

22. This may well have been the intended role of the SS-N-24, which would marry a well-developed naval technology with a newly available launch platform, the ex-SSBN Yankees.

23. N.P. V'iunenko, B.N. Makeev, and V.D. Skugarev, *Voenno-morskoi flot: Rol', perspektivy razvitiia, ispol'zovanie* (Moscow: Voenizdat, 1988). S.G. Gorshkov contributed a foreword to the book, which was produced under his leadership.

24. For an analysis of the navy's mission structure as it emerged in the 1960s, see Michael MccGwire, "Soviet Power and Global Strategy," in *Soviet Military Thinking,* ed. Derek Leebart (London: Allen and Unwin, 1981), 125–81; and Michael MccGwire, "Naval Power and Soviet Global Strategy," *International Security* 3 (Spring 1979): 134–89. At the time that piece was written, I had not identified the doctrinal shift in late 1966 and did not realize that Gorshkov was arguing within the context of a two-phase world war.

25. Note 41 outlines the genesis of this requirement.

26. On this subject, see Floyd Kennedy, "The Reorganization of Soviet Military

Aviation and its Effect on the New Soviet Carrier," United States Naval Institute *Proceedings* (forthcoming).

27. According to a Soviet informant, there were some delays in preparing the book for publication, but these were for editorial reasons; he did not know of any political obstacles that were put in its way. The book was scheduled for publication in the second quarter of 1988, but it was typeset June 26, 1987, and signed to the press October 19, 1987, so it may have been available earlier to a selected readership. The scheduled print run was 30,000 copies, but only 25,000 copies were actually published. This compares with the 60,000 copies of each edition of *Seapower of the State* (1976, 1979).

28. See MccGwire, *Military Objectives*, 307–31.

29. D.F. Ustinov, "For High Combat Readiness," *Krasnaia zvezda*, November 12, 1983.

30. Stephen Shenfield, *The Nuclear Predicament: Explorations in Soviet Ideology*, Royal Institute of International Affiars, Chatham House Papers No. 37 (London: Routledge & Kegan Paul, 1987). 27. My summary of the ideological background is based on Shenfield's outstanding analysis of the core values of peace and socialism in the Soviet ideology of international affairs.

31. N.V. Ogarkov, "On the 40th Anniversary of the Great Victory: Unfading Glory of Soviet Arms," *Kommunist vooruzh-nnykh sil* (Communist of the armed forces); no. 21 (1984), and his *Istoriia uchit bditel'nost'* (History teaches vigilance) (Moscow: Voenizdat, 1985), 85–90. This evidence is analyzed in MccGwire, "Rethinking War," 9.

32. S.A. Tiushkevich, ed., *Vtoraia mirovaia voina: itogi i uroki* (The Second World War: Results and lessons) (Moscow: Voenizdat, 1985), 414. This comes in a six-page "conclusion" that was almost certainly added to the galleys after they had been finally sent to the printer, and subsequent to Gorbachev's being elected general secretary. The use of the present tense in Ogarkov's writings and the convoluted and peculiar choice of words concerning the noninevitability of war support the assessment that a recent decision, not the 1956 doctrinal reformulation, is being referred to.

33. Ibid., 417.

34. References to "averting world war" or "averting war" are the only substantive amendments to the entries for "military doctrine" and "military strategy" in the 1983 edition of *Voennyi entsiklopedicheskii slovar'* (Military encyclopedia dictionary) 2d ed. (Moscow: Voenizdat, 1986), 240, 712.

35. This was General Secretary Yuri Andropov's opinion as expressed in an interview with *Pravda*, March 27, 1983. Several Western commentators have suggested an analogy between the 1985 summit and Khrushchev's meeting with Eisenhower in 1959."

36. *Pravda*, May 31, 1987.

37. For the rather odd case of the two Russian fishing vessels seized by the Ghanaian navy in 1969, see David K. Hall, "Naval Diplomacy in West African Waters," in *Diplomacy of Force: Soviet Armed Forces as Political Instrument*, ed. Stephen S. Kaplan (Washington, D.C.: Brookings, 1981), 521–31.

38. Naval forces supplied to Egypt, Indonesia, and Algeria from the mid-1950s through early 1960s came into this category.

39. See Michael MccGwire, "Soviet-American Naval Arms Control," in *Navies and Arms Control*, ed. George H. Quester (New York: Praeger, 1980), 44–100.

40. See MccGwire, *Military Objectives*, 488–96; and Michael MccGwire, "Why the Soviets Are Serious about Arms Control," *Brookings Review* 5 (Spring 1987): 13–16.

41. The urgency of the threat from the Polaris-armed SSBN stemmed from its potential to deny the Soviet Union the use of NATO Europe as an alternative socio-economic base from which to rebuild the devastated socialist economies as provided for in the 1960s strategy. In 1961–1962 the Soviets appear to have embarked on a typical three-stage response to the problem, pursuing the three possible ways of countering Polaris: area defense, trailing, and ocean search and surveillance. The initial response involved extending and elaborating the established concept of antisubmarine defense zones. The interim response was to develop a high-speed deep-diving submarine capable of trailing an improved Polaris using active sonar. The high-speed deep-diving Alpha SSN prototype went to sea in 1971, a lead time consistent with the main 1961–1962 decision period. The final response required developing some means of detecting submarines that did not require access to surrounding coastlines and massive computer power, both of which the Soviet lacked. This excluded the option of sieving the ocean for sound (a SOSUS system) and favored the use of air- or space-borne sensors to detect surface and other anomalies caused by the presence of a submerged submarine.

9
Alternative Models of Soviet Naval Behavior

Donald C. Daniel

B y the late 1970s a model started to take hold in the West of how the
Soviet Navy would act prior to and in the initial period of a North
Atlantic Treaty Organization (NATO) war. This view of Soviet naval
behavior, which may be called the strategic defensive model, contrasts with
an alternative, which may be termed the strategic offensive model. The purpose of this chapter is to examine whether recent arguments in behalf of the
strategic offensive model should cause the West to abandon its reliance on
the strategic defensive paradigm.

An important aspect of the strategic defensive model is the assumption
of the Soviet Navy's dispersal of its nuclear-powered ballistic missile submarines (SSBNs) to waters adjacent to the homeland, where they would remain
ready to execute authorized launch orders. While some SSBNs might participate in initial (retaliatory) nuclear strikes, a high proportion would be retained in the nation's strategic reserve—the rationale being their lessened vulnerability to sudden nuclear attack compared to fixed land-based missile
systems.

Submarines, however, are more vulnerable to gradual attrition from attacks by conventional weapons from Western antisubmarine submarines, surface ships, and aircraft. Hence, dispersing the missile submarines in adjacent
waters and keeping them there is intended among other things to facilitate
their protection. The SSBNs would benefit as friendly general purpose forces
establish around the homeland a maritime defense perimeter encompassing
sea control and sea denial areas. The navy would attempt to maintain control
of all or major portions of the Kara, Barents, Norwegian, Greenland, Baltic,
Black, Japan, and Okhotsk seas, as well as that portion of the Pacific alongside the Kamchatka Peninsula. It would also seek to deny its enemies freedom
of movement in outlying seas and oceans as far as 2,000 kilometers or more
from the homeland. All (or nearly all) units in the Baltic and Black Sea fleets
would remain within the defense perimeter; so too would "virtually all available Northern and Pacific Ocean Fleet surface combatants [and] combat aircraft, and about 75 percent of available attack submarines."[1] The number of

units expected to remain in the perimeter means that vital Western sea-lines of communications (SLOCs) "will initially be threatened by relatively few forces."[2] A greater threat would arise only in a protracted war where SLOCs become critical to the outcome.

The model posits that the vast bulk of the forces in the defense perimeter would perform several tasks, including:

- Dedicated escort of some (perhaps most) SSBNs.
- Defense-in-depth of approaches to SSBN deployment areas.
- Augmenting of command and control links to SSBNs.
- Early warning of and defense of the homeland against bombers and cruise missiles approaching from oceanic vectors.
- Destruction of enemy aircraft carriers and land attack cruise missile ships or submarines.
- Protection of coastal sea, land, and air lines of communications.
- Amphibious, gunfire, logistical, transportation, and other support to ground forces fighting on the coasts.

When this model of the Soviet Navy's behavior was first advanced, many in the West greeted it with great skepticism. Harkening back to the crucial maritime resupply and reinforcement battles of World War II and sensitive to the relatively large size of the Soviet submarine fleet, the skeptics fully expected a major assault on the sea-lanes from the first moment of a new world war. Reinforcing their view were the increasingly high profile that the Soviet Navy exhibited on the high seas since the mid-1960s, the large cutbacks suffered by the U.S. Navy in the early through mid-1970s, and the sense of disquiet that grew throughout the 1970s that qualitative Soviet Navy improvements put at risk not only the sea-lanes but also high-value combatants, including aircraft carriers.

Nevertheless, the model was accepted as the principal projection of expected Soviet Navy behavior. Better than alternative models, it seemed to fit the evidence of what was seen in Soviet writings, in naval-related hardware developments, and in deployment and exercise patterns. The model fit as well with the sense that the Soviet Navy needed to be judged on its own terms; as the saying went, one needed "to think Russian" and avoid mirror imaging. If the result was that the Soviet Navy did not conform to generally held Western assumptions of what great power navies are supposed to be about—far-forward offensive operations—then the need for a model that set the record straight was considered paramount.

Although the new model became widely (but not universally) adopted, many adherents hedged their intellectual bets. They stressed the possibility of the Soviet Navy's adopting sooner or later an offensive strategy centered on submarines hotly contesting the sea-lanes from the onset of war.

The Case for an Alternative Strategic Offensive Model

Several arguments support the proposition that the strategic offensive model is now or will soon be a better basis for planning than the strategic defensive alternative. One is that overall Soviet military doctrine seems increasingly to accept that a war with NATO could well remain conventional and last weeks or months. The preference, of course, would be to win it as quickly as possible. A major and early effort to interdict the sea-lanes could contribute to that end. NATO's short-term survivability depends, among other things, on its successful execution of the Rapid Reinforcement Plan (RRP), which is supposed to be implemented prior to the start of a war. Political or technical delays are very plausible and could leave much critical RRP shipping open to attack after a war begins.

A second argument is that Soviet naval writings of the last decade, and especially in the 1980s, exhibit heightened interest in SLOC warfare. According to some dedicated American readers of Soviet literature, this is evidenced in the quantity and the content of relevant articles in the official Soviet naval journal (*Morskoi sbornik*), especially in the early 1980s. As one reader, David Hildebrandt, put it, the "SLOC interdiction mission was a topic of lively discussion, perhaps even debate, in the pages of *Morskoi sbornik* between 1981 and 1984, with some ... authors appearing to refer to it as 'strategic.'"[3] Hildebrandt adds that interest in the topic in that journal subsequently subsided but that it did receive increased emphasis in the 1987 public statements of the Soviet naval commander, Fleet Admiral V.N. Chernavin. In addition, a new book published in 1988, *The Navy: Its Role, Prospects for Development, and Employment,* the main text of which was written by a rear admiral and two senior captains, expresses the view that NATO's sea-lanes are important. It also predicts that "the trend toward an expansion of warfare on the oceanic and sea lines of communication and an increase in its significance will be maintained in the future as well."[4] While it cannot be said that Soviet writings indicate any significant increase in the relative importance of the anti-SLOC task compared with participating in a nuclear (retaliatory) strike and defending the homeland and SSBNs, the heightened interest in the task may suggest an increase in absolute importance.

A third argument is that a large-scale early threat to the sea-lanes, evidenced by the movement of many Soviet submarines toward them during a crisis presaging war, is exactly what it would take to preempt or outflank the U.S. Navy's Maritime Strategy and put all of NATO's navies on the defensive.

After all, the strategic defensive model of the Soviet Navy was a fundamental assumption for the formulators of the Maritime Strategy. They envisioned forward offensive operations by the NATO navies as reinforcing Soviet defensive proclivities at sea. Hence, the best way for the Soviet Navy to turn the tables on that strategy would be to go on the offensive first; NATO's navies would then have to abandon their own plans in order to deal with the Soviet wolf lurking in their backyard. Key to this argument are the assertions of NATO's maritime commanders that unless the Soviet Navy's forces are tied down within the Soviet maritime defense perimeter, the alliance will lose the SLOC war for lack of enough escorts to guard critical transport ships against concerted opposition.

A fourth, follow-on argument is that the Soviet Navy has enough submarines to mount a concerted opposition. In the Northern Fleet (expected to provide nearly all the units assigned for distant anti-SLOC operations in the Atlantic and the Mediterranean), there are about seventy-five nuclear-powered and about forty diesel-powered cruise missile– or torpedo-firing submarines. Since open-ocean antisubmarine warfare (ASW) is highly labor intensive, involving detection, classification, localization, and attack, NATO's navies would be straining to deal with a sizable proportion of the 100 or so of these submarines operationally available for combat at the start of a war.

A fifth argument is that Soviet military forces are slowly but surely adding to their capabilities to defend the maritime defense perimeter. The Soviet Navy itself now has large aircraft carriers (two *Tbilisi*-class units, the first of which is now fitting out), quiet submarines (the Akula and Sierra classes), formidable antiship cruise missile-firing platforms (such as the Oscar submarine, with twenty-four missiles, the *Kirov* cruisers, with twenty missiles, and the Backfire bombers, with their long ranges). The Soviet Union is improving its surveillance capabilities to monitor activities in the maritime perimeter, and it acquired operationally important information about U.S. submarine and antisubmarine warfare operations from the Walker and Whitworth spy ring. A possible result is that fewer Soviet submarines may be needed to defend the perimeter; those freed up could instead be assigned to sink naval and transport ships outside the perimeter.

Additionally, if tactical submarines are dedicated to supporting their ballistic missile–carrying counterparts, then three developments could possibly release tactical units to operate outside the defense perimeter. One is that modern SSBNs have become better able to protect themselves. They are quieter, can patrol under ice, and have such long-range missiles that they can fire from very large areas. A second development is that there may be fewer SSBNs to protect if a strategic arms reduction agreement limiting overall warhead numbers is signed. Such an agreement could mean a drop in the SSBN inventory from sixty-three to between fourteen and thirty-four. A third development is the deployment of mobile land-based SS-24 and SS-25 intercontinental ballistic missiles (ICBMs). If perceived as being less vulnerable than the SSBNs and as having better communications with national command authorities, then these ICBMs could lessen the SSBNs' relative importance as strategic nuclear reserves that must be protected at all costs.

In sum, several related arguments support the proposition that the time has come, or is certainly approaching, to move toward a strategic offensive model of Soviet naval behavior in a NATO–Warsaw Pact war contingency. The arguments focus on: (1) changes in overall Soviet military doctrine premised on the possibility of conventional, possibly protracted, conflict; (2) increased Soviet interest in the anti-SLOC mission as evidenced in naval writings; (3) the logic of outflanking the U.S. Maritime Strategy by invalidating its premise of a strategically defensive Soviet Navy; (4) a tactical submarine inventory whose size raises the specter of an anti-SLOC campaign; and (5) changes in Soviet military and naval capabilities that could lessen the number of tactical submarines needed to protect the maritime defense perimeter and SSBNs retained therein. There is a logic and flow to these arguments that makes them attractive, but it is best to suspend final judgment until arguments for continued acceptance of the strategic defense model are presented.

The Case for Retaining the Strategic Defensive Model

The case for the strategic defensive model is in two parts. The first addresses the tradition of employing the Soviet Navy defensively. It provides an overall context for the specific arguments based on benefits and costs presented in the second part.

Arguments Based on the Overall Context

Traditions can be difficult to change, and an important Soviet military tradition is strategic defensive employment of the navy consistent with a continental orientation characteristic of that nation's strategic planners. This orientation centers on the belief that the country's security and well-being, if not its destiny, are first and foremost linked to events and conditions occurring in territories adjacent to its land borders and the land borders of its imperium in Eastern Europe and Asia. The threat of nuclear attack gave Soviet thinking an intercontinental dimension, but, except possibly in the Nikita Khrushchev years, there was probably no absolute lessening of concern for continental developments. Furthermore, increasing confidence in deterring nuclear war is probably reinforcing the relative importance of the continental orientation.

In line with this orientation is a strategic planning process that evaluates the potential contribution of the navy in narrow terms. The Soviet Navy is only one of five military services, the others being the strategic rocket forces, the air forces, the air defense forces, and the ground forces. The distribution of high-level appointments in the military hierarchy makes clear which service is the most prominent. All combat officers who have become ministers of defense and all first deputy ministers (including the highly influential chiefs of the general staff and all chiefs of the main political administration) have come from the ground forces. Even the present chiefs of the strategic rocket forces and of the air defense forces, Generals Yu.P. Maksimov and Ivan Tretiak, are ground forces officers. In contrast to the U.S. land-based missile forces, which arose from and remain in the air force, the Soviet strategic rocket forces arose out of the artillery arm of the ground forces. The traditions, viewpoints, and uniforms of the strategic rocket forces are imbedded in their parent service. As for the air defense forces, they have been commanded by a ground forces or an air forces officer since their founding in 1950. All commanders of TVDs, the Russian acronym for a theater of military action, identified to date have been ground forces officers. Finally, whereas the other services have about two individuals on the Central Committee, the ground forces usually have ten to twenty.

In contrast to the ground forces, the navy is the least influential service, a fact that has frustrated its leaders. This is evident in the writings of the recently deceased chief of the Soviet Navy, Admiral Sergei Gorshkov. In a series of articles written in the early 1970s, for example, he addressed "Russia's Difficult Road to the Sea" and criticized "falsifiers of military history" who "assert that all of Russia's victories have been gained only by the army and that it can be powerful only by strengthening the army at the expense of the navy."[5] In a 1976 book extolling the virtues of maritime power, Gorshkov differentiated between "fleet against fleet" and "fleet against shore" activities and stated that the latter have become dominant since the advent of naval nuclear land-attack systems.[6] He then vitiated his own categorization by placing all fleet-against-fleet tasks, including attacking enemy naval and merchant ships, under the fleet-against-shore heading. His logic is confusing until one realizes that his was an exercise in circumlocution justifying traditional fleet-against-fleet tasks to an audience overwhelmingly concerned with land warfare. Gorshkov pointedly addressed that audience in the 1979 edition of this same book, where he added a follow-on section, "The Strategic Employment of the Fleet." In it he readily criticized Napoleon, the epitome of the ground forces marshal, for not properly appreciating the naval dimensions of war. He criticized as well Russia's military leadership in the 1904–1905 war with Japan, for although Russia's military leadership, he said, had "thoroughly worked out" the land strategy for the conflict, the nation was defeated nonetheless because its leaders gave "insufficient attention . . . to theoretical thinking on the patterns of armed combat in sea theaters."[7]

Gorshkov wrote in his foreword to the 1988 book, *The Navy: Its Role, Prospects for Development, and Employment,* of a "smoothing over of significant differences" in the roles of the services in combat.[8] Nevertheless, he and the authors of the main text continually make the case that a navy is valuable. They go so far as to call for retaining the principle that forces traditionally assigned as primarily responsible for operations in a particular medium ought to continue to be the primary war fighters there.[9] They particularize their argument with assertions throughout the book about the significance or special features of naval forces for conducting operations in maritime theaters. As a consequence, a reader is left to wonder if there are debates in the Soviet Union not only about the relative importance of maritime theaters but also about the relative importance of naval forces for fighting in them.

It should not be surprising that the great bulk of the navy would do the bidding of others in war. SSBNs (and probably land-attack cruise missile shooters) would, of course, be under the control of the national command authority. The ground forces officers commanding continental TVDs along the periphery of the Soviet Union–Warsaw Pact regions would have wartime operational control of most of the general-purpose naval units deployed in the adjacent waters, possibly out to great distances. Somewhat similarly, naval units directly involved in homeland air defense would probably function as part of a coordinated strategic aerospace defense network together with the air defense forces and elements of the air forces. The entire network would respond to the commander of the air defense forces, whose incumbent is now a ground forces officer.

Only general purpose naval units operating in distant ocean TVDs (to interdict SLOCs, for instance) would remain fully under naval operational control. Soviet strategic planners as a matter of habit would probably be unenthusiastic to proposals to dedicate large numbers of naval units to such TVDs—where they would not be readily available to do the bidding of continental and aerospace defense commanders—unless the benefits seemed worthwhile.

Arguments Based on Benefits and Costs

It is generally accepted that overall Soviet military strategy today—notwithstanding Gorbachev's emphases on defensive defense—remains one that calls for a full-scale conventional offensive in the center of Western Europe with limited offensives or holding actions on the flanks. The central offensive is to be as rapid as possible in order to deliver a knockout blow or at least ensure that the initial period of the war is decisively in the Soviets' favor.

Within that overall strategy, Soviet writings do acknowledge that SLOC interdiction could become very important, but often as not, the importance is specifically related to the length of conflict. For example, *The Navy* states that the "battle of the SLOCs" will be "manifested especially strongly in the course of a long war."[10] The implication is that interdiction would not be as important in short wars, exactly the kind of war Soviet military strategists are aiming for.

A Soviet switch to a defensive military doctrine probably means that any war would be protracted. Whether long or short, however, Soviet writings also indicate that interdicting sea-lines of communications (SLOCs) can consist of more than sinking ships at sea. Ports and harbors are parts of SLOCs, and these can be captured, sabotaged, bombed, or mined.

It is not enough, furthermore, that NATO succeed in getting supplies to reception ports. Supplies must eventually make it to the fighting fronts, and even a defensive doctrine does not preclude attacking the land lines of communications over which supplies would flow. For the most part, land lines are also easier to find and probably easier to interdict.

In short, sinking ships at sea is not the only way to stop the flow of supplies. Naval writers also point out that it is not enough just to sink ships as Germany did in World War II.[11] One must husband resources and sink only those carrying valuable military cargoes. It will probably be very difficult to single out the ships with critical cargoes in the midst of all the others that must sail so as to provide Europe with economic goods. To attack many of the latter ships would probably quickly exhaust the weapons on available Soviet submarines, for it is not believed that the Soviet Union has many submarines to spare to the task, especially since it must expect to lose some as they transit through Western antisubmarine defenses (both when they go out to the Atlantic and when they return home to rearm).

But, the reader may ask, it was asserted earlier that the Soviet Navy has many submarines. Are the numbers not sufficient after all? The proponents of the strategic defensive paradigm would say not. They point out, first, that Soviet submarine numbers will surely drop in the 1990s. The Soviets built about seventy-five submarines a year in the mid-1950s, about twenty a year in the mid-1960s, about twelve to fourteen a year in the mid-1970s, and about half that a year for their own navy in mid-1980s. Soviet spokesmen have stated that increased submarine force capabilities will come from better quality, not from greater quantity.[12]

The restructuring of Soviet economic priorities associated with Mikhail Gorbachev's reforms may mean that the decade of the 1990s may be especially austere for the navy (as the least influential of the services) and slow the pace of improvements in its capabilities. That fact can be important since confidence in protecting the maritime defense perimeter may not be increasing. Soviet planners, who tend to be conservative by nature when estimating military requirements, probably see the perimeter not as a solid wall but rather as one with many gaps or openings.

The U.S. Maritime Strategy makes clear an intent to force those openings, and the recent qualitative and quantitative buildup of U.S. naval forces (with over a hundred ships added to the fleet in the 1980s) evidences an increased capability to do so. Ambitious U.S. and NATO naval exercises in the Norwegian Sea provide additional proof of a determination, if there were a conflict, to bring the maritime war to the Soviet Navy.

As a result, Soviet strategic planners may have few incentives to release supposedly freed-up units for operations against distant SLOCs in the early periods of a war. Rather, there may be an increase in their propensity for strategically defensive naval operations. Indeed, since 1985 there has been a gradual and fairly steady drop in the average number of units deployed in far distant waters. Similarly, major exercises have since then been conducted closer to the homeland. The U.S. director of naval intelligence, Rear Admiral William O. Studeman, addressed possible reasons for these changes:

> We believe [they] . . . reflect—among other things—economic constraints; increased emphasis on the Navy's role in close-in, combined arms operations; and/or an intention to develop more flexible employment options for naval forces and to increase their combat readiness to counter the U.S. Maritime Strategy's deployment of forces near Soviet territory and SSBN operating areas at the outset of hostilities.[13]

While there may be fewer Soviet SSBNs in the future, thereby reducing the number that need to be protected, each SSBN becomes that much more important, especially if overall strategic warhead levels decrease significantly in a nuclear arms reduction agreement. Thus, devoting general purpose forces to protect them may be viewed as important as ever, especially in the light of a potentially increasing threat to land-based missiles as the United States deploys more hard-target-kill MX and Trident II weapons. In addition, U.S. deployment of the B-1 and B-2 bombers and (if news accounts are true) of satellites that "see" through clouds can only heighten Soviet concerns about the potential vulnerability of mobile land-based systems, thereby reinforcing concern to ensure the survivability of sea-based missiles.

In short, while a major threat of an offensive against Western resupply ships might indeed outflank the Maritime Strategy and bring other benefits, the Soviet naval response to the strategy and to U.S. improvements in strategic and general purpose forces may be the traditional or habitual one of employing general purpose units defensively. In the Soviet mind such employment may provide the best relative return.

This is not to argue that there will be no submarines employed offensively early in a war. A few will probably be dedicated to an anti-SLOC mission, if for no other reason than to tie down Western ASW assets. Similarly, some may deploy to challenge Western SSBNs, but because the prospects of succeeding are so poor, it is expected that few would be assigned this task.

Should the Soviets ever achieve a breakthrough in ASW detection and tracking, that development more than any other might justify to Soviet strategic planners a major naval offensive early on in a war. That Western tactical submarines might attack Soviet SSBNs (as the Maritime Strategy suggests) is a frustrating possibility for the Soviet Navy, not only because it must devote considerable resources to SSBN protection but also because it can pose no comparable threat to U.S. strategic missile submarines. *The Navy* does speak, however, of a major Soviet campaign to that end. The book lists main missions "vitally important to the state," and under the rubric of "repelling an enemy aerospace attack," the authors state that the increasing threat (resulting from improvements in SSBNs, in submarine-launched ballistic missiles, and in submarine-launched land-attack cruise missiles) means that

> in the nearest foreseeable future, as prospects for the development of submarines and their weapons show, the missions of combating them may rise to the level of a national mission (*obshchegosudarstvennaia zadacha*), and then one may speak of the antisubmarine defense of the country in the same manner as we speak of the air defense of the country.[14]

This mission is described as encompassing great geographic scope since, the authors point out, Poseidon and Trident missile submarines can patrol and fire from 4,600 to 11,000 kilometers from targets in the Soviet Union. While acknowledging that "aviation, air defense forces, missile forces, and space means" will share in the mission, the authors also point out that

> the principal burden of combating groupings of missile-armed submarines rests with the naval forces, inasmuch as they are the only branch of the armed forces capable of overcoming enemy opposition, entering into immediate contact with strategic weapons platforms, accomplishing lengthy and concealed tracking of them while it is still peacetime, and destroying them with its own weapons immediately at the outbreak of war.[15]

This immediate destruction of submarines "before their missiles are launched" is viewed as being "of special significance to both of the opposing sides."[16]

Are we to infer that Soviet naval forces will soon deploy in large numbers to find, track, and, if war occurs, immediately destroy Western SSBNs? The desire to do so is clear, but there does not seem to be evidence of an actual or foreseeable capability to threaten a significant portion of the sea-based nuclear deterrent of the United States. Indeed, the discussion in *The Navy* has an element of advocacy to it, especially when the authors suggest the possibility that antisubmarine defense of the nation may become a mission comparable to national air defense. The authors may be trying to make a case that, in an era of tight budgets, funding for ASW should be viewed as no less important than for aerospace defense. No doubt advocates of the latter are arguing just as strongly for a Soviet Strategic Defense Initiative and for systems to counter the B-1 and B-2 bombers, stealthy U.S. cruise missiles, and the advanced technology fighters.

In sum, there is probably only one development that might well result in a significant increase in Soviet naval units operating offensively from the first moment of a war. This is an ASW breakthrough against ballistic missile submarines, but such a development is not yet foreseeable. It may never occur; but if it does, it should do so very slowly in view of competing research priorities in an era of fiscal austerity.

Conclusion

There are two models of Soviet naval behavior in the initial period of a NATO–Warsaw Pact (conventional) war. The strategic defensive model became generally accepted in the 1980s as the prime model for explaining and predicting Soviet naval developments. The strategic offensive alternative has been the first runner-up for adoption should evidence suggest that the strategic defensive model falls short.

Has the time come to move the offensive model to the forefront? No. Although the arguments for that model are attractive, all can be countered by arguments offered in favor of the strategic defensive alternative. In addition, the latter has the weight of Russian tradition or habit in its favor; no operational evidence exists that that tradition has changed.

Nevertheless, the offensive model ought not to be dismissed. It must continue to serve as a foil for testing the validity of the strategic defensive model of Soviet naval behavior. Otherwise Western observers of the Soviet Navy could fall victim to complacency and self-delusion.

Notes

1. Statement of Rear Admiral William O. Studeman, U.S. Navy, Director of Naval Intelligence, before the Seapower and Strategic and Critical Materials Subcommittee of the House Armed Services Committee, on Intelligence Issues, March 1, 1988, 4.

2. Ibid., 12.

3. David Alan Hildebrandt, "The Soviet Trend toward Conventional Warfare and the Soviet Navy: Still No Anti-SLOC?" (Master's thesis, Naval Postgraduate School, 1988), 131. James McConnell of the Center of Naval Analyses and Charles Peterson, formerly of the same center, are both regular readers of Soviet literature and in unpublished works both have written of a trend of increased emphasis on the importance of sea-lines of communications.

4. Rear Admiral N.P. V'iunenko, Captain 1st Rank B.N. Makeev, and Captain 1st Rank V.D. Skugarev, *Voenno-morskoi flot: Rol', perspektivy razvitiia, ispol'zovanie* (The Navy: Its role, prospects for development, and employment) (Moscow: Voenizdat, 1988), 23. Admiral of the Fleet Sergei G. Gorshkov contributed a foreward to the book, which was produced under his leadership.

5. S.G. Gorshkov, "Voenno-morskie floty v voinakh i v mirnoe vremia" (Navies in war and peace)," *Morskoi sbornik*, no. 3 (1972): 20.

6. S.G. Gorshkov, *Morskaia moshch' gosudarstva* (Sea power of the State) (Moscow: Voenizdat, 1976), chap. 4, esp. 360.

7. Ibid., 2d ed. supplemented (1979), 308–18.

8. Gorshkov, foreword to V'iunenko, Makeev, and Skugarev, *Voenno-morskoi flot*, 15.

9. V'iunenko, Makeev, and Skugarev, *Voenno-morskoi flot*, 34–35.

10. Ibid., 244.

11. Ibid., 248.

12. See Richard L. Haver, "Soviet Navy Perspectives," U.S. Naval Institute *Proceedings* 114 (May 1988): 238.

13. Statement of Rear Admiral William O. Studeman," 39–40.

14. V'iunenko, Makeev, and Skugarev, *Voenno-morskoi flot*, 233.

15. Ibid., 220–21.

16. Ibid., 222.

Part V
What Use for a Navy?

The Soviet Navy must participate in a combined arms defense of the Eurasian landmass. Advocates have always arisen, and continue to arise, for the navy to play a broader role as a worldwide instrument of policy in peace and war. The Soviet Navy is not built for the projection of power into the Third World. Also, the failure of past Soviet policy and the requirements of the new do not argue well for increased Soviet naval presence in the Third World. Yet significant naval capabilities are at the disposal of Soviet leaders who are unlikely to abandon the need to project the Soviet Union as a superpower with worldwide interests.

In chapter 10 Richard B. Remnek examines the costs and benefits of Soviet naval support facilities in the Third World. The results are quite mixed. The navy has benefited but often at significant political and economic cost. Soviet leaders are faced with powerful reasons to reduce such commitments. Yet, as Steve F. Kime argues in chapter 11, a reduced threat in Europe and arms control could legitimize the freeing of naval forces for roles other than perimeter defense. Should policy require a presence in the Third World, the navy is ready. Persian Gulf operations are a recent case in point. Finally, as Kime reminds us, the Soviet Navy lacks an established identity, and so its mission could change. To the degree that Gorbachev's agenda is successful, the Soviet Navy may increasingly become a powerful force in search of a purpose.

10
Soviet Access to Overseas Naval Support Facilities: A Military and Political Analysis

Richard B. Remnek

W hen General Secretary Mikhail Gorbachev offered in September 1988 to relinquish the Soviet Navy's access to Vietnam's Cam Ranh Bay in exchange for the elimination of U.S. military bases in the Philippines, public attention once more focused on the Soviet use of overseas naval support facilities.[1] Thus far, the U.S. government has not responded favorably to Gorbachev's offer. However, if the superpowers' arms control agenda were eventually to be expanded to include limitations on naval deployments, restricting the development and use of overseas military facilities may very well become a focal point of the negotiations. In that event, Soviet naval support facilities overseas will receive more careful scrutiny than they have warranted so far. In the past Soviet naval bases tended to receive sensationalized attention in the Western press, usually in connection with exaggerated claims about the Soviet naval threat to the West.

In reality, the wartime role of these facilities is far less ominous than is frequently assumed. In fact, the peacetime role of Soviet access to overseas naval facilities is more important. They have enabled the Soviets to establish a military presence in distant regions, and as a tangible expression of Moscow's security commitments, that presence has been an important instrument of its Third World diplomacy. Soviet naval access to overseas facilities has also been an objective of that diplomacy. The quest for naval access has induced Soviet leaders to cultivate relations with regimes on littoral nations, some of which would otherwise be too small and insignificant to warrant such attention. On occasion, it has led the Soviets to undertake commitments to a host government that they would have rather avoided. Hence, the political aspects of Soviet naval access would appear to be just as important as the military considerations. This chapter explores these military and political dimensions of Soviet naval access.[2]

Access Privileges versus Base Rights

Naval access privileges are different from base rights. Foreign military bases are secured through leasehold treaties and can be employed in any way the user wishes for as long as the treaties remain in legal force. By contrast, access privileges are granted (and can be abridged or withdrawn) at the host nation's discretion. In general, the sovereignty of host nations has been better protected by access arrangements than by leasehold treaties granting base rights.

This does not mean that access arrangements have no legal basis, for Soviet access privileges have been codified in secret protocols concluded with host countries. The protocols do not appear to have had the same legal weight as leasehold treaties for base rights. For example, the existence of access agreements prevented neither Egypt nor Somalia from abrogating access privileges before the expiration dates of the agreements. In Egypt, the annulment occurred in 1976, two years before a renewed five-year access agreement was to have lapsed.

Another difference is that access arrangements usually provide for extensive host nation control over the development and use of facilities. Such control has both formal and substantive aspects. As a rule, Soviet ensigns do not fly over facilities ashore in the Third World. Moreover, Soviet installations are guarded by local troops. In many cases, the Soviets need local permission for naval visits or for the staging of reconnaissance aircraft from local airfields. Soviet pressures to obtain greater operational control over their support activities have often been successfully resisted.

Yet the Soviets have had some success in achieving significant operational control, as the following examples attest. First, they gained exclusive and unrestricted use of Egypt's Cairo West airfield, which they used during the 1971 Indo-Pakistan War to transship arms and material to India—the wrong country in Egypt's view. Second, when the Soviets have been able to install communications and intelligence collection stations ashore, they have usually been able to use them without local interference. Here Soviet needs for military secrecy concerning such relatively sophisticated installations have taken precedence over host nation desires to maximize control. In these cases the host's concerns are likely to be met in a pro forma manner—for example, by the posting of local guards outside an exclusive Soviet installation. This occurred in Somalia in the mid-1970s when Somali military personnel stood guard over the long-range communications station at Berbera, to which only the Soviets apparently had access.[3] Third, the Soviets have a similar arrangement (but on a larger scale) in Vietnam today. Vietnamese Army units reportedly guard two peripheral checkpoints to Cam Ranh Bay, the most elaborate military support complex the Soviets have ever developed overseas, while the Soviets maintain direct control over check points in the inner ring of the complex.[4]

Occasionally an incident has occurred revealing the Soviets' exclusive use of installations, despite the fact that they had not acquired extraterritorial base rights. In one instance, a Department of Defense delegation of technical experts led by Senator Dewey Bartlett (R.–Oklahoma) was denied entry to the communications station at Berbera in 1975 despite the personal intervention of the head of Somalia's secret police (and President Siad Barre's son-in-law), Ahmed Suleiman. In denying Colonel Suleiman's request, the Somali sentries on duty outside the station appear to have acted on instructions from Soviet personnel inside. A similar incident occurred at the western Egyptian port of Mersa Matruh, which prior to July 1972 the Soviets were developing for their own exclusive use. In early 1972, President Anwar Sadat and Libyan president Muammar Qaddafi were initially refused entry to the Mersa Matruh complex by the local Soviet commander.[5] It was only after the intercession of the Soviet ambassador in Cairo that Sadat and his guest were permitted entry. Aside from the embarrassment, the political fallout of these incidents was not severe, probably because exclusive Soviet access was arranged through mutual consent and met Soviet operational and security requirements deemed legitimate by the host nation. If these incidents raised fears that Egypt and Somalia had granted the Soviets base rights, such fears should have been laid to rest once these states expelled the Soviets with ease.

Another important aspect of the distinction between access and base rights relates to Soviet terminology. By long-standing Soviet definition, naval bases are protected zones supporting permanently stationed naval forces and containing an administrative staff and other support infrastructure ashore. The Soviet definition applies clearly to their own home fleet bases. However, this customary definition does not seem to apply to their naval support facilities overseas, which today are largely mobile and support naval forces deployed on rotation from the Soviet home fleets.

In recent years, however, the Soviets have created some ambiguity on this point. In the 1983 and 1986 editions of the Soviet *Military Encyclopedic Dictionary,* the entry for "military base" includes this statement: "Capitalist states, and especially the USA, for expansionist and aggressive purposes acquire military bases beyond their borders."[6] Since the mid-1950s—when the Soviet Union abandoned its base rights, secured by leasehold treaties, to Porkkala-Udd (Finland) and Port Arthur (China)—the Soviets have disclaimed any interest in acquiring overseas base rights. Until the 1983 publication of the *Military Encyclopedic Dictionary,* the Soviet line was that only imperialist states had overseas bases. The 1983 change in formulation raises the possibility that the Soviets have reserved the right to acquire foreign base rights for themselves, albeit for nonaggressive purposes. Since the only major new development in Soviet naval support activities overseas took place in Vietnam, it is possible that the Soviets adjusted their formulation to account for their acquisition of a major support base at Cam Ranh Bay, a complex that Rear Admiral John L. Butts, U.S. director of naval intelligence, has described as "Moscow's first true overseas base."[7] It should be kept in mind, however, that from Moscow's perspective, Vietnam is not a Third World state but rather a member of the "socialist commonwealth of nations." As we shall discuss later, the distinction between Third World and socialist states appears to have influenced recent Soviet naval access policy.

The Importance of Access to the Soviet Union

The importance of overseas support facilities to the Soviet Union becomes clear from a survey of the specific benefits they provide. The advantages of overseas access to Moscow occur both in promoting a Soviet peacetime political presence in the Third World and in improving Soviet training and intelligence collection for wartime operations. The primary concrete military benefits are three: logistics, maintenance, and crew rest. Improved direct support of Soviet naval operations has had a measurable impact on Soviet Third World deployments. Additionally, overseas facilities provide indirect support for naval units through communications and aerial reconnaissance. Finally, overseas airfields might play a significant role in Soviet combat operations in wartime.

Naval Access for Peacetime and Wartime

In peacetime, the Soviet Navy performs primarily, but not exclusively, a politico-military mission in Third World waters. First and foremost, it constitutes a presence that local actors must take into account. Thus, the operational benefits the navy derives from the use of facilities in the Third World are in peacetime principally applied to the pursuit of the Soviet Union's political objectives.

This is not to deny that the Soviet use of overseas naval facilities in peacetime has general benefits improving the Soviet Union's ability to prepare for war. For example, the Soviets see prolonged forward naval deployments as useful for training. Even the limited routine training and naval exercises the Soviets occasionally undertake in the forward area to some extent increase their ability to perform various wartime missions. Furthermore, Soviet naval units deployed out of area also collect intelligence and intercept communications of Western and Chinese military and civilian targets. This practice improves overall Soviet military preparedness in numerous and indeterminate ways. One might add here that since U.S. carrier forces deployed in Third World waters operate in peacetime at tempos far higher and under conditions far closer to those that would be probably experienced in wartime than do Soviet naval forces in the forward area, the intelligence collected by the Soviets against Western warships in these waters is likely to be significantly more useful militarily than whatever information the West obtains about Soviet naval operations there.

Some observers have commented that the Soviet Navy's political mission in the Third World has largely coincided with and reinforced its war-related mission of countering Western carrier forces in these regions.[8] However, although many of the Soviet naval forces deployed in Third World regions are configured for the anticarrier role, this does not mean that they would necessarily be used in wartime to attack carrier groups in Third World waters. To a large extent how Soviet naval forces deployed in peacetime in the forward area would be used in war depends on how the West would employ its naval forces. Should U.S. and other Western naval forces be withdrawn from the Mediterranean or Indian Ocean, say during a crisis leading to a North Atlantic Treaty Organization (NATO)–Warsaw Pact war, the Soviets might pull their forces out of those areas too if they felt no alternative objectives, such as military installations (for example, Diego Garcia) or economic objectives (for example, oil terminals) were worth targeting there with naval forces.[9] The main point is that Soviet forces deployed in distant waters in peacetime may not be there in wartime. Their wartime use is thus highly scenario dependent.

Even if Moscow's naval forces were to be engaged in combat in forward areas against Western forces, probably they would not survive long enough once hostilities erupted to need shore-based support. Thus the wartime value of Soviet use of overseas facilities mainly depends on the quality of naval support activities during peacetime. By increasing the combat readiness and capabilities of these forces on the eve of war, support facilities ashore can help the Soviet Navy give a better account of itself, regardless of whether its deployed forces would be used for engaging Western carrier groups in naval battles lasting little more than the first salvo or for reassignment to other missions closer to Soviet home waters.

Concrete Military Benefits of Naval Access

Nevertheless, the Soviet Navy derives concrete military benefits from using overseas facilities. It uses shore-based support overseas primarily for logistics, maintenance, and crew rest. Although Soviet combatants can and do receive supplies from naval auxiliaries, civilian cargo vessels, and tankers in international waters, it is easier and more efficient for the Soviets to supply their warships directly from shore. Hence they have usually developed or expanded significantly petroleum, oils, and lubricants (POL) and storage facilities in their main support complexes.

Similarly, although the Soviet Navy can and does perform minor repairs at sea, it needs access to protected harbors to perform more extensive maintenance and repairs. Many of these repairs can be performed with the assistance of auxiliary tenders; more extensive maintenance and overhauls for combatants as large as destroyers can be done in the floating drydocks the Soviets have stationed at Dahlac, Ethiopia; Luanda, Angola; Tartus, Syria; and other locations. Soviet submarines and minor surface combatants have also been overhauled on a routine basis in repair yards in Yugoslavia, Tunisia, and, prior to 1976, in Egypt. In addition Soviet naval auxiliaries flying civilian ensigns have been overhauled in shipyards in Singapore and Greece. The repair of Soviet auxiliaries by foreign shipyards has increased in recent years, despite the reduced tempo of Soviet naval operations in forward areas and the limited availability of hard currency due to declining oil export revenues.[10] For more extensive repairs and overhauls of combatants, the Soviets use repair yards in their home ports.

The rest that Soviet crews receive ashore in the Third World enables them to stretch their sea legs—but little more. By Western standards the quality of their rest and recreation ashore leaves much to be desired. Most of the Third World ports that the Soviets have used for this purpose are extremely hot and uncomfortable during the summer months and lack many basic amenities. Yet for sailors, many of whom are assigned to small vessels with even fewer amenities (insufficient water for taking daily showers and no air conditioning, for example), even brief visits ashore can provide some relief from the tedium of very lengthy deployments in tropical climates.

The Consequences of Improved Direct Support of Naval Operations

However limited these support services may be, they have nevertheless had a tangible impact on Soviet naval operations. Through the use of shore-based facilities, the Soviet Navy has been able to support forward-deployed combatants with fewer support vessels and to prolong combatant deployments significantly. For example, prior to gaining extensive access to facilities at Berbera, Somalia, in 1972, the average Soviet warship assigned to the Indian Ocean stayed there for roughly five months; in 1973 Soviet combatant deployments to the Indian Ocean lasted for around a year, though they declined in subsequent years.[11] In 1977 the Soviets were expelled from Berbera.

Lengthening combatant deployments has important operational advantages. First, it reduces the overall proportion of time wasted by Soviet warships in transit from home fleet areas to forward operating stations. In some cases these reductions are significant. In the 1970s, for example (before the Soviet Indian Ocean Squadron began to make occasional use of Cam Ranh Bay for en route logistic and maintenance support), it took Soviet naval units approximately three weeks with normal transit speeds of 10 to 12 knots to reach the Gulf of Aden, their normal Indian Ocean operating station at that time, from their Vladivostok home port (a distance of 6,700 nautical miles). Prior to 1973, when Soviet naval deployments in the Indian Ocean averaged five months, to keep one combatant on station continuously in the Gulf of Aden Soviet warships spent roughly four months per year in transit. By more than doubling the length of combatant deployments in 1973, the Soviets were able to cut the amount of transit time by more than half.

Second, lengthening deployments gives the Soviet Navy the ability to meet their force requirements with a smaller inventory of ships, thereby reducing overall operating costs as well as freeing units for other tasks. To be sure, only some of the general purpose forces the Soviets deploy forward—such as submarines and the more modern, missile-equipped surface combatants—could be used effectively to perform higher-priority missions of strategic significance elsewhere. Other units have limited combat capabilities and are therefore well suited to perform relatively nondemanding politico-military missions in the Third World and little else. This applies particularly to the older combatants the Soviets used to deploy, such as 900-ton T-58-class patrol ships and 1,100 ton Petya-class frigates, first introduced into service when the Soviets had only a day-sailing navy.[12] Indeed, the Soviets appear to have risked Indian Ocean deployments for the Petyas (whose small size and low endurance made them particularly ill suited for open ocean operations) only after they had gained routine access to Berbera. The ready availability of local support facilities there appears to have enabled them to prolong the useful service life of warships that might otherwise have been scrapped or sold to foreign countries. (In fact, as Petyas have been delivered to several Third World states, more modern frigates have taken their place among deployed Soviet naval contingents.)

Communications and Aerial Support of Naval Operations

Besides direct support of deployed Soviet naval units, overseas facilities also provide indirect support for them through communications and aerial reconnaissance. The Soviets now operate a long-range high-frequency communications station at Aden, the same station they used at Berbera until 1977. They have more sophisticated communications stations in Cuba and Vietnam, where they also have electronic intelligence-gathering installations. These communications stations facilitate Soviet military communications worldwide. The intelligence collection facilities in Vietnam and Cuba undoubtedly obtain highly valuable information about Western military operations and civilian activities of strategic significance, such as oil tanker traffic.

The Soviets have staged routine surveillance flights from many foreign airfields (including Egypt, Somalia, and Guinea in the 1970s; Cuba, Vietnam, Angola, Syria, Libya, South Yemen, and Ethiopia today). Most often the Soviets have used for this purpose Il-38 May antisubmarine warfare (ASW) planes, whose limited range does not allow them to perform more than aerial surveillance in support of deployed naval forces. However, the Soviets also stage long-range Tu-95 Bear-D maritime reconnaissance aircraft from airfields in Angola, Cuba, and Vietnam. They have used Vietnamese and Cuban airfields to support Tu-142 Bear-F ASW surveillance flights. This affords the aerial surveillance of wide expanses of the North and South Atlantic, Western Pacific, and South China Sea. It also provides the Soviets with reconnaissance of military operations and civilian activities along the shore in such important locations as the U.S. bases in the Philippines and Chinese bases in southern China and on Hainan Island. Such maritime reconnaissance flights can provide real-time intelligence. For example, Tu-95 Bear-Ds staging from Luanda during the 1982 Falklands-Malvinas War conducted limited surveillance of British naval forces en route to Ascension Island.[13] Bear-Ds are also capable of providing targeting data for sea-launched cruise missiles, a valuable asset in peacetime naval exercises as well as in wartime, assuming that the Bear-Ds would survive long enough to be able to relay the data.

Third World airfields have also received Soviet strike aircraft. Tu-16 Badgers were stationed at Aswan, Egypt, until 1972. Today the Soviets station Badgers in Syria and Vietnam. As far as we know, none of these Badgers has ever flown a maritime mission. Each of these Badger deployments can and presumably has been rationalized as a response to regional security threats to the host nation. Regardless of whether the host nations would consent, that the Soviets could and would be able to use these rather obsolete bombers effectively in a coalition war remains very doubtful.

Wartime Employment of Overseas Airfields

Nevertheless, the advantages to Moscow of staging bombers from Third World airfields in wartime are obvious. Doing so would extend the range and on-station operating time of high-performance aircraft, such as the Backfire, assuming the Soviets would be willing to place in jeopardy these valuable assets, and it would enable the Soviets to employ, however effectively, shorter-range Badgers in distant theaters.

Moreover, the Soviets do not need to deploy strike aircraft to forward airfields prior to the outbreak of hostilities to make effective use of those facilities in wartime. For example, should a coalition war be fought in the Mediterranean, Libyan airfields could advantageously be used for the recovery and turnaround of surviving Soviet aircraft launched from Warsaw Pact air bases. By using Libya's ordnance and POL storage facilities, Moscow could rearm and refuel its bombers for missions against NATO targets in the western Mediterranean. Libya's improving air defense capabilities would afford some protection for Soviet aircraft staging from Libyan airfields. Vietnam, whose air defense capabilities are probably more effective than those in Libya, could offer similar support to Soviet aircraft should a major war break out in the Asian Pacific region. And finally, should a conflict that started in Southwest Asia escalate horizontally, with U.S. carriers routed around the Cape of Good Hope to the Atlantic, airfields in South Yemen and Ethiopia could be used for recovery and turnaround of Backfires, flying from Soviet home bases against carriers in transit. Although the less protected airfields in those countries could place Soviet bombers in jeopardy, the Soviets might nevertheless risk using these airfields to extend the range of their strike aircraft if they felt they had a reasonable chance of disabling a U.S. carrier thereby. The Soviets appear to have real needs for access to Third World airfields, but not port facilities, after the initiation of hostilities in a major war.

These scenarios for Soviet air combat operations are not simply hypothetical musings. We know that the Soviets built into their infrastructure in Somalia in the 1970s, and reportedly today in Vietnam, capabilities specifically designed to support Soviet combat operations. For example, the so-called missile-handling and storage facility at Berbera was capable of handling a wide variety of air- and sea-launched conventional tactical missiles, as well as other ordnance far more sophisticated than those the Somalis had or were ever likely to receive.[14] The ordnance storage facility's proximity to both the large airfield then under construction and the port suggests its potential use for naval combatants and bomber aircraft alike.

Just what contingencies the Soviets had in mind in the mid-1970s when they built into their support infrastructure at Berbera the capability to support strike aircraft is mystifying. Before the shah of Iran's fall and the U.S. military buildup in the Indian Ocean area, no conceivable regional scenario would have justified the acquisition of such capabilities. I have speculated at length elsewhere that the Soviets may have had a Mediterranean scenario in mind.[15] According to this scenario, Badgers deploying from Soviet airfields could have been refueled and loaded with ordnance at Berbera in order to attack U.S. carrier groups in the eastern Mediterranean. The initiation of construction of air combat support facilities at Berbera—about a year after the Soviets had been forced to withdraw their Badgers from Egypt—suggests that Berbera may have been seen by Moscow as an alternative to Egyptian facilities.

Another possible explanation is that the Soviets developed these air combat support facilities at Berbera without any scenario in mind. Perhaps they replicated an existing ordnance storage facility in the Soviet Union without taking into account the negative publicity that predictably ensued once the wide capabilities of the facility became common knowledge. This interpretation implies that Soviet development of overseas military support facilities may be planned far less deliberately, and scrutinized far less carefully by the Soviet foreign ministry, than Western analysts have generally assumed.

While the use of Third World airfields in various combat scenarios may seem advantageous from Moscow's perspective, it is far less certain whether host nations would be willing to permit the Soviets to use their airfields in a NATO–Warsaw Pact conflict. With the possible exception of Libya's Qaddafi, no Third World leader has displayed a willingness to see his country become a battlefield in a coalition war. Even countries that support the Soviet Navy and rely heavily on Soviet arms imports and security assistance continue to depend primarily on Western economic trade, aid, and private investment. With their nonsubsistence economies tied to the West, they would have much to lose from such a conflict, especially if it left the Western economies in ruin. Hence, they would hardly be likely to throw in their lot with the Soviets in a coalition war.

In certain situations, however, the Soviets might be able to use local airfields when they need it, despite local opposition. The most likely situations would be ones in which the Soviets enjoyed exclusive access to airfields at locations remote from local capitals and population centers, where local armed forces were few or nonexistent. Local forces could be neutralized by Soviet technical advisers immobilizing weapons systems (as they did to Afghan Army tanks just before the December 1979 Soviet intervention), or cutting communications to the local Defense Ministry, or be countered by rapid insertion of Soviet airborne forces to defend airfields and other important installations. These conditions generally applied in Berbera, which is distant from both the capital at Mogadishu and the regional military headquarters at Hargeisa. Also, the Somali armed forces were heavily dependent on Soviet technical support. More recently, such conditions have been approximated in Cam Ranh Bay, where the Soviets enjoy exclusive access and maintain a contingent of roughly 2,000 personnel, far larger reportedly than the token force of Vietnamese Army troops stationed there.[16] Moreover, Cam Ranh Bay is remote from major Vietnamese cities.

The Soviets derive concrete operational benefits from the use of overseas naval support facilities in peacetime. In a major war, however, access to overseas airfields would be far more important to them than the use of local port facilities. And in certain situations, the Soviets might be able to use these airfields regardless of the host nation's will.

Access and Soviet Foreign Policy

Given the clear military importance of these facilities, how has the quest for access to them affected Soviet foreign policy? Has naval access been so important as to alter the thrust of Soviet regional policies? If so, what were the consequences?

The Soviet Quest for Access

The quest for access has undoubtedly given impetus to Moscow's cultivation of relations with Third World regimes. It helps to explain why the Soviets over the past decade in particular have established military ties with many small and poor Third World littoral states (such as, Guinea, Somalia, the Yemens, Guinea, Cape Verde, Benin, and Guinea-Bissau), where Soviet military aid is likely to have a greater political impact. Although the port facilities in these states are rudimentary, the Soviet Navy probably would find them useful nevertheless. That is because Soviet warships have been able to keep their needs for shore-based support to a minimum by towing smaller combatants to and from station, by remaining immobile, in port or at sea, for roughly two-thirds of their time on station, and by practicing routine maintenance and logistics at sea. That the Soviets do not need much shore-based support to sustain a naval presence was clearly demonstrated during the Ogaden War. After the Soviets were expelled from Berbera in November 1977, they were able to augment their Indian Ocean squadron by 50 percent and then employ it extensively for six months in its most demanding (noncombat) mission to date, before an alternate support base became available.[17]

The Question of Soviet Policy Distortion

By extending their military assistance to more littoral nations, the Soviets undoubtedly have increased their access options and improved their bargaining power with each potential or actual donor. This means that the Soviets will probably be able to avoid the kind of compromises they made in the early 1970s when they felt compelled to turn to Somalia for support of their Indian Ocean Squadron.

In the early 1970s the need for access definitely distorted Soviet policy in the Horn of Africa. When they decided to buy access to Somali facilities with modern weapons, Soviet leaders ignored the warnings of their Africanists about the dangers of dealing with an irredentist regime and pursued the policy of "painting nationalism red."[18] They seem to have taken a calculated risk that a strong U.S.-backed Ethiopia would deter any Somali military adventures. Without the need for access, the Soviets would never have aligned themselves so closely with what the rest of Africa regarded as a pariah state. The 1974 Ethiopian revolution, which eventually altered the military balance in the Horn far enough to tempt the Somalis to invade Ethiopia, apparently caught the Soviets by surprise. When instability in Ethiopia stimulated Somali nationalism and raised the danger that Soviet weapons supplied to Somalia could be used to trigger a regional conflict, the Soviets did not temper their support for Somalia. In fact, they increased their military aid in exchange for additional access privileges while securing Somalia's pledge, written into their 1974 friendship treaty, to use that aid for "defensive purposes" only. Had the Soviets not bought access to Somali facilities with roughly $400 million worth of weapons, becoming involuntary accomplices to Somalia's aggression, they would not have had to supply Ethiopia with anywhere near the $1.3 billion worth of weapons they delivered in 1977 and 1978 in order to resist that aggression. Nor would they have had to bear the probably larger material and political costs connected with the intervention of over 13,000 Cuban troops in Ethiopia. Had the Soviets not furnished Somalia with the wherewithal to fight a major war, the conflict in the Ogaden would have been about as noteworthy as the Polisario conflict in the western Sahara.

With respect to the political underpinnings of Soviet access, however, Somalia is an exceptional case. Generally the quest for access has not altered the fundamental thrust of Soviet foreign policy. For example, concern for the preservation of extensive access privileges in Egypt and Somalia (in 1976–1977) did not prevent the Soviets from taking actions that diverged from the interests of those nations. When relations with Egypt soured and Sadat began trying to barter for arms with Moscow's remaining access privileges, the Soviets looked elsewhere for naval access. Although the Soviets "pulled their punches" in dealing with Mogadishu until they were expelled from Berbera in November 1977, they never acquiesced to Siad Barre's demand that they cease supporting Ethiopia.[19] In both the Egyptian and Somali cases, the Soviets appear to have assumed that submitting to Third World blackmail over access could establish a dangerous precedent, entailing even greater problems in the long term with respect to maintaining their status as a bona-fide superpower than losing access. The evidence that granting access privileges to the Soviets gives the donor country extensive bargaining leverage thus appear to be mixed.

The Interests of Host Nations in Granting Soviet Access

The Somali case is exceptional in another sense. The Soviet-Somali arms for access relationship was a classic quid pro quo relationship, subject to intense bargaining, construction delays, and other problems. When we study other cases of Soviet access carefully, we find that most donors have a direct interest in supporting the Soviet Navy. These interests are usually based on security needs, which has probably been the most important factor in the cases of Egypt prior to the October 1973 war, Syria, South Yemen, Ethiopia, Angola, and to a lesser extent Libya and Algeria. Security concerns also play a prominent role in non–Third World cases of Soviet access—Cuba and Vietnam.

Egypt's Practical Security Needs

Soviet access has met the security needs of these states in different ways. In several countries, a Soviet naval presence met the donor's practical security requirements. For example, after its defeat in the June 1967 Middle East war, Egypt was virtually defenseless for some time against Israeli air power. Soviet warships in Egyptian ports represented not only a deterrent to Israeli attacks, but they also possessed the only operative air defense assets on Egyptian territory. Even after Egyptian air defense capabilities improved and the large Soviet military presence ashore was withdrawn in 1972, Cairo still had a stake, albeit more limited, in supporting the Soviet Navy, which was seen as a counter to the U.S. 6th Fleet, still regarded in many Arab capitals as Israel's strategic reserve.

Ethiopia: The Eritrean Dilemma

The Ethiopian security interest in Soviet access is qualitatively different from those of Arab states in conflict with Israel and the United States. In early 1978 Soviet ships evacuated Ethiopian forces besieged by Eritrean guerrillas at Massawa.[20] There is also one unconfirmed BBC (British Broadcasting Corporation) Radio report that Soviet warships fired their guns on the insurgents. Regardless of the accuracy of this report, the Soviets were apparently prepared to lend combat support to beleaguered Ethiopian troops at the height of the Ogaden War. In early 1978, they augmented their Indian Ocean Squadron with Riga-class frigates, whose shallow drafts and shore guns made them suitable for fire support at close range.[21] Since the Ogaden War, the Soviet Navy has occasionally provided logistic support for Ethiopian forces operating against Eritrean guerrillas.

In general, Soviet naval access to Ethiopian facilities gives the Soviet Union a stake in the Ethiopian pacification of Eritrea. The strife there has impaired Soviet naval support activities, particularly at the airfield at Asmara, which has repeatedly come under guerrilla attack. In fact, in May 1984 the insurgents destroyed several Il-38 May ASW aircraft on the ground at Asmara, and Soviet surveillance flights were suspended thereafter.[22] A pacified Eritrea would not only remove the insurgent threat to Soviet aircraft, but might also enable Soviet ships to make greater use of the Ethiopian naval base of Massawa, which the Soviet Navy would probably prefer over the Dahlac Islands, since the latter do not possess a source of fresh water.

It is worth noting that Moscow in 1988 pressed Addis Ababa to negotiate seriously with the insurgents in the hope of reaching a political settlement, which might entail a federated status for Eritrea.[23] That the Soviets seem willing to promote a peace settlement in Eritrea that undoubtedly would place their access privileges in jeopardy suggests Soviet naval access holds a lower priority in Moscow's current policy than resolving the three-decades-old insurgency in Eritrea, which has drained enormous Ethiopian and significant Soviet resources.

Vietnam: A Fraternal Socialist Country

The Soviet naval presence in Vietnam symbolizes a Soviet security commitment to a fraternal socialist country. When the Soviets acquired naval access to Cam Ranh Bay in the late 1970s, Sino-Vietnamese relations were deteriorating sharply over Kampuchea. At that time Hanoi probably saw a local Soviet military presence primarily as a deterrent against China. Although Vietnam obtains direct military benefits, such as intelligence and reconnaissance on Chinese military activities in southern China and Hainan island, from its support of roughly twenty-five Soviet ships and forty Soviet reconnaissance, ASW, strike, and fighter aircraft,[24] this military force seems far larger than Vietnam would need to protect its coastal flanks against China, whose capabilities to launch an attack against Vietnam from the sea remain weak. Perhaps Gorbachev's recent willingness to barter Soviet withdrawal from Cam Ranh Bay for the elimination of U.S. bases in the Philippines reflects a growing awareness in both Hanoi and Moscow that the Soviet military presence in Vietnam is largely superfluous to Vietnam's security needs. Moreover, it represents an impediment to Soviet and Vietnamese efforts to improve relations with China. It seems reasonable to expect a reduction in the Soviet military presence in the region as Soviet and Vietnamese relations with China further normalize.

Albania: A Former Fraternal Socialist Country

Just as the Soviet military force in Vietnam represents a symbolic security commitment to a Southeast Asian outpost of the socialist community of nations, the small Soviet submarine presence in Albania—an early prototype of Soviet access—may have played a similar role. From 1958 to 1961 (before the Soviet Navy established routine forward deployments), the Soviets stationed six Whiskey-class attack submarines at Valona Bay, Albania.[25] This submarine contingent may have symbolized a Soviet security commitment to what was then a friendly socialist state, cut off from Warsaw Pact nations by hostile Yugoslavia. The simplest explanation for the deployment is that the Warsaw Pact treaty, to which Albania was a signatory, gave the Soviets the right, while the U.S. 6th Fleet gave them the reason, to station their naval forces in the only Soviet bloc outpost on the Mediterranean. But the timing of the deployment was apparently related to the state of Soviet-Yugoslav relations. The arrival of the submarines in Albania marked the nadir of post-Stalin Soviet-Yugoslav relations and the zenith of Soviet-Albanian ties. Within two years, the situation was reversed as Soviet relations with the socialist states on the Adriatic became enmeshed in the emergent Sino-Soviet dispute. Within three years the Soviets had pulled out of Valona, and the rest of Albania as well. The loss of Albanian access became a casualty of the Sino-Soviet-Albanian schism.

Yugoslavia's Commercial Model

Another type of Soviet access relationship in which the donor has a direct interest is based on economic incentives. The overhaul and repair of Soviet submarines in Yugoslav shipyards since 1974 is exemplary.[26] By the early 1970s repair work at Yugoslav shipyards had sharply slackened due to a worldwide recession in the shipping industry. These shipyards also needed to be modernized if Yugoslavia were to remain competitive. The Soviet naval high command must have recognized the potential value of Yugoslavia's Tivat yard (on Kotor Bay near Albania) as a supplement to, or even substitute for, Egypt's Al-Gabbari shipyards. And it was equally clear that Tivat could use the Soviet Navy's business. Soviet initiatives began to have positive results during a period when Belgrade's relations with Moscow were improving and those with the United States, Greece, and Italy were worsening.

A 1974 revision of Yugoslavia's coastal sea law opened its shipyards to any nation "not participating in aggression," but only the Soviet Union was interested. The revised law went far toward reconciling Yugoslavia's economic interest in Soviet Navy business with the political sensitivities of the nonaligned movement concerning foreign base rights. Essentially the law restricted Yugoslav support for the Soviet Navy to the water's edge. A limited number of small combatants and naval auxiliaries were allowed to be repaired, only by Yugoslav workers and for periods no longer than six months. Also, only those members of the crew essential to assist in the repair work could remain in the port while the ship was repaired. Prior to entering the yard, all ordnance was to be transferred to Yugoslav custody for safekeeping; no storage of foreign repair equipment or POL was permitted. These restrictions were probably intended to keep Soviet naval support operations from coming ashore as they had in Egypt.

The Yugoslav policy may have set a precedent for emulation by other non-aligned states. A few years later, Tunisia, whose shipyards were also underutilized, began to repair small Soviet combatants on a commercial basis. And Soviet naval auxiliaries, flying civilian ensigns, have been repaired in shipyards of several Third World states, including Singapore. Thus, even some pro-Western states have participated in this trend toward the commercialization of support for the Soviet Navy.

Lessons from the Soviets Access Experience

This selective review of examples illustrating the diverse political underpinnings of Soviet access suggests that the Soviets have been far more successful when their access partners had a direct stake in supporting the Soviet Navy. When donor interest was indirect—when Soviet access was valued as a means to obtain Soviet weapons (as in Somalia and post-1973 Egypt)—access relationships were trouble prone. Perhaps it is more than coincidental that in both of Moscow's failed Third World relationships access was based on a quid pro quo. It is possible that Moscow may have learned that using arms to extract access privileges is not good policy, for none of its current access relationships is based on the exchange principle.

Another lesson the Soviets may have learned from their Somali experience is that candor is the best policy when dealing with Western publicity about Soviet naval support operations. In Somalia they practiced deception, and this eventually harmed their interests. In fact, the Soviets went to great pains to disguise their military presence at Berbera. Guided tours were arranged in early 1975 so that visiting Arab journalists and other groups would not detect Soviet military activities. On one occasion the repair vessel the Soviets normally stationed dockside was towed far enough offshore so that only Somali sailors were visible topside under a Somali ensign.

The U.S. Department of Defense exposed this subterfuge in June 1975 through Defense Secretary James Schlesinger's congressional testimony and the follow-up inspection visit to Berbera by Pentagon experts led by Senator Dewey Bartlett. The negative publicity garnered by the so-called missile handling and storage facility cost the Soviets more than embarrassment. A U.S. Senate resolution to suspend further construction of what was then an austere naval communications station at Diego Garcia was defeated. The Soviets subsequently never used the ordnance storage facility even for repair of faulty missiles from their warships.

From this episode, the Soviets may have learned that their interests can be damaged when they engage in deception or build facilities whose employment cannot be easily rationalized in terms of regional security requirements. It is worth noting that in 1988 when Western newspapers disclosed that the Soviets had expanded their naval support operations at Tartus, Syria, the Soviet press responded fairly quickly with a reasonably candid disclosure of the nature of the support activities there.[27] It would seem that Gorbachev's policy of *glasnost'* has made the Soviets more forthcoming with respect to their naval access overseas.

As a result of their experience in Egypt and Somalia, the Soviets have learned to cope with the uncertainty of naval access in the Third World by acquiring multiple access options as a hedge against loss and as a means of increasing their bargaining leverage. The Somali experience also seems to have taught them to rely on portable installations.

To understand why the loss of Berbera was a shock to the Soviets, we must realize that when they began to develop a major support infrastructure there, they assumed that Somalia would remain dependent upon Soviet military assistance indefinitely and that their naval access would be secure. Hence, they were willing to spend hundreds of thousands of dollars to construct fixed military installations ashore, not only at Berbera (for example, the airfield and the ordnance storage complex) but also at other locations, such as Chisimaio, Dafet, and Baidoa, for joint or Somali use only. Further, when they decided to support Ethiopia militarily, they evidently did not believe that this would lead necessarily to the loss of Somali access privileges.[28] They appear to have overestimated Somali dependence upon Soviet assistance or underestimated the strength of Somali nationalism, or both.

Since the loss of Berbera, Soviet military writers have complained about the unreliability of Third World access donors and have praised the value of mobile support facilities.[29] In fact, the Soviets have not built facilities in the Third World as extensive or permanent as the ones they lost at Berbera. At Dahlac, which replaced Berbera as the Soviet Indian Ocean squadron's main base of logistic support and maintenance, the Soviets have employed mostly portable equipment, such as floating piers, water and fuel storage tanks, and the same 8,500-ton-capacity floating drydock that they had earlier anchored at Berbera. So far, the Soviets have not pressured Ethiopia to allow them to move their naval support operations ashore. According to a high-ranking Ethiopian defector, Dawit Wolde Giorgis, who served as the governor of Eritrea in the early 1980s, during his tenure there the Soviets asked only for less restrictive use of Asmara airfield for routine surveillance flights.[30]

Probably because of the susceptibility of Asmara and other Third World airfields to guerrilla attacks, the Soviets apparently have decided to reduce significantly their dependence on Third World airfields for staging maritime reconnaissance flights. The Soviets have developed a large seaplane, the TAG-D, which is similar in size to the TU-95 Bear-D maritime reconnaissance plane and a potential replacement for the IL-38 May ASW aircraft. If the TAG-D is employed as anticipated, the Soviets would be enabled to centralize their Indian Ocean naval support activities in the Dahlac Islands.[31]

Vietnam represents an exception to this general trend toward the scaling down of the Soviet Navy's overseas support infrastructure. The Soviets have made further improvements at Cam Ranh Bay, which the United States had earlier developed as a major base during the Vietnam War. Now the most elaborate support complex used by the Soviet Navy in the forward area, Cam

Ranh Bay's facilities include seven piers, expanded and protected POL and ordnance storage facilities, a FIX-24 high-frequency direction-finding site, an electronic intelligence collection complex, and a command post ashore. In addition, Bear-D maritime reconnaissance and Bear-F ASW planes, Badger-G strike aircraft, and Flogger interceptors stage routine flights from the airfield there.[32] The Vietnam case suggests that the Soviets may have adopted a two-track approach toward naval access. While they have scaled down their support infrastructure in Third World "states of socialist orientation," which Soviet writers increasingly view as unstable and potentially unreliable, they have continued to develop major facilities in socialist Vietnam, although these too may be cut back should Sino-Soviet-Vietnamese relations improve.

The general reduction of the Soviet Navy's overseas naval support infrastructure seems to be consistent with a general decline in the tempos of Soviet naval operations in the forward area. The lower Soviet military profile ashore and at sea also reflects the declining role of military power as an instrument of Soviet diplomacy and the growing appreciation of the risks of aggravating regional conflicts and creating superpower confrontations that could ensue from deepening security commitments to unstable Third World regimes.

To some extent, these policy changes may reflect the lessons the Soviets appear to have learned about access to overseas naval support facilities. In their experience, access relationships have proved less troublesome where supporting the Soviet Navy met the donor's direct security or economic interests. The Soviets have also learned to become more candid about their naval support activities and to cope with the uncertainty of access by acquiring multiple access options and by relying heavily on movable installations. In managing its own troubled access relationships in Third World states, the United States can profit from the Soviet experience.

Notes

1. Mikhail S. Gorbachev, speech in Krasnoiarsk, *Pravda*, September 18, 1988, trans. in *Current Digest of the Soviet Press*, October 19, 1988, 6.

2. The chapter relies heavily on published research on this subject contained in: George S. Dragnich, "The Soviet Union's Quest for Access to Naval Support Facilities in Egypt Prior to the June War of 1967," in *Soviet Naval Policy*, ed. Michael MccGwire, Ken Booth, and John McDonnell (New York: Praeger, 1975), 237–77; Robert G. Weinland, "Egypt and Land-Based Support for the Soviet Fifth Eskadra," *Survival*, 20 (March–April 1978), 73–79; and my "The Politics of Soviet Access to Naval Support Facilities in the Mediterranean," in *Soviet Naval Diplomacy*, ed. Bradford Dismukes and James M. McConnell (New York: Pergamon, 1979), 357–403; and "The Soviet-Somali 'Arms for Access' Relationship," *Soviet Union/Union Sovietique* 10, pt 1 (1983): 59–81.

3. Senate Committee on Armed Services, *Soviet Military Capability in Berbera, Somalia,* 9th Cong., 1st Sess., July 1975, 15.

4. For detailed information on Soviet use of the Vietnamese facilities, see "The Cam Ranh Syndrome," *ASEAN Forecast* (Special Supplement) (June 1984): 100.

5. *Washington Star,* Aug. 24, 1972.

6. *Voennyi entsiklopedicheskii slovar'* (Moscow: Voenizdat, 1983), 60; *Voennyi entsiklopedicheskii slovar'* (Moscow: Voenizdat, 1986), 60.

7. Statement of Rear Admiral John L. Butts, U.S. Navy, Director of Naval Intelligence, before the Seapower and Force Projection Subcommittee of the Senate Armed Services Committee on the Naval Threat, 99th Cong. 1st Sess., February 26, 1985, 14.

8. James M. McConnell and Bradford Dismukes, "Conclusions," in their *Soviet Naval Diplomacy,* 294–95.

9. For further discussion of the potential uses of Soviet naval forces deployed in the Mediterranean, Indian Ocean, and off the west coast of Africa, see my *Soviet Strategic Military Interests in Africa in the 1980s,* Army War College, Strategic Studies Institute, *Final Report* (Carlisle Barracks, Pa.: Army War College, May 1986).

10. Department of Defense, *Soviet Military Power* (Washington, D.C.: Government Printing Offices, 1988), 92.

11. Senate Committee on Foreign Relations, *U.S. Foreign Policy Objectives and Overseas Military Installations,* 96th Cong., 1st sess., 1979, 91.

12. Remnek, *Soviet Military Interests in Africa in the 1980s,* 4.

13. Department of the Navy, *Understanding Soviet Naval Developments,* 5th ed. (Washington, D.C.: Government Printing Office, 1985), 10.

14. Congress, Senate Committee on Armed Services, *Disapprove Construction Projects on the Island of Diego Garcia,* Hearings, 94th Cong., 1st sess., June 10, 1975, 7.

15. Remnek, *Soviet Military Interests in Africa in the 1980s,* 7–8.

16. "The Cam Ranh Syndrome," 100–101.

17. "The Soviet Navy as a Political Instrument," in *Strategic Survey 1979* (London: International Institute for Strategic Studies, 1980), 23.

18. Remnek, "The Soviet-Somali Arms for Access' Relationship," 61–62.

19. For further elaboration of this argument, see my "Soviet Policy in the Horn of Africa: The Decision to Intervene," in *The Soviet Union in the Third World: Successes and Failures,* ed. Robert H. Donaldson (Boulder, Colo.: Westview, 1981), 125–49.

20. "The Soviet Navy as a Political Instrument," 23.

21. Kenneth G. Weiss, *The Soviet Involvement in the Ogaden War,* Professional Paper 269 (Alexandria, Va.: Center for Naval Analyses, 1979).

22. Department of Defense, *Soviet Military Power* (Washington, D.C.: Government Printing Office, 1985), 123.

23. *Indian Ocean Newsletter,* April 9, 1988, 1–2. *See also* Moscow Radio Domestic Service in Russian, March 30, 1989, translated in Foreign Broadcasting Information Service, *Soviet Union Report,* March 31, 1987, p.32.

24. *Soviet Military Power* (1988): 83.

25. Remnek, "The Politics of Soviet Access to Naval Support Facilities in the Mediterranean," 362–64.

26. Ibid., 382–86.

27. *Krasnaia zvezda,* September 15, 1988; trans. in Foreign Broadcast Information Service, *Soviet Union Daily Report,* September 16, 1988, 18–19.

28. For further elaboration, see Remnek, "Decision to Intervene," 132–40.

29. See V. Gulin and I. Povaliaev, "Dve podkhoda k odne teme," *Morskoi sbornik,* no. 11 (1979): 80; and I.E. Shavrov, ed. *Lokal'nye voiny: isoriia i sovremennost'* (Moscow: Voenizdat, 1981), 264.

30. Interview with the author, February 26, 1987.

31. *Statement of rear Admiral Thomas A. Brooks, U.S. Navy, Director of Naval Intelligence* before the Seapower, Strategic, and Critical Materials Subcommittee of the House Armed Services Committee on Intelligence Issues, 101st Cong., 1st Sess., February 22, 1989, 15.

32. See Department of Defense, *Soviet Military Power,* 87.

11
The Soviet Navy in a Changing World

Steve F. Kime

The Soviet Navy is a foreign policy instrument as well as a military force. It is not clear to many observers, however, how the political and military roles of the Soviet Navy relate to one another. I first addressed the question two decades ago, before it was fashionable to write about the Soviet Navy and while the nuclear-age Soviet Navy was completing its formative stage and beginning to be noticed on the high seas.[1] It was apparent then that the post-Stalinist Soviet Navy was first and foremost a military creature of the nuclear age and of the threat of escalation to intercontinental nuclear warfare. Indeed, the threat of escalation was the key to understanding the complex interrelationship between the political roles of the Soviet Navy and its war-fighting roles.

Soviet naval power was easier to describe twenty years ago. Two factors dominated development of the Soviet Navy. The long-standing geopolitical categories of continental and maritime powers had been blurred by intercontinental nuclear striking power, and the Soviet image of another world war was an inevitable all-out nuclear holocaust. These factors, and the position of the navy in the Soviet political and military scheme of things, helped to define both new capabilities and inherent limitations of the navy. The navy of an intercontinental nuclear superpower, even if that superpower had traditionally been considered continental, could credibly interpose itself on the high seas with the navy of a traditional maritime power. It could not do this in all cases, however, because the threat of nuclear escalation is not always credible, and a Soviet pretension to engage in limited conflict would have been incompatible with the Soviet view of war.

Now that a full generation has passed since the nuclear revolution began in military affairs, it is time to reexamine the nature of Soviet naval power. The long-term effects of unused ultimate weaponry, changing Soviet views of the probable course of another war, and the possibility of new Soviet atti-

The views expressed in this chapter are those of the writer and are not to be construed as official or reflecting the views of the Department of the Navy.

tudes about the prospect of nuclear escalation are major considerations affecting any contemporary attempt to determine the role of the navy in Soviet foreign and defense policy.

The Policy Setting

When considering the role of the Soviet Navy in Soviet defense and foreign policy, it is necessary to understand that defense policy comes before foreign policy in the Soviet mind-set. Military security considerations dominate Soviet thinking about both domestic and foreign policy. Foreign policy instruments are closely connected to the domestic Soviet preoccupation with the security of the homeland. This is especially true of military instruments of foreign policy, and it has been emphatically true of the Soviet Navy. There has been a direct connection between Soviet naval development and the Soviet phobia for security of the homeland. This connection has both given license for naval expression and restricted it.

The Soviet Navy is a military instrument built first for military reasons. Within Soviet defense policy, war-fighting comes first. Deterrence and other political, perception-oriented notions play a secondary role in Soviet defense policy.[2] Soviet naval forces must be justified in terms of prevailing Soviet views on the probable course of the next war, not in terms of management of peacetime relationships. The political utility of the Soviet Navy has been a spinoff of Soviet intercontinental nuclear superpower status and the opportunities and dangers inherent in that military status.

Within the Soviet defense establishment, the Soviet Navy is a subordinate institution. It is both literally and conceptually a peripheral part of the Soviet answers to core concerns. In military terms, the Soviet core concern is to maintain the capacity to dominate the Eurasian landmass in the event of war. The justifications for the Soviet Navy's existence must be persuasively tied to Soviet continental concerns, even if Soviet ships are deployed well beyond the Eurasian landmass. The policies and doctrines that address Soviet core concerns are far beyond the ken of the Soviet Navy, which acts as a kind of chameleon within the Soviet defense establishment. It must change complexion as broader policies and doctrines shift.

Soviet policies and doctrines do indeed shift. The modern Soviet Navy is a creature of the nuclear age, a reflection of the fact that its very existence is the product of the biggest change of all in Soviet military doctrine—the adjustment to the nuclear and technological revolution in military affairs. That the Soviet Navy is a chameleon, required to change its color as Soviet views of war in the nuclear age evolved, is a judgment difficult for Western observers to accept. We have a longing for a Soviet Mahan and a Soviet naval strategy understandable in classical sea power terms.

The Shifting Context for Soviet Naval Advocacy

Naval advocacy should not be confused with naval strategy. Axe-grinding to justify ships and submarines is not surprising, but Soviet naval advocacy is likely to be successful only to the extent the Soviet Navy is integrated with, rather than separated from, other Soviet forces. The closest the Soviet Navy came to independence was in the 1970s when Admiral of the Fleet of the Soviet Union S.G. Gorshkov published his book, and the contributions of naval science enjoyed some recognition. This was a far cry from any claim to a distinct naval strategy, and even this modicum of individual identity for the Soviet Navy was reversed in the early 1980s.[3]

It is no surprise, then, that an investigation of the Soviet Navy two decades ago resulted in a description of a complex interrelationship of a mixed bag of naval capabilities rather than a coherent naval strategy. Naval forces built at different times with varying primary missions in mind created a unique profile of naval power. It was the interrelationship between varying naval capacities and the rest of the Soviet military establishment, and Soviet view of the nuclear escalation ladder, that described Soviet naval power.[4]

Soviet naval capabilities, the interrelationships between Soviet military and naval capabilities, and the Soviet view of the escalation ladder have changed. Soviet naval development, and the politico-military expression of its navy, are limited but not fixed in the role of chameleon. The challenge to the United States is probably more complex than would be produced by a clean-cut, coherent, and unchanging Soviet naval strategy. Western military analysts cannot confine themselves to a search for the Soviet grand naval strategy and then simply hope to place the Soviet ships they see into that strategy. We are compelled to decide where the Soviet Navy stands in the light of several changing factors. The crucial questions are:

- What is the current Soviet view of the probable nature of the next war?
- How do the forces currently on hand, sometimes built with past missions in mind, relate to the naval missions that fit the prevailing Soviet view of the likely course of war?
- What is the current Soviet view of the risk of escalation, especially to nuclear levels of conflict, and how does this affect political and lower-level military uses of the Navy?

Systemic Support for the Soviet Navy

Geography has not been kind to Russian and Soviet sea power, but history and politics have provided plenty of support. The navy will never be first in line to get scarce resources, and if there were not sufficient resources made available, the navy might be the first in trouble, but no real trouble seems to be in sight.

There are enduring, basic notions about war that should be borne in mind as other factors change.[5] Soviet naval forces are the products of a Soviet singlemindedness about military power.[6] War, the prospect of war, and the instruments of war are national preoccupations in the Soviet Union. The very legitimacy of the ruling position of the Communist party of the Soviet Union (CPSU) is intertwined with this preoccupation. It is the role of the CPSU as guarantor of Soviet security, a role consolidated in the Great Patriotic War, that is the basis of the right to rule. It is not economic development, expansion of civil liberties, or even technological progress that justifies the system and the privileged position of the elite that controls the system. Therefore, it is feckless to hope that need for change in these sectors will alter the central role that military considerations play in Soviet policymaking.[7]

The threat of war is real in the Soviet mind. Ordinary Soviet citizens feel that they live in a potential future battlefield as well as a past one. They are prepared to do what is necessary to fight and win the next war. This attitude spawns perspectives that are alien to Americans, who think much differently about war. The United States had difficulty, for example, accepting the "shoot first and ask questions later" mentality reflected in the shooting down of the Korean airliner and the murder of Lieutenant Colonel Arthur D. Nicholson, Jr. Americans insisted on concluding that these were cases of policymaking run amok or lack of control over local tactical elements. Instead, these events are logical outcomes of a different way of looking at the use of force in human relationships.[8]

Soviet perspectives on war are distinctly focused on the Eurasian landmass, but geopolitical theories about what is a natural continental or sea power will not prevent them from doing anything that can help them to fight and win the next war. Modern, expensive Soviet naval forces were justified and built when the Soviet image of war was a global nuclear conflagration. If, in an era of negotiation and U.S.-Soviet agreement to defuse the risk of global nuclear war, the kind of war envisioned by the Soviets becomes more nearly fightable and winnable, the Soviet Navy's mission might grow.

A Big War Mentality

The Soviets do not think of war in limited ways. The national preoccupation with war does not seem to extend, at least in the 1980s, to direct Soviet military involvement at distances. The student of Soviet military politics is made to wonder if the legitimacy of the CPSU regime, steeped as it is in the military security of the homeland, extends to any active forms of direct military adventurism very far from the Soviet Union. Naval forces, like all other

Soviet military forces, have been understood and justified in terms of their functions in a major conflict of nuclear superpowers. It is a "big war" mentality. This has had fundamental implications for the Soviet Navy:

- Projection forces exist, but they are spinoffs of forces built for the big war.

- Intercontinental nuclear offensive and defensive missions tend to dominate Soviet naval construction. This is because conventional "phases" of war, or even major conventional war with a superpower adversary, are lesser included cases of a worst-case conflict.

- Integration always outweighs independence in Soviet naval matters. No matter how distant or even how nonnuclear Soviet naval missions become, the postwar question is, Who controls Eurasia? The Soviet Navy's ability to contribute to a combined arms effort to answer this question is its reason for existence.

- The contemporary Soviet interpretation of how the big war will be played is crucial, especially for its navy. There will always be tension between dominant nuclear war contingencies and conventional war missions. Varying kinds of naval forces are required for a potentially vast array of different kinds of naval missions, and mission priorities, that might evolve if the Soviet view of how the big war will be fought changes.

Escalation in the Soviet View of War

As the newness of the nuclear and missile age wears off, we must not forget that the modern Soviet Navy is a creature of intercontinental nuclear striking power for which the threat of nuclear escalation has been critical. Manifestations of Soviet naval power, especially at long distances from home, have been tied to the existence of the intercontinental nuclear umbrella. For example, interposition strategies, in which a smaller force can deter a larger one, are based on the credibility of escalating beyond the level and site of a limited conflict situation. To some extent the Soviet Navy, though it certainly was not built for the purpose, could exploit the concept of interposition to devalue the use of naval force for the world's greatest sea power. Even at nonconflict levels, the credibility and prestige of the Soviet Navy flowed from its potential to act equally with the U.S. Navy. Showing the flag by Soviet naval units was display of the flag of an intercontinental nuclear superpower.

A generation has passed, and nuclear weapons have not been used. The Soviet Navy was part of the Soviet adjustment to the nuclear revolution, but the nuclear revolution is a peculiar phenomenon in the history of military thought because it has been almost entirely theoretical. Time is bound to erode mere theory, especially in a country where thoughts about war in an almost palpable, hands-on sense are an integral part of everyday politics. Continuing adjustments to the nuclear missile age are inevitable.

A change in the Soviet view of the threat of escalation to nuclear levels in a major superpower confrontation has profound effects on naval missions, naval construction, and expressions of naval power at distances from the Soviet Union. There are solid Soviet reasons to want to decouple the intercontinental nuclear threat from the determination of who controls Eurasia? in a major war. Soviet conventional military power would generally loom larger, but the impact on the Soviet Navy would probably be quite uneven. Just as the nuclear age and its threat of escalation ushered in new license for the Soviet Navy, a significant change in the relevance of nuclear escalation to naval power would alter that license. Show the flag and interposition would take on different meaning for the Soviet Navy.

Some analysts are concerned that the reduction of nuclear weapons on the potential European battlefield is the first step toward making the world safe for conventional war. If this is so, Soviet naval planners must be watching very closely. There is a crucial difference to the Soviet Navy between relying on near-automatic escalation and aiming at keeping a conflict at conventional levels.[9] All the conventional naval missions of two world wars come back into play. To some degree, the old geopolitical categories of continental powers and sea powers become relevant again. Precious Soviet intercontinental strategic nuclear attack forces—nuclear-powered ballistic missile submarines (SSBNs)—must be protected better and for a longer period of time.

The Projection of Soviet Naval Power: A Changing Context?

For most of the nuclear era, Soviet willingness to project military power has been assessed, at least by me, in limited terms.[10] Soviet leaders have been alert to opportunities, but they are careful calculators of risk versus gain. The Soviet preference in Third World meddling has been for indirect methods where the potential gains and losses are not connected with survival of the homeland or Eurasian dominance. A reasonably clear distinction between peripheral, continental projection of power and more distant applications of Soviet force was easier in the past. The logic of this kind of thinking was quite persuasive before the Soviets achieved nuclear parity and even seemed sound as the Soviets achieved equality as long as their image of the big war involved near-certain escalation to nuclear levels. How does the Soviet calculation of risk versus gain in Third World conflict situations change in a world where superpower conflict might be limited to conventional levels? Does the prospect of containing conflict in Europe carry with it a similar prospect of containing lesser conflicts in remote areas where the stakes are much lower, or are such potential lower-level conflicts likely to escalate at least to major confrontation in Eurasia between the nuclear superpowers? These are questions with great implications for the entire range of Soviet economic, political, and military power. The Soviet Navy is only one of the instruments involved in what could turn out to be a new context for the projection of Soviet power.

In the past, the notion of war at sea between the navies of the superpowers did not seem credible because the limited stakes of any dispute to be settled at sea would have been far out of proportion to damage to the Soviet homeland that had to be considered highly probable. Insulation of the superpowers' homelands from nuclear, and perhaps even conventional, attack changes the calculations. To the extent that the stakes of some distant dispute must be balanced only against the potential losses on the spot, Soviet leaders could find Third World opportunities more tempting. This is a two-edged sword: if Soviet projection forces are more nearly disconnected from escalation that would endanger the homeland, they are more subject to the geopolitical limitations that have always plagued Russian navies. The nuclear age gave license to the twentieth-century version of the Russian Navy, and any success at putting the nuclear genie back into the bottle threatens to remove that license.

We cannot know what effect a changing Soviet view of the course of the next war will have on Soviet attitudes toward displaying and projecting military power, but it seems likely that there will be some effect. Soviet naval presence on the high seas was cut back as adjustments to the SSBN bastion concept were made and, perhaps, as Soviet leaders began to discount the value of showing the flag under the nuclear umbrella, but the utility of the navy as a politico-military instrument might be rediscovered toward the end of this century. This rediscovery could well occur as the Soviet Union finds itself with more and better instruments available for the projection of naval power and as the regime needs successes abroad to compensate for failed reforms at home. The military legitimacy of the regime has not in the past extended to direct Soviet military involvement in foreign conflicts away from the Soviet periphery. Further, the big-war mentality has so far tended to make small wars difficult to justify. How much these facts have changed is a major question in determining the future role of the Soviet Navy in Soviet foreign and defense policy.

Conclusion

The Soviet Navy continues to be a force in transition. It is a military and political instrument that must adjust to the winds of change, and change is in the air. The Soviet Navy, as distinguished from the traditionally limited navy of continental Russia, is a product of the Soviet adjustment to the nuclear revolution in military affairs, but the nuclear revolution has not yet run its course. Since the beginning of the nuclear age, there has been a variety of justifications for building Soviet naval forces as Soviet doctrine evolved, as the military balance shifted in Soviet favor, and as time and technology altered perceptions about the probable course of the next war. The Soviet Navy, the chameleon of the defense establishment, has thrived in this changing environment but has not established a coherent identity or naval strategy that would make absolutely clear its future directions.

Some of the major factors that dictate the future of the Soviet Navy, and some major trends in those factors, are visible. The preoccupation of the Soviet populace with the prospect of war and the resultant political legitimacy that the regime enjoys from its role as military guarantor of the Soviet homeland are highly relevant to the future of all Soviet military forces. These sociopolitical factors are especially relevant to the Soviet Navy, a peripheral force. A big-war mentality produces enough military resources for everyone and will continue to do so. It remains to be seen if a less cataclysmic view of the next major war will be popularly accepted and in time legitimize smaller, more discrete, overt uses of naval force in potential conflict situations with other major powers.

Soviet military forces are built for major war, and the Soviet image of how that war will be conducted will dominate naval construction and deployment. Two extremely important processes are at work that bear close watching: the evolution of the Soviet view of the next major war and the efforts at nuclear arms control that might insulate the superpowers from the threat of nuclear escalation. To the extent that the prospect of a prolonged conventional phase or a totally conventional war is accepted in the Soviet Union, Soviet naval missions could be dramatically affected. New missions involving more distant deployments, and Soviet willingness to support those deployments, might be dictated by a changed risk versus opportunity calculus.

Political utility is a spinoff of combat capabilities of Soviet military forces. The role of the Soviet Navy in Soviet foreign policy will flow from the changing role of the Soviet Navy in Soviet defense policy. In the past, the threat of nuclear escalation yielded limited political utility for forces built to conduct a future global nuclear war. The future seems to promise a Soviet Navy attuned to the possibility of prolonged conventional conflict where the threat of nuclear escalation is attenuated or even eliminated. In such a future, the relationship between the political and military roles of the Soviet Navy would change. There will be new opportunities and new risks for both of the superpower navies as adjustments are made to this change.

Notes

1. Steve F. Kime, "The Rise of Soviet Naval Power in the Nuclear Age" (Ph.D. diss., Harvard University, 1971). Robert Herrick had made his landmark contribution, *Soviet Naval Strategy* (Annapolis: U.S. Naval Institute, 1968).

2. This point is amplified in my essay, "The Soviet View of War," *Comparative Strategy* 2, no. 3 (1980): 205–21.

3. Michael MccGwire makes this point succinctly in his "Contingency Plans for World War," in James L. George, ed., *The Soviet and Other Communist Navies* (Annapolis: U.S. Naval Institute Press, 1986), 74.

4. This profile of Soviet naval power is described in detail in my *Soviet Naval Strategy for the 1980s,* National Security Affairs Monograph (Washington, D.C.: National Defense University, 1978), 6–9.

5. Dimitri Simes, in a well-balanced and insightful essay on Gorbachev's regime, points out that "Gorbachev is not inclined to depart from the fundamentals of Soviet strategy," though he "uses a refreshing tactical flexibility in the pursuit of traditional Soviet objectives." Dimitri K. Simes, "Gorbachev: A New Foreign Policy?" *Foreign Affairs* 65, no. 3 (1987): 478.

6. For an elaboration of this subject, see my "War and Politics in the Soviet Union." *Strategic Review* 15 (Fall 1987): 44–54.

7. William Odom speaks of the "primacy of military affairs" in his "Soviet Force Posture: Dilemmas and Directions," *Problems of Communism* 34 (July–August 1985): 1–14. Odom also sheds light on changes in Soviet doctrine.

8. Marshal A.I. Koldunov, the same marshal promoted after the Korean Airlines shootdown, was fired after a small plane from Finland landed on Red Square on May 28, 1987, without being destroyed for penetrating Soviet airspace. The minister of defense and the Moscow air district commander were among those fired. "Military Shakeup Widens in Moscow," and "Public Criticism," *Washington Post,* June 18, 1987, A25. See also "Flight Has Left Soviet Military Vulnerable to Public Criticism," *Washington Post,* June 18, 1987, p. A32.

9. The West must not fall into the trap of simply assuming that a conventional conflict scenario poses only advantages for the Soviet Union. Some of the limitations of changing the nature of the expected war in Europe are suggested in my "Warsaw Pact: Juggernaut of Paper Tiger?" *Air Force Magazine,* 65 (June 1982): 67–69.

10. Steve F. Kime, "Power Projection, Soviet Style," *Air Force Magazine,* 63 (December 1980): 50–54.

Afterword

A broad consensus runs through these chapters on certain major themes. The Russian and Soviet navies have long held oceanic pretensions even if constrained by continental requirements. There is no separate naval strategy. The Soviet Navy is subordinate to an army-dominated General Staff and politically established military doctrine. Soviet foreign policy and military posture have not brought security to the Soviet state. There are political as well as economic imperatives for "new thinking." The military are losing influence in Soviet decision making. The navy's primary role in national strategy will be perimeter defense.

Other issues continue to be debated. How much does the tradition of a strategic culture mold perceptions and decisions and how much the objective circumstances of the situation? Is there more continuity than change in Soviet strategy, even in an age of "defensive" doctrine? In what ways does Soviet naval conduct depend on purely Soviet factors, and in what ways is it a reaction to Western developments and actions? What are the prospects that naval capabilities will define roles? Are we likely to see in the future more or less Soviet naval presence in the Third World?

As we pursue our questions and test our conclusions we would do well to distinguish what we know from what is unclear. Even more fundamentally, we would do well to identify and examine our assumptions. How much are we projecting our own peculiar ethnocentric assumptions onto our evaluations and predictions of Soviet behavior? To what extent is their (or our) behavior determined by an enduring culture and modes of thought, or by the rigors of objective logic? If we are to understand ourselves as well as the Soviets, perhaps the most difficult task, but the most necessary, is to challenge our own assumptions.

Index

About the Contributors

Robert B. Bathurst, has written widely on Soviet and Russian cultural questions, which he has studied since 1952. Among the events in his life are: interpreter for the Khrushchev visit to Camp David, and initator of the Hot Line, assistant naval attaché in Moscow, naval operations professor at the U.S. Naval War College, Ph.D. in comparative literature, and visiting scholar at the Harvard Russian Research Center and the Hoover Institution.

Kenneth Booth holds a personal chair in the Department of International Politics at the University College of Wales, Aberystwyth. In 1977 he served as scholar-in-residence at the Center for Advanced Research at the U.S. Naval War College, and from 1979–1981 he was senior research fellow at Dalhousie University in Canada. Among his books are *Navies and Foreign Policy, Strategy and Ethnocentrism,* and *Law, Force and Diplomacy at Sea.*

Donald C. Daniel, director of the Strategy and Campaign Department at the Center for Naval Warfare Studies of the Naval War College, received a doctorate in political science from Georgetown University. Prior to his present position, he was a professor in the National Security Affairs department of the Naval Postgraduate School in Monterey, California. His most recent book, *Antisubmarine Warfare and Superpower Strategic Stability,* was chosen by the U.S. Naval Institute as a 1986 notable naval book.

Robert W. Herrick, an analyst with Rekenthaler Technology Associates, is a retired U.S. Navy commander who served in Moscow as an assistant naval attaché and holds a doctorate in international relations from Columbia University. He is the author of *Soviet Naval Strategy* (1968) and *Soviet Naval Theory and Policy: Gorshkov's Inheritance* (1988).

Steve F. Kime is the director of Servicemembers' Opportunities Colleges, a consortium of 13 higher educational institutions and 500 of their member institutions. He holds a doctorate from Harvard University and has written extensively on Soviet political and military matters. He served twice as U.S. naval attaché to the Soviet Union and has been associate dean at the National War College and a division director at the U.S. Naval Academy.

Jacob W. Kipp is a senior analyst with the Soviet Army Study Office of the U.S. Army Combined Arms Center at Fort Leavenworth, Kansas. He received a doctorate in Russian history from Pennsylvania State University in 1970. Prior to his present position, he taught at Kansas State University for fifteen years. Dr. Kipp has published extensively in the areas of Soviet military and naval history.

Rear Admiral Ronald J. Kurth, USN, currently president of the U.S. Naval War College, is a graduate of the U.S. Naval Academy and holds a Ph.D. from Harvard University. He has served in the Office of the Secretary of Defense and has served twice in Moscow (as naval attaché and defense attaché). In 1971 he helped negotiate the U.S.-Soviet Incidents at Sea Agreement.

Michael MccGwire has been a senior fellow at the Brookings Institution in Washington, D.C., since 1979. Prior to this appointment, he served as a professor of maritime and strategic studies at Dalhousie University in Canada. He is the author of *Military Objectives in Soviet Foreign Policy* (1987) and *Perestroika and Soviet National Security* (forthcoming). Mr. MccGwire served in the British Royal Navy from 1942 to 1967.

William H.J. Manthorpe, Jr., serves in the Office of the Chief of Naval Operations. He graduated from the U.S. Naval Academy, earned a master's degree in international affairs from George Washington University, and did further graduate work at American University. Mr. Manthorpe served in the U.S. Navy for more than twenty years and retired at the rank of captain in 1978. He served as naval attaché to the Soviet Union in the early 1970s.

Richard B. Remnek is a research associate of the Institute of International Studies at the University of California, Berkeley. His research interests focus on the military dimensions of Soviet–Third World relations. He has written extensively on such topics as Soviet military interests in Africa and Soviet access to overseas naval support facilities.

Jürgen Rohwer, from 1959 to 1989 the director of the Bibliothek für Zeitgeschichte in Stuttgart, is an internationally renowned and widely published naval historian. He served as editor of the influential naval journal *Marine-Rundschau* for almost three decades. He is vice-president of the International Commission on Military History and holds a position in several defense organizations, as well as in Stuttgart University.

Harry D. Train II, Admiral, U.S. Navy (ret.), is president of SRMS Inc. While on active duty in the U.S. Navy, he served for four years as commander in chief of the U.S. Atlantic Command, as NATO supreme allied commander-Atlantic, and as commander in chief of the U.S. Atlantic Fleet. He is on the academic advisory board of the NATO Defense College and holds the first Henry Clay Hofheimer chair of military professionalism at the U.S. Armed Forces Staff College.

About the Editors

Willard C. Frank, Jr., is director of graduate studies in history and associate professor of history at Old Dominion University, and adjunct professor at the U.S. Naval War College. He is coordinator of Old Dominion's strategy and policy program and specializes in naval history. Dr. Frank, who received a doctorate from the University of Pittsburgh, served on active duty in the U.S. Navy between 1957 and 1959 and in the reserves between 1962 and 1977. His publications mainly concern sea power and the Spanish Civil War.

Philip S. Gillette, is director of the graduate program in international studies and associate professor of political science at Old Dominion University. He received a M.A. in regional studies—Soviet Union—and a Ph.D. in political science from Harvard University. Dr. Gillette has taught on the faculties of Columbia University, Rutgers University, and Kalamazoo College. He is the coauthor with John A. Fahey of *Military Liaisons between NATO and the Warsaw Pact* (1988).